# teach<sup>®</sup> yourself

## swahili
joan russell

D1216579

For UK order enquiries: please contact Bookpoint Ltd, 130 Milton Park, Abingdon, Oxon, OX14 4SB. Telephone: +44 (0) 1235 827720. Fax: +44 (0) 1235 400454. Lines are open 09.00–17.00, Monday to Saturday, with a 24-hour message answering service. Details about our titles and how to order are available at www.teachyourself.co.uk

For USA order enquiries: please contact McGraw-Hill Customer Services, PO Box 545, Blacklick, OH 43004-0545, USA. Telephone: 1-800-722-4726. Fax: 1-614-755-5645.

For Canada order enquiries: please contact McGraw-Hill Ryerson Ltd, 300 Water St, Whitby, Ontario, L1N 9B6, Canada. Telephone: 905 430 5000. Fax: 905 430 5020.

Long renowned as the authoritative source for self-guided learning – with more than 50 million copies sold worldwide – the **teach yourself** series includes over 500 titles in the fields of languages, crafts, hobbies, business, computing and education.

Teach Yourself Swahili is also available in the form of a pack containing this book and two cassettes/CDs. If you have been unable to obtain the pack, the cassettes/CDs can be ordered separately through the bookseller.

*British Library Cataloguing in Publication Data*: a catalogue record for this title is available from the British Library.

*Library of Congress Catalog Card Number*: on file.

First published in UK 1996 by Hodder Education, part of Hachette Livre UK, 338 Euston Road, London, NW1 3BH.

First published in US 1996 by The McGraw-Hill Companies, Inc.

This edition published 2003.

The **teach yourself** name is a registered trade mark of Hodder Headline.

Copyright © 1996, 2003 Joan Russell

Typeset by Transet Limited, Coventry, England.
Printed in Great Britain for Hodder Education, part of Hachette Livre UK, 338 Euston Road, London, NW1 3BH, by Cox & Wyman Ltd, Reading, Berkshire.

The publisher has used its best endeavours to ensure that the URLs for external websites referred to in this book are correct and active at the time of going to press. However, the publisher and the author have no responsibility for the websites and can make no guarantee that a site will remain live or that the content will remain relevant, decent or appropriate.

Hachette Livre UK's policy is to use papers that are natural, renewable and recyclable products and made from wood grown in sustainable forests. The logging and manufacturing processes are expected to conform to the environmental regulations of the country of origin.

Impression number   26 25 24 23 22 21
Year              2010

iii

**contents**

# Acknowledgements

I am most grateful to my language consultant, Rehema Rajabu, for her painstaking checking of the manuscript and for many helpful suggestions.

Many people have indirectly influenced the content of this book, from friends, colleagues and chance acquaintances in Kenya and Tanzania to several generations of students at the University of York who took Swahili electives; I am indebted to them all. This debt extends to Valerie Perrott, author of the first *Teach Yourself Swahili*, and to Ethel Ashton, whose book, *Swahili Grammar*, has influenced our understanding of the structure of the language for over half a century.

My thanks go to people who – knowingly or unknowingly – have provided direct input, either with linguistic or social information or in some other way: Amina Ali, Jacob & Virgilia Amuli, Susie Bowen, Olwyn Fonseca, Brian Justice, Ken Kaduki, Margaret Kumbuka, Joshua Madumulla, Steve Nicolle and Alison Ross.

I am particularly pleased that Eileen McClelland undertook to do the drawings.

My grateful thanks go to Debbie Phillippo for so efficiently producing a clear manuscript from the untidy and not always very legible drafts and also to Caty Blacktop and Muriel Wood for helping out during the occasional emergency.

The author and publishers would like to thank the following for permission to reproduce copyright material:

The Institute of Kiswahili Research, University of Dar es Salaam, for the extract from *Kipande cha Akili*, in the collection of folktales *Fasihi-Simulizi ya Mtanzania: Hadithi*, published by Dar es Salaam University Press; E. Kezilahabi for the poem *Ngoma ya Kimya* in the collection of his poems *Karibu Ndani*, published by Dar es Salaam University Press; S. Ndunguru, for the extract from Chapter II of *Urithi Wetu*, published by Ndanda Enterprises (T) Ltd.

**introduction**

## About Swahili

Swahili is the most extensively used of the hundreds of Bantu languages spoken in many areas of sub-Saharan Africa. A knowledge of Swahili will enable you to make yourself understood throughout much of east and central Africa.

Swahili is a language that developed and spread through the trading links that the coastal towns had with the interior of Africa and with the lands around the Indian Ocean. Until the early part of the nineteenth century its use was largely confined to the people of the coastal and island towns, stretching from what is now the Somali Republic southwards to Mozambique.

The expansion of the trade-routes between the island of Zanzibar, the coast and the interior gave an impetus to the use of Swahili as a means of communication between people at trading-places who did not share the same 'home language'. Most of the major trade-routes went through modern Tanzania. It is in Tanzania that the use of Swahili is the most widespread. Even in remote areas far from towns, where people have little need to use a language other than their home language, there are likely to be at least some people who know Swahili. For many Tanzanians, Swahili, even if not the first language acquired in childhood, is now the language they use most during the working day. It is the country's national language, and is used in government administration, in schools and in the media.

Pre-twentieth-century links between the coast of Kenya and the interior were much less extensive than those further south and so the use of Swahili did not spread inland to the extent it did in Tanzania. However, all along the Kenya coast and islands, in the inland towns and wherever there is a mixed population of speakers of different languages, Swahili is in use. As in Tanzania, Swahili is a national language, and is used in schools and the media.

Uganda's history and geographical position has not favoured the use of a 'standard' east coast form of Swahili. There was no indigenous Swahili-speaking community from whom the use of the language might have spread. Nevertheless, it is used in Kampala and some of the larger towns.

In these three countries Swahili shares its function as *lingua franca* (auxiliary language) with English in certain domains of use – in the tourist trade, for example. Further west it is French that fulfils this function.

Swahili is also spoken in the eastern part of the Democratic Republic of Congo (formerly Zaire), and is officially recognized as one of the country's four national languages. D.R.C. (Zairean) Swahili differs in some respects from the kind spoken further east, but it is recognizably Swahili; if you go to the Democratic Republic of Congo it is better to know some Tanzanian/Kenyan **Kiswahili Sanifu** than to know none at all. Swahili is also understood in parts of Rwanda and Burundi.

On the margins of the Swahili-speaking area, and this includes the border areas of northern Malawi and Zambia as well as the southern Somali coast and the northern end of the Mozambique coast, you should not expect everyone to know Swahili. In some places it may only be a small proportion of the men in the population who have a working knowledge of it. You should also not be surprised to hear something which at first sounds as if it might be Swahili but turns out to be the local language, which has absorbed words from Swahili.

Since millions of people who use Swahili in east and central Africa have acquired it as a second or third language, people are very relaxed about talking to someone who speaks it rather differently from the way they do. An unfamiliar way of speaking is a source of interest rather than the subject of criticism. No one is going to be horrified or offended if you make mistakes, or have a strong accent to start with. People will be pleased that you are learning Swahili, whether it is their own language or one that they have just picked up or learnt at school. The important thing is to want to talk to people!

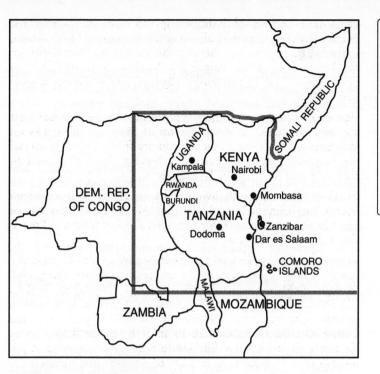

## How to use this course

The course is divided into two parts. Units 1–6 form Part One, a basic survival package for people who do not have time to work through the whole course but would like to get some idea of how the language works, and want something more than a phrase book. Units 7–18, in Part Two, build on the foundation of Part One, and are for people who would like to do more than just 'survive' with the language. Each unit builds on what you have learnt in the previous units, and opens with a short list of what you will know how to say after working through the unit.

Each unit starts with a dialogue: two dialogues per unit in Part One, and one per unit in Part Two. These dialogues, marked by the symbol ▶, are at the heart of each unit and introduce the new words and grammatical structures in the context of an everyday situation.

Then comes a boxed list of the new words and phrases in the order in which they occur in the dialogue.

Next is a section of background information to help you put the dialogue into the context of life in eastern Africa. This is marked **i**.

The next section, the Grammar section, explains the new structures used in the dialogue. Grammatical terms are kept to a minimum and only used where absolutely necessary to give you 'short cuts' to learning. The terms are introduced, with English examples, at the point where they are needed in an explanation.

The final section of each unit is the Practice section. This provides a range of activities which will help you to check your understanding of the dialogue and your ability to use the new words and structures. You will find the answers in the Key to the Exercises following Unit 18.

The Appendix (pp.278–82) contains summaries of the grammatical information taught in the course.

At the end of the book there are Swahili–English and English–Swahili vocabulary lists containing words taught in the course.

## How to use the course with the recording

You will find it helpful to do some listening before you start working through the course. If you are using the recording you should listen to the pronunciation of the sounds and words. If you do not have the recording and are already in a Swahili-speaking area, listen to as much Swahili as you can.

You can see what is in the recorded material from the symbol **▶** next to passages in the book. When you work through a unit, read the dialogue several times (listening to the recording if you have it) using the boxed vocabulary to help you understand it. When you think you have understood most of it read through (and listen) again. It is the dialogue that is most likely to give you a 'feel' for the language and you should not go on to the Grammar section until you have a good grasp of the dialogue.

## How to study

Try to set aside a certain amount of time each day for working on the course. Half an hour each day would be more helpful than one longer session per week. You need frequent practice when you are starting on a language, or trying to brush-up a half-forgotten one.

Set a definite – but realistic – goal for each Swahili-learning session, e.g. aim to work through one dialogue, to learn one list of vocabulary, or to read and understand two sections of a Grammar section. When you learn anything by heart, whether single words, phrases (groups of words) or whole sentences, try to imagine yourself using them in real situations and say them to yourself aloud. Writing things down will also help you to remember them. Try putting lists of vocabulary where you will see them every day – near the bathroom mirror, in the kitchen or by your bed. Try to link your language-learning with activities in your everyday life: for instance, write part of a shopping list in Swahili, keep a daily diary in Swahili – even if, to start with, it is only a sentence or two.

One of the interesting features of Swahili which will help your vocabulary learning is that it has a number of English 'loan-words' in it. A loan-word is a word used in a language other than the one where it originated. Like English, Swahili has a very rich vocabulary because of the words it has absorbed from other languages. Many have come from Arabic and Persian as well as from Gujerati, Hindi, Portuguese and – more recently – English. The reason that you already know the word *safari* in English is because it is a loan-word from Swahili; but it was originally taken into Swahili from Arabic. Loan-words are pointed out from time to time in the course because they 'behave' differently from words of Bantu origin.

You will find that you need to keep a very open mind about language structure; don't expect Swahili to work like English or any other language you know, although here and there you may find similarities. One big difference is in the way the words are composed. For example, in English when we talk about more than one of anything we usually add something to the end of the noun, as in *cat* → *cats*, or we change one or more of its sounds as in *mouse* → *mice*, or we even do both, as in *child* → *children*. But in Swahili it is the beginning of the noun that changes: **mtoto** (*child*) → **watoto** (*children*); **kikapu** (*basket*) → **vikapu** (*baskets*). (This is how it works most of the time, but there is a pleasant surprise in store for you in Unit 2.)

There are also differences in the way words are *organized* in sentences. One very obvious difference is the way 'qualifiers' are used with nouns. (Examples of nouns: *cat, house, mouse, woman, child, basket, happiness, tree.*) A qualifier is a word or group of words used with a noun to add some more information. The words attached to *tree(s)* in the following examples are all qualifiers: *tall trees*; *three trees*; *our trees*; *other trees*; *all trees*; *this tree*; *trees with long roots*; *the tree itself*; *any tree at all*. You will notice that most of the qualifiers come in front of the noun *tree(s)*. In all these examples Swahili puts the qualifier after the noun. So in Swahili we would say: *trees tall*, *trees three*, *trees our*, *trees other* – and so on.

There are other differences to look out for, and you will be introduced to them gradually as you go through the units. Points which are especially important are indicated by '*Note*'.

## Abbreviations

| | |
|---|---|
| (syll.) | syllable |
| (sing.) | singular |
| (pl.) | plural |
| lit. | literally |
| -ni | something must precede **ni** |
| ki- | something must follow **ki** |
| -ta- | something must precede *and* follow **ta** |

**pronunciation**

The best way to acquire good Swahili pronunciation is to imitate native-speakers or people who learned Swahili at school and use it as their primary means of communication. There are two basic rules which will help you to get off to a good start:

1 *Note*: In Swahili the stress of a word almost always falls on the next-to-last syllable. The ´ shows the stressed syllable in the following words: **bába** (2 syllables), **mtóto** (3 syllables), **amepáta** (4 syllables), **aliyekúja** (5 syllables).

2 Keep your voice level, and do not try to emphasize a word by giving it extra stress or raise the pitch of your voice to show surprise. Swahili does, of course, have its own patterns of intonation (rise and fall), which you will acquire naturally, through imitation, but the extent of the rise and fall is much less than in English.

## ▶ Vowels

| Letter | Approximate sound | Example |
|---|---|---|
| a | pronounced rather like the **a** in *father* but halfway towards *bat* | **baba** *father* |
| e | pronounced rather like e in *get*, but it should feel slightly longer | **pete** *ring* |
| i | pronounced like ee in *see* | **kisu** *knife* |
| o | pronounced like o in *olé*, with the lips kept well apart throughout the sound | **boga** *pumpkin* |
| u | pronounced like **oo** in *tooth* | **dudu** *pest* |

*Notes:*

1 When **a** comes at the end of a word it should be pronounced more like a beginning or middle **a** than like *er*. For example, **baba** should not be made to sound like *barber*. This means that you need to keep your mouth well open for the final **a**.

2 When two different vowels occur together each keeps its own sound and forms a separate syllable: **faida: fa-i-da** (3 syllables); **aibu: a-i-bu** (3 syllables).

3 Two similar vowels occurring together count as two syllables, as far as stress is concerned, and are pronounced as a long vowel. For example, **kúfa** (*to die*) has two syllables and **kufáa** (*to be suitable*) has three. (These double vowels are very often the result of the loss of an earlier **l** between the vowels. Later on, you will see that, in certain circumstances, the **l** reappears.)

# ▶ Consonants

In writing Swahili, the only letters of the alphabet that are not used are **q** and **x**.

In the first group of consonants each sound is represented by one letter. The Swahili sound is much the same as the English sound represented by the same letter, but take note of the special comment on **b**, **d**, **g** and **j**.

| Letter | Approximate sound | Example |
|--------|-------------------|---------|
| b | like **b** in *book* | **baba** *father* |
| d | like **d** in *day* | **dada** *sister* |
| f | like **f** in *father* | **fimbo** *stick* |
| g | like **g** in *get* | **gari** *vehicle* |
| h | like **h** in *hot* | **habari** *news* |
| j | like **j** in *job* | **joto** *heat* |
| k | like **k** in *keep* | **kiti** *chair* |
| l | like **l** in *like* | **leo** *today* |
| m | like **m** in *make* | **mama** *mother* |
| n | like **n** in *no* | **na** *and* |
| p | like **p** in *pot* | **pata** *get* |
| r | like **r** in *carrot* | **chura** *frog* |
| s | like **s** in *soft* | **sasa** *now* |
| t | like **t** in *bat* | **bata** *duck* |
| v | like **v** in *voice* | **vuka** *cross* |
| w | like **w** in *wait* | **watu** *people* |
| y | like **y** in *yet* | **yetu** *our* |
| z | like **z** in *zoo* | **zetu** *our* |

*Note on* **b, d, g** *and* **j**

If you have the recording or have listened quite a lot to people speaking Swahili you may have noticed that when these sounds come at the beginning of a word or between vowels – **baba** is a good example – they have a slightly 'hollow' sound. This is because they are produced with a downward movement of the 'voice-box' and an intake of breath. In words such as **mbegu**, **ndefu**, **ngoma** and **njema** they sound (and are produced) much more like the English sounds. The two different kinds of **b, d, g** and **j** don't make a difference to the meaning, so if you cannot manage the 'gulped' ones just use the English sounds.

The **j** sound, except when it follows **n**, needs your tongue-tip to be behind your lower teeth and the main part of your tongue to be touching the roof of the mouth, behind the hard ridge at the back of your upper teeth. If you eventually aim for native-speaker pronunciation you should try to manage this, but it is best practised by watching someone making this sound.

*Notes on* **m**

(Come back to this after Units 1, 2 and 5.)

1 Two groups of words, the singular nouns of classes M/WA (Unit 1) and M/MI (Unit 5), have **m** at the beginning, as a syllable:

**mtu** (2 syllables)    **mtoto** (3 syllables)    **mnanasi** (4 syllables)

If **w** follows **m** in words of these two classes, the **m** is not a separate syllable:
**mwana** (2 syllables)   **mwanangu** (3 syllables)

2 If **m** comes at the beginning of a word in the N class of nouns (Unit 2) it is not a separate syllable. It 'merges' into the next sound which is always either **b** or **v**. So don't linger on the **m** in **mbegu** (2 syllables) or **mvua** (2 syllables).

▶ In the second group of consonants each sound is represented by two letters.

| Letter | Approximate sound | Example |
|---|---|---|
| ch | like **ch** in *chop* | **chakula** *food* |
| dh | like **th** in *this* | **dhahabu** *gold* |
| gh | like **ch** in Scots *loch* (see **kh** below) but voiced | **ghali** *expensive* |

| kh | like **ch** in Scots *loch* or German *Bach* | **Khamisi** *man's name* |
| ng' | like **ng** in *song* | **ng'ombe** *cow* |
| ny | like **n** in *new* and the first **n** in *onion* | **nyama** *meat* |
| sh | like **sh** in *ship* | **shauri** *advice* |
| th | like **th** in *thin* | **thelathini** *thirty* |

*Voiced and voiceless sounds*
(to help with **gh** and **kh,** and with the N class words in Unit 2)

Before trying **gh** and **kh,** make sure you can tell the difference between a voiced sound and a voiceless one. Make the English sounds **p** (voiceless) and **b** (voiced) alternately, with a finger resting lightly on the front of your throat. When you make the **b** sound you should be able to feel the movement in your throat caused by the vibration of the vocal cords in your 'voice-box'. Then try **k** and **g**, and finally **kh** and **gh**. The **kh** and **gh** sounds occur in words of Arabic origin. You need only use the **kh** sound for words that have **kh** in the spelling; it occurs in some Muslim names, such as **Khadija,** and a few greetings. You may hear native-speakers using **kh** in some of the words spelt with **h,** but as this is only appropriate in certain words, it would be best to always pronounce written **h** as **h.**

*Notes on ny, ng and ng'*
1 Remember that **ny** represents a single sound. In Swahili it must never be pronounced like **nigh.**

2 **ng** without the following apostrophe represents the **ng** sound in *finger, hunger, longer,* where the **g** is sounded.

3 **ng'** has no **g** sound in it.

# ▶ Pronunciation practice

1 Practise the double vowels
  (The words with a hyphen at the beginning are verbs.)

| aa | ee | ii | oo | uu |
|------|--------|--------|--------|-------|
| -faa | mzee | hii | choo | buluu |
| -kaa | niletee | mtalii | koo | mguu |
| saa | pekee | utalii | kondoo | wakuu |

2 Practise using **m**. In the first column **m** is a syllable, in the
  second and third columns it is not.

| mfinyanzi | mwana | mbati |
|-----------|----------|--------|
| mgeni | mwalimu | mbavu |
| mtoto | mwezi | mbegu |
| mtu | mwili | mvua |

Notice that in **mtu** the **m** is stressed.

3 Nasal sounds: **ng'**, **ng** and **ny**.

  a  Practise **ng'**, after checking it in the second list of
     consonants. For most (not all) English-speakers this is the
     sound at the end of *sang*, *wrong*, *hung*, etc., and in the
     middle of *hangar*, *singer*, etc. There is no **g** sound.

     Try separating *hangar* like this: *ha-ngar*, then drop the
     *ha*, and say the second part several times. Then just do
     **ng'** with all the Swahili vowels, so that you say: **ng'a,
     ng'e, ng'i, ng'o, ng'u**.

     Then practise these words:

     | ng'ambo | ng'ombe |
     |---------|---------|
     | ng'oa | |
     | ng'ofu | -ng'ong'ona |

  b  The letters **ng** (without the apostrophe) represent two
     sounds, as they do in English: *finger*, *hunger*, *longer*, etc.
     You will need to get used to having these sounds together
     at the beginning of a word. Try these:

     | ngamia | ngoma |
     |--------|-------|
     | ngiri | |
     | ngoja | nguvu |

c The letters **ny** represent only one sound. Have a look at the two English examples in the second list of consonants. If you know any French you can use the sound represented by **gn** in *magnifique* and *agneau*. Remember, **ny** is never a separate syllable.

Practise these words:

| | |
|---|---|
| **nyama** (2 syllables) | **-nyonya** |
| **nyemelea** (4 syllables) | **nyota** |
| **nyerere** | **nyuki** |
| **nyika** | **nyuma** |
| **-nyima** | |

How many syllables do the rest of the words have?

4 Grand finale!
Try saying this word – it has two of the sounds you have been practising, and one of those occurs twice:
**-nyang'anya**
How many syllables are there?

*Note*: In 3(c) **nyerere** has 3 syllables and the other words each have 2 syllables.
In 4 **-nyang'anya** has 3 syllables.

# 01

# hujambo?

how are you?

**In this unit you will learn**
- how to exchange greetings
- how to say where you come from
- how to identify yourself and others

# ▶ Dialogue 1

Alison and John have just arrived in Tanzania. Their friend Mohamed calls at their hotel to see them.

| | |
|---|---|
| **Mohamed** | (*to John*) Hujambo, bwana? |
| **John** | Sijambo. |
| **Mohamed** | (*to Alison*) Hujambo, bibi? |
| **Alison** | Sijambo, bwana. |
| **Mohamed** | Habari za safari? |
| **John** | Njema. |
| **Alison** | Safari njema. |

One of Mohamed's colleagues, Asha, is on her way to work and sees him coming out of the hotel with John and Alison.

| | |
|---|---|
| **Asha** | Hujambo, bwana? |
| **Mohamed** | Sijambo, mama. Habari za asubuhi? |
| **Asha** | Nzuri, bwana. (*to John and Alison:*) Hamjambo? |
| **John and Alison** | Hatujambo, mama. |

| | |
|---|---|
| **hujambo** | *how are you?* (to one person) |
| **bwana** | *sir, Mr, gentleman* |
| **sijambo** | *I'm fine* |
| **bibi** | *lady, Mrs, Miss, Ms* |
| **habari za ...** | *how is/was...* (lit. news of) |
| **safari** | *journey, trip* |
| **njema** (-ema) | *good* |
| **mama** | *Mrs, Miss, Ms, mother, woman* |
| **asubuhi** | *morning* |
| **nzuri** (-zuri) | *good, fine* |
| **hamjambo** | *how are you?* (to more than one person) |
| **hatujambo** | *we're fine* |

## ℹ Hujambo / sijambo; hamjambo / hatujambo

These are the most commonly used greetings and responses. Notice that, in Dialogue 1, Mohamed could have greeted John and Alison jointly with **'Hamjambo?'** as Asha did. This greeting is appropriate for two or more people together.

If you are younger than the people you are going to talk to, you should greet them first. Also, a person newly arrived in a place always greets first the person or people already there.

**Jambo** can mean *affair*, *business*, *circumstances*, or *matter for discussion* according to the context. It is only in greetings that it is attached to **hu-**, **si-**, **ham-** and **hatu-**; these will be explained in Unit 2.

# ℹ️ Bwana, bibi, mama

It is courteous in Swahili (and courtesy is very important wherever Swahili is spoken) to use these as titles when addressing people. They can be used on their own or followed by the person's name, e.g. Mohamed's friends could address him as either **Bwana Mohamed** or **Bwana**. People can be referred to in the same way when they are not present.

In Tanzania, but not elsewhere, **ndugu** (*relation*) can sometimes be heard as a term of address to mean *comrade* or *friend*. Its use has the effect of emphasizing the solidarity of the speaker with the person addressed.

**Bibi** is usually shortened to **Bi.** when followed by the woman's name, e.g. **Bi. Ruth**. **Bibi** is probably rather more common at the coast than inland. Where both **mama** and **bibi** are in use, **bibi** is slightly more formal, and some speakers tend to use it for younger rather than older women. (**Bibi** is also in use as a word for *grandmother* but the context of use usually makes it clear who is being referred to.)

Sometimes a married woman is addressed, and referred to, as **Mama** followed by the name of her eldest or last child, so **Mama Fatuma**, Mohamed's mother, may well be referred to, by family and friends, as **Mama Mohamed**. Also **Mwana** is still heard, in some coastal and island communities, as a very respectful title for a woman, followed by her own name. Note that where two names are used, e.g. **Bi. Rehema Daudi**, the second name is usually the name of the person's father – in this case the names refer to Rehema, daughter of Daudi. Some professional families have adopted the custom of a wife taking one of her husband's names, e.g. his father's name, and using it as a surname.

# ▶ Dialogue 2

The next morning, Mohamed takes Alison to meet his mother, Mama Fatuma, who lives north of Dar es Salaam. They approach her house and stand outside the door, which is slightly open.

| | |
|---|---|
| **Mohamed** | Hodi! |
| **Mama Fatuma** | (*from inside*) Karibu! (*She comes to the door, and sees Alison with Mohamed.*) Karibuni! |
| **Mohamed** | Shikamoo, mama. |
| **Mama Fatuma** | Marahaba. |
| **Mohamed** | Hujambo? |
| **Mama Fatuma** | Sijambo, mwanangu. |
| **Mohamed** | Habari za asubuhi? |
| **Mama Fatuma** | Salama tu. |
| **Alison** | (*to Mama F.*) Shikamoo, mama. |
| **Mama Fatuma** | Marahaba. Karibu sana. Unatoka wapi, bibi? |
| **Alison** | Natoka Uingereza. |
| **Mama Fatuma** | Wewe si Mmarekani? |
| **Alison** | Ndiyo, si Mmarekani. Mimi ni Mwingereza. |

| | |
|---|---|
| **hodi** | *May I / we come in?* |
| **karibu** | (here:) *Come in* (addressed to one person) |
| **karibuni** | *Come in* (to more than one person) |
| **shikamoo** | greeting to an older person or someone the speaker considers to be of higher status |
| **marahaba** | the standard reply to **shikamoo** |
| **mwanangu** (mwana wangu) | *my child, son* or *daughter* |
| **salama** | *safe, in good health* |
| **tu** | *just, simply* (also *only* and *merely*) |
| **karibu sana** | *you're very welcome* |
| **unatoka** | *you come from* |
| **wapi** | *where?* |
| **natoka** | *I come from* (**nina → na**) |
| **Uingereza** | *UK, Britain, England* |
| **Wewe si Mmarekani?** | *You are not an American?* (person from USA) (**Mwamerika** is also used) |
| **ndiyo** | *yes, that is so* |
| **si** | *am not / are not / is not* |
| **Mimi ni Mwingereza** | *I am British* |
| **ni** | *am / are / is* |

*Notes*:

1 You can also call out **Hodi!** if you are trying to make your way through a crowd.

2 There is no English equivalent of **Marahaba**. It cannot be used to initiate a greeting. Only use it as a reply to **Shikamoo**.

# Grammar

## 1 Asking how things are / what's new

**Habari za...** can be used for a variety of different greetings, including ones for different times of the day. In Dialogue 1, Mohamed asked Asha how things were that morning. Here are some more examples of its use:

| | |
|---|---|
| Habari za mchana? | *How's everything today?* |
| Habari za jioni? | *How's everything this evening?* |
| Habari za siku nyingi? | *How's everything since I last saw you?* (some time ago) |
| Habari za tangu jana? | *How's everything been with you since yesterday?* |
| Habari za kazi? | *How's work?* |
| Habari gani? | *What news?* |

| | | | |
|---|---|---|---|
| **mchana** | *daytime* | **kazi** | *work* |
| **jioni** | *evening* | **gani** | *what* |
| **siku nyingi** | *many days* | **nyumbani** | *at home* |
| **tangu jana** | *since yesterday* | | |

Greetings should be kept very general. A man would not, for example, ask about another man's wife, unless he had been told she was ill, or knew the family very well. To enquire about a person's family, say:

| | |
|---|---|
| Habari za nyumbani? | *How's everything at home?* |
| Hamjambo nyumbani? | *Are you all well at home?* |

Sometimes **Habari** is omitted, so that an exchange of greetings might be:

| | |
|---|---|
| A: Za nyumbani? | *(How's everything) at home?* |
| B: Nzuri, za kazi? | *Good, (how's everything) at work?* |

The replies to **Habari za** in the two dialogues are all in common use. **Safi** (*in order, correct*) is also commonly used as a reply. These replies are all positive; one or other of them should always be used as an immediate reply. If there is some bad news to be communicated, that can follow later.

Note that **Shikamoo** is only used to greet someone older or of higher status than the speaker.

Telephone conversations tend to begin with 'Hello' followed by one or more of the **Habari...?** variants.

## 2 Nouns and noun-prefixes

Words for people, places, things or ideas – nouns – function in various 'classes' in Swahili. Most of these noun-classes group together similar types of nouns. The class membership of a noun can be recognized, in most cases, by the bit at the beginning – the *noun-prefix*. For example, the word **mtu**, which means *person*, is made up of two parts, and the prefix is **m-**. If you want to talk about more than one person, the prefix is **wa-**: **watu** means *people*.

| Singular: m- | | Plural: wa- | |
|---|---|---|---|
| **mtu** | *person* | **watu** | *people* |

## 3 Mmarekani, Mwingereza and other M/WA class nouns

**Mtu** and **watu** are in the M/WA class of nouns. In this class, if the main part of the noun begins with a *vowel* (a, e, i, o, u), the singular prefix is **mw-** instead of **m-**, e.g. **mwana** (*son/daughter*). The plural prefix follows these rules: **wa + a** makes **wa-**, **wa + e** makes **we-**, **wa + i** makes **we-**: e.g. **wana** (*sons / daughters*). The only exceptions are words for nationalities or other established group names, in which cases the vowel of the main part of the word is retained, as in **Waingereza**.

| Singular: | | Plural: | |
|---|---|---|---|
| **mwana** | *son/daughter* | **wana** | *sons/daughters* |
| **Mwingereza** | *British person* | **Waingereza** | *British people* |

The words below are also in the M/WA class. You should learn all these by heart as soon as you can; they will be used in subsequent units. More M/WA words will be introduced in the units that follow. Almost all the words in this class refer to people – two exceptions are **mnyama** (*animal*) and **mdudu** (*insect*).

| M/WA class nouns | | |
|---|---|---|
| | Singular | Plural |
| **Mfaransa** | French (person) | **Wafaransa** |
| **mfinyanzi** | potter | **wafinyanzi** |
| **mgeni** | guest, visitor, stranger | **wageni** |
| **mgonjwa** | sick person | **wagonjwa** |
| **Mhindi** | Indian (person) | **Wahindi** |
| **Mjerumani** | German (person) | **Wajerumani** |
| **Mkristo** | Christian (person) | **Wakristo** |
| **mkulima** | farmer | **wakulima** |
| **mpokeaji** (or **mpokezi**) | receptionist | **wapokeaji** |
| **mtalii** | tourist | **watalii** |
| **mtoto** | child | **watoto** |
| **mwalimu** | teacher | **walimu** or **waalimu** |
| **mwanafunzi** | student, pupil | **wanafunzi** |
| **mwanamke** | woman | **wanawake** |
| **mwanamume** | man | **wanaume** |
| **Mwislamu** | Muslim (person) | **Waislamu** |
| **mwuguzi** | nurse | **wauguzi** |
| **mzee** | old person | **wazee** |
| **Mzungu** | European (person) | **Wazungu** |

## 4 Verbs and verb-prefixes

**a** Verbs are words or combinations of words which refer to actions, events and states. In the following sentences, for example, the words printed in italics are all verbs:

They *gave* her some food.   I *will read* it tomorrow.
He *will be leaving* for Cairo.   The manager *received* a complaint.
She *has* malaria.   We *don't like* mushrooms.
*Unatoka* wapi, bibi?   Where *do you come from*, madam?
*Natoka* Uingereza.   I *come from* Britain.

In Swahili, a verb is made up of several parts, as in **unatoka** (*you come from*):

| | |
|---|---|
| **u-** | you (singular) |
| **-na-** | present time |
| **-toka** | *come from* (this is the verb 'stem'; in dictionaries it is the stem of the verb which is given, so **-toka** can be found under T) |

**b** The first part of the verb, **u-** in the case of **unatoka,** will be referred to as the *verb-prefix.* This prefix stands for the subject of the verb (like *it, I, you, he, she, we, they* in English): in this case, *you* (one person only). In a sentence the verb has to be closely linked to its subject, and this linking is done through the **verb-prefix.** Most noun-classes each have a pair of verb-prefixes, one for singular subjects (*it*) and one for plural subjects (*they*). It is only the **M/WA** class that has six.

So that you can talk about yourself and about other people, you need to learn all the verb-prefixes for the M/WA class of nouns:

| | | | |
|---|---|---|---|
| ni- | I | tu- | we |
| u- | you (sing.) | m- | you (pl.) |
| a- | he / she | wa- | they |

The following sentences show how these prefixes work:

| | |
|---|---|
| **Ni**natoka Manchester. | *I come from Manchester.* |
| **U**natoka Nairobi? | *Do you (sing.) come from Nairobi?* |
| **A**natoka Marekani. | *He comes from the USA.* |
| | *She comes from America.* |
| **Tu**natoka Uingereza. | *We come from the UK/Britain.* |
| **M**natoka Kenya? | *Do you (pl.) come from Kenya?* |
| **Wa**natoka Kisumu? | *Do they come from Kisumu?* |

If you need to mention who the subject is, just put the word or words at the beginning:

| | |
|---|---|
| Mohamed anatoka Dar es Salaam. | *Mohamed comes from Dar es Salaam.* |
| Mama Fatuma anatoka Tanzania. | *Mama Fatuma comes from Tanzania.* |
| Bi. Alison na Bw. John wanatoka Uingereza. (**na** = *and*) | *Alison and John come from Britain.* |

## 5 Ndiyo *It is so*

Although **ndiyo** is often translated as *yes* and does have a *yes* function in Swahili, it really means *it is so,* i.e., *it is as you say.* In Dialogue 2, Alison is mistaken for an American. Mama Fatuma says to Alison, '**Wewe si Mmarekani?**' (*'You're not American?'*). When Alison replies, '**Ndiyo, si Mmarekani**', she is saying, *'That's right, (I'm) not American.'*

If the question addressed to you is 'Ni Mwingereza?' or 'Wewe ni Mwingereza?' the correct reply – if you *are* British – is 'Ndiyo, ni Mwingereza.'

## 6 Names of countries

Many Swahili-speakers inevitably have a very hazy idea of the composition of the UK, just as many English-speakers (wherever they live) have difficulty in identifying African countries and places within them. **Uingereza** is used variously to refer to the *United Kingdom*, *Britain* or just *England*. There are no well-established Swahili names for Scotland, Wales and N. Ireland, and if people need to refer specifically to any of these they are likely to have sufficient knowledge of the English language – and European geography – to use the English names. Not all Swahili names of countries have a U- prefix, but quite a few do, and they form one set of words that belong to the U class of nouns which will be dealt with in Unit 6.

a  Countries (U class nouns):

| | | | |
|---|---|---|---|
| **Ubelgiji** | *Belgium* | **Uingereza** | *UK, Britain, England* |
| **Uchina** | *China* | **Ujerumani** | *Germany* |
| **Ufaransa** | *France* | **Ulaya** | *Europe* |
| **Uganda** | *Uganda* | **Ureno** | *Portugal* |
| **Ugiriki** | *Greece* | **Urusi** | *Russia* |

b  Countries without the U- prefix:

| | | | |
|---|---|---|---|
| **Afrika ya Kusini** | *South Africa* | **Marekani** | *USA* |
| **Bara Hindi** | *India* | **Misri** | *Egypt* |
| **Hispania** | *Spain* | **Msumbiji** | *Mozambique* |

## Practice

1  How would you:

   a  Reply to a child who greets you with '**Shikamoo**'?
   b  Ask someone how his/her journey was?
   c  Reply to the greeting '**Hujambo**'?
   d  Ask someone how things are this morning?
   e  Ask to come in to someone's house? (See Dialogue 2.)

**f** (Together with a companion) reply to 'Hamjambo'?

**g** Reply to 'Habari za mchana'?

**h** Welcome a visitor into your home? (See Dialogue 2.)

**i** Ask someone how everything is at home?

**j** Welcome a group of people into your home? (See Dialogue 2.)

2 How would you say:

**a** I come from America.

**b** Where do you (sing.) come from?

**c** She comes from Liverpool.

**d** Do they come from Kenya?

**e** They come from Nairobi.

**f** Where do you (pl.) come from?

**g** Does he come from Germany?

**h** Do you (pl.) come from Uganda?

3 Rearrange the list of person words (List B) so that each of them is next to the appropriate country.

e.g. Marekani (*USA*) Mmarekani (*American person*)

| A | B |
|---|---|
| Kenya | Mtanzania |
| Uchina | Mfaransa |
| Uingereza | Mrusi |
| Uganda | Mganda |
| Ufaransa | Mwingereza |
| Tanzania | Mkenya |
| Urusi | Mjerumani |
| Ujerumani | Mchina |

4 Write a suitable question for each of the following answers. The first one has been done for you.

**a** **Hodi!** Karibu, Bi. Alison.

**b** —————— Hatujambo, mama.

**c** —————— Njema tu.

**d** —————— Safari nzuri.

**e** —————— Tunatoka Marekani.

**f** —————— Sijambo, bwana.

**g** —————— Marahaba.

**h** —————— Ndiyo, ni Mwingereza.

**i** —————— Ndiyo, si Mmarekani.

5 Make up an exchange of greetings between yourself and the person or people in each of the following pictures. If you are learning Swahili with a friend or in a group, do some role-plays of different greeting sequences.

6 Identify the people in these pictures:

A          B          C

Jeanne na Pierre     Bw. Musa          Mama Amina

**D**   **E**   **F**

Bw. Ramadhani    Bi. Bertha    Lulu na Abdu

e.g. **A** Jeanne na Pierre ni watalii. (*Jeanne and Pierre are tourists.*)

Then answer the following questions, using **ndiyo** or **siyo** and **ni** or **si**.

e.g. **a** Siyo, Bi. Bertha si mtalii. Bi. Bertha ni mwuguzi.

**a**   Bi. Bertha ni mtalii?
**b**   Pierre ni mpokeaji?
**c**   Bw. Ramadhani ni mwalimu?
**d**   Lulu na Abdu ni wapokeaji?
**e**   Jeanne ni mtalii?
**f**   Mama Amina ni mwuguzi?
**g**   Bw. Musa ni mpokeaji?
**h**   Abdu ni mwanafunzi?

*Note:*
Do remember that the greetings are absolutely essential for successful communication. Make sure you know all the **M/WA** class nouns introduced here before you go on to Unit 2. Also make sure that you can remember the six verb-prefixes. Try practising them by making up sentences about yourself and your friends, e.g. **Ninatoka Birmingham, Bill anatoka Washington, Heidi na Otto wanatoka Berlin...**

You will be delighted to know that each of the other noun-classes, one per unit in Part One, has only two verb-prefixes – because, of course, you only need words for *it* and *they* when things, rather than people, are involved.

# 02

## kwenda posta
going to the post office

**In this unit you will learn**
- how to ask and understand simple directions
- how to ask where something is located
- how to count
- how to buy stamps at the post office

# ▶ Dialogue 1

John is on his way from the hotel to the post office.

| | |
|---|---|
| **Dereva** (*taxi driver*) | Hujambo, bwana? Teksi? |
| **John** | Sijambo, bwana. Habari za asubuhi? |
| **Dereva** | Safi sana, bwana. Teksi? |
| **John** | Hapana. Nakwenda posta tu. Iko karibu? |
| **Dereva** | Iko karibu sana. Nenda moja kwa moja, halafu pinda kushoto. Nenda moja kwa moja, moja kwa moja, halafu utaona posta, upande wa kulia. |
| **John** | Haya, asante sana, bwana. Kwa heri! |
| **Dereva** | Haya, bwana. Karibu tena! |

| | |
|---|---|
| **dereva** | *driver* (here: *taxi-driver*) |
| **teksi** | *taxi* |
| **sana** | *very, very much* |
| **hapana** | *no* |
| **nakwenda** (ni-na-kwenda) | *I'm going (to)* |
| **posta** | *post office* |
| **iko** | *it is (located)* |
| **karibu** | *near, nearby* |
| **nenda** | *go (to one person)* |
| **moja kwa moja** | *straight on* |
| **halafu** | *then* |
| **pinda** | *turn* |
| **kushoto** | *left* |
| **utaona** (u-ta-ona) | *you will see* |
| **upande wa kulia** | *(on) the right side* (lit. *side of right*) |
| **haya** | *OK* |
| **asante** | *thanks* |
| **kwa heri** | *goodbye* |
| **karibu tena** | a polite farewell (lit. *welcome again*) |

In some areas people say **naenda** rather than **nakwenda**, meaning *I'm going/I'm on my way*.

kushoto        kulia

# ℹ Street transactions

If the taxi driver's question seems rather brusque and insistent, it should be remembered that overseas visitors, whether temporary workers or tourists, represent a potential source of income for which there is fierce competition in the capital cities and larger towns of Africa. Urban taxi drivers and street traders in east Africa get used to dealing with tourists who have little or no knowledge of Swahili and who may be in a hurry. People with services to offer are good at modifying their language to suit the circumstances and will often use very simple Swahili until they have assessed a visitor's knowledge of the language. Transactions are carried out at a more leisurely pace away from the large towns.

# Grammar

## 1 Teksi, posta and other N class nouns

a Teksi and posta, like many other loan-words, function as members of the N class of nouns. This class is so called because some of the words of Bantu origin in it begin with a 'nasal' sound, written as **m**, **n**, **ny** or **ng'**. A few of the commonly used words with this nasal prefix are given in the N class vocabulary box below, along with some non-prefixed ones, including those introduced in this unit and Unit 1.

| N class nouns | | | |
|---|---|---|---|
| **asubuhi** | *morning* | **nguo** | *garment* |
| **barua** | *letter* | **njia** | *road* |
| **chai** | *tea* | **nyumba** | *house* |
| **chumvi** | *salt* | **posta** | *post office* |
| **habari** | *news* | **safari** | *journey* |
| **kahawa** | *coffee* | **shilingi** | *shilling* |
| **kompyuta** | *computer* | **stampu** | *stamp* |
| **mvua** | *rain* | **sukari** | *sugar* |
| **ndizi** | *banana* | **teksi** | *taxi* |

You will find some of these words in the next dialogue. As is clear from the nouns in the box, the N class is rather a ragbag as far as meaning is concerned. But it does contain one group of words for living beings, and these will be dealt with separately. This class contains many loan-words, which have no prefix, and some words of Bantu origin which have lost their prefix.

One good thing about the N class from a learner's point of view is that the singular and plural forms of the nouns are the same.

| Singular | | Plural | |
|---|---|---|---|
| **nyumba** | *house* | **nyumba** | *houses* |
| **ny - umba** | | **ny - umba** | |

  ↑   ↑                  ↑   ↑

prefix stem                prefix stem

Although in other noun classes the form of the prefix remains virtually the same whatever noun-stem it is attached to, in the N class the form of the prefix varies according to the first sound in the stem. The 'stem' is the main part of a noun – the part to which the prefix is attached. It is worth noting here the rules for the nasal prefix because they also apply to *adjectives* ('describing words' like *good*, *bad*, *short*, *tall*, etc.) and other qualifiers which must be made to agree with their noun by having the same prefix. You can leave the learning of these rules until later if you like, and just learn the N class nouns in the vocabulary box.

*Notes to Grammar section 1a*

1 Loan-words, and noun-stems of Bantu origin beginning with the voiceless consonants **p**, **f**, **s**, **ch**, **k** and **t**, do not take a prefix. The only exceptions are the few stems of this sort that have a single syllable. Like all single-syllable stems of Bantu origin in this class, they take a prefix, which carries the stress, e.g. **ńchi**.

2 Stems beginning with a vowel take the prefix **ny-**, e.g. **nyumba**.

3 Stems beginning with **b**, **v** or **w** take the prefix **m-**, e.g. **mvua**. In addition, **w** becomes **b**, e.g. **m + wili** becomes **mbili** (**-wili** is the stem for *two*). Do not confuse this **m** with the singular prefix of the M/WA class. In the N class the only reason that **m** occurs as a prefix is that it is the appropriate nasal prefix for noun-stems beginning with sounds made with the lips closed or partly closed.

4 Stems beginning with **d**, **j**, **z** or **g** take the prefix **n-**, e.g. **ndizi**, **njia**, **nguo**. Although we write **n-** as the prefix for stems beginning with **g**, its *sound* is like the sound at the end of *thing*, not *thin*. (See the guide to pronunciation, pages xvi and xvii.)

**5** Stems beginning with **l** or **r** also take the prefix **n**, and the **l** or **r** changes to **d**, e.g. **n** + **limi** (*tongues*) becomes **ndimi**, **n** + **refu** (*long*) becomes **ndefu**.

The prefix for this class must originally have been something like **ni-**, which contracted to **ny-** and **n-**. If you try pronouncing **n** before **b** or **v** you will feel how easily it changes to **m**.

You would probably find it helpful at this point to listen several times to the N class nasal prefixes in the pronunciation guide at the beginning of the recording.

**b** Verb prefixes
This is where the difference between singular and plural shows up.

Singular: **i-**          Plural: **zi-**

Teksi **i**natoka wapi?      Teksi **zi**natoka wapi?
*Where is the taxi coming*    *Where are the taxis coming*
   *from?*                      *from?*

Words for 'uncountables' like **mvua** (*rain*), **sukari** (*sugar*), etc., use the singular verb-prefix only.

**c** People and other creatures in the N class
Most words for animals and insects, and some words for people, are in this class. Two occurred in Unit 1 – **mama** and **ndugu**. They are like the other N nouns in that singular and plural are the same; but they take the verb-prefixes of the M/WA class. Here are a few of the most frequently used N class 'animates':

| | | | |
|---|---|---|---|
| **askari** | *soldier* (also used for *policeman*, which is *askari polisi* in full) | **mbuzi** | *goat* |
| | | **mbwa** | *dog* |
| | | **ng'ombe** | *cow* |
| **baba** | *father* | **nyoka** | *snake* |
| **dada** | *sister* | **paka** | *cat* |
| **kaka** | *brother* | **rafiki** | *friend* |
| **kuku** | *chicken, hen* | **samaki** | *fish* |
| **mbu** | *mosquito* | | |

| Askari anatoka wapi? | *Where does the policeman come from?* |
| Askari **wa**natoka wapi? | *Where do the policemen come from?* |
| Paka anatoka wapi? | *Where does the cat come from?* |
| Paka **wa**natoka wapi? | *Where do the cats come from?* |

## 2 Being in a place

The **ni/si**, *is/is not*, forms used in Dialogue 2 of Unit 1 cannot be used to talk about people or objects being in a place. For this a particular structure is used:

$$\underset{\substack{\uparrow \\ \text{verb prefix}}}{\text{i}} + \underset{\substack{\uparrow \\ \text{place-marker}}}{\text{ko}} \rightarrow \text{iko}$$

Using **wapi** (*where*) and a few N class nouns, we can ask:

Sukari iko wapi? *Where is the sugar?*
Nguo ziko wapi? *Where are the clothes?*

Similarly, using M/WA verb-prefixes:

| Niko wapi? | *Where am I?* |
| Mohamed yuko wapi? | *Where is Mohamed?* |
| Tuko wapi? | *Where are we?* |
| John na Alison wako wapi? | *Where are John and Alison?* |

Note that the form meaning *he/she is located...* is **yuko**, and not 'ako' as you might have expected.

There are three place-markers:

**-ko** refers to indefinite location, and is therefore the form used when asking where someone or something is.

**-po** refers to definite location, as in **yupo posta**, *she's at the post office*, not necessarily inside it – she might be waiting just outside.

**-mo** refers to location inside, as in **yumo posta**, *she's inside the post office* – perhaps sheltering from heavy rain.

The use of any one of these is dependent on the circumstances as the speaker sees them, but you can restrict yourself to **-ko** until you have gained more experience with the language.

In the post office, John goes towards one of the windows at the counter.

| | |
|---|---|
| **John** | (*to a young woman nearby*) Habari gani, bibi? |
| **Bibi** | Nzuri, bwana. |
| **John** | Nitapata stampu hapa? |
| **Bibi** | Hapana, hutapata stampu hapa. Angalia juu! (*She reads aloud the notice above the counter:*) 'Hundi za posta'. Simama pale. Utapata pale. |
| **John** | (*to the counter clerk at the correct window*) Naomba stampu kwa barua hizi, kwenda Uingereza kwa ndege. |
| **Karani** (*clerk*) | Una barua ngapi? |
| **John** | Nina barua tatu. |
| **Karani** | Haya. Stampu tatu za shilingi mia moja na sabini ni shilingi mia tano na kumi. |
| **John** | Na barua hii nataka kupeleka Mwanza. |
| **Karani** | Moja tu? |
| **John** | Ndiyo, moja tu. |
| **Karani** | Unataka stampu ya shilingi arobaini. Jumla ni shilingi mia tano na hamsini. (*John passes a Sh 1000/– note to the clerk who then gives him the change.*) Haya, chukua chenji ya shilingi mia nne na hamsini. Karibu tena. |
| **John** | Asante sana. |

| | |
|---|---|
| **nitapata** (ni-ta-pata) | *I will get* |
| **hapa** | *here* |
| **hutapata** (hu-ta-pata) | *you will not get* |
| **angalia** | *look, pay attention* |
| **juu** | *up, above, top* |
| **hundi za posta** (N)* | *postal orders* |
| **simama** | *stand* |
| **pale** | *over there* |
| **utapata** (u-ta-pata) | *you will get* |
| **naomba** (ni-na-omba) | *I want* |
| **kwa** | *for* |
| **barua** (N)* | *letter* |
| **hizi** | *these* (with N nouns) |
| **kwenda** (ku-enda) | *to go* |
| **kwa ndege** (N)* | *by air* (**ndege** is *aeroplane* and *bird*) |

| karani | clerk |
| --- | --- |
| **una** (u-na) | you have |
| **ngapi?** | how many? (referring to N class nouns) |
| **nina** (ni-na) | I have |
| **tatu** | three |
| **za** | of |
| **shilingi** | shilling |
| **mia moja na sabini** | 170 |
| **mia tano na kumi** | 510 |
| **hii** | this |
| **nataka** (ni-na-taka) | I want, need |
| **kupeleka** (ku-peleka) | to send |
| **moja** | one |
| **ya** | of |
| **arobaini** | 40 |
| **jumla** (N)* | total |
| **mia tano na hamsini** | 550 |
| **chukua** | take |
| **chenji** (N)* | change |
| **mia nne na hamsini** | 450 |

*Note*: New N class nouns in the vocabulary box are indicated by (N). After a noun class has been introduced, new nouns in that class which occur in subsequent units will be labelled, e.g. nouns in the 'Human' class will have (M/WA) attached to them from here on.

## ℹ️ Post offices

It is only in large post offices in the cities and larger towns that people like John may find themselves going to the wrong window if they fail to read the signs above the counter. We can assume that John was in the post office in Maktaba Street in Dar es Salaam (still referred to by residents as **posta mpya** – the 'new post office') where only certain counters are allocated to the sale of stamps. The spelling can vary between **stampu** and **stempu**.

Post offices are always busy places, not only because of the transactions inside but because people who rent mail boxes come to collect their letters from them. Only the holder of the key to a particular numbered box has access to that box and can collect letters from it. Addresses must therefore contain the correct P.O. Box number:

*Bibi Amina Omari*

*S.L.P. 584*

*Musoma*

*Mkoa wa Mara*

| **S.L.P. (sanduku la posta)** | *P.O. Box* |
|---|---|
| **la** | *of* |
| **Mkoa wa Mara** | *Mara Region* |

# ℹ️ Money

Kenya, Tanzania and Uganda all have the **shilingi** (*shilling*) as their unit of currency, but its value varies markedly from one country to another. One hundred shillings is abbreviated as 100/– or Sh.100.

There are three words in current use meaning *money* and all are in the N class: **fedha**, **hela**, and **pesa**. Note that **fedha** also means *silver*. Hela is only likely to be heard in Tanzania and is used much less frequently than the other two words.

# Grammar

## 3 How many?

**Ngapi** (*how many*) is one of the words that takes the same prefix as the noun to which it refers. Since it already begins with a nasal sound we do not have to attach a nasal prefix to make it agree with an N class noun:

| Barua ngapi? | *How many letters?* |
|---|---|
| Nyumba ngapi? | *How many houses?* |
| Shilingi ngapi? | *How many shillings?* |

N class words for humans and other creatures take M/WA prefixes on qualifiers. This means that when **ngapi** follows one of these words it must be prefixed with **wa-**:

| Askari **wangapi**? | *How many soldiers?* |
|---|---|
| Mbuzi **wangapi**? | *How many goats?* |
| Ng'ombe **wangapi**? | *How many cows?* |
| Paka **wangapi**? | *How many cats?* |

| 1 | **moja** | (-moja) | 11 | **kumi na moja** | (-moja) |
|---|----------|---------|----|-------------------|---------|
| 2 | **mbili** | (-wili) | 12 | **kumi na mbili** | (-wili) |
| 3 | **tatu** | (-tatu) | 13 | **kumi na tatu** | (-tatu) |
| 4 | **nne** | (-nne) | 14 | **kumi na nne** | (-nne) |
| 5 | **tano** | (-tano) | 15 | **kumi na tano** | (-tano) |
| 6 | **sita** | | 16 | **kumi na sita** | |
| 7 | **saba** | | 17 | **kumi na saba** | |
| 8 | **nane** | (-nane) | 18 | **kumi na nane** | (-nane) |
| 9 | **tisa** | | 19 | **kumi na tisa** | |
| 10 | **kumi** | | | | |

## 4 Numbers

This box, like the following two boxes, shows the *cardinal numbers* (*one, two, three*, etc.). You will need to know these in order to make *ordinal numbers* (*first, second, third*, etc.), which will be dealt with later.

Numbers 1–5 and 8 have to agree with the noun they qualify:

| mtu **m**moja | *one person* |
|---------------|--------------|
| watu **wa**wili | *two people* |

In counting and mathematics, 1, 2, 3, 4, 5 and 8 are used as if in agreement with N class nouns; this is the form shown in the box. These numbers take a prefix even when they are used with **kumi** (*ten*) as part of a larger number:

| watu kumi na **wa**wili | *12 people* |
|-------------------------|-------------|
| watu kumi na **wa**nane | *18 people* |

The stems of those numbers that need a noun-class agreement prefix when they qualify a noun are shown in brackets in the box above.

| 20 | **ishirini** | 60 | **sitini** |
|----|--------------|----|------------|
| 22 | **ishirini na mbili** | 66 | **sitini na sita** |
| 30 | **thelathini** | 70 | **sabini** |
| 33 | **thelathini na tatu** | 77 | **sabini na saba** |
| 40 | **arobaini** | 80 | **themanini** |
| 44 | **arobaini na nne** | 88 | **themanini na nane** |
| 50 | **hamsini** | 90 | **tisini** |
| 55 | **hamsini na tano** | 99 | **tisini na tisa** |

None of the words for 20, 30, 40, etc., takes a prefix. The prefixed numbers 1–5 and 8, when used with **ishirini**, **thelathini**, **arobaini**, etc., to form a number, behave as they do when used with **kumi** – they take a prefix:

| | |
|---|---|
| watoto ishirini na **wa**tatu | *23 children* |
| watoto arobaini na **wa**tano | *45 children* |
| watoto sitini na **wa**nane | *68 children* |

| | | | |
|---|---|---|---|
| 100 | **mia** | 250 | **mia mbili na hamsini** |
| 101 | **mia na moja** | 999 | **mia tisa, tisini na tisa** |
| 200 | **mia mbili** | 1000 | **elfu** |

The word for *hundred*, **mia**, is in the N class. Notice that if you want to talk about a number of hundreds, the word for that number follows **mia**.

| | |
|---|---|
| wanafunzi mia tatu, hamsini na wanne | *354 students* |
| wanafunzi mia sita, thelathini na tisa | *639 students* |

In referring to numbers in which hundreds of thousands are involved, the qualifying number is usually put before **elfu** instead of after it, to avoid confusion.

| | |
|---|---|
| mia tano elfu, na moja | *500,001* |
| elfu moja mia tano na moja | *1,501* |

## 5 Talking about the future

Future time is marked by putting **-ta-** between the verb-prefix and the verb:

| | |
|---|---|
| nitatoka | *I will leave* |
| tutatoka | *we will leave* |

Notice that **nitatoka** can mean in English *I will leave*, *I will be leaving*, *I am leaving* (at some future time) and *I leave* (at some future time).

## 6 The negative forms of verb-prefixes

*Not doing* or *being* something is indicated by putting the negative prefix **ha-** immediately in front of the verb-prefix.

In the N class the negative forms of the verb-prefixes are absolutely regular, as they are in all the other classes except the M/WA class:

| | | | |
|---|---|---|---|
| **hai-** | | **hazi-** | |
| negative + it (N class) | | negative + they (N class) | |

In the M/WA class, some contraction has taken place, and the negative forms of the verb-prefixes are:

| | | | |
|---|---|---|---|
| **si-** | (*not* hani-) *I* | **hatu-** | *we* |
| **hu-** | (*not* hau-) *you* (sing.) | **ham-** | *you* (pl.) |
| **ha-** | (*not* haa-) *he / she* | **hawa-** | *they* |

    Sitapata stampu.     *I will not get stamps.*
    Hawatapata hundi za posta.   *They will not get postal orders.*

These negative verb-prefixes remain the same, whatever the tense (present, future, etc.). In the present tense you also have to change the end of the verb to make it negative; this will be explained in Unit 3.

## 7 Having

*To have*, in Swahili, is to 'be with', and in all tenses other than the present, the verb **kuwa** (*to be*) is used followed by **-na**. **Na** is a word that expresses association. In the present tense only **-na** is required, attached to the verb-prefix.

| | | | |
|---|---|---|---|
| **nina** | *I have* | **tuna** | *we have* |
| **una** | *you have* (sing.) | **mna** | *you have* (pl.) |
| **ana** | *he / she has* | **wana** | *they have* |

The negative forms of the verb-prefixes with **-na** are as explained above under section 6.

    Una barua?     *Have you a letter?*
    Sina barua.     *I haven't a letter.*
    Wana stampu?     *Do they have stamps?*
    Hawana stampu.     *They have no stamps.*

Now you can see that the greetings using **jambo**, introduced in Unit 1, have developed in the course of time out of negative **-na** forms.

| Huna jambo? | *You have no problem?* | is now **Hujambo?** |
| Sina jambo | *I have no problem.* | is now **Sijambo.** |
| Hamna jambo? | *You (all) have no problem?* | is now **Hamjambo?** |
| Hatuna jambo | *We have no problem.* | is now **Hatujambo.** |

Using the full form **kuwa na** with the future marker **-ta-** enables you to say, for example:

| Atakuwa na shilingi mia. | *She will have Sh 100.* |
| Hawatakuwa na pesa. | *They won't have any money.* |

## 8 Telling someone to do something

In Dialogue 2 the young woman says to John, '**Angalia juu!**' Here the verb has no verb-prefix or tense-marker. The same is true of **simama** in the same dialogue. In Dialogue 1, **pinda** and **nenda** are similarly used.

These verb-stems are being used as *imperatives*, or orders, like the verbs in these English sentences: '*Look!*', '*Sit down!*', '*Come here!*' There are only four irregular imperatives:

| **lete!** | *bring!* | from the verb **-leta** |
| **nenda!** | *go!* | from the verb **-enda** |
| **njoo!** | *come!* | from the verb **-ja** |
| **kula!** | *eat!* | from the verb **-la** (**kula** also means *to eat*) |

# Practice

1

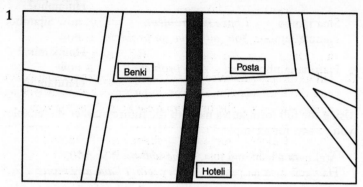

Using the information on the map and assuming you and the enquirer are facing in the direction of the required destination:

- **a** Tell someone who is at the hotel how to get to
  - the post office
    e.g. Nenda moja kwa moja, halafu pinda kulia.
    Nenda moja kwa moja, halafu utaona posta upande wa kushoto.
  - the bank

- **b** Tell someone who is at the bank how to get to the hotel.
- **c** Tell someone who is at the post office how to get to the hotel.

| | | | |
|---|---|---|---|
| **benki** (N) | *bank* | **barabara** (N) | *main road* |
| **hoteli** | *hotel* | **vuka** (verb) | *cross* |

The shaded road on the map is a **barabara**; the unshaded roads are narrower minor roads, **njia**. *Cross the main road is* **Vuka barabara.**

- **d** Tell someone who is at the bank how to get to the post office.
- **e** Tell someone who is at the post office how to get to the bank.

2 Fill in the gaps in the following questions:

- **a** Wageni _____ko wapi?
- **b** Chai _____ko wapi?
- **c** Mbuzi _____ko wapi?  (N class animate)

d   Mtoto _____ko wapi?
e   Kahawa _____ko wapi?
f   Posta _____ko wapi?
g   Wajerumani _____ko wapi?
h   Dada _____ko wapi?        (N class animate)

3   Fill in the gaps and also provide a suitable reply, using **posta** and the four words in the vocabulary box below, as well as names of towns. The first two have been done for you.

| **baa** (N) | *bar* | **sinema** (N) | *cinema* |
|---|---|---|---|
| **benki** (N) | *bank* | **stesheni** (N) | *station* |

a   Baba _____ko wapi?        Baba yuko Kampala.
b   Wanafunzi _____ko wapi?   Wanafunzi wapo baa.
c   Mzee _____ko wapi?        _____
d   Bw. Omari _____ko wapi?   _____
e   Ali na Amina _____ko wapi? _____
f   Mama _____ko wapi?        _____
g   Askari _____ko wapi?      _____
h   Wauguzi _____ko wapi?     _____

*Note:*

Although it would be acceptable at this stage to use **-ko** in all your replies, try to think of circumstances which would require the use of **-po** or **-mo** to convey a more precise meaning. If necessary look back at section 2 of the Grammar in this unit – 'Being in a place' – to revise the functions of the three place-markers **-po**, **-ko** and **-mo**. You will need to imagine the locations and their size, and whether you want to convey that the people referred to are in the general area of the place, precisely at it or right inside it.

4   If you want to tell someone that Mr Athumani is not in the bank, he's at the post office, you say:

**Bw. Athumani hayupo benki, yupo posta.**

The negative forms of the verb-prefixes referring to humans, introduced in section 6, can be used with **-ko**, **-po** and **-mo**, as well as with full verbs and **-na**.

Try these:

a   Juma is not at the post office, he's at the station.
b   The tourists are not in Dar es Salaam, they're in Tanga.
c   Miss Ruth is not in Nairobi, she's in Mombasa.
d   The students are not at the cinema, they're at the bar.
e   The French person is not at the station, he's in the bar.

Try not to be influenced by the English prepositions *in* and *at*; think about the size of the locations and how precisely you can locate the people in relation to them.

5   With a partner, develop some of the questions and replies that you did for Practice question 3 into short dialogues, by adding a question using **ipi**, *which*, used only in questions, and a reply using **karibu na**, *near* (a place).

The ending -pi takes the verb-prefix. The i- in **ipi** is the N class singular verb-prefix; this is the only noun-class involved here because you will only be using **baa**, **benki**, **posta**, **sinema** and **stesheni**, all N class nouns. Here is an example to start you off:

A. Wanafunzi wako wapi?
B. Wapo baa.
A. Baa ipi?
B. Karibu na stesheni.

6   Write, in words, the amount you need to pay for each of the following purchases at the post office. **Nunua** = *buy*.

a      Nunua stampu tano.
**Shilingi ishirini.**

b      Nunua stampu tatu.
**Shilingi _____**

c      Nunua stampu mbili.
**Shilingi _____**

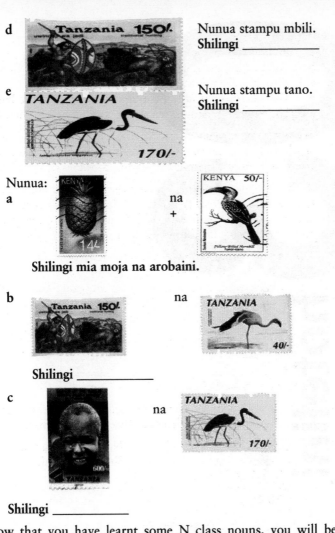

**d**

Nunua stampu mbili.
**Shilingi** _____

**e**

Nunua stampu tano.
**Shilingi** _____

7   Nunua:
**a**                        na
                             +

**Shilingi mia moja na arobaini.**

**b**                        na

**Shilingi** _____

**c**                        na

**Shilingi** _____

Now that you have learnt some N class nouns, you will be pleased to know that no other class has so many complications of the noun-class prefix. Don't worry if you found the rules set out in section 1 of the Grammar a bit daunting; they are there for reference. For the moment, just make sure you can remember most of the nouns in the boxes. It's a good idea to start with the English loan-words, and then go on to words for things you use frequently in everyday life. So, on to Unit 3 and the next noun-class, which has verb-prefixes identical to the noun-prefixes – a real incentive to keep going!

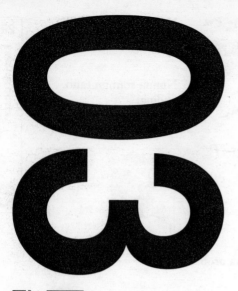

# 03

## hotelini
### in the hotel

**In this unit you will learn**
- how to enquire about a hotel room
- how to use ordinal numbers
- how to express likes and dislikes
- how to apologize
- how to identify some dishes in a restaurant

# ▶ Dialogue 1

A new guest arrives at the **mapokezi** (*reception desk*).

| | |
|---|---|
| **Mgeni** | Habari za hapa? |
| **Mpokeaji** | Safi sana, bwana. Habari za safari? |
| **Mgeni** | Salama tu. Jina langu Mathew Dunstan. Chumba changu kiko wapi? |
| **Mpokeaji** | Chumba chako? |
| **Mgeni** | Ndiyo, chumba changu. Nilipiga simu jana, kuwekesha chumba. |
| **Mpokeaji** | (*consulting the booking sheet*) Sina habari hapa. Samahani! Subiri, bwana. |
| | (*He goes into the office behind the reception desk, talks to someone, and soon returns.*) Unataka chumba cha mtu mmoja? Leo? |
| **Mgeni** | Ndiyo. Naomba chumba chenye choo na bafu. |
| **Mpokeaji** | Kipo kimoja kwenye ghorofa ya tatu. |
| **Mgeni** | Sipendi ghorofa ya juu. Mimi napenda ghorofa ya kwanza. |
| **Mpokeaji** | Kipo kimoja kwenye ghorofa ya kwanza, lakini kidogo. |
| **Mgeni** | Si kitu. Chumba kidogo kitafaa. Nitaondoka kesho. |
| **Mpokeaji** | Sawa. |

| | |
|---|---|
| **hotelini** (hoteli-ni) | *in / at the hotel* |
| **mapokezi** | *reception counter, desk* |
| **jina langu** | *my name* |
| **chumba changu** | *my room* |
| **nilipiga simu** | *I telephoned* |
| **jana** | *yesterday* |
| **kuwekesha** | *to reserve, book* (a room) |
| **samahani!** (or **msamaha**) | *apologies!* |
| **-subiri** | *wait* |
| **chumba cha mtu mmoja** | *a single room* |
| **leo** | *today* |
| **chenye** | *with, having* |
| **choo** | *lavatory, toilet* |
| **bafu** | *bath, shower* |
| **kwenye** | *at/on* |
| **ghorofa ya tatu** (N) | *third floor* |
| **sipendi** | *I don't like / want* |
| **-penda** | *like* |
| **ghorofa ya juu** (N) | *top floor* |
| **ghorofa ya kwanza** (N) | *first floor* |

| lakini | *but* |
| kidogo | *small* (room) |
| si kitu (kitu means *thing*) | *it's nothing, it doesn't matter* |
| kitafaa | *it* (i.e. the room) *will do, will be suitable* |
| -ondoka | *leave a place, set off* |
| kesho | *tomorrow* |

*Note*: In some places, e.g. Zanzibar, **mfereji** is used for *shower*.

*Note:* From this unit onwards, new verbs in the vocabulary boxes, if they occur in the dialogue with a prefix and tense-marker that have already been introduced, will be shown in their stem form only, like **-penda** and **-ondoka**.

## ⓘ Hotels

The word **hoteli** covers a very wide range of types of accommodation and eating-places. At one end of the scale are the 'international' hotels such as the most expensive ones in the capital cities and at the coast. At the other end of the price-range are small rural hostelries, hardly distinguishable from nearby village houses, apart from sometimes displaying a soft drink advertisement outside. This is the sort of place, remote from towns, that you would encounter during a refreshment stop on a long-distance bus journey.

John and Alison's hotel, the setting for the dialogues in this unit, is a no-frills middle-range one with three floors. It has one restaurant with a short menu listing mainly local dishes; this contrasts with the 'international' hotels which have an array of restaurants, grills, carveries, bruncheries, coffee shops, etc. There is always at least one receptionist on duty at the reception counter. Note that **mpokeaji** (*receptionist*), its alternative **mpokezi**, and **mapokezi** are all derived from the verb **-pokea** meaning *receive*.

## Grammar

### 1 The -ni suffix

Hoteli, like most nouns other than names of places and words for people and animals, takes the ending **-ni** to convey *at*, *in*, *on*, *to*, *from*, etc. The rest of the sentence and the context of use make clear the exact nature of the location or direction.

hotéli → **hotelíni** *in/at/to/from the hotel*
chúmba → **chumbáni** *in/at/to/from the room*
Watalii wapo hotelíni. *The guests are at the hotel.*
Alison yumo chumbáni. *Alison is in the room.*

(The stress marks are a reminder that as soon as you add a syllable to the end of a word, you have to shift the stress to the right, to keep it on the penultimate syllable.)

The words introduced in Unit 2 which do not take **-ni** (**baa, benki,** etc.) are used as if they are place names:

Joel yuko Uganda?    Yuko Uganda.
Francis yupo posta?    Yupo posta.

The small number of words that never use **-ni** are nearly all loan-words, although one that is not is the word for *shore/beach/coast* – **pwani** (N). There is, however, a definite tendency for phrases (groups of words) denoting specific places to be used without **-ni**. Two examples of such phrases are those meaning *police station* and *airport* in the KI/VI vocabulary box on page 34.

## 2 Chumba, choo, kitu and other KI/VI class nouns

**a** In this noun-class, **ki-** is the prefix for singular nouns and **vi-** for plurals. When the noun-stem begins with **a, e, o** or **u, ki-** changes to **ch-** and **vi-** changes to **vy-** (with just a few exceptions).

e.g.   ki + umba → **chumba**
vi + umba → **vyumba**

Notice that we have also had **-umba** with an N class prefix – **nyumba**.

Loan-words which begin with **ki-** or **ch-** tend to be absorbed into this class and develop plural forms in **vi-** or **vy-**, as in the cases of **kitabu**, *book* (from Arabic) and **cheti**, *note* (from Hindi).

This class includes words for:

- inanimate objects
- people and animals (very restricted)
- diminutive forms of nouns in other classes
- a few body-parts

| KI/VI class nouns | |
|---|---|
| Singular | Plural |
| **chakula**  food | **vyakula** |
| **chandalua**  mosquito net | **vyandalua** |
| **cheti**  note, brief letter, receipt | **vyeti** |
| **chungu**  earthenware cooking pot | **vyungu** |
| **kiatu**  shoe | **viatu** |
| **kiazi**  sweet potato | **viazi** |
| **kichwa**  head | **vichwa** |
| **kijiko**  spoon | **vijiko** |
| **kikapu**  basket | **vikapu** |
| **kikombe**  cup | **vikombe** |
| **kisu**  knife | **visu** |
| **kitabu**  book | **vitabu** |
| **kitanda**  bed | **vitanda** |
| **kiti**  chair | **viti** |
| **kituo cha ndege**  airport | **vituo vya ndege** |
| (also **kiwanja cha ndege**) | (**viwanja vya ndege**) |
| **kituo cha polisi**  police station | **vituo vya polisi** |

**b** The verb-prefixes are the same as the noun-prefixes:

Singular: **ki-**              Plural: **vi-**

Chumba kitafaa?               Vyumba vitafaa?
*Will the room do?*            *Will the rooms do?*
*Will the room be suitable?*   *Will the rooms be suitable?*

Kitabu kiko wapi?             Vitabu viko wapi?
*Where is the book?*           *Where are the books?*

**c** Some of the most common words for people and animals in this class are listed in the next vocabulary box. They, like the N class animates, take the verb-prefixes of the M/WA class.

| KI/VI class: people and animals | |
|---|---|
| Singular | Plural |
| **kiboko**  hippopotamus | **viboko** |
| **kifaru**  rhinoceros | **vifaru** |
| **kijana**  young person, older child (pre-adolescent) | **vijana** |
| **kiongozi**  leader | **viongozi** |
| **kipofu**  blind person | **vipofu** |
| **kiwete**  lame person | **viwete** |
| **kiziwi**  deaf person | **viziwi** |

Viongozi wanakwenda Arusha. *The leaders are going to Arusha.*

# 3 Possessives

These are words meaning *my/mine*, *your/yours*, *her/hers*, etc., as in *It's my book*, *The book is mine*.

These are the stems for possessives:

| | | | |
|---|---|---|---|
| -angu | *my, mine* | -etu | *our, ours* |
| -ako | *your, yours* (sing.) | -enu | *your, yours* (pl.) |
| -ake | *his/her, his/hers* | -ao | *their, theirs* |

These forms take the verb-prefix of the noun they qualify (i.e., the noun they are giving more information about).

**a Possessives with M/WA nouns**

As the *he/she* verb-prefix is **a-** and the *they* prefix is **wa-** you would expect **a-** to be prefixed to possessives qualifying singular nouns and **wa-** to possessives qualifying plural nouns. But **wa-** is in fact used for *both* singulars and plurals; it is reduced to **w-** in front of the possessives:

| | | | |
|---|---|---|---|
| **wangu** | *my* | **wetu** | *our* |
| **wako** | *your* | **wenu** | *your* |
| **wake** | *his/her* | **wao** | *their* |

| | | | |
|---|---|---|---|
| mgeni wangu | *my visitor* | wageni wangu | *my visitors* |
| mgeni wetu | *our visitor* | wageni wetu | *our visitors* |

(There are several more unpredictable irregularities in the way the singular nouns of this class agree with qualifiers. They will be pointed out later.)

**b Possessives with N nouns**

Singular: **i-** (becomes **y-**)          Plural: **zi-** (becomes **z-**)
**yangu, yetu**, etc.          **zangu, zetu**, etc.

| | | | |
|---|---|---|---|
| nyumba yangu | *my house* | nyumba zangu | *my houses* |
| nyumba yetu | *our house* | nyumba zetu | *our houses* |

| | |
|---|---|
| Nyumba ndogo ni yangu. | *The small house is mine.* |
| Nyumba ndogo ni zetu. | *The small houses are ours.* |

*Notes to Grammar section 3b:*

Although almost all qualifiers of N nouns denoting people or animals take M/WA class prefixes – whether noun-prefix or verb-prefix – the possessives are an exception and take the **i-** (**y-**) and **zi-** (**z-**) prefixes like this:

- With words for people, in both singular and plural:

  rafiki yangu  *my friend*        rafiki zangu  *my friends*
  rafiki yetu   *our friend*       rafiki zetu   *our friends*

- With words for animals, in the plural only, with the singular taking the M/WA class prefix **wa-** (**w-**):

  ng'ombe wangu  *my cow*         ng'ombe zangu  *my cows*
  ng'ombe wetu   *our cow*        ng'ombe zetu   *our cows*

c Possessives with KI/VI nouns
  Singular: **ki-** (becomes **ch-**)      Plural: **vi-** (becomes **vy-**)
  **changu, chetu,** etc.                  **vyangu, vyetu,** etc.

  kikapu changu  *my basket*      vikapu vyangu  *my baskets*
  kikapu chetu   *our basket*     vikapu vyetu   *our baskets*

- *Note*: A note on word order: as well as remembering that qualifiers almost always follow the noun, note too that if you use a possessive and another qualifier as well, such as a numeral or a descriptive adjective (e.g. **-dogo**, *small*) it is the possessive which comes first:

  mbuzi zangu wanane  *my eight goats*
  chumba chetu kidogo  *our small room*

- The form **-ao** (*their*) is only used when referring to possession by people and animals. When the possessor is inanimate, **-ake** has to be used, for plurals as well as singulars. For example, when referring to the price of bananas: **bei yake**, *their price*.

## 4 -a *of*

This is another form that takes the verb-prefix. In the dialogue the receptionist asks the guest if he wants a **chumba cha mtu mmoja**, a *single room* – literally a 'room of one person'. The source of **cha** is **ki + a**. You had another example of 'verb-prefix + a' in Unit 1 in the greeting **Habari za asubuhi?** which literally means *News of the morning?*; in that case the verb-prefix was **zi-**, the appropriate prefix for **habari**, an N class plural noun.

'Verb-prefix + **a**' has an *of* function and one of its common uses is to refer to something that is 'possessed', when the owner or associate is also mentioned.

Any slight change in the shape of a verb-prefix when it is attached to **-a** is exactly the same as when it is attached to the possessives beginning with **-a** (in fact the possessive stems contain this **-a** within them). The irregularity noted in section 3 for the agreement of possessives with M/WA class nouns applies to **-a** too.

| | |
|---|---|
| mtoto wa Bw. Juma | *Mr Juma's child* |
| kahawa ya mwalimu | *the teacher's coffee* |
| vyandalua vya wanafunzi | *the students' mosquito nets* |

There is quite a lot of flexibility in the use of **-a** with N class animates. Some Swahili-speakers use the same rule as for the possessives **-angu**, **-ako** etc. (see section 3), and others use the M/WA verb-prefix **wa-**, reduced to **w-**:

*Either* mbuzi za mwalimu
    *or* mbuzi wa mwalimu   *the teacher's goats*
*Either* rafiki ya mtalii
    *or* rafiki wa mtalii    *the tourist's friend*

Note that it is the word for what is 'possessed' that comes first in the phrase; it is this word that **-a** must agree with. The word for the 'possessor' comes at the end of the phrase.

An alternative way of saying the same thing is to use the possessives, like this:

| | |
|---|---|
| mtoto wake Bw. Juma | *Mr Juma's child* |
| wazee wake Bi. Amina | *Miss Amina's old people/parents* |

Another function of **-a** is to make adjectives, as in **ghorofa ya tatu, ghorofa ya juu, ghorofa ya kwanza** in the dialogue.

## 5 Ordinal numbers: -a kwanza, etc.

As noted in section 4 above, numbers denoting order are made with **-a**. Except for *first* and *second* the actual number-words used are the cardinal numbers given in Unit 2. The only new words you need to learn are:

| -a kwanza | *first* | -a mwisho | *final/last* |
|---|---|---|---|
| -a pili | *second* | | |

mgeni wa kwanza      *the first visitor*
Mfaransa wa pili     *the second French person*
nyumba ya tatu       *the third house*
chungu cha mwisho    *the final pot*

## 6 Omission of ni in 'is' sentences

In the dialogue there are two sentences where **ni** (*am, are, is*: see Unit 1) might be used in more formal or written Swahili, but where it is left out in everyday conversation:

Jina langu (   ) Mathew Dunstan.  *My name is Mathew Dunstan.*

Kipo kimoja kwenye ghorofa ya    *There is one on the*
kwanza, lakini (   ) kidogo.     *first floor but it's small.*

These sentences show two typical contexts in which **ni** is commonly omitted.

## 7 Past tense: -li-

There is one example in the dialogue of a verb in the past tense: **nilipiga simu**, *I telephoned* (**-piga** means *hit* or *beat* and gets used with a variety of following nouns to make different verb-meanings). Like **-na-** (for the present tense) and **-ta-** (for the future tense) it is placed immediately after the verb-prefix; this is where all Swahili tense-markers occur.

Nilinunua viatu.   *I bought some shoes.*
Ulinunua chai?     *Did you buy some tea?*

To make the negative of the past tense:

- add **ha-** to the verb-prefix (remembering that the M/WA singular verb-prefixes become **si-, hu-, ha-**), and
- change **-li-** to **-ku-**

Sikununua viatu.              *I didn't buy any shoes.*
Hukununua chai?               *Didn't you buy any tea?*
Hamkuenda Kisumu?             *Didn't you (pl.) go to Kisumu?*
Chumba chake hakikufaa.       *Her room wasn't suitable.*

(Notice that **-ku-** replaces the **-kw-** in **kwenda**.)

# 8 Adjectives: single words, with prefix

An adjective is a word used with a noun to represent some quality of whatever is denoted by that noun. *Small, tall, heavy, black, red, horrible, attractive* are all examples of English adjectives. Words like these are sometimes called qualitative adjectives, for obvious reasons. All single-word adjective stems of Bantu origin take the noun-prefix, like **-dogo** in the dialogue, and **-zuri** and **-ema** (both meaning *good*) which were introduced in Unit 1.

Adjectives used with N class animates take the M/WA prefixes.

| | |
|---|---|
| watoto wazuri | *good children* (pleasant; well-behaved) |
| watoto wema | *good children* (of good character) |
| habari njema | *good news* |
| paka wadogo | *small cats* (N animate) |
| kisu kizuri | *a good knife* (serviceable) |

Note the difference in meaning between **-zuri** and **-ema**, especially when applied to people.

Here are a few more qualitative adjective stems:

| | | | |
|---|---|---|---|
| **-baya** | bad | **-kubwa** | large |
| **-chache** | few | **-pana** | broad, wide |
| **-embamba** | narrow, thin | **-pya** | new, recent, modern |
| **-ingi** | many | **-refu** | long, tall |
| **-ingine** | some of / other / different | | |

*Note:* The following few 'special cases' should be noted:

- **-pya with N class nouns**
  This stem was used in **posta mpya** in the explanation about post offices on p.20. It can only qualify nouns denoting non-living things. It is the only adjective that is a single syllable, and even though it begins with a voiceless consonant – which would not normally be given an N prefix – it takes the prefix **m-** when qualifying N class nouns. The **m-** is stressed and functions as a syllable, so **mpya** has two syllables.

- **KI/VI prefixes and adjective stems beginning with -i**
  Instead of changing to **ch-** and **vy-** these prefixes stay as **k(i)** and **v(i)**, e.g. **kingine, vingi**. One **i** gets 'lost': **i + i** gives **i**.

• **-ema with N class nouns**
When this qualifies an N class noun it takes the form **njema**, as in **habari njema**, *good news*. With all other adjective-stems beginning with -e the N class noun-prefix follows the rule set out on p.16, e.g. **nyembamba**.

## ▶ Dialogue 2

Alison and John go into the hotel dining-room with Mohamed.

| | |
|---|---|
| **Mohamed** | Tukae wapi? |
| **Alison** | Tukae pale, karibu na dirisha. |
| | (*They sit at a table near the window, and consult the menu*.) |
| **Mohamed** | Je, mnapenda chakula gani? |
| **Alison** | Mimi napenda wali kwa samaki. |
| **Mohamed** | Samaki wa namna gani? |
| **Alison** | Sijui. (*Checking the fish dishes on the menu*:) Wana changu na 'kingfish'. |
| **John** | Ala! 'Kingfish!' Jina lake kwa Kiswahili? |
| **Mohamed** | 'Kingfish' ndio nguru. |
| **Alison** | Haya basi, wali kwa nguru. |
| **Mohamed** | (*to John*) Na wewe, kaka? |
| **John** | Mimi napenda wali kwa nyama. |
| **Mohamed** | Hupendi biriani? |
| **John** | Biriani ni chakula gani? |
| **Mohamed** | Ni wali kwa nyama, pamoja na viungo vingi. |
| **Alison** | Viungo? |
| **Mohamed** | Viungo, ndiyo, kama iliki, dalasini ... na bizari. |
| **John** | (*Noticing the price*:) Naona biriani ni ghali. |
| **Mohamed** | Si ghali sana. Ninyi ndio wageni wetu! |
| **John** | Haya basi. Nitakula biriani ya nyama ya ng'ombe. |
| **Mohamed** | Haya, vizuri. Mi napenda wali kwa kuku. (*He calls the waiter who is standing nearby*.) Kaka! |

| | |
|---|---|
| **tukae wapi?** | *where shall we sit?* (here: **-kaa** = sit) |
| **tukae pale** | *let's sit over there* |
| **dirisha** | *window* |
| **je** | *well, now then, hi there!* |
| **wali** | *cooked rice* |
| **kwa** | *with* |
| **samaki** (N) | *fish* |
| **namna** (N) | *kind, sort, type* |
| **gani** | *what* |
| **sijui** | *I don't know* |
| **changu** (N) | *a kind of sea-fish (also* **tangu***)* |
| **ala!** (alá) | *an expression of surprise* |
| **jina lake** | *its name* |
| **kwa Kiswahili** | *in Swahili* |
| **ndio** | *an emphatic form of* **ni***, is or* (in this case) *are* |
| **nguru** (N) | *kingfish* |
| **basi** | *so, now, well* |
| **haya basi** | *OK then, well now* |
| **biriani** (N) | *a highly-spiced rice and meat dish* |
| **kabisa** | *extremely, very ... indeed* |
| **pamoja na** | *together with* |
| **viungo** (KI/VI) | *spices and seasonings, flavourings* |
| **kama** | *like, such as* |
| **iliki** (N) | *cardamom seeds* |
| **dalasini** (N) | *cinnamon* |
| **bizari** (N) | *curry powder, ingredients of curry powder* |
| **-ona** | *see, feel* |
| **ghali** | *expensive* |
| **ninyi** (or **nyinyi**) | *you* (pl.) |
| **-(ku)la** | *eat* |
| **nyama ya ng'ombe** (N) | *beef* (lit. meat of cow) |
| **mi** | short form of **mimi**, *I* |

*Note*: Structures like **tukae** will be explained in Unit 6.
Notice the use of **kaka** (*brother*) for calling the waiter.

# ℹ️ Eating out, and local food

The major components of **biriani** (sometimes called **birinzi**) are rice and meat, but they are cooked with many more spices than the ones mentioned by Mohamed. Similar, but less rich and easier to prepare, is **pilau** (N). The simpler, everyday, dishes are like those chosen by Alison and Mohamed. The basic part of the meal is either **wali** or **ugali**, a kind of polenta made with maize flour or, – in some places – cooked bananas, and it is this that really counts as **chakula**. The accompaniment, called **kitoweo** (KI/VI), is a meat, fish or vegetable stew; the meat can be beef, goat or chicken. Pork is not much used; even if it had been on the menu Mohamed, being Muslim, would not have chosen it. In the hotel dining-room the waiter would probably have also brought them small individual dishes of **kachumbari** (N), a mixture of chopped tomatoes, onions and perhaps cucumber.

The tourist hotels and some restaurants tend to have cosmopolitan menus, with one section reserved for local dishes. Drinks and snacks are available in cafés. For more casual eating in town, there are roadside foodstalls selling snacks such as roasted maize-cobs and thin wedges of cassava, spicy kebabs, nuts and a variety of sweetmeats and cakes. Among the more common of the cakes are the doughnut-like **maandazi** and **mahamri**, both containing cardamom seeds, and also **vitumbua** and **vibibi**.

| | |
|---|---|
| **kuku** (N) | *chicken* |
| **maandazi, mahamri** | *doughnut-like buns containing cardamom seeds* |
| **matango** | *cucumbers* |
| **mishikaki** | *kebabs* |
| **mahindi** | *maize (sweetcorn)* |
| **gunzi** | *maize cob* |
| **muhogo** | *cassava root and plant* |
| **nyama ya mbuzi** (N) | *goat meat* |
| **nyanya** (N) | *tomatoes* |
| **vibibi** (KI/VI) | *small pancakes* |
| **vitumbua** (KI/VI) | *rice buns* |
| **vitunguu** (KI/VI) | *onions* |

# Grammar

## 9 Present tense negatives

In the conversation there are two examples of present-tense verbs used in the negative:

sijui                *I don't know*
hupendi biriani?     *Don't you like biriani?*

There is also an example of **sipendi** (*I don't like*) in the first dialogue in this unit, where the new guest tells the receptionist he doesn't like the top floor. And **sipendi** is what John could have said instead of **hapana** to the taxi driver in the fourth line of the first dialogue of Unit 2. **Sipendi** or its plural form **hatupendi** is the usual polite way of declining goods and services.

The negative prefixes are as given in section 6 of the Grammar in Unit 2, repeated here as part of the negative form of **-jua**, *know*, in the present tense with all the 'persons' of the M/WA class:

| | | | |
|---|---|---|---|
| **si**jui | *I don't know* | **hatu**jui | *we don't know* |
| **hu**jui | *you* (sing.) *don't know* | **ham**jui | *you* (pl.) *don't know* |
| **ha**jui | *he/she doesn't know* | **hawa**jui | *they don't know* |

Notice that there is no tense-marker, and the final -a of the verb-stem is changed to -i. The following examples use **-faa**, *be suitable*:

. . . with N class subjects:

Nyama haifai     *The meat isn't suitable.*
Bizari haifai    *The curry powder isn't suitable.*

. . . with KI/VI class subjects:

Kisu hakifai     *The knife isn't suitable.*
Vitabu havifai   *The books aren't suitable.*

So, to talk about *not* doing something, in the present tense:

• Add **ha-** to the verb prefix (remembering the exceptions to this in the M/WA singulars).
• There is no tense-marker.
• The final -a of the verb changes to -i. This only happens with negatives in the present tense.

## 10 Kwa Kiswahili

### Kwa

One of the functions of **kwa** is to introduce a word or phrase that denotes the means by which something is done, or the purpose for which it is done.

| | |
|---|---|
| Sema kwa Kiswahili. | *Say it in Swahili.* |
| Kwa nini? (lit. 'For what?') | *Why?* |

### Ki-

The **ki-** prefix means *in the manner of* so Kiswahili must once have meant *'in the manner of the Swahili people'*. It will turn up again later in the book but for the moment, just note that it is the appropriate prefix to denote a language when attached to a stem referring to a nationality/country. If you turn back to the list of countries with the U- prefix, in the vocabulary box on p.9, you can make a list of language names by replacing U- with Ki- (ignore Ulaya and Ubelgiji):

| | |
|---|---|
| Sema kwa Kiingereza. | *Say it in English.* |
| | (Only to be used as a last resort!) |

## 11 Adjectives: single words, without prefix

There is one of these adjectives (**ghali**, *expensive*) in the conversation where John says '**Naona biriani ni ghali.**' *'It looks to me as if biriani's expensive'* would be an equivalent thing to say in English. Here are a few more adjectives that do not take a prefix; they are of Arabic origin:

| | | | |
|---|---|---|---|
| **hodari** | brave | **safi** | clean, honest, |
| **maskini** | poor | | straightforward |
| **rahisi** | easy/cheap | **tajiri** | rich |

**Safi** has already been introduced as one of the suitable replies to a **Habari...?** greeting.

*Note*: The next two do not take prefixes either, but need special mention because they go *before* the noun:

| | |
|---|---|
| **kila** | each |
| **kina (or akina)** | the group associated with ... |

**Kila** is quite straightforward to use:

kila mtu     *each person*
kila nyumba  *each house*

**Kina**, sometimes **akina**, is only used to refer to a group (family, clan, colleagues or some other grouping) associated with the person referred to. You can only use **kina / akina** successfully if you are sure your hearer knows which particular group you have in mind:

(a)kina mama  *the womenfolk*  (a)kina Mohamed  *Mohamed's lot*

## 12 Mimi, wewe, yeye *I, you, he/she, etc.*

These are called *personal pronouns*. In Swahili the single-word personal pronouns are used only for emphasis in situations where in English we would put heavy stress on the pronoun, e.g. '*I like rice and meat, even though she doesn't*', '*What are you going to have? I've told you what I'm going to have*' etc. These pronouns are not given heavy stress in Swahili.

Here are all the personal pronouns; you have already been introduced to three of them:

| | | | |
|---|---|---|---|
| **mimi** | *I* | **sisi** | *we* |
| **wewe** | *you* (sing.) | **ninyi (nyinyi)** | *you* (pl.) |
| **yeye** | *he/she* | **wao** | *they* |

When a full verb (e.g. **penda**) or a place-marker (e.g. **ko**) is used with an M/WA class subject, the verb-prefix itself functions as a personal pronoun. This is why **mimi**, **wewe**, etc., are needed only for emphasis.

In the case of **ni** and **si**, which are not full verbs, the single-word personal pronouns are necessary in sentences such as:

Yeye ni Mmarekani,     *He is American, I'm German.*
  mimi ni Mjerumani.

But in casual conversation the **ni** can be omitted from sentences like this.

# 13 Verbs of one syllable, and ku-

There are only a few verbs with a stem of one syllable; **-la**, *eat*, used in the dialogue, is one of these. John says '**Nitakula biriani ya nyama ya ng'ombe**' *I'll have* (lit. 'eat') *beef biriani*.

The **ku-** in **kula** is like the **ku-** in **kuwekesha** (see Dialogue 1) and usually functions like the *to* in English *to go, to eat, to see,* etc. But the monosyllabic verbs keep the **ku-** with all the tenses you have learnt so far. These are among the tense-markers that cannot carry stress so the inclusion of **ku-** prevents them from occurring as the penultimate syllable.

| Present tense: | -na- | Tunakula. | *We are eating.* |
|---|---|---|---|
| Future tense: | -ta- | Atakula biriani. | *He will eat biriani.* |
| Past tense: | -li- | Walikula ugali. | *They ate polenta.* |

But the negative forms you have learnt allow the **ku-** to be dropped:

| Past negative: | siku ____ | Sikula pilau. |
|---|---|---|
| (-li- → -ku-) | | *I didn't eat pilau.* |
| | hawaku ____ | Hawakula samaki. |
| | | *They didn't eat fish.* |

The **-ku-** in the above examples is the past tense negative marker.

| Present negative: | si ____ i | Sili kuku. |
|---|---|---|
| (-a → -i) | | *I don't eat chicken.* |
| | hawa ____ i | Hawali nyama. |
| | | *They don't eat meat.* |

Remember that the present negative does not have a tense-marker.

Here are four more monosyllabic verbs. **Kuwa** was mentioned in Unit 2 on p.24.

| | | | |
|---|---|---|---|
| **ku-ja** | *(to) come* | **ku-pa** | *(to) give* |
| **ku-nywa** | *(to) drink* | **ku-wa** | *(to) be* |

*Note*: Two verbs which have more than one syllable but tend to follow the rules of the monosyllabic verbs are: **(kw)isha**, *finish*, and **(kw)enda**, *go*.

# Practice

1  This is a receipt from a one-night stay at a small hotel.

   a  Write in words the sum you would have to pay for three days' accommodation.
   b  Suggest the meaning of (1) **hundi** (2) **sahihi**.
   c  Suggest the meaning of **Nimepokea**. Although the tense-marker has not yet been introduced, you should already know the verb-prefix and the verb, and the context should give you a good idea of the meaning.

---

No.  *63*                    Tarehe ......*9/8*....20..*02*....

Nimepokea kutoka kwa  *Mwl. T.C. Kondo*

...................................*NA. 13*...................................

Kiasi cha Shilingi.......*Elfu kumi*...........................

kwa malipo ya  *malazi ya siku moja tu*

Shs.  *10,000/–*                    *P.L Mwenzi*

TASLIM/HUNDI No. .........          SAHIHI YA MPOKEAJI

---

| **kiasi** (KI/VI) | amount | **malazi** | accommodation, bedding |
| **kutoka (kwa)** | from | **taslim** (N) | total cash payment |

▶ 2  Match the questions on the left with the answers on the right:

| | | | |
|---|---|---|---|
| a | Mtoto huyu ni wako? | 1 | Iko karibu na benki. |
| b | Chumba hiki ni chako? | 2 | Siyo, ni ndogo. |
| c | Hoteli yetu iko wapi? | 3 | Siyo, sitakwenda pale. |
| d | Wageni wenu wanakwenda wapi? | 4 | Ndiyo, yeye ni wangu. |
| | | 5 | Aliomba kimoja tu. |
| e | Nyumba ya wazee ni kubwa? | 6 | Siyo, ni cha Bwana Omari. |
| f | Vitabu hivi vitafaa? | 7 | Havitafaa. |
| g | Utakwenda kituo cha polisi? | 8 | Wanakwenda nyumbani. |
| h | Aliomba vyote? | | |

3   You have arranged to meet a friend near the reception desk of your hotel. While you are waiting, you overhear two conversations. Reconstruct them from the information given below, then act them out, or write them.

   a   **Mpokeaji na Bwana Clement**
       The receptionist and Bw. Clement exchange greetings, then Bw. Clement asks for a single room. The receptionist asks if the second floor will do, and Bw. Clement says yes, it will be OK.

   b   **Mpokeaji na Bw. Robert**
       They exchange greetings. Bw. Robert asks for a room for three people, adding that one of the people is a small child. The receptionist says they have a large room with (**chenye**) two beds; will it be suitable? Bw. Robert replies that it will.

4   Fill in the gaps in the following sentences using suitable adjectives from the box. The ones with a hyphen will need the appropriate noun-class prefix. In **b** 'hawa' means 'these'.

   | -dogo   -embamba   -pya   ghali   hodari   kila |
   |---|

   a   Askari ni _____ sana.
   b   Mbuzi _____ hawa ni wake?
   c   Visu vikubwa ni _____; vidogo ni rahisi.
   d   Njia za Nairobi si _____, ni pana sana.
   e   Kisu hakifai; nitapata kisu _____.
   f   _____ mwalimu ana nyumba yake.

5   Mohamed thinks Alison is a bit fussy about food, so he asks her to tell him exactly what she likes and doesn't like. Say what she tells him (mostly tongue in cheek!), using the information below. The first sentence has been done for you.

   I don't like meat but I like fish. I like rice but I don't like polenta. I don't like cardamom but I like cinnamon. I like doughnuts but I don't like rice buns. I don't like onions but I like tomatoes.

   **Sipendi nyama lakini napenda samaki.**

## As the saying goes . . .

Learn these three proverbs:

> Ahadi ni deni.
> *A promise is a debt.*

> Kuuliza si ujinga.
> *To ask is not stupidity.*

> Mtu ni watu.
> *A person is people* (or *No man is an island*).

Swahili is very rich in proverbs, and they are used in everyday conversation to emphasize a point or sum up an argument. Quoting a proverb to children is a way of teaching desirable behaviour and attitudes, or admonishing them, in a non-confrontational way, for unacceptable behaviour. More proverbs later!

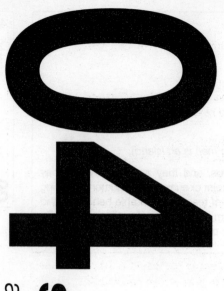

# 04

## sokoni

at the market

**In this unit you will learn**
- how to ask the price of market produce
- how to do simple bargaining to reduce the price
- how to say goodbye
- how to order drinks and food
- how to talk about doing things for other people

# ▶ Dialogue 1

Alison is with Regina at a market. They stop at a stall piled with oranges and other fruit.

| | |
|---|---|
| **Alison** | Unahitaji matunda gani leo? |
| **Regina** | Nahitaji machungwa. (*She calls to the stall-holder who is chatting to a friend nearby:*) Ebu, njoo bwana! Habari za asubuhi? |
| **Mwuzaji** | Njema tu, mama. Habari zako? |
| **Regina** | Salama, bwana. Machungwa haya, bei gani leo? |
| **Mwuzaji** | (*indicating two piles of oranges in front of him*) Haya shilingi ishirini ishirini, haya ishirini na tano. |
| **Regina** | Ala! Ghali mno! Punguza bei, bwana, nahitaji mengi. |
| **Mwuzaji** | Unataka mangapi? |
| **Regina** | Naomba arobaini. |
| **Mwuzaji** | Basi, chukua! Kwa shilingi kumi na tano, madogo haya. |
| **Regina** | Vizuri. (*She puts them in her basket with Alison's help, then turns her attention to pawpaws:*) Mapapai, je, unauza bei gani? |
| **Mwuzaji** | Mapapai ni shilingi thelathini. |
| **Regina** | Kwa nini ghali hivi? |
| **Mwuzaji** | Siyo ghali, ndiyo bei yake. |
| **Regina** | Hebu punguza bei bwana, ninahitaji matatu. |
| **Mwuzaji** | Haya, mama. Nitakufanyia shilingi ishirini na tano. (*Regina opens her purse.*) |
| **Alison** | Hutanunua matunda mengine? Hapa pana ndizi. |
| **Regina** | Sihitaji mengine. Haya yatatosha. Tuna migomba shambani. (*Suddenly Regina's husband, Francis, arrives with John. They have been looking for Regina and Alison.*) |
| **Francis** | Jamani! Bado mpo hapa? Tunakwenda mkahawani – tuna kiu sana! |
| **Regina** | (*paying the fruit-seller*) Haya, kwa heri, bwana! |
| **Mwuzaji** | Kwa herini! |

| | |
|---|---|
| **soko(ni)** | *(at the) market* |
| **-hitaji** | *need* |
| **matunda** | *fruit* (pl.) |
| **machungwa** | *oranges* |
| **ebu** (also **hebu**) | a call to attract attention |
| **haya** | *these* |
| **bei** (N) | *price* |

| | |
|---|---|
| **shilingi ishirini ishirini** | *twenty shillings each* |
| **mno** | *extremely, too* |
| **-punguza** | *reduce, decrease* |
| **-chukua** | *take* |
| **mapapai** | *pawpaws (papayas)* |
| **-uza** | *sell* |
| **kwa nini** | *why* |
| **hivi** | *like this, in this manner, thus* |
| **siyo** | *emphatic form of* **si** *is/are not* |
| **nitakufanyia . . .** | *I'll make it . . . for you* |
| **hapa pana** | *here are* |
| **ndizi** | *bananas* |
| **-tosha** | *be enough, suffice* |
| **migomba** | *banana trees* |
| **shamba(ni)** | *(in the) smallholding* |
| **jamani!** | *you lot! y'all!* (only used in informal situations, to people you know well) |
| **bado** | *still* (i.e. still at a place or carrying out an action) |
| **mkahawa(ni)** | *(to the) café* |
| **kiu** (N) | *thirst* |
| **tuna kiu sana** | *we're very thirsty* |
| **kwa heri** (to one person) | *goodbye* |
| **kwa herini** (to two or more) | *goodbye* |

# 🛈 Markets and marketing

Markets range in size from small displays of fruit and vegetables neatly arranged on the ground in front of the sellers to large covered markets with permanent stalls, in towns. The town markets sell a wide range of produce including meat and dried fish, as well as household goods and clothes.

Dry goods such as rice, flour (maize or wheat), beans and sugar would, in most places other than towns, be more likely to be found in the nearest shop than at the market; they are sold by the kilo. Paraffin, i.e. lamp-oil or kerosene, is also usually bought at a shop. It is stocked in four-gallon rectangular tins which, when empty and cleaned, make very useful containers.

In markets, larger fruit and vegetables are usually priced singly, with smaller items like peppers, tomatoes and onions arranged in small piles, the seller's starting price, e.g. **'Shilingi kumi kumi!'** referring to a whole pile. Bananas (**ndizi**) are sometimes sold by the 'hand' (a stem containing several bunches), as well as by the bunch or singly. Green vegetables such as spinach and cassava leaves are sold by the bundle, as are lengths of sugar-cane.

Bargaining is an essential procedure in shopping at markets and wayside stalls but it needs to be done cheerfully and with patience. The sellers will not expect to get the first price they quote, and it is standard practice for customers to use ploys like Regina's to get the price reduced – **'Kwa nini ghali hivi?'** or **'Punguza bei!'** Other possibilities are:

| | |
|---|---|
| **Siwezi kulipa bei hii.** | *I can't pay this price.* |
| **Siwezi kulipa shilingi . . .** | *I can't pay . . . shillings.* |
| **Nitalipa shilingi . . .** | *I'll pay . . . shillings.* |

Note that **asante**, *thanks/thank you* (used by John to the taxi driver in Unit 2), does not appear at all in this conversation. It should be used much more sparingly than *thank you* is in British English. Alternatives are **vizuri** and **vema**, both meaning *good/fine*. Politeness is also indicated by body-language; for example, if the stall-holder decided to give Alison an orange as a gift (a not impossible scenario) she should extend both hands, the left underneath and slightly behind the right hand, with which the gift is received. In ordinary transactions, when gifts are not involved, give and take just with the right hand. It is also the right hand that is used when eating. The banana trees which Regina refers to as being **shambani** might be a few trees growing near the house, or a larger number on a smallholding or plantation further away.

| | |
|---|---|
| **kilo** (N) | *kilo* |
| **mchele** | *rice* (uncooked grain) |
| **mchicha** (N) | *spinach* |
| **mkungu wa ndizi** | *hand of bananas* (esp. of green bananas) |
| **muwa** | *sugar-cane* |
| **pilipili hoho** (N) | *red pepper(s)* |
| **unga wa mahindi** | *maize flour* |
| **unga wa ngano** | *wheat flour* |

# Grammar

## 1 Tunda, papai, chungwa, shamba, soko and other (JI)/MA class nouns

**a** The first three of these words occur in the plural in the dialogue:

**ma**tunda *fruit*   **ma**papai *pawpaws*   **ma**chungwa *oranges*

In this noun-class most singular nouns have no prefix, but a small number have the prefix ji-. Plural nouns have the prefix **ma-**.

The first vocabulary box below has a few of the many words without a singular prefix that denote inanimates; you will recognize one from Unit 3. Note that most of the words for fruit are in this class and are of the type in the first box:

| (JI)/MA class nouns | |
|---|---|
| Singular | Plural |
| **debe**   *large oil tin* | **madebe** |
| **dirisha**   *window* | **madirisha** |
| **duka**   *shop* | **maduka** |
| **embe**   *mango* | **maembe** |
| **haragwe**   *(kidney) bean* | **maharagwe** |
| **jani**   *leaf* | **majani** (also *grass*) |
| **limau**   *lemon* | **malimau** |
| **nanasi**   *pineapple* | **mananasi** |
| **sanduku**   *box* | **masanduku** |
| **shamba**   *cultivated field* | **mashamba** |
| **yai**   *egg* | **mayai** |

In the following box are examples of words with ji- as the singular prefix. It is used in its full form on noun-stems that have only one syllable, and gets reduced to j- on the front of stems that begin with a vowel. Notice that in some cases the ji- or j- is retained in the plural form:

| Singular | Plural |
|---|---|
| **jambo**   *matter, affair, thing* (abstract) | **mambo** |
| **jicho**   *eye* | **macho** |
| **jiko**   *cooking-place, kitchen* | **meko** (ma-iko) |
| **jino**   *tooth* | **meno** (ma-ino) |
| **jembe**   *hoe* | **majembe** |
| **jibu**   *answer, reply* | **majibu** |
| **jina**   *name* | **majina** |

**b** The use of the singular noun-prefix on *adjectives* is similar to its use on the nouns themselves:

- Use **ji-** when the adjective stem has only one syllable:

  | | |
  |---|---|
  | duka **ji**pya | *a new shop* |
  | sanduku **ji**pya | *a new box* (or *suitcase*) |

- Use **j-** when the adjective begins with a vowel:

  | | |
  |---|---|
  | debe **j**ingine | *another paraffin tin* |
  | dirisha **j**embamba | *a narrow window* |

- No prefix is necessary when the adjective-stem begins with a consonant:

  | | |
  |---|---|
  | duka kubwa | *a big shop* |
  | nanasi dogo | *a small pineapple* |

The plural noun-prefix is used on all adjectives (that take a prefix) qualifying a plural noun. As with noun-stems, the **ma-** gets modified slightly on the front of stems beginning with a vowel (just as the **wa-** prefix does):

| | |
|---|---|
| madebe **ma**tano | *five paraffin tins* |
| masanduku **me**ngi (ma-ingi) | *many boxes* (or *suitcases*) |
| mambo **ma**pya | *new matters* |
| majembe **me**mbamba (ma-embamba) | *thin hoes* |

**c** Verb-prefixes for (JI)/MA nouns

| | |
|---|---|
| Singular: **li-** | Plural: **ya-** |
| Debe moja **li**tatosha. | *One paraffin tin will be enough.* |
| Mananasi yake **ya**tatosha. | *His pineapples will be sufficient.* |
| Majembe mapya **ya**nafaa. | *The new hoes are suitable.* |

Remember that **ha-** goes at the beginning for negatives:

| | |
|---|---|
| Debe moja **ha**litatosha. | *One paraffin tin won't be enough.* |
| Mananasi yake **ha**yatatosha. | *His pineapples won't be sufficient.* |
| Majembe mapya **ha**yafai. | *The new hoes are not suitable.* |

When verb-prefixes are used on possessives and **a-**, *of*, predictably, **li-** reduces to **l-** and **ya-** reduces to **y-**:

| | |
|---|---|
| debe langu, debe lako | *my paraffin tin, your paraffin tin* |
| malimau yangu, malimau yako | *my lemons, your lemons* |
| duka lake Musa | *Musa's shop* |
| duka la Musa | *Musa's shop* |
| macho ya mtoto | *the child's eyes* |

The verb-prefixes used on place markers:

| | |
|---|---|
| Duka lake liko wapi? | *Where is his shop?* |
| Duka lake lipo Bukoba. | *His shop is at Bukoba.* |
| Maharagwe yako wapi? | *Where are the beans?* |
| Yamo kikapuni. | *They are in the basket.* |

**d** There is a group of words in this class which are always used in the plural. Some denote things, either concrete or abstract, which cannot be counted and for which a singular word would be used in English. Others denote things which are countable and for which English-speakers would typically use a singular noun. **Matatizo**, the plural form of **tatizo**, can be used in contexts where *problem* would be used in English. The agreement-prefix, whether noun-prefix (on adjectives) or verb-prefix, is always plural. Here are a few examples:

| | | | |
|---|---|---|---|
| **maendeleo** | *development, progress* | **maji** | *water* |
| **mafuta** | *oil* (for cooking or lamps) | **mapokezi** | *reception desk* |
| **mafuta ya taa** | *paraffin* (lamp-oil) | **matatizo** | *problems* |
| **majani** | *grass* | | |

(**Majani** is included here because, although – if you needed to – it would be possible to refer to a single blade of grass, the word is usually used in the plural.)

Some words for people operate in this class, in that they take the **ma-** prefix for their plurals; the singular forms have no prefix. They are mostly words of foreign origin for titles or occupational status. Like the words for people in the N class they take M/WA noun and verb-prefixes except for some possessives (and note **bibi yangu**, but **bwana wangu**). The three words noted here all have been introduced in earlier units.

| Singular | | Plural |
|---|---|---|
| **bibi** | *lady* | **mabibi** |
| **bwana** | *gentleman* | **mabwana** |
| **karani** | *clerk* | **makarani** |

| | |
|---|---|
| Mabibi watakwenda Mombasa. | *The ladies will be going to Mombasa.* |
| Mabwana wawili walivuka njia. | *Two gentlemen crossed the road.* |
| Makarani hawapo posta. | *The clerks are not at the post office.* |

More will be said later, in Part Two, about **ma-**.

## 2 -hitaji and other verbs of foreign origin

The verb -hitaji, *need*, is used at the start of the dialogue. This is a verb of Arabic origin. If a verb-stem in its unprefixed or 'dictionary' form does not have a final -a, it is not of Bantu origin, and does not change its final vowel for the negative of the present tense. In Unit 3 -subiri, *wait*, was used in the first dialogue; that behaves just like -hitaji. Not all verbs of Arabic origin end in -i; some have final -u, as in -dhuru, *harm*, or -e as in -samehe, *forgive*, and they all keep their original vowel in present-tense negatives.

## 3 Kwa herini! *Goodbye!*

This is the plural form of kwa heri (to one person). It is only in saying *goodbye* that the same basic formula is exchanged; greetings, as explained in Unit 1, have question-and-answer routines.

The source of this -ni plural suffix is ninyi, *you* (plural). Kwa heri ninyi has become shortened to kwa herini. This -ni is used to make a singular imperative into a plural. Using three of the verbs already introduced in their imperative form on p.57, we can make plurals by adding -ni. Notice that the final -a of the verb-stem gets changed to -e.

Angalieni!  *Look/take care, both/all of you!*
Leteni!  *Bring (it, them), both / all of you!*
Nendeni!  *Off you go, both / all of you!*

*Note*: This form of the verb is used when *telling* people what to do. For conveying the equivalent of *Would you please . . .?*, *Would you mind -ing?*, *Could you . . .?*, *I'd be grateful if you would . . .*, etc., a different form of the verb is used, and this will be explained in Unit 6.

## ▶ Dialogue 2

Francis and John have persuaded Regina and Alison to join them for a drink in a café near the market. They find a table and, as Regina puts down her basket, Francis comments on the quantity of oranges she has bought.

**Francis**  Machungwa mengi sana!
**Regina**  Ndiyo. Nitawatengenezea wageni maji ya machungwa.

| | |
|---|---|
| **Francis** | Aa, vizuri sana! Mtapika chakula gani jioni? |
| **Regina** | Tutapika biriani. |
| **Francis** | Vizuri kabisa. (*Looking at Alison*:) Lakini, dada hapendi nyama. |
| **Regina** | Ndiyo, hapendi nyama. Tutampikia biriani ya mboga. (*The waiter is hovering.*) |
| **Francis** | Haya, basi. Mtakunywa nini? |
| **Regina** | (*to Alison*) Dada, unapenda kunywa soda? |
| **Alison** | Sipendi kunywa kinywaji baridi. Napenda chai ya rangi. |
| **Francis** | (*to John*) Na wewe, bwana. Chai? Kahawa? Soda? |
| **John** | Napenda soda. |
| **Regina** | Nitakunywa kahawa. Na wewe, je? |
| **Francis** | Maziwa baridi. Basi. Kaka! Lete chai moja ya rangi, kahawa moja, soda moja na maziwa gilasi moja. |
| **Regina** | Je, chakula? |
| **John** | Sina njaa sana, lakini naona sambusa pale. |
| **Francis** | Mnapenda sambusa? |
| **John** | Sana! |
| **Alison** | Napenda sambusa za mboga. |
| **Francis** | (*to the waiter*) Basi, vinywaji pamoja na sambusa mbili mbili. Bibi huyu, mletee sambusa za mboga. |

| | |
|---|---|
| **-tengeneza** | *prepare* (also *mend*) |
| **nitawatengenezea wageni** | *I'm going to make the visitors* |
| **maji ya machungwa** | *some orange juice* |
| **aa!** | *an expression of pleasure* |
| **-pika** | *cook* |
| **vizuri kabisa** | *very good, excellent* |
| **tutampikia biriani ya mboga** | *we'll cook vegetable biriani for her* |
| **soda** (N) | *bottled fizzy drink, non-alcoholic* |
| **kinywaji** (KI/VI) | *a drink* |
| **chai ya rangi** (N) | *tea without milk* (lit. *tea of colour*) |
| **gilasi** (N) | *glass* |
| **njaa** (N) | *hunger* |
| **sina njaa sana** | *I'm not very hungry* |
| **sambusa za mboga** | *vegetable samosas* |
| **sambusa** (N) | *samosas* |
| **mbili mbili** (N) | *two* (here: samosas) *each* |
| **mletee** | *bring for her* |

# ℹ️ Drinks

More or less any bottled flavoured drink that is not alcoholic is referred to as 'soda', even if it is not fizzy.

The word **rangi** (N), *colour*, is used in the phrase **chai ya rangi**, with the literal meaning *tea of colour*. In cafés, if you ask just for **chai** you are likely to get a cup of tea with the milk already in it. The milk and tea are often brewed up together; if condensed milk is used, the result can be a fairly thick and sweet liquid. Tea served in people's homes is sometimes spiced, particularly with ginger, and it is worth searching this out in cafés too. In towns, particularly at the coast, street coffee-sellers advertise their black coffee by clinking together the small cups in which they serve it.

There are several different varieties of commercially-produced bottled beers. These are quite different from the alcoholic brews made from locally grown fermented grain, e.g. maize, rice, millet, or fruit, e.g. bananas. These brew-ups are the equivalent of 'scrumpy' and inclined to be very powerful. Wine is available in town supermarkets and large hotels and restaurants.

One of the pleasures of being at (or not too far from) the coast is drinking coconut milk, which is extracted from young, slightly under-ripe coconuts. Note that there are different words for coconuts at this stage and fully ripe ones (see vocabulary box below). Do not confuse the liquid that can be drunk from the young coconut with the juice made by adding water to grated (fully ripe) coconut and then straining it – the resulting liquid is used in cooking rice, for example. The young coconuts can be bought at markets and from street stalls or from the young boys who congregate at long-distance bus stops hoping to tempt thirsty travellers with their local produce. The seller will make a hole in the coconut for you to drink from.

| | |
|---|---|
| **bia** (N) | *commercially produced bottled beer* |
| **dafu** (MA) | *young, slightly under-ripe coconut* |
| **divai** (N) | *wine* |
| **maji ya madafu** | *coconut milk* (for drinking) |
| **nazi** (N) | *fully ripe coconut* |
| **pombe** (N) | *locally produced beer from fermented grain or fruit* |
| **tui** (N) | *juice (or 'milk') extracted from grated coconut* |
| **tangawizi** (N) | *ginger* |

# 4 Adjectives: phrases with -a (of) + noun

In this unit there are two examples of adjectives made in this way. The stem **-a**, *of*, takes the verb-prefix; if necessary look back to Unit 3 pp.36–7 to revise the verb-prefixes attached to **-a**.

maji ya machungwa    ya + a → **ya**
biriani ya mboga    i + a → **ya**

It is the noun that is qualified by an adjective, i.e. the first noun, that controls the verb-prefix on **-a**.

Here are some more examples from previous units:

| | | |
|---|---|---|
| hundi za posta | *postal orders* (lit. cheques of P.O.) | zi + a → **za** |
| chumba cha mtu mmoja | *single room* | ki + a → **cha** |
| ghorofa ya juu | *top floor* | i + a → **ya** |
| nyama ya ng'ombe | *beef* (lit. meat of cow) | i + a → **ya** |

# 5 -tengenezea, -pikia, etc.: doing things for people

In the dialogue there are two verbs, **-tengeneza**, *prepare* (also *mend*) and **-pika**, *cook*, which are used with an extra vowel between the verb-root and the final **-a**. Think of **-tengenez-** and **-pik-** as the root of these verbs. We need to make a distinction between a verb-stem, e.g. **-pika** (also **-pikia**, **-pikwa**, **-pikika**, **-pikisha**, etc.) and a verb-root, e.g **-pik-**. The root is the minimal part of a verb without anything added to it (including the final **-a** of Bantu verbs) and carries its meaning.

The **-e-** following **-tengenez-** and the **-i-** following **-pik-** perform the function that *for* performs in English, in sentences like *I cooked supper for them*. *For* is one of several 'prepositions' in English; others include *to* as in *They gave it to me*, and *at* as in *They laughed at it*. Prepositional functions of this kind are fulfilled in Swahili by adding a particular vowel to the root of the verb.

The vowel of this prepositional form of the verb is either **i** or **e**, according to what the final vowel of the verb-root is.

- If the final or only vowel of the verb-root is: **i**, **a** or **u**:
  -andik-        -tak-        -uz-
  *write*        *want*        *sell*
  the extra vowel is **i**.

• If the final or only vowel of the verb-root is **e** or **o**:
  -tengenez-          -som-
  *prepare*           *read*
  the extra vowel is **e**.

In the examples below, notice that if the verb-root ends in a vowel, **l** is inserted in front of **i** or **e**:

| Verb-root | | Prepositional vowel is **i** |
|---|---|---|
| -andik- | *write* | -andikia |
| -fu- (nguo) | *wash* (clothes) | -fulia |
| -pat- | *get* | -patia |
| -nunu- | *buy* | -nunulia |
| -pik- | *cook* | -pikia |
| -pig- simu | *make a phone call* | -pigia simu |

| Verb-root | | Prepositional vowel is **e** |
|---|---|---|
| -let- | *bring* | -letea |
| -pelek- | *send, take* | -pelekea |
| -poke- | *receive* | -pokelea |
| -som- | *read* | -somea |
| -tengenez- | *prepare* (or *mend*) | -tengenezea |

The forms on the right, above, have more than one potential meaning: *for/to/on behalf of*. When listening to or (later on) reading Swahili, the context will usually make the precise meaning clear. In speaking Swahili, concentrate, to start with, on the functions shown in the example sentences at the end of the next section.

Note that not all verbs need a prepositional vowel when you want to refer to doing something for someone; some verbs have an 'inbuilt' prepositional function:

| -eleza | { | *explain* (something) |
| | | *explain* (something) *to someone* |
| -faa | { | *be useful* |
| | | *be useful to someone* |
| -onyesha | { | *show* (something) |
| | | *show* (something) *to someone* |
| -pa | | *give* (something) *to someone* |

*Note*: **-pa** is one of the small number of monosyllabic verbs (see Unit 3).

Verb-roots will be needed again in several units in Part Two, for adding more functions to verbs and for making nouns out of verbs.

# 6 Me, you, him/her, etc. – object-markers

In the sentence **John anapenda biriani** (*John likes biriani*) the subject of the verb is **John** and the object of the verb is **biriani**. Other examples of objects in English sentences are *garden* in *John dug the garden*, *beans* in *Mary planted the beans*, *it* in *John dug it* and *them* in *Mary planted them*.

In Swahili the objects meaning *it* and *them* are not separate words as they are in English, neither do they follow the verb. *John likes it*, where *it* refers to **biriani** is: **John anaipenda**.

The verb-prefixes are used for *it* and *them*; **i** is the appropriate prefix to represent **biriani** which is an N class singular noun. Forms with this function will be referred to as *object-markers*; they always come immediately before the verb-stem. More will be said in Unit 5 about verb-prefixes functioning as object-markers. This section will concentrate on the six object-markers for humans and animals, because they differ in some cases from the M/WA class verb-prefixes.

## M/WA object-markers

| | | | |
|---|---|---|---|
| **-ni-** | *me* | **-tu-** | *us* |
| **-ku-** | *you* (sing.) | **-wa-** | *you* (pl.) |
| **-m-** | *him/her* | **-wa-** | *them* |
| (**-mw-** before a vowel) | | | |

Their use is shown with **-penda** which can mean *love* as well as *like* when used with human objects:

| | | |
|---|---|---|
| -ni- | Regina ananipenda. | *Regina loves me.* |
| -ku- | Mama anakupenda. | *Mother loves you.* |
| -m- | Mohamed anampenda Zahra. | *Mohamed loves Zahra.* |
| -tu- | Baba anatupenda. | *Father loves us.* |
| -wa- | Tunawapenda. | *We love you (all).* |
| -wa- | Ninawapenda/Nawapenda. | *I love them.* |

The object-marker **-wa-**, meaning *both/all of you* as well as *them* should not be a problem; the context of use should prevent ambiguity. But in some places alternatives are used for *you* (pl.):

| | |
|---|---|
| nawapendeni | *I love all of you* (collectively). |
| nakupendeni | *I love each of you.* |

*Note:* M/WA object-markers are used for N class objects which denote animates.

Try to learn these M/WA object-markers as soon as you can. A good way is to make up sentences about people you know, using -penda in all of them so that you only have to concentrate on getting the object-marker right. A lot of our everyday conversation involves talking about ourselves and other people so the use of the object-markers is really crucial. Another useful verb to practise with, before going on to the 'prepositional' verbs, is -pa, *give*, which involves a recipient, represented by the object-marker, and the thing given, which goes after the verb.

| | |
|---|---|
| Alinipa pesa. | *S/he gave me some money.* |
| Nitakupa machungwa. | *I will give you some oranges.* |

If speaker and hearer(s) know what has been or will be given it need not be mentioned:

| | |
|---|---|
| Nitakupa. | *I will give you* (the oranges we've been talking about). |

If you need to identify the recipient, that word must follow immediately after the verb, and the word for the thing(s) given goes right to the end:

| | |
|---|---|
| Nitampa Francis mananasi. | *I will give Francis some pineapples.* |
| Tuliwapa watoto mayai. | *We gave the children eggs.* |

With the verb -pa, one of the single-syllable verbs, it is the object-marker that is stressed, because it is the penultimate syllable; this means that **m** in **nitampa** functions as a syllable and receives stress.

Note that -pa, like other monosyllabic verbs, does not need its **ku-** when it is preceded by an object-marker.

The following sentences show some of the verbs from the previous section with the prepositional vowel and a 'recipient' object-marker.

| | |
|---|---|
| Juma aliniandikia barua. | *Juma wrote me a letter.* |
| Ninamnunulia mtoto viatu. | *I am buying the child some shoes (now).* |
| Hakutupikia ugali. | *She did not cook us polenta.* |
| Ulimpigia Mohamed simu? | *Did you 'phone Mohamed?* |
| Nitawaletea vitabu vya Kiswahili. | *I will bring you (all) some Swahili books.* |
| Niliwasomea watoto jana. | *I read to the children yesterday.* |

## Summary

- The object-marker representing the recipient/beneficiary comes immediately before the verb-stem.
- If the recipient is identified by means of a noun (e.g. **watoto**) or a noun-phrase (e.g. **watoto wake Juma**) it must go immediately after the verb.
- The object, i.e. the word(s) for the thing written, bought, cooked, sold, etc., goes at the end, following the recipient.

# Practice

1   **Unahitaji vitu gani?** *What things do you need?*
    You have offered to do some shopping for Mama Fatuma. Fill in her replies to your questions. The first reply has been done for you.

    **You**        Unahitaji machungwa?
    **Mama F.**   *Says she doesn't need oranges, there are oranges in the kitchen:* **Sihitaji machungwa, pana machungwa jikoni.**
    **You**        Unahitaji mananasi?
    **Mama F.**   *Says yes, she needs two pineapples.*
    **You**        Unahitaji ndizi?
    **Mama F.**   *Says she doesn't need bananas, there are (**kuna**) many banana trees in the shamba.*
    **You**        Unahitaji malimau?
    **Mama F.**   *Says yes, she needs five lemons.*
    **You**        Unahitaji mayai?
    **Mama F.**   *Says no, she doesn't need eggs, her friend brought her some.*

2   Re-read Dialogue 1 and complete the following sentence by inserting in words the amount of money Regina gave the fruit-seller:

    **Regina alimpa mwuzaji Sh. _____ .**

3   When Mohamed was ill with malaria (**homa ya malaria**) his colleagues and friends rallied round and helped him in various ways. Using the pictures and verb-clues, say or write what they did. Remember to add the prepositional suffix to the verb-root.

a **Asha alimpikia chakula** (or **wali, ugali, biriani,** etc.!)

a

Asha (**-pika**)

b

Juma (**-fua**)

c

Francis (**-piga simu**)

d

Ruth (**-leta**)

e

Khadija (**-nunua**)

f

John (**-soma**)

4 Today it is your turn to do the ordering in a café. This is what you and your friends have decided you want:

You: Tea without milk and a rice bun.
Ruth: Coffee and a small pancake.
Omari: Coffee and two doughnuts (MA pl.)
Regina: A fizzy drink.
Mohamed: Coffee and a rice bun.

Call the waiter over, tell him how many of each kind of drink to bring, using '**Lete . . .**' and then order the food in the same way.

5 Two of you have recently moved into a house, and neighbours have been calling in with gifts. You are now trying to remember who brought what. Match the answers on the right with the questions on the left.

| | | | |
|---|---|---|---|
| a | Nani alituletea mayai? | 1 | Ndiyo, walituletea nazi. |
| b | Mzee alituletea nanasi? | 2 | Alituletea makubwa. |
| c | Nani alituletea ndizi? | 3 | Siyo, hakutuletea nanasi, alituletea maharagwe. |
| d | Nani alituletea mchele? | | |
| e | Watoto walituletea nazi? | 4 | Ndiyo, alituletea kuku. |
| f | Mwalimu alituletea machungwa yapi? | 5 | Sijui, labda mwuguzi alileta mchele. |
| g | Nani alituletea machungwa madogo? | 6 | Regina alituletea mayai. |
| | | 7 | Bwana Juma alituletea ndizi. |
| h | Mohamed alituletea kuku? | 8 | Mama Zainabu alituletea machungwa madogo. |

> **nani...?** *who...?*     **labda** *perhaps*

6 Fill in each of the blanks with a suitable word from the list below.

a Mwalimu aliwapa _____ vitabu.
b Tulimpa mgonjwa _____.
c Nilimfulia mama _____.
d Baba atanipigia simu _____.
e Mgeni wetu alitununulia _____ mkahawani.
f Bi Khadija alininunulia _____ dukani.

> sukari   kesho   watoto   soda   matunda   nguo

Now write out the English equivalent of the completed sentences.

# 05

## kwenye duka
## la sanaa
at the craft shop

**In this unit you will learn**
- how to make introductions and respond to an introduction
- how to name colours
- how to say what people are wearing
- how to express sympathy
- how to refer to months and seasons

# ▶ Dialogue 1

Alison and her friend Ruth go into a craft shop. Alison wants to
buy some fabric to make herself a dress, and possibly buy a few
gifts.

| | |
|---|---|
| **Alison** | Mama Fatuma atanisaidia kushona gauni. |
| **Ruth** | Ana cherehani? |
| **Alison** | Ndiyo, anayo. |
| **Ruth** | (*indicating lengths of cloth*) Unapenda kitambaa hiki? |
| **Alison** | Napenda nakshi yake, lakini sipendi rangi nyekundu. |
| **Ruth** | Unapenda rangi gani? |
| **Alison** | Napenda rangi ya kijani na buluu. |
| | (*They wander over to a rail of ready-made garments.*) |
| **Ruth** | Unapenda mavazi haya? |
| **Alison** | Sana. Nayapenda, ila sipendi sana magauni. Sipendi mtindo huu. Mikono ni myembamba sana. Tena, ni ghali sana. |
| | (*A sales assistant approaches, and Ruth recognizes him.*) |
| **Ruth** | Bwana Khamisi! Hujambo? |
| **Msaidizi** | Sijambo sana. Za siku nyingi? |
| **Ruth** | Njema. Za nyumbani? |
| **Msaidizi** | Salama tu. Karibuni! |
| **Ruth** | Kutana na Bi. Alison, mgeni wetu. |
| **Msaidizi** | Karibu, bibi. Habari yako? |
| **Alison** | Njema, bwana. |
| **Msaidizi** | Unatafuta kitambaa cha namna gani, bibi? Kanga? Kitenge? Batiki? |
| **Alison** | Una batiki? |
| **Msaidizi** | Tunazo. Zipo karibu na mlango. Hukuziona? Basi nitakuonyesha. |
| **Ruth** | Vizuri. Mimi nakwenda sokoni sasa. Nitarudi baada ya nusu saa! |

| | |
|---|---|
| **sanaa** | *art, craft* |
| **-saidia** | *help* |
| **kushona** (ku-shona) | *to sew* |
| **gauni** (MA) | *dress* |
| **cherehani** (N) | *sewing-machine* |
| **anayo** | *she has one* |
| **kitambaa** (KI/VI) | *fabric* |
| **hiki** | *this* (i.e. cloth) |
| **nakshi** (N) | *pattern* |
| **rangi** (N) | *colour* |

| | |
|---|---|
| **rangi nyekundu** | *the colour red* |
| **rangi ya kijani** | *green* |
| **buluu** | *blue* |
| **mavazi** (MA) | *clothes* |
| **haya** | *these* (i.e. clothes) |
| **ila** | *but, except* |
| **mtindo** | *style, fashion* |
| **huu** | *this* (i.e. style) |
| **mikono** | *sleeves, arms* |
| **tena** | *also, moreover* |
| **msaidizi** (M/WA) | *assistant* |
| **-kutana na** | *meet (someone)* |
| **-tafuta** | *look for* (also *find*) |
| **kanga** (N) | *matching pair of patterned lengths of fabric* |
| **kitenge** (KI/VI) | *patterned fabric* |
| **batiki** (N) | *batik-printed and 'tie-dyed' fabric; dresses made from these types of fabric* |
| **tunazo** | *we have some* (i.e. batik, etc., fabrics) |
| **mlango** | *door* |
| **-onyesha** | *show* |
| **-rudi** | *return* |
| **baada ya nusu saa** | *after half an hour* |

# ℹ Craftwork, clothes and souvenir shops

The craftwork displayed in souvenir shops and on stalls includes wood carvings, baskets, mats, beadwork and (in some places) pottery. The more portable items of this sort are also offered for sale by the young men who try to make a living by selling to tourists around the beach hotels.

The **kanga** and **kitenge** fabric mentioned by the sales assistant in Dialogue 1 might well be on sale in a craft shop, but not necessarily. There is likely to be a better selection in shops aimed at local trade rather than tourists and on stalls in the larger markets. **Kangas** (referred to as **leso** in some places) are worn only by women. They are sold as a single length of material incorporating two identical rectangular blocks of bold pattern, often including a proverb or (sometimes provocative) saying. **Kitenge** fabric is rather heavier and more expensive, and can be bought by the metre as well as in dress-lengths. Fabric shops and markets are also the places where the

**kikoi** can be found. This is a length of fabric, often white with a coloured border at waist and hem, worn sarong-like by some men, particularly at the coast. Adult men tend to wear trousers rather than shorts, which are mainly (although not exclusively) worn by young boys – and male tourists.

The garment associated with Muslim men is the long-sleeved ankle-length **kanzu** but it is not worn all the time by all Muslim men; some wear it only for worship at the mosque, or on special family or community occasions. The **kofia** has given its name to any kind of hat, but the original **kofia** is the shallow fez-shaped cap worn by Muslim men. The traditional outdoor garment for Muslim women is the black **buibui**, an enveloping garment rather like the Iranian 'chador'. These are still to be seen but an increasing number of Muslim women are adopting a more tailored style of modest outdoor garment.

Tie-dyed and batik-printed fabrics can be bought as dress-lengths or by the metre, and are popular among fashion-conscious town-dwellers who can afford them. Both types of material are used for loose, collarless shirts as well as women's dresses. Much use is made of the services of local tailors.

| | |
|---|---|
| **buibui** (N) | outdoor garment worn by Muslim women |
| **mshonaji** (M/WA) <br> **fundi** (MA) **wa cherehani** } | tailor |
| **kanzu** (N) | long white garment worn by Muslim men |
| **kaptura** (N) | shorts |
| **kikoi** (KI/VI) | men's 'sarong' |
| **kofia** (N) | hat |
| **koti** (MA) | jacket, coat |
| **mita** (N) | metre |
| **shati** (MA) | shirt |
| **soksi** (N) | socks |
| **suruali** (N) | trousers |

*Note:* **Kanzu** can also mean a woman's dress, in Zanzibar.

# Grammar

## 1 Making introductions

The way in which Ruth introduced Alison to her acquaintance Bw. Khamisi was very informal, and quite typical of brief introductions between younger people familiar with English and whose Swahili is sometimes influenced by English usage. A rather more formal introduction might go like this:

**Ruth**  Bibi huyu ni mgeni wetu, jina lake Bi. Alison.
**Mzee**  Hujambo, Bi. Alison. Nimefurahi kukutana nawe.
**Alison**  Sijambo mzee. Na mimi nimefurahi. Habari yako?

| | |
|---|---|
| **nimefurahi kukutana nawe** | *I'm happy to meet you* |
| **-furahi** | *be happy* |

**Nimefurahi** has a tense-marker -me- which will be explained in section 8 of this unit.

If the elderly man in this last example had been introduced to more than one person, he would say, '. . . kukutana nanyi', instead of '. . . kukutana nawe.' **Nanyi** and **nawe** are the contracted forms of **na nyinyi** and **na wewe** respectively.

## 2 Mkono, mlango and other M/MI class nouns

**a** In this class **m**- is the prefix for singular nouns and **mi**- for plurals.

In Dialogue 1, **mkono** was used in its plural form, **mikono**. In Unit 4 several M/MI class words were introduced, e.g. **mkungu** (**wa ndizi**) – plural **mikungu** – and **mchele** which is usually used as a singular (note that it means husked rice that has not yet been cooked).

As in the case of the M/WA class, **m**- usually changes to **mw**- before a vowel, e.g. **mwembe**.

| M/MI class nouns | |
|---|---|
| Singular | Plural |
| **mchungwa** *orange tree* | **michungwa** |
| **mfuko** *bag, pocket* | **mifuko** |
| **mgomba** *banana plant* | **migomba** |
| **mguu** *leg* | **miguu** |
| **mhindi** *maize plant* | **mihindi** |
| **mji** *town* | **miji** |
| **mkate** *bread, loaf* | **mikate** |
| **mlimau** *lemon tree* | **milimau** |
| **mnanasi** *pineapple plant* | **minanasi** |
| **mnazi** *coconut palm* | **minazi** |
| **mti** *tree* | **miti** |
| **mto** *river, pillow* | **mito** |
| **mwaka** *year* | **miaka** |
| **mwembe** *mango tree* | **miembe** |
| **mwili** *body* | **miili** |

This noun-class contains most of the words for trees and plants, and you have probably recognized some noun-stems that occur in the (JI)/MA class as names of fruit. Mostly, the same noun-stem is used for a fruit and the tree it grows on. An exception to this is **mgomba** and the word for *banana(s)* – **ndizi** (N). It will probably be helpful to think of this as the 'tree class' and to concentrate, to start with, on the names of trees whose fruit you met in the (JI)/MA class in Unit 4.

Apart from trees and plants it is not possible to group M/MI words together on any obvious basis, but you might like to link together **mji, moshi, moto, mto** and also **mwili, mguu, mkono.** What you can be sure of is that there are no words for humans or animals in this class.

There are two exceptions to the rule of **mw-** before a vowel. Some (not all) noun-stems beginning with **-o** take **m-**, rather than **mw-**, as their prefix:

| Singular | Plural |
|---|---|
| **moshi** *smoke* | **mioshi** |
| **moto** *fire, heat* | **mioto** |
| **moyo** *heart* | **mioyo** |

The second exception is that the original form of this prefix, **mu-**, is retained in a few words. Two of the most common of these are shown below; they have both appeared in previous units in their singular form:

| Singular | | Plural |
|---|---|---|
| **muhogo** | *cassava* | **mihogo** |
| **muwa** | *sugar-cane* | **miwa** |

**b** As with all the noun-classes these noun-prefixes are used on the front of single-word adjective-stems to make the adjectives 'match' their nouns. The singular prefix is **mw-** before a vowel. The plural prefix is **my-** before **-e**; when the plural prefix comes before **-i**, one **i** disappears: **mi** + **i** makes **mi**.

| | |
|---|---|
| mchungwa mkubwa | *a large orange tree* |
| miji mingi | *many towns* |
| miwa myembamba | *thin sugar-canes* |

**c** Verb-prefixes:

| Singular: **-u** | Plural: **i-** |
|---|---|
| Mkate mmoja **u**natosha | Mikate miwili **i**natosha. |
| *One loaf is enough.* | *Two loaves are enough.* |

The prefix **u-** becomes **w-** before a vowel, and **i-** becomes **y-**.

| | | |
|---|---|---|
| mgomba **w**angu | *my banana tree* | migomba **y**angu |
| | | *my banana trees* |
| mti **w**a kwanza | *the first tree* | |

## 3 'This' and 'these'

In Dialogue 1 there are three examples:

| | |
|---|---|
| kitambaa hiki | *this fabric* |
| mavazi haya | *these clothes* |
| mtindo huu | *this style* |

The words for *this* and *these* vary according to the class of the noun they qualify, as you would expect, but their formation is very straightforward:

- they all begin with **h-**.
- they all end with the verb-prefix.

| Noun-class | *this* | *these* |
|------------|--------|---------|
| M/WA | h–yu | h–wa |
| KI/VI | h–ki | h–vi |
| N | h–i | h–zi |
| (JI)/MA | h–li | h–ya |
| M/MI | h–u | h–i |

What is missing is a vowel; all you have to do is fill the gap with the vowel of the verb-prefix. This gives you: **huyu, hawa, hiki, hivi,** etc.

| | | | |
|---|---|---|---|
| mgeni huyu | *this visitor* | wageni hawa | *these visitors* |
| kitabu hiki | *this book* | vitabu hivi | *these books* |
| barua hii | *this letter* | barua hizi | *these letters* |
| embe hili | *this mango* | maembe haya | *these mangoes* |
| mkate huu | *this loaf* | mikate hii | *these loaves* |

Use M/WA verb-prefixes for N class animates.

## 4 Kushona, kukutana, etc. – the infinitive

The **ku-** form of verbs was referred to briefly in section 13 of the second Grammar section in Unit 3. From now on it will be given its grammar name, the *infinitive*.

In this unit there are two examples of its use. In Dialogue 1, Alison says:

Mama Fatuma atanisaidia     *Mama Fatuma will help me to*
  kushona gauni.             *sew (make) a dress.*

In section 1 of the Grammar the elderly man in the example says to Alison:

Nimefurahi kukutana nawe.   *I'm happy to meet you.*

Here are two more examples, with verbs you already know, **kusoma** and **kununua,** to illustrate the use of the infinitive:

Tunapenda kusoma vitabu     *We like to read German books.*
  vya Kijerumani.
Bi. Mariamu anataka         *Miss Mariamu wants to buy*
  kununua maembe.             *some mangoes.*

Notice that in the first example the verb in the English version could have been in the form 'reading'.

# 5 More about object-markers

**a** In Unit 4 the object-markers referring to people were introduced:

| | |
|---|---|
| Tulimwona mzee. | *We saw the old man.* |
| Tulimwona. | *We saw him.* |

In casual conversation the object-marker can be omitted if the object noun, e.g. **mzee** in the first sentence above, is indefinite, that is if speaker and hearer(s) do not know the identity of the old man:

| | |
|---|---|
| Tuliona mzee. | *We saw an old man.* |
| Tuliona mzee mmoja. | *We saw a certain old man.* |

The more formal the context of use, the more likely is the object-marker to be used, even if the object noun is indefinite.

The object-marker is also used to denote the recipient or beneficiary of an action, which may or may not involve an object as well:

| | |
|---|---|
| Bi. Rehema alimpikia mgeni wali. | *Rehema cooked rice for the visitor.* |
| Bi. Rehema alimpikia wali. | *Rehema cooked rice for her.* |
| Bi. Rehema alimpikia. | *Rehema cooked for her/ did some cooking for her/ did her cooking.* |

The final object-marker you will need for referring to people is **-ji-** which is used to denote *myself, yourself, himself,* etc.

| | |
|---|---|
| Alijikata kwa kisu hiki. | *She cut herself with this knife.* |
| Nitajipatia nyumba. | *I will get myself a house.* (i.e. *for myself*) |

But the use of **-ji-** can change the meaning of some verbs, e.g. **-fanya**, *do*, and **-ona**, *see*:

| | |
|---|---|
| walijifanya watalii | *they pretended to be* (or *disguised themselves as*) *tourists* |
| anajiona | *he is conceited* |

**b** In the other noun-classes the verb-prefixes are used quite straightforwardly as object-markers to denote *it* and *them*; they remain the same before a vowel:

| Noun-class: | *it* | *them* |
|---|---|---|
| N | -i- | -zi- |
| KI/VI | -ki- | -vi- |
| (JI)/MA | -li- | -ya- |
| M/MI | -u- | -i- |

| | |
|---|---|
| Uliinunua nguo hii? | *Did you buy this garment?* |
| Niliinunua. | *I bought it.* |
| Ulizinunua nguo hizi? | *Did you buy these clothes?* |
| Nilizinunua. | *I bought them.* |
| Ulikinunua kiti hiki? | *Did you buy this chair?* |
| Nilikinunua. | *I bought it.* |
| Ulivinunua viti hivi? | *Did you buy these chairs?* |
| Nilivinunua. | *I bought them.* |

c The objects in the questions above are definite – *this garment, these clothes*, etc. An object is a definite one if all the participants in a conversation know what is being referred to; this might be because of the use of *this* or it might be because the thing referred to by the object noun has already been mentioned in the conversation. In Swahili, only when the non-human object is definite or the speaker wants to focus attention on the object (rather than on the action) is the object-marker used. Extra emphasis can be given by putting the object noun before the verb instead of after it, in which case the object-marker must definitely be used:

Nguo hizi, ulizinunua? *These clothes, did you buy them?*

The focus here is very much on *these clothes*.

Non-definite objects do not require an object-marker:

| | |
|---|---|
| Ulinunua machungwa? | *Did you buy any oranges?* |
| Nilinunua. | *I bought some.* |
| Sikununua. | *I didn't buy any.* |

## ▶ Dialogue 2

Outside the craft shop Ruth meets John coming in to join Alison. His rucksack is full of market shopping and he looks very hot. They exchange greetings.

**Ruth**   Pole, bwana!
**John**   Nimeshapoa. Alison yumo dukani bado?

| **Ruth** | Bado yumo. Haya, nakwenda sokoni sasa. |
| **John** | Soko limejaa watu! Je, utarudi hapa? |
| **Ruth** | Ndiyo, nitarudi baadaye kidogo. |
| | *(John walks into the shop, sees Alison still choosing fabric and goes to look at a display of carvings. The manager comes over to him.)* |
| **Meneja** | Karibu, bwana. Unavipenda vinyago hivi? |
| **John** | Vinanipendeza sana, hasa kikubwa hiki. |
| **Meneja** | Kinyago kikubwa hiki ni cha Kimakonde, mtindo wa 'binadamu'. Tazama – wapo baba, mama na watoto saba. |
| **John** | Bila shaka ni kizito sana. Sipendi kununua kitu kizito. Labda nitanunua mfinyango mdogo. |
| **Meneja** | Tazama mfinyango huu. Mzee amekaa. Anapiga ngoma. |
| | *(John realizes he has no money, but fortunately Alison appears.)* |
| **John** | Una pesa? Mimi sina. |
| **Alison** | Ninazo, lakini kidogo tu. Nimenunua vitambaa vingi. |
| **John** | Mbona umenunua vingi? |
| **Alison** | Kwa sababu, kwanza nitakushonea shati, halafu nitajishonea gauni . . . |

| | |
|---|---|
| **pole** | an expression of condolence |
| **nimeshapoa** | formulaic reply to *pole!* |
| **soko limejaa watu** | *the market is full of people* |
| **-rudi** | *return* |
| **baadaye kidogo** | *in a little while, soon* |
| **vinyago** (KI/VI) | *carvings* |
| **vinanipendeza** | *I like them (lit. they please me)* |
| **hasa** | *especially, particularly* |
| **Kimakonde** | *Makonde-type* |
| **binadamu** (N) | *human being* |
| **-tazama** | *look* |
| **bila shaka** | *probably, doubtless* |
| **(ki)zito** | *heavy (thing)* |
| **labda** | *perhaps* |
| **mfinyango** (M/MI) | *pottery figure* |
| **-piga ngoma** | *beat a drum* |
| **kidogo** | *small amount* |
| **mbona . . .?** | *why . . .? (expressing surprise)* |
| **kwa sababu** | *because (lit. for the reason)* |
| **kwanza** | *first of all, to start with* |

The structure of **nimeshapoa** will be explained in Unit 6, section 6.

Makonde carvings

# ℹ️ Expressing sympathy

**Pole, bwana/mama/bibi/mzee**, etc., and the plural **poleni** if you are addressing more than one person, can be used to express sympathy in a wide range of situations, for example in illness, whether serious or minor, and for commiserating with someone over small mishaps such as stumbling, or dropping or spilling something. It is also used to show sympathy with someone who has been involved in discomfort or extra exertion.

In the dialogue, Ruth's first words to John, after a brief exchange of greetings to him, are **Pole, bwana!** because she has noticed his heavy rucksack and realizes that, as a newcomer to the coast during the hottest time of the year (December to March), he is feeling the heat.

If you yourself are the cause of someone else's discomfiture, say **Samahani** (like the receptionist in the first dialogue of Unit 3 when he can't find the new guest's booking) or **Nisamehe** (a structure related to **Samahani** and which will be explained later).

If you find yourself in the sad position of needing to offer condolences to someone on the death of a relative or friend, say **Rambirambi zako**, roughly translatable as *my/our sympathy to you*.

# Grammar

## 6 Seasons of the year (majira) and months (miezi)

| | | |
|---|---|---|
| Kiangazi | December–March | Hottest time of year, with north-east monsoon, **Kaskazi** |
| Masika | April–May | Period of heaviest rain |
| Kipupwe | June–August | Coolest time of year |
| Vuli | September–November | Period of lightest rainfall, and onset of **Kaskazi** |

These time-spans are necessarily approximate. The onset and intensity of rainfall can vary considerably from one place to another. 'Cool' is a very relative term, and means something very different in Mombasa or Dar es Salaam, compared with, say, Nairobi – or halfway up Mount Kilimanjaro!

> **mwezi**  *month*                    (pl.) **miezi**

As you see, **mwezi** is another M/MI class noun. It is sometimes used with **-a**, *of*, in referring to a particular month: **mwezi wa Oktoba, mwezi wa Januari**, etc.

All you have to do as far as the months are concerned is adjust the pronunciation, the stress (penultimate syllable) and the spelling of what is already familiar to you:

| | | | |
|---|---|---|---|
| Januari | Aprili | Julai | Oktoba |
| Februari | Mei | Agosti | Novemba |
| Machi | Juni | Septemba | Desemba *or* Disemba |

People sometimes refer to the months by using the ordinal numbers:

Mwezi wa kwanza / wa pili / wa tatu / wa nne, etc.

## 7 Kinyago kikubwa hiki: word-order in the noun phrase

In the case of more than one qualifier following a noun, the usual word-order is as follows.

a A qualitative adjective comes before *this, these* and *that, those*:

kinyago kikubwa hiki          *this large carving*

and before a numeral:

    vinyago vikubwa viwili    *two large carvings*

**b** A possessive comes before a qualitative adjective:

    kinyago changu kikubwa    *my large carving*

and before a numeral:

    vinyago vyangu viwili    *my two carvings*

**c** The rules for word-order, given above, are for unemphatic speech. In order to emphasize one of the qualifiers, Swahili-speakers change the word-order. They do NOT do what English-speakers do – put heavy stress on the word to be emphasized. In Swahili noun-phrases the word to be given emphasis is placed at the end. So in order to draw attention to a large carving near you, and distinguish it from smaller carvings nearby, you would say:

    kinyago hiki kikubwa   *instead of*   kinyago kikubwa hiki

Never try to emphasize words by stressing them; Swahili does not work like that!

**d** When two qualitative adjectives follow the verb (and therefore function like nouns), they are joined by **na** or **tena**:

| | |
|---|---|
| Vinyago vyake ni vikubwa na vizuri. | *His carvings are large and beautiful* (or '*are large and beautiful ones*'). |
| Vinyago vyao ni vidogo tena rahisi. | *Their carvings are small and cheap* (or '*are small and cheap ones*'.) |

## 8 Soko limejaa watu; mbona umenunua vingi? The -me- tense

In Dialogue 2 the verbs **-jaa**, *be full*, and **-nunua**, *buy*, both have the tense-marker **-me-**, usually referred to as the perfect tense. The marker **-me-** is used when referring to a state, as in **limejaa**, or a completed action as in **umenunua**.

**a** Expressing a state
This is done through the meaning of the verb together with the use of **-me-**. It will help you to understand the function of **-me-** if you remember that **Soko limejaa watu** can be put into English

not only as *The market is full of people* but also as *The market has become* (or *got*) *full of people* or *The market has filled with people*. The state is the result of a process. Some more verbs denoting a state are:

| | |
|---|---|
| **-choka** | *become tired, feel weary* |
| **-furahi** | *be happy* |
| **-isha (kwisha)** | *be finished, used up* |
| **-potea** | *be lost* |
| **-shiba** | *be full up, satisfied with food* |
| **-vaa** | *wear, be wearing* |

| | |
|---|---|
| Tumechoka. | *We are tired, have become tired.* |
| Mchele umekwisha. | *The rice is finished/all used up/ there's no more rice.* |
| Nimeshiba. | *I'm full up/satisfied/ I have had enough to eat.* |

*Note*: **-vaa** also means *put on clothes*. With this meaning use **-na-** in the present tense.

**b** Expressing a completed action
Verbs denoting activities like taking, sending, buying, selling, eating, cooking – activities that people initiate and carry out – take **-me-** to express the completion of the action:

| | |
|---|---|
| Umeipeleka barua? | *Have you sent the letter?* |
| Nimenunua cherehani. | *I have bought a sewing-machine.* |
| Ameuza ng'ombe? | *Has he sold some cows?* |
| Wamekula ugali. | *They have eaten polenta.* |

At the time of speaking the action has been completed, and the results of the action may well be in evidence – the sewing-machine installed, the remains of the polenta in the pot, etc. The questions refer to a possible action in the recent past. Note that with **-me-** the monosyllabic verbs, such as **-la**, retain the infinitive **ku-**, as they do with the tense-markers **-li-**, **-na-** and **-ta-**.

The negative will be dealt with in Unit 6.

# 9 Kimakonde, kidogo – two more uses of ki-

The **ki-** prefix on the first word above really has the same general function of *in the manner of* as the **ki-** in **Kiswahili**, except that here it is a type of object associated with or produced by a group that is being referred to – a Makonde carving. The Makonde people are called, in Swahili, **Wamakonde** and their language **Kimakonde**; similarly, for example, the Nyamwezi people and their language are **Wanyamwezi** and **Kinyamwezi**.

**Kidogo** in **lakini kidogo tu,** near the end of the dialogue, is not in agreement with a KI noun. It refers to Alison's money being small in quantity. When it has this meaning, rather than small in size, the **ki-** prefix stays the same whatever noun it qualifies.

Ana michungwa midogo.    *She has some small orange trees.*
Ana michungwa kidogo.    *She has a few orange trees.*

## 10  Anayo, tunazo, ninazo – the -o form

The -yo in **anayo**, near the beginning of Dialogue 1, refers back to **cherehani** (N sing.); **-zo** in **tunazo** near the end of the same dialogue refers back to **batiki** (N pl.); **-zo** in **ninazo** at the end of Dialogue 2 refers back to **pesa** (N pl.).

Being with something, or *having something* as we usually express it in English, was explained in Unit 2 and takes the form **nina, una,** etc. The form **-na** does not take an object-marker in front of it as full verbs do, but it does use the verb-prefix, attached to **-o** in the following way:

| Noun-class | | | |
|---|---|---|---|
| M/WA | Sing. (irregular form) | | ye |
| | Pl. | wa + o | *makes* o |
| N | Sing. | i + o | yo |
| | Pl. | zi + o | zo |
| KI/VI | Sing. | ki + o | cho |
| | Pl. | vi + o | vyo |
| (JI)/MA | Sing. | li + o | lo |
| | Pl. | ya + o | yo |
| M/MI | Sing. | u + o | o |
| | Pl. | i + o | yo |

This verb-prefix + **o** form is attached to **nina, una, ana,** etc. Its functions are as follows:

**a** To act as a pronoun, i.e. stand in place of a noun or nounphrase:

Una ndizi? Ninazo.
*Have you any bananas?*
*We have **some**.*

Wana vitabu vya Kiswahili? *Have they any Swahili books?*
Wanavyo.
*They have **some**.*

The negative does not need the -o form, as in the dialogue when John says **Mimi, sina** (*As for me, I haven't any*).

**b** To mark definiteness:

Unazo ndizi?
*Have you the bananas?*
Ninazo.
*I have got **them**.*
Wanavyo vitabu vya
*Have they got the Swahili*
Kiswahili?
*books?*
Wanavyo.
*They've got **them**.*

The verb-prefix + **o** form has several other uses, to be dealt with later in the book, and nearly all of them have a referring-back function.

# Practice

1  -vaa: *wearing* or *putting on clothes* (-me- or -na-)

Using the verb -vaa and either -na- or -me- as the appropriate tense-marker, write a sentence for each of the pictures to say what the person is doing:

Mzee Khamisi

Mtalii

Bi. Pendo

Mama Lela

Mama Zubeda

Bw. Francis

2   **Jibu maswali haya.** Answer these questions.
    (They refer to the two dialogues.) The first one has been
    done for you.

> **kwa sababu**   *because, for the reason that*
> **badala ya**    *instead of*

a   Nani atamsaidia Bi. Alison kushona gauni?
    **Mama Fatuma atamsaidia Bi. Alison kushona gauni.**
b   Bi. Alison hapendi rangi gani?
c   Kwa nini (*why*) Bi. Alison hapendi magauni dukani?
    (**Bi. Alison . . . kwa sababu . . .**)
d   Nani anamwonyesha Bi. Alison vitambaa?
e   Bw. John ametoka wapi sasa?
f   Kinyago kipi kinampendeza dukani?
g   Kwa nini Bw. John hakinunui kinyago kikubwa cha
    Kimakonde?
    (*Use* **kwa sababu** *in this answer.*)
h   Anapenda kununua kitu gani badala ya kinyago?

3   Fill in each gap with the correct word for *this* and *these*
    chosen from the list below.

a   Bi. Asha ameninunulia kitambaa _____.
b   Utanisaidia kupika maharagwe _____?
c   Msaidizi alituonyesha vitabu _____.
d   Rafiki yangu ameniandikia barua _____.
e   Akina mama wanamtafuta mtoto _____.
f   Tutapata machungwa mengi, mwaka _____.
g   Nyumba kubwa _____ zinawapendeza wageni.
h   Jembe _____ limenisaidia sana shambani.

> huyu   hizi   hiki   hii   hivi   haya   hili   huu

Now write out the English version of each sentence.

4   Regina is planning a party – **karamu** (N). She and her
    daughter Anastasia are checking on what things are already
    in the food store. Fill in Anastasia's replies to Regina's
    questions according to whether there is a tick or a cross at
    the end of the answer-line. The first two have been done for
    you:

| **Regina** | Tuna mchele? | |
|---|---|---|
| **Ana** | Tunao. | ✓ |
| **Regina** | Tuna unga wa ngano? | |
| **Ana** | Hatuna. | ✗ |
| **Regina** | Tuna unga wa mahindi? | |
| **Ana** | _____ | ✗ |
| **Regina** | Tuna viazi? | |
| **Ana** | _____ | ✓ |
| **Regina** | Tuna ndizi? | |
| **Ana** | _____ | ✓ |
| **Regina** | Tuna nyanya? | |
| **Ana** | _____ | ✓ |
| **Regina** | Tuna malimau? | |
| **Ana** | _____ | ✗ |
| **Regina** | Haya, basi. Twende (*let's go*) sokoni! | |

5   A river-bridge has collapsed and several busloads of
    assorted people, one of whom is yourself, have had to take
    refuge in the nearest small town, which is now crammed.
    Before you fall asleep there is just time to make a brief entry
    in your diary which you are (of course!) keeping in Swahili.
    Write your diary entry using the following information:

    *The river is full of water. The hotel is full of tourists. The
    teachers' houses are full of elderly people. The bar is full of
    students. We and Bw. Juma are in the school. The food is
    finished!*

### As the saying goes . . .

Two more proverbs to learn!

Mkono mmoja hauchinji ng'ombe.
*One hand cannot slaughter a cow.*

(**-chinja**, *slaughter an animal for food*)

Mke ni nguo, mgomba kupalilia.
*A wife is clothes, a banana tree (is) weeding.*

Migomba

Mke ni nguo, mgomba kupalilia.
*A wife is clothes, a banana tree (is) weeding.*

# 06

## matembezi jioni!
### an evening walk

**In this unit you will learn**
- how to tell the time
- how to make polite requests and suggest future action
- how to say whether something has or has not yet occurred
- how to refer to the days of the week and dates

# ▶ Dialogue 1

Mohamed has arranged to meet John and Alison at about 4 p.m.
not far from Dar es Salaam harbour. Alison has not yet arrived.
Mohamed and John are commenting on some of the buildings.

| | |
|---|---|
| **John** | Mafundi wamemaliza kukarabati kanisa lile? |
| **Mohamed** | Bado. Wamekarabati paa, lakini kuta bado. (*Looking at his watch*:) Sasa ni saa kumi u nusu. Dada yuko wapi, basi? |
| **John** | Sijui. Baada ya chakula cha mchana alisema atakwenda maktaba asome magazeti ya Kiingereza. |
| **Mohamed** | Afadhali asome magazeti ya Kiswahili! <br> (*At that moment Alison appears. She exchanges brief greetings with Mohamed whom she has not seen since the previous day*.) |
| **Alison** | Jamani, samahani! Nimechelewa sana. |
| **John** | Mbona umechelewa hivi? |
| **Alison** | Nilitoka maktaba mapema. Mara niliona shanga zangu nyeupe zimepotea. Nilianza kuzitafuta njiani, karibu na maktaba. |
| **John** | Umezipata? |
| **Alison** | Sikuzipata. |
| **Mohamed** | Pole dada. |
| **Alison** | Asante. |
| **John** | Basi, twende wapi? |
| **Mohamed** | Tuendelee kutembea karibu na bahari? |
| **John** | Haya, twende. |
| **Mohamed** | Mtapata nafasi kwenda Zanzibar kwa boti? (*Indicating a row of ticket offices ahead of them along the waterfront*:) Mtapata tiketi ofisini pale. Ukutani pana ratiba. |
| **John** | Afadhali twende Zanzibar kwa ndege. Ni safari ya dakika ishirini tu. |
| **Mohamed** | Lakini ni ghali zaidi! |

Waiting for Alison near the harbour

*Notes:*
- **maktaba** is one place-word that does not take the **-ni** suffix.
- **-chelewa** is one of the 'state' verbs that takes the **-me-** tense-marker.
- Mohamed's use of **dada** (*sister*), to address Alison expresses friendliness.

| | |
|---:|---|
| **matembezi** (MA) | *walk, stroll* |
| **jioni** | *evening* |
| **mafundi** (MA) | *skilled craftsmen* |
| **-maliza** | *finish* |
| **-karabati** | *renovate, repair* |
| **kanisa** (MA) | *church* |
| **lile** | *that* (i.e. church) |
| **bado** | *not yet* |
| **paa** (N) | *roof* |
| **kuta** | *walls* |
| **sasa** | *now* |
| **saa kumi u nusu** | *half-past four* (the tenth hour, and a half) |
| **-jua** | *know* |
| **baada ya chakula cha mchana** | *after the midday meal* |
| **mchana** | *daytime* |
| **maktaba** (N) | *library* |
| **asome** | *(that) she might/should read* |
| **magazeti** (MA) | *newspapers* |
| **afadhali** | *better, preferably* |
| **Jamani!** | *Hi, there!* |
| **-chelewa** | *be late* |
| **hivi** | *like this, thus* |
| **-toka** | *leave* |
| **mapema** | *early* |
| **mara** | *suddenly* |
| **-ona** | *realize* (in this context) |
| **shanga** | *beads* |
| **-anza** | *begin, start* |
| **twende wapi?** | *where should we go?* |
| **tuendelee** | *let's continue* |
| **kutembea** | *to walk* |
| **bahari** (N) | *sea* |
| **nafasi** (N) | *opportunity, time* |
| **boti** (N) | *small motorized boat* |
| **tiketi** (N) | *ticket* |
| **ofisi** (N) | *office* |
| **ukuta** | *wall* |
| **ratiba** (N) | *timetable* |
| **dakika** (N) | *minutes* |
| **zaidi** | *more* |

# ℹ️ Cities in Kenya, Uganda and Tanzania

The cities in the countries where Swahili is spoken have developed by very different routes. Nairobi grew out of a base-camp for engineers' workshops and stores at the foot of an escarpment during the difficult building of the Mombasa–Kisumu railway line during the 1890s; the site of the camp was near a crossing-place over a stream which the local Maasai people called Enkare Nairobi. It was the building of this railway that helped to restore something of the earlier prosperity of Mombasa which, at the beginning of the sixteenth century, was a wealthy port, functioning like a city-state, and engaged in international trade.

Kampala, built on several hills, with the city centre on one of them, was established as the new capital of the Baganda kingdom in the early 1860s, and has been expanding, on and off, ever since.

Although Dodoma is officially the capital of Tanzania, it is Dar es Salaam, the 'haven of peace', which houses most of the government ministries, the embassies and high commissions, and is the place of arrival for most visitors to Tanzania. There has been settlement in the Dar es Salaam area for centuries, and to the south of the present city lay a starting-point for one of the trade-routes that linked Zanzibar with the interior during much of the nineteenth century.

The cities, and the larger towns, act as magnets for ambitious young people from other parts of the country, intent on seeking their fortune. And all of them, to varying degrees, provide scope for the development of lifestyles which are hugely different from those of people living in rural areas. The city populations are linguistically very mixed, and Swahili's role as a *lingua franca* is of great importance. Urban living provides continuing impetus for the expansion of the language. It is not only in the coining and spread of new Swahili vocabulary that urban-dwellers are innovative; in Nairobi, for example, a Swahili–English mixture has developed which is used by streetwise young people as a sort of 'in-group' badge of identity.

# Grammar

## 1 Saa ngapi? *What's the time?*

**a** Working out the time

In the dialogue Alison should have met the others at about 4 p.m.: **saa kumi**, '*hour ten*' or '*the tenth hour*'.

The six-hour difference in working out time is because in

Swahili the numbering of the hours is in accordance with twelve hours of daylight and twelve hours of darkness, the first hour of each twelve-hour period being **saa moja,** the second **saa mbili,** and so on. So if you relate the hours of the Swahili day to what you would say in English at the same hour, 7 a.m. – the beginning of the first full hour of daylight after sunrise – would be **saa moja,** 8 a.m. would be **saa mbili,** 9 a.m. **saa tatu,** and so on up to 6 p.m. which would be **saa kumi na mbili.**

Until you get used to the system a useful rule for converting 'English-speaking time' to Swahili time is to *subtract* six hours from 'English-speaking time' during the morning, starting at 7 a.m. (7 – 6 = 1, **saa moja**) and to *add* six hours from 1 p.m. onwards up to 6 p.m. (6 + 6 = 12, **saa kumi na mbili**). The same rule can be applied to the twelve hours of night, beginning at 7 p.m.

| | |
|---:|:---|
| **kucha** | *the whole night* |
| **kutwa** (sometimes **kuchwa**) | *the whole day* |
| **mchana** (no pl.) | *daylight, daytime* |
| **saa** (N) | *hour,* also *clock, watch* |
| **siku** (N) | *day* |

**b** Parts of the day

| | | | |
|:---|:---|:---|:---|
| **\*alfajiri** | *dawn* | **\*alasiri** | *afternoon (2–4ish)* |
| **asubuhi** | *morning* | **jioni** | *evening* |
| **mchana** | *middle part of day* | **\*magharibi** | *around sunset* |
| **\*adhuhuri** | *midday* | **usiku** | *night* |

\*These are the names of four of the prescribed Muslim prayer-times. The fifth one, which has not given its name to a period of the day, is **isha,** at around 8 p.m.

Because **saa** is an N class noun, the number used with it is in its N class agreement form (always easy because it is the form you use in counting) and so is **-a,** *of,* when it is used. In order to pinpoint an hour within day or night, phrases like these are used (**ya** is shown in brackets because it is often omitted):

| | |
|:---|:---|
| saa tatu (ya) asubuhi | *9 a.m.* |
| saa nane (ya) mchana | *2 p.m.* |
| saa kumi na mbili (ya) jioni | *6 p.m.* |
| saa nne (ya) usiku | *10 p.m.* |

You can manage with just **mchana** and **usiku,** to start with.

**c** Half-hours, quarter-hours and minutes

*Half past* is expressed by **u nusu**; *quarter past* by **na robo**; and *quarter to* by **kasa robo**. *Minute* is **dakika** (N); to express minutes after the hour you say **na dakika**, and before the hour **kasa dakika**:

| | |
|---|---|
| saa mbili u nusu | 8.30 |
| saa mbili na robo | 8.15 |
| saa tatu kasa robo | 8.45 |
| saa mbili na dakika tano | 8.05 |
| saa tatu kasa dakika mbili | 8.58 |

*Second* varies between **sekunde** and **nukta**.

## 2 Ushanga, ukuta, usiku and other U class nouns

**a** U class nouns sort themselves out quite neatly into groups, and the three nouns above, all in their singular form, are in the same group. This group have U as their singular prefix but make their plurals like the N class plurals. We shall call this group U/N nouns. If you look back at Unit 2 and check the rules for the N prefix, you will see why the plurals of the three words above are **shanga**, **kuta** and **siku**; their stems begin with a voiceless consonant and do not take a nasal prefix. Here are a few more U/N nouns. Notice that they tend to denote either long objects, or masses like hair, **nywele**, and beads, **shanga**, with the singular form referring to a single item of the mass, i.e. **unywele**, *a single hair*, and **ushanga**, *a single bead*.

| U/N nouns | |
|---|---|
| Singular | Plural |
| **ubao** *plank of wood* | **mbao** |
| **ufagio** *broom* | **fagio** |
| **ulimi** *tongue* | **ndimi** |
| **unywele** *single hair* | **nywele** |
| **wavu** (u-avu) *net* (fishing, trapping) | **nyavu** |
| **wimbo** (u-imbo) *song* | **nyimbo** |

**b** Another group of U class nouns are those which refer to some substance which cannot be counted; they do not have a plural form. You already know some of these:

| U class nouns (uncountables) | |
|---|---|
| **udongo** *earth, soil, clay* | **unga** *flour* |
| **ugali** *polenta* | **wali** *cooked rice* |
| **uji** *liquid porridge, gruel* | |

c The last group of U class nouns to be dealt with here are those which denote abstract concepts. They are made from nouns by changing the class prefix to **u-**, or to **w-** before a vowel, and from adjectives by prefixing **u-** to the stem. They can also be made from verb-roots. They do not have a plural. You should already be familiar with the noun and adjective stems from which all but one of these are made (the exception is **umri**, which is a loan word).

| U class nouns (abstract) | | | |
|---|---|---|---|
| **ubaya** | *badness* | **umri** | *age* |
| **udogo** | *smallness* | **utoto** | *childhood* |
| **ugonjwa** | *illness* | **uzee** | *old age* |
| **ukubwa** | *size* | | |

Some of these words also have a MA plural:

**magonjwa** *diseases*      **mabaya** *bad actions*

d The group of U class nouns denoting countries was introduced in Unit 1.

e Prefixes on adjectives and other qualifiers taking the noun-prefix

Unlike the other noun classes, the singular prefix on qualifiers that take the noun-prefix – qualitative adjectives and **-ingine** as far as singulars are concerned – is *not* the same as the prefix on the noun. Instead of **u-** the prefix is **m-**, or **mw-** before a vowel:

| ufagio mrefu | *a long broom* |
| ugali mzuri | *good polenta* |
| utoto mwema | *a good childhood* |
| wavu mwingine | *another net* |

Qualifiers used with plural nouns (this, of course, applies only to words like those in the first box) take the appropriate N class prefix, **ny-**, **n-**, **m-** or no prefix if the stem begins with a voiceless consonant. As well as adjectives and **-ingine**, the numbers and **-ingi** also need an N class prefix (the only reason that **-ngapi** does not take one is that it already begins with a nasal sound):

| mbao nzuri | *good planks of wood* |
| nyavu mbili | *two nets* |
| nyimbo nyingi | *many songs* |
| fagio ngapi? | *how many brooms?* |

f The verb-prefixes are:

| | |
|---|---|
| Singular: **u-** | Plural: **zi-** |
| Wavu huu **u**tafaa. | Nyavu hizi zitafaa. |
| *This net will do.* | *These nets will do.* |
| Wavu **u**ko wapi? | Nyavu ziko wapi? |
| *Where is the net?* | *Where are the nets?* |
| wavu **w**angu | nyavu **z**angu |
| *my net* | *my nets* |

and so on, for **wa** (u + a), **za** (zi + a), **huu, hizi, ninao** and **ninazo**, etc.

## 3 'That' and 'those'

In the dialogue John refers to **kanisa lile**, *that church*. The **li-** is the verb-prefix for singular nouns in the (JI)/MA class. In section 3 of Unit 5 it was noted that the verb-prefixes are involved in the formation of the words for *this* and *these*, to agree with the nouns they qualify. *That* and *those* are formed by adding **-le** to the verb-prefix.

| Noun-class: | *that* | *those* |
|---|---|---|
| M/WA | yule | wale |
| KI/VI | kile | vile |
| N | ile | zile |
| (JI)/MA | lile | yale |
| M/MI | ule | ile |
| U/(N) | ule | zile |

For example:

| | |
|---|---|
| mkulima yule | *that farmer* |
| wakulima wale | *those farmers* |
| kiti kile | *that chair* |
| viti vile | *those chairs* |

## 4 Twende, asome, tuendelee – the -e form of verbs

Verb-forms like these enable people to convey a range of attitudes towards the action, including suggestion, purpose, obligation and polite request. The stems of these three verbs are: **-enda**, *go*, **-soma**, *read*, **-endelea**, *continue*. Only the verb-prefix and the verb-stem are used, with the final -a of the stem changed to -e. There is no tense-marker.

| | |
|---|---|
| twende (tuende) | *let's go* |
| asome | *she should read* |
| tuendelee | *let's continue* |

The spelling **twende** rather than **tuende** reflects normal pronunciation.

**a** In the next two examples a suggestion is put in the form of a question:

| | |
|---|---|
| Basi, twende wapi? | *Well, where shall we go?* |
| Tuendelee kutembea karibu na bahari? | *Shall we go on walking near the sea?* |

**b** The purposeful function, *in order to*, is shown in this example:

| | |
|---|---|
| . . . alisema atakwenda maktaba asome magazeti ya Kiingereza. | *. . . she said she would be going to the library (in order to) read English newspapers.* |

After verbs of coming and going, the infinitive is sometimes used for the following verb, instead of the -e form, but this is only possible if there is no change of person:

| | |
|---|---|
| Atakwenda benki kuchukua pesa. | *He will go to the bank to get (take out) some money.* |
| Atakwenda benki nipate pesa. | *He will go to the bank so that I get some money.* |

*(c)* The functions of 'saying something ought to be done' range from *should* to *must*, when following certain words. **Afadhali** (*better, preferably*) gives the following -e verb a *should* function:

| | |
|---|---|
| Afadhali asome magazeti ya Kiswahili! | *She should read Swahili newspapers!/ It would be better for her to read Swahili newspapers!* |
| Afadhali twende Zanzibar kwa boti. | *We should go to Zanzibar by boat./We ought to go to Zanzibar by boat.* |

**Afadhali** can be preceded by **ni** (*is*) but often is not.

> **(ni) lazima** *(it is) necessary*

Following (ni) lazima, -e verbs have a strong *must* meaning:

Lazima aende maktaba.    *She must go to the library.*

d Polite requests:

Usimame hapa.    *Please stand here./Would you mind standing here?*

Ununue samaki kesho.    *Please buy some fish tomorrow./ I'd be glad if you would buy some fish tomorrow.*

Note also:

e The single-syllable verbs drop the ku- prefix when used in the -e form:

Watoto wale matunda.    *The children should eat fruit.*

f Negatives are made by inserting -si- between the verb-prefix and the verb-stem:

Tusiende maktaba.    *Don't let's go to the library.*

Wasipike jioni?    *Aren't they supposed to cook this evening?*

Note that this negative form also functions as the negative of imperatives:

Nunua nyama!    *Buy some meat!*

Usinunue nyama!    *Don't buy any meat!*

g Object-markers also come between the prefix and the verb-stem:

Avilete vitabu.    *She should bring the books.*

The object-marker follows -si- in negatives:

Usizipike.    *Please don't cook them. You shouldn't cook them.* (-zi- could refer, for example, to bananas)

Verbs without a final -a do not change their ending. This will be dealt with in Unit 7.

## ◨ Dialogue 2

Alison, John and Mohamed have continued along the harbour front and are now almost opposite the railway station.

**Mohamed**    Haya, tuvuke sasa.
(*They cross the road and wander into the station.*)

| Alison | Tukienda Mbeya tutapata gari moshi hapa? |
|---|---|
| **Mohamed** | Hapana. Lazima mwende stesheni ya TAZARA. Umeshaiona, siyo? |
| **John** | Hatujapata nafasi bado. Ni kama stesheni hii? |
| **Mohamed** | Si kama stesheni hii. Stesheni hii ilijengwa zamani. Stesheni ya TAZARA ilijengwa mnamo miaka ya sitini. |
| **Alison** | Tunakusudia kwenda Tanga. Twende kwa basi? |
| **Mohamed** | Ndiyo, afadhali mwende kwa basi. Mtapata basi Mnazi Mmoja. Mnakusudia kusafiri siku gani? |
| **John** | Labda Ijumaa. |
| **Mohamed** | Afadhali mnunue tiketi Jumatano au Alhamisi. Twende Mnazi Mmoja sasa, niwaonyeshe kituo cha mabasi. *(They leave the station and walk to the Mnazi Mmoja area so that Mohamed can show them where the bus terminus is. They leave the terminus at 5.30 p.m. and head in the direction of Alison and John's hotel.)* |
| **Mohamed** | Hoteli yenu iko karibu. Mimi nakwenda kusali. Msikiti uko karibu. Baada ya safari yenu nitawapelekeni kuona jumba la makumbusho. Kwa herini sasa. |
| **John and Alison** | Kwa heri, bwana. |
| **Mohamed** | Safari njema! |

| | |
|---|---|
| **tukienda** | *if we go* |
| **gari moshi** (MA), also **treni** (N), esp. in Kenya | *train* |
| **stesheni** | *station* |
| **TAZARA** | Tanzania–Zambia rail link |
| **umeshaiona, siyo?** | *you've already seen it, haven't you?* |
| **hatujapata nafasi bado** | *we haven't had time yet* |
| **nafasi** (N) | *time, opportunity* |
| **kama** | *like* |
| **ilijengwa** | *(it) was built* |
| **zamani** | *a long time ago* |
| **mnamo miaka ya sitini** | *in the 1960s* |
| **-kusudia** | *intend* |
| **-safiri** | *travel* |
| **Ijumaa** | *Friday* |
| **Jumatano** | *Wednesday* |
| **Alhamisi** | *Thursday* |
| **kituo cha mabasi** (KI/VI) | *stop, terminus* |
| **-sali** | *pray* |

| msikiti (M/MI) | mosque |
| jumba la makumbusho (MA) | museum |
| safari njema! | (have a) good trip! |

# Grammar

## 5 Days of the week, dates, period of time

a

| Jumamosi | Saturday | Jumatano | Wednesday |
| Jumapili | Sunday | Alhamisi | Thursday |
| Jumatatu | Monday | Ijumaa | Friday |
| Jumanne | Tuesday | | |

**Juma** (MA) means *week*, and a useful way to learn the days is to start with Saturday, the first day of the Muslim week. Think of **mosi** as a variant of **moja** (*one*); the other numbers used in the words for Sunday to Wednesday should already be familiar to you. Another word for *week* is **wiki** (N).

b

| tarehe (N) | date |

Remember **mwezi** means *month*:

| tarehe moja (*or* mosi), mwezi wa Machi | 1st March |
| tarehe pili (*or* mbili), mwezi wa Mei | 2nd May |
| tarehe tatu, mwezi wa Oktoba | 3rd October |
| tarehe ishirini na nne, mwezi wa Novemba | 24th November |
| tarehe kumi na tano, mwezi wa nane, mwaka (wa) elfu mbili | 15th August 2000 |

c

| muda (M/MI) | period of time |

| muda wa miaka miwili | a period of two years |
| muda wa miezi mitano | a period of five months |
| muda wa majuma sita | a period of six weeks |
| muda wa wiki kumi | a period of ten weeks |
| muda wa siku tatu | a period of three days |
| Walikaa pale muda wa wiki mbili. | They stayed there (in that place) for a period of two weeks. |

## 6 Umeshaiona, siyo?
*You've already seen it, haven't you?*

Two verbs are involved in **umeshaiona**; it is a 'collapsed' form:

| umekwisha | + | kuiona | → | umeshaiona |
|---|---|---|---|---|
| *you have finished* | | *to see it* | | *you have already seen it* |

There is an example of a 'collapsed' form using the verb **kwisha** (**ku-isha**, *to finish*), in the second dialogue of Unit 5:

| nimekwisha | + | kupoa | → | nimeshapoa |
|---|---|---|---|---|
| *I have finished* | | *to feel better* | | *I'm already feeling better* |

The form **-mekwisha** has an *already* function:

| Ameleta matunda. | *He has brought some fruit.* |
|---|---|
| Amekwisha kuleta matunda. | *He has already brought some fruit.* |
| Amesha kuleta matunda. | *He has already brought some fruit.* |
| Ameshaleta matunda. | *He has already brought some fruit.* |

Although the full forms are not used in everyday conversation, they do occur in formal Swahili, such as speeches or lectures, and they are used in the written language.

## 7 Hatujapata nafasi  *We haven't had time yet*

The **-ja-** immediately before the verb is another tense-marker, the 'not yet' tense.

| Umepika wali? | *Have you cooked the rice?* |
|---|---|
| Sijapika wali. | *I haven't yet cooked the rice* (but I will eventually). |
| Mmenunua sukari? | *Have you (pl.) bought sugar?* |
| Hatujanunua sukari bado. | *We haven't yet bought any sugar* (but we will). |

Note that **bado**, *not yet*, can be used at the end of a sentence with **-ja-**, to emphasize that something has not yet happened.

If it is clear that the action will not take place, the past tense negative is used. In Dialogue 1 John asks Alison:

| Umezipata? | *Have you found them?* |
|---|---|

Being quite sure that she now has no chance of finding them, she replies:

| Sikuzipata. | *I haven't found them.* |
|---|---|

# Practice

▶ 1 Public clocks usually display 'English-speaking time' and some people set their watches like this too. Give the Swahili time for each 'English-speaking time'.

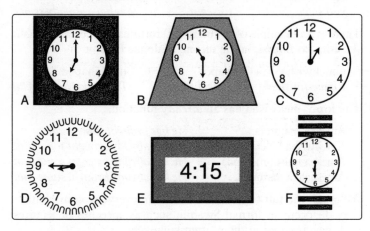

2 In Dialogue 1:
   a  What is the time (English-speaking!) when Mohamed looks at his watch?
   b  Why is Alison late in meeting the other two?
   c  What is on the wall of the ticket-office?
   d  Why does John think they should fly to Zanzibar?

   In Dialogue 2:
   e  Which day are John and Alison planning to go to Tanga?
   f  When does Mohamed suggest they get their tickets?
   g  What is the time, in Swahili, when they leave the bus terminus?
   h  What is Mohamed going to do after the walk?

3 Fill in each gap with a suitable word from the list below.

   a  Shanga _____ Bi. Alison zimepotea.
   b  Dada amewapikia watoto uji _____.
   c  Nywele zake ni _____.
   d  Mama ana ufagio _____.
   e  Watoto wanapenda nyimbo _____ Kifaransa.
   f  Watakarabati ukuta _____ kanisa.

   | wa | ndefu | zake | huu | za | mzuri |

**4** Write out these sentences putting the verbs in brackets in their correct form. There are two possibilities in **a**.

a John amekwenda posta (**-nunua**) stampu.
b Tulimpa Alison pesa (**-leta**) matunda.
d Ninawatafuta wageni (**-pa**) barua zao (*that I may give them*).
d Regina alinunua mchele (**-pika**) pilau.
e Mwalimu alinipa kitabu cha Kiswahili (**-soma**).
f Tulimnunulia Otto gazeti lile (**-soma**) Kiswahili.

**5** This is a newspaper advert:

a On which day of the week was the Twiga Band playing?
b What time was the music due to begin? (English-speaking time!)
c What do you think **mahali** means?
d Write out the date in Swahili words.
e What do you think **twiga** means?

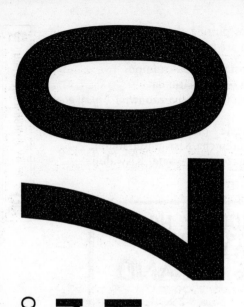

# 07

## kupika kwa mama mzee

### cooking at grandmother's

**In this unit you will learn**
- how to offer to help someone
- how to ask what someone is doing
- how to tell people politely not to do things
- how to refer to procedures used in preparing a meal

# ▶ Dialogue

Regina and Francis are on a visit to Francis' parents' home in southern Tanzania; they have brought with them a visiting American student, Steve. Other family members, including Francis' grandmother, **mama mzee**, live nearby. It is late afternoon.

**Steve**    Regina yuko wapi?

**Francis**    Yupo msituni. Kina mama walikwenda kukata kuni. Tangu walipokwenda ni masaa mawili. Ila mama mzee yupo.

(*Steve finds* **mama mzee** *sitting at the back of her house, with two baskets of large leaves.*)

**Steve**    Je, mama, nikusaidie? Unafanya nini?

**Mama mzee**    (*laughing*) Aa, mwanangu! Ndiyo kazi yangu. Nachambua majani ya muhogo.

**Steve**    Ulinunua sokoni?

**Mama mzee**    Sikununua. Nilichuma shambani. Si uliona shambani pana mihogo? Ni lazima nichume majani laini. Nitapika kisamvu.

**Steve**    Kisamvu?

**Mama mzee**    Ndiyo, mboga ya kisamvu. Kazi yangu ni kuchambuachambua na kuponda, halafu kuchemsha.

**Steve**    Nikuletee maji?

**Mama mzee**    Haya, mwanangu. Debe lenye maji lipo pembeni pale, na sufuria ipo hapa.

(*Steve pours water from the* **debe** *into a large* **sufuria**.)

Vizuri. Weka juu ya mafiga. Moto unawaka. Tia na chumvi kiasi. Usitie nyingi sana!

*Later:*

**Steve**    Maji yamechemka!

**Mama mzee**    Nitie majani sasa. (*She puts the cassava leaves into the boiling water.*)

**Steve**    Nikoroge?

**Mama mzee**    Usikoroge sasa. Funika tu. Baadaye nitatia vitunguu na tui, ndipo utakoroga. Njoo ukatekate vitunguu!

(*Regina appears.*)

**Regina**    He! Unajifunza namna ya kupika kisamvu!

**Steve**    Ndiyo, mimi ni mpishi sasa.

**Regina**    Tutakula kisamvu kwa ugali. Sasa hivi nimeanza kupika ugali. Naona umezoea meko ya mama mzee. Mimi ninapika ugali juu ya jiko la makaa.

*Later, after supper:*

**Steve**     Nitakaporudi Nairobi nitajipikia kisamvu.
**Francis**   Lazima ununue majani ya muhogo sokoni; hamna shamba huko, siyo?
**Steve**     Hatuna.
**Mama mzee** Tena, usisahau kutia chumvi ya kutosha!

| | |
|---|---|
| **kwa mama mzee** | *(at) grandmother's place* (home) |
| **msitu** (M/MI) | *woodland* |
| **kuni** (U/N) | *firewood* (pl. form) |
| **tangu walipokwenda** | *since they went* |
| **-po-** | *when* |
| **masaa mawili** (MA) | *two hours* |
| **-fanya** | *do* |
| **kazi** (N) | *work* |
| **-chambua** | *clean, pick over, sort out* |
| **-chuma** | *gather, pick* (leaves, fruit) |
| **laini** | *tender, delicate, soft* |
| **kisamvu** | *vegetable dish made from cassava leaves* |
| **-ponda** | *pound* (leaves, seeds) |
| **-chemsha** | *boil* (something) |
| **debe lenye maji** | *the debe containing water* |
| **-enye** | *having* |
| **pembe** (N) | *corner* |
| **sufuria** (N) | *large metal cooking pot without handles* |
| **juu ya** | *on* |
| **mafiga** (MA) | *three stones to support a cooking pot over a fire* |
| **-waka** | *be burning well* |
| **tia na chumvi kiasi** | *put in enough* (a suitable amount of) *salt* |
| **kiasi** (N) | *amount, quantity* |
| **-chemka** | *be boiling* |
| **nitie majani sasa** | *let me put in the leaves now* |
| **-koroga** | *stir* |
| **-funika** | *cover, put lid on* |
| **ndipo** | *then, that is when* |
| **he!** | *exclamation to draw attention to someone* |
| **-jifunza** | *learn* |
| **namna ya** | *how to, the way to* |
| **mpishi** (WA) | *cook* |
| **sasa hivi** | *right now, just now* |
| **-zoea** | *get used to, be familiar with* |

| | |
|---|---|
| **meko** | the place in the kitchen or cooking-area where the three hearth stones are |
| **jiko la makaa** | *charcoal stove* |
| **jiko** (MA) | *hearth, cooking-place, kitchen, stove, cooker* |
| **makaa** (MA) | *charcoal* |
| **nitakaporudi** | *when I return* |
| **huko** | *up there* |
| **-sahau** | *forget* |
| **chumvi ya kutosha** | *enough salt* |

Notice that when **saa** means a period of time, it takes the MA plural.

# 🛈 Background to the dialogue

Imagine the following scene, for it is typical of many areas, give or take some variation in the details. The group of houses where Francis' extended family lives is part of a village of scattered homesteads each containing one or more houses, with their grainstores, and a few fruit trees growing nearby. Hens peck around the houses and a few goats graze not far away. Family **shambas** growing maize, millet and cassava can be seen beyond the houses, and further away are plantations of cashew trees, which provide an annual cash crop.

Mama mzee's house, like some of the others, has a thatched roof, which needs replacing every few years; re-thatching is done by the menfolk. Francis' parents' house, rather larger than his grandmother's, is built of locally produced bricks and roofed with sheets of corrugated iron, fixed in place with the help of a local **fundi** (*skilled worker*).

For cooking, mama mzee uses the traditional hearth of three large stones to support a **sufuria** or an earthenware cooking-pot over a wood fire. The firewood is collected by the younger womenfolk who go in small groups, with their machetes, to an area of woodland about half an hour's walk away, and bring home the wood in large bundles on their heads (it is only in very hilly areas that loads are carried on the back rather than on the head).

The charcoal for the stove in Francis' parents' house is bought by the sack in the small town, thirty miles away. It is transported for part of the journey either by bus or in the lorry of a trader-friend. Whichever form of transport Francis' father manages to get, he and the charcoal travel the last ten miles home by bicycle. He uses this to get to and from the main road, leaving it at the house of a friend near the crossroads while he goes to the town.

In some cattle-keeping areas, dry cow-dung provides a constant supply of fuel. It is mainly in large towns that the finding of cooking fuel can be a problem, either because firewood is very expensive to buy or is unobtainable. Charcoal is usually available, but at a price. An increase in the population of towns has motivated attempts to produce alternative fuels, hence the availability, in some places, of briquettes, commercially produced from agricultural by-products such as husks. Some small-scale experimental work, on solar stoves for example, is aimed at the possibility of eventually reducing dependence on the burning of wood in confined spaces.

Note that the verb -**ponda**, used in the dialogue to refer to pounding the cassava leaves, should not be used when referring to the pounding of grain. A different verb is used for that, even though both activities involve the use of a pestle and mortar. The grinding of grain into flour, either with grindstones or mechanically in a flour mill, also has its own verb.

And, finally, it might be useful to note an idiomatic use of -**tia chumvi**, *put salt in*: it can be used to mean *exaggerate*.

| | |
|---|---|
| **bati** (MA) | *sheet of corrugated iron* |
| **-ezeka** | *roof a house* |
| **kinu** (KI/VI) | *mortar* |
| **korosho** (N) | *cashew nuts* |
| **mchi** (M/MI) | *pestle* |
| **mkorosho** (M/MI) | *cashew tree* |
| **mtama** (M/MI) | *millet, plant and grain* |
| **panga** (MA) | *machete* |
| **-saga** | *grind grain into flour* |
| **tofali** (MA) | *brick* |
| **-twanga** | *pound grain to remove husks* |

# Grammar

## ▶ 1 Walipokwenda, nitakaporudi – -po-, when

-**po**-, meaning *when*, follows immediately after the tense-marker when used with the three tenses -**li**-, -**na**- and -**ta**-. When it is used with the marker of future time, -**ta**- becomes -**taka**-, as in the second example above, from the dialogue.

| Wanawake walipokwenda msituni walikata kuni nyingi. | *When the women went to the woodland they cut a lot of firewood.* |
| Anapopika kisamvu anatia chumvi nyingi sana. | *When she cooks kisamvu she puts a great deal of salt in.* |
| Tutakapokwenda Nairobi tutamwona rafiki yetu. | *When we go to Nairobi we shall see our friend.* |

If an object-marker is needed, it follows -**po**-:

| Nilipowaona niliwapa magazeti. | *When I saw them I gave them the newspapers.* |

With -**po**-, monosyllabic verbs keep their **ku**- prefix:

| Alipokuja alinipa korosho. | *When he came he gave me some cashew nuts.* |

-**po**- is one of a set of *relative pronouns*. In English, relative pronouns are separate words like *when*, *where* as in *the place where they went*, *who* as in *the man who sold it to me*, *which*, as in *the thing which really annoys me*. The other relative pronouns in Swahili take the same position as -**po**- does, immediately after the tense-marker -**li**-, -**na**- or -**taka**-, and they are also formed with -**o**. They will be dealt with later, in Unit 8.

## 2  Si uliona . . .? *Didn't you see . . .?*

This is an alternative to **Hukuona . . .?** If **Si uliona . . .?** is used, the implication is that you should have seen. It is a more emotionally loaded way of asking a negative question than **Hukuona?**

| Si mtaondoka leo? | *Aren't you leaving today?* |
| | *(I'm sure you told me you were!)* |

## 3  Another noun-class – PA; also ku- and mu-

**a**  In the dialogue we have:

| shambani pana mihogo | *there are cassava plants in the field* |

and in the first dialogue of Unit 6:

| ukutani pana ratiba | *there is a timetable on the wall* |

Here **pana** is functioning just like **ana** and **ina** in:

| Mohamed ana gazeti. | *Mohamed has a newspaper.* |

Nyumba ina madirisha manne.   *The house has four windows.*

A more literal translation of the first two sentences is:

| shambani | pana | mihogo |
|---|---|---|
| *in-the-field* | *has* | *cassava plants* |
| ukutani | pana | ratiba |
| *on-the-wall* | *has* | *a timetable* |

Since their introduction in Unit 3 we have been using the nouns with the -ni ending as place adverbials. An *adverbial* is a word or phrase or larger unit that adds information to the verb about where, when, how or why the action takes place. Phrases in English like *in the house, to the supermarket, on the wall* are place adverbials, like **nyumbani** and **msikitini** here:

| Baba yupo nyumbani. | *Father is at home.* |
|---|---|
| Mohamed alikwenda msikitini. | *Mohamed went to the mosque.* |

These nouns with the added -ni can also be used as the subject of a sentence. In this case a special agreement-prefix denoting place is put on the front of the verb, or on -na as in the first two examples. The nouns **shamba** and **ukuta** have come out of their usual classes, MA and U/N respectively, and been put into the PA class.

Apart from its temporary -ni members, the PA class contains only one noun:

---

**PA *noun-class***
**mahali** or **pahali**          *place*
One prefix for all qualifiers and the verb: **pa-**

---

| mahali pazuri | *a good place* |
|---|---|
| mahali pengine (**pa + ingine**) | *another place* |
| mahali pana miti mingi | *the place has a lot of trees* |
| mahali pamejaa watu | *the place is full of people* |

**b** Unlike **mahali**, which can *only* take the **pa-** agreement-prefix, the -ni 'adverbial nouns' can be used with either **pa-**, as in the first two examples of this section, or with **ku-** or **mu-**, depending on whether definiteness (**pa-**), indefiniteness or movement to or from (**ku-**), or insideness (**mu-**) is involved. This idea of a three-way choice for denoting place should be familiar to you; if it isn't, look back now to the explanation of -ko, -po and -mo in Grammar section 2 of Unit 2. Those three place-markers are made from a place-prefix + o: ku + o makes -ko; pa + o makes -po; mu + o makes -mo.

The -ni form of a noun, rather than its 'ordinary' form, is used as the subject of a sentence in order to emphasize some aspect of the place in relation to the event or action, perhaps its suitability or size, for example.

Nchini kuna watalii wengi.    Lit. *In-the-country has a lot of tourists.*

Chumbani pamejaa watoto.    Lit. *In-the-room is full of children.*

Kikapuni mna mayai.    Lit. *In-the-basket has eggs.*

*Note:*

• the use of **ku-**, **pa-** or **mu-** has little to do with whether you would use *in*, *at*, etc., in the equivalent English sentences.
• **mu-** usually gets reduced to **m-**.

When one of these place-prefixes is attached to **-na**, the word can come at the beginning of the sentence:

Kuna watalii wengi nchini.    *There are many tourists in the country.*

Mna mayai kikapuni.    *There are eggs in the basket.*

c Negatives are made, as usual, by prefixing **ha-**.

Hakuna makaa. *There is no charcoal* (anywhere around).
Hapana makaa. *There is no charcoal* (in the specific place).
Hamna makaa. *There is no charcoal* (inside).

d Although the adverbial nouns made with -**ni** do not take adjectives, they can be used with -**a**, *of*:

Mtoto yumo chumbani    *The child is in the nurse's room.*
  mwa mwuguzi.

and with possessives:

Yumo chumbani mwangu.    *She is in my room.*

and with words for *here* (*this place*) and *there* (*that place*):

pembeni hapa    *in this corner*
pembeni pale    *in that corner*

e Look at previous dialogues to find examples of **hapa**, *here* (specific place) and **pale**, *there* (specific place); you will find them in Units 2, 3, 4 and 6 as well as in the dialogue in this unit. Looking back at the Grammar section on *this* and *that* in Units

5 and 6 will help you to see how **hapa** and **pale** fit into those patterns. Note also:

| | | | |
|---|---|---|---|
| huku | (*hereabouts*) | kule | (*somewhere over there*) |
| humu | (*in here*) | mle | (*inside there*) |

## 4 Kuchambuachambua; ukatekate – repeating words

The use of repetition is a common and very useful way of intensifying or extending the meaning of words. Depending on the meaning of a verb, repeating it can imply a continuation of the action over a period of time and/or thoroughness and attention to detail in carrying out the action.

**Kuchambuachambua,** in the dialogue, means to pick over and clean (the leaves) *thoroughly*, removing any unsuitable ones. The verb **-chambua** can be used whenever you want to refer to separating suitable from unsuitable things. Depending on the type of crop, it can refer to the cleaning process, e.g. of cotton or cloves.

The repetition of **-kata**, as in **ukatekate**, extends the meaning *cut* to *cut into small pieces*.

## 5 More on the -e form of verbs

**a** In the dialogue, mama mzee says to Steve:

Njoo ukatekate vitunguu!    *Come and cut up the onions!*

One of the functions of the **-e** form is to express the second of two commands or requests. Here the first verb is an imperative (one of the few irregular ones). The first verb can also be an **-e** form:

Usome gazeti hili uongeze         *Read this newspaper (so that)*
   maarifa ya Kiswahili.          *you increase (your)*
                                *knowledge of Swahili.*

**b** The **-e** ending is used when you need to have an object-marker with an imperative. As no verb-prefix is used, to indicate *you* (either singular or plural), this structure is really a kind of imperative, but is included in this section because of its **-e** ending.

| | |
|---|---|
| Yasome. | *Read them* (newspapers). |
| Kisome. | *Read it* (the book). |
| Vinunue. | *Buy them* (the potatoes, shoes or books!). |

The same applies when the object-marker refers to a recipient or beneficiary.

Mpe chakula.        *Give her some food.*
Mwandikie barua.    *Write him a letter.*

At the end of Grammar section 4 in Unit 6 it was noted that verbs without a final -a do not change their ending. There is an example of one of these verbs, in the negative, in mama mzee's parting shot to Steve in the dialogue: *Don't forget to put in enough salt!* Usisahau . . . ! Verbs of this sort are of Arabic origin.

## 5 Chumvi ya kutosha – more on adjective phrases

This example from the dialogue means *enough salt*, literally 'salt of to-be-enough'. In Unit 4 we had one kind of adjective phrase using -a, *of*:

sambusa za mboga    *vegetable samosas* (samosas of vegetables)

As well as making an adjective phrase with a noun following -a you can use the infinitive form of a verb:

sufuria ya kufaa    *a suitable cookpan*
kuni za kutosha    *enough firewood*

Prepositional forms of the verb are used in this way, to show the purpose of something:

kasha la kuwekea nguo        *a clothes chest*
                              (a chest for putting clothes in)

kikapu cha kutilia matunda    *a fruit basket*
                              (a basket for putting fruit in)

---

**kasha** (MA)    *storage chest*

---

## Practice

1   Unafanya nini? Mnafanya nini?    *What are you doing?*
    Write a question-and-answer sequence between yourself and
    the person or people in each picture, using these activities:

-jifunza Kiswahili              -shona shati
-ezeka nyumba                   -koroga kisamvu
-chuma machungwa                -andika hadithi

*Example:*

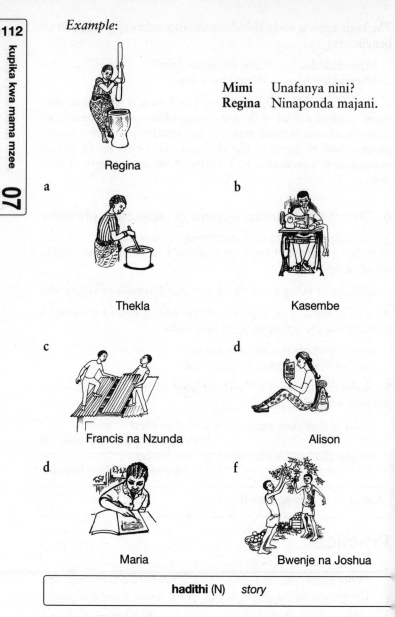

**Mimi** Unafanya nini?
**Regina** Ninaponda majani.

Regina

a

Thekla

b

Kasembe

c

Francis na Nzunda

d

Alison

d

Maria

f

Bwenje na Joshua

| **hadithi** (N) | *story* |

Then choose three of your mini-dialogues and lengthen
them by asking if you can help the person or people
(**Ni_____e?**), and then getting the reply: *OK, welcome!*

If you are working with someone else or in a group, do these as role-plays, and exchange greetings at the beginning.

2 Complete the sentences on the left from the choices listed on the right.

a Baada ya kutia majani . . .          tuliposahau kuosha sufuria.
b Alipotuona . . .                      walikula chakula cha jioni.
c Watakapopata pesa . . .              watakarabati kanisa.
d Njooni . . .                          tutakwenda benki.
e Tutakapofika Nairobi . . .           mchemshe maji!
f Watakapopata matofali . . .          funika chungu.
g Watalii walirudi                      alitupa korosho.
     hotelini . . .
h Mama alikasirika sana . . .          watanunua mabati.

3 These sentences are incorrect statements about the dialogue. Correct and rewrite them.

a Kuchambua majani ya muhogo si kazi ya mama mzee.
b Mama mzee hakuchuma majani ya muhogo.
c Steve anajifunza namna ya kupika wali.
d Regina anapika ugali juu ya mafiga.
e Atakaporudi Nairobi Steve hatajipikia kisamvu.
f Francis hayupo.

4 Fill in the subject of each sentence from the list below.

| **kutoka** | *from* |
| --- | --- |

a _____ kuna wageni kutoka Ujerumani.
b _____ mna mayai kumi.
c _____ pana watu wengi.
d _____ kuna boti nyingi.
e _____ mna pesa kidogo.
f _____ pana kuni za kutosha.

| Kanisani | Mfukoni | Baharini | Mjini |
| --- | --- | --- | --- |
| | Kikapuni | Jikoni | |

5 Regina and Francis have returned to Dar es Salaam after their trip to the south. Regina wants to prepare a special family meal to celebrate their return and she calls on anyone who happens to be near the kitchen to help. Write out (in Swahili!) what she says:

*Grace, come and boil some water! Adam, come and cut up these tomatoes! Maria, give me some salt! I'm going to prepare these fish, then I'm going to make some orange juice.*

| | | |
|---|---|---|
| **tayari** *ready* | | **-tayarisha** *prepare* |

*Note:* -tayarisha is a verb made from an adjective; verbs like this will be explained in Unit 16. Remember that the word for *fish* is a N class animate.

---

### As the saying goes . . .

| | | |
|---|---|---|
| **kitendawili** (KI/VI) *riddle* | | **-tega** *set, put ready* |

This time there are some riddles to learn, instead of proverbs. These are well-known ones, so if you try them out on Swahili-speaking children they might well know the answers. But they will be delighted at your familiarity with the riddles and no doubt introduce you to more. In general people are fascinated by the clever use of words and have great respect for good story-tellers, orators and poets, and old ladies in particular have a seemingly endless supply of riddles and proverbs, as well as stories. So, if you want to know more – ask a grandmother!

The opening formula for posing a riddle is:

**You**  Kitendawili!          **The listener**  Tega!

Then you say the riddle.

**i**  Nyumba yangu haina mlango.
   *My house has no door.*

**ii**  Nyumbani mwangu hamkosekani unga.
   *In my house there's never any shortage of flour.*

**iii**  Kamba yangu ndefu lakini haiwezi kufunga kuni.
   *My rope is long but it can't tie up a load of firewood.*

| | | |
|---|---|---|
| **-kosekana** *be missing* | **kamba** (N) *rope* |
| **majivu** (MA) *ashes* | **-funga** *tie up* |

(Yai) (*Egg*)          ii (Majivu) (*Ashes*)          iii (Njia) (*Road*)

# 08

## kusafiri ni kuzuri!

travelling is good!

**In this unit you will learn**
- how to discuss travel arrangements
- how to agree with a suggested course of action
- how to explain where towns are located

# ▶ Dialogue

Regina and Francis have returned to Dar es Salaam. Steve has extended his stay with Francis' parents; he is discussing his travel plans with Francis' father, Elvan.

**Steve**    Sijui kama nitapata nafasi kutembelea pwani ya kusini. Bila shaka Kilwa ni mahali pa kupendeza?

**Elvan**    Ndiyo, hata miji ya Lindi na Mtwara. Ni lazima urudi Nairobi, mwisho wa mwezi?

**Steve**    Si lazima. Kabla sijaenda Nairobi nitakuwa na shughuli huko Dar es Salaam. Tena napenda kumtembelea rafiki yangu anayekaa huko.

**Elvan**    Anafanya kazi Dar es Salaam?

**Steve**    Ndiyo. Natumaini atakuwepo, nitakapofika. Anasafiri mara kwa mara kwa ajili ya kazi.

**Elvan**    Basi, ukiwa na nafasi, ukae kwetu mpaka kaka yangu aje.

**Steve**    Yule anayekaa Tunduru?

**Elvan**    Ndiye yeye. Atakuja wiki kesho. Kwa kawaida anakaa kwetu siku mbili tu, halafu anaendelea na safari yake mpaka Mtwara. Yeye ni mtu wa biashara. Afadhali uende naye.

**Steve**    Ni safari ndefu?

**Elvan**    Ni safari ya siku mbili tu. Mkiondoka hapa asubuhi mtafika mjini jioni. Kuna hoteli mbili* mjini. Mtapata vyumba vizuri, na chakula cha jioni. Siku ya pili yake mtapanda basi ya kwenda Mtwara. Mabasi huondoka kila saa moja wakati wa mchana. Ni safari ya masaa machache. Utakubali kufuatana naye?

**Steve**    Nitakubali. Nitafurahi kwenda naye. Sipendi kusafiri peke yangu.

**Elvan**    Labda utakuwa na nafasi kwenda Kilwa, uangalie magofu?

**Steve**    Ikiwezekana. Kilwa iko kusini ya Lindi?

**Elvan**    Siyo. Iko kaskazini.

**Steve**    Na Tunduru, iko upande gani wa hapa?

**Elvan**    Tunduru iko magharibi ya hapa. Una ramani? Nitakuonyesha sisi tuko wapi hasa.

**Steve**    Kwa bahati mbaya niliacha ramani yangu kwa Francis, lakini si kitu.

**Elvan**    Kweli, haidhuru. Umejua Kiswahili sasa. Unaweza kuuliza maswali; kuuliza si ujinga! Unapenda kusafiri, siyo?

**Steve**    Sana! Kusafiri ni kuzuri!

*In the recorded material Elvan says 'mahoteli mawili'; both are acceptable.

| | |
|---|---|
| **kama** | *if, whether* |
| **-tembelea** | *visit* |
| **pwani** (N) | *coast, shore* |
| **kusini** (N) | *south* |
| **hata** | *even* (also *not even*) |
| **kabla** | *before* |
| **shughuli** (N) | *business, commitments* |
| **huko** | *over there* |
| **anayekaa** | *(that one) who lives* |
| **-tumaini** | *hope* |
| **atakuwepo** | *he will be there* |
| **mara kwa mara** | *from time to time* |
| **mara** (N) | *time, occasion* |
| **kwa ajili ya** | *because of, for the sake of* |
| **ajili** (N) | *cause, sake, reason* |
| **ukiwa na nafasi** | *if you have time* |
| **kwetu** | *at our home* |
| **mpaka** | *until, as far as* |
| **wiki kesho** (N) | *next week* |
| **kwa kawaida** | *usually* |
| **kawaida** (N) | *custom, rule* |
| **biashara** (N) | *trade* |
| **naye (na yeye)** | *with him* |
| **mkiondoka** | *if you (both) set off* |
| **-ondoka** | *set off, leave* (a place) |
| **-fika** | *arrive* |
| **siku ya pili yake** | *on the second day* |
| **-panda** | *get on, into a vehicle; climb* |
| **huondoka** | *(they) always leave* |
| **wakati wa** | *during* |
| **wakati** (U) | *period of time* |
| **-kubali** | *agree* |
| **-fuatana na** | *accompany* |
| **peke yangu** | *on my own* |
| **-angalia** | *have a good look at* |
| **magofu** (MA) | *ruins* |
| **ikiwezekana** (**i** = *it*) | *if it's possible* |
| **-wezekana** | *be possible* |
| **kaskazini** (N) | *north* |
| **upande** (U/N) | *direction, side* |
| **magharibi** (N) | *west* |
| **ramani** (N) | *map* |
| **hasa** | *exactly, completely* |
| **kwa bahati mbaya** | *unfortunately* |
| **bahati** (N) | *luck, good luck* |
| **kwa Francis** | *at Francis' place, home* |
| **kweli** (noun is N) | *true, truth* |
| **haidhuru** (**i** = *it*) | *it doesn't matter* |
| **-dhuru** | *harm, damage, hurt* |

# ℹ️ Getting around

If, like Steve, you are resident in an East African country for more than just a few weeks without your own transport, and want to see places and meet people beyond your immediate area, you will inevitably be dependent on local contacts for practical help, as well as information and advice. Locals who work in a city are very likely to have relatives and friends in another part of the country.

Road travel is generally faster than train, and buses, particularly the luxury ones on the major hard-surfaced roads, provide a good and relatively cheap means of travel. On dirt roads, which in many cases get insufficient maintenance, bus travel can be difficult, particularly after heavy rain, and travellers need to be prepared to be very flexible about departure and arrival times. In some places departure times are variable even without problems like floods, muddy roads or mechanical failure, and buses do not leave until they are full. Some routes are very popular and it is wise to buy a ticket several days before planning to travel, where it is possible to do so.

On major routes, between cities and towns, shared taxis are a popular way of travelling, faster than buses because of fewer stops but necessarily somewhat more expensive.

The least comfortable and most crowded, but usually the cheapest, form of public transport is the privately owned minibus. These supplement the regular bus services in the cities and, in some places, go beyond the city and compete with the long-distance buses. In Tanzania they are called **daladala** (N) and in Kenya **matatu** (N). Fares are unlikely to be higher than those of the local regular buses, and are usually cheaper. Apart from providing a much needed service for city centre workers who live on the outskirts, they enable small-scale entrepreneurs who can find the money for a (usually second-hand) bus and a driver to generate an income.

Elvan's solution to the problem of getting his brother and Steve as far as the main road, if they don't fancy walking, might be to lend them bicycles or, through one of his many local contacts, get a lorry driver to make a detour and pick them up.

If you are not in a great hurry and your destination is on one of the railway routes, train travel is a good idea. Bedding can be hired on the train, unless you travel third class, and the dining-car provides generally well-cooked meals. On the TAZARA line meals can be ordered to be brought to your compartment. First-class travel on the trains is, however, definitely not cheap.

Internal air flights are worth considering if money is not a problem but time and long distances are.

# Grammar

## 1 Kabla *Before*

**a** Use the **-ja-** ('not yet') tense after **kabla**, as in **kabla sijaenda Nairobi**, in the dialogue.

| | |
|---|---|
| kabla hajaenda msituni | *before she went to the woodland* |
| kabla hatujapanda basi | *before we got on the bus* |

**b** An alternative is to use **kabla ya** + infinitive:

| | |
|---|---|
| kabla ya kwenda msituni | *before going to the woodland* |
| kabla ya kupanda basi | *before getting on the bus* |

Both these ways of using **kabla** can apply to past, present or future time.

| | |
|---|---|
| Kabla hajaenda msituni alitafuta panga lake. | *Before she went to the woodland she looked for her machete.* |
| Kabla ya kupanda basi tununue matunda. | *Before getting on the bus let's buy some fruit.* |

## 2 Huko (+ place name)

**Huko** is used, either on its own or *in front of* a place name, as in **huko Dar es Salaam** in the dialogue. It means *somewhere there*, when the *there* is out of sight or a long distance away. The same word will turn up again later, but with a very different function.

## 3 More about being in a place: kuwepo / kuwapo

In the dialogue Steve says **Natumaini atakuwepo**, *I hope he'll be there*, referring to the friend in Dar es Salaam whom he is hoping to see eventually. The verb is **kuwa**, *to be*, with one of the place-markers attached to it. In many areas people say **atakuwapo** rather than **atakuwepo**. Whichever one you use makes no difference at all to the meaning; they are just variants of the same word.

You were introduced to the present-tense forms for *being in a place* in Unit 2 – **nipo, upo, yupo**, etc. All the other tenses need **kuwa** + **-ko**, **-po** or **-mo**:

| | |
|---|---|
| Nilikuwako Kenya | *I was in Kenya.* |
| Walikuweko Kenya? | *Were they in Kenya?* |
| Amekuwepo mjini? | *Has he been in the town?* |
| Tutakuwemo ofisini. | *We'll be right inside the office.* |

Remember that you only need **-ko**, **-po** or **-mo** on the end of **kuwa** when you are talking about people being in a place. For referring to someone being thin, or ill, or a driver, you use **kuwa** on its own, or **ni** when referring to present time:

| | |
|---|---|
| Masanja ni dereva. | *Masanja is a driver.* |
| Masanja alikuwa dereva. | *Masanja was a driver.* |
| Masanja alikuwa mgonjwa. | *Masanja was ill.* |
| Masanja alikuwapo nyumbani. | *Masanja was at home.* |

## 4 -ki- *if*

**a** There are two examples of **-ki-** meaning *if/when* in the dialogue.

| | |
|---|---|
| ukiwa na nafasi | *if you have time* |
| mkiondoka hapa | *if you set off from here* |

This **-ki-** occupies the tense 'slot'. The examples show parts of sentences. The part of a sentence containing **-ki-**, usually the first part, states a condition, and the second part says what will or should happen if that condition is fulfilled.

The verb in the first example is **kuwa**, one of the verbs with a single-syllable stem. The use of **-ki-** with a monosyllabic verb allows the **ku-** to be dropped because, unlike the tenses **-li-**, **-na-**, **-me-** and **-ta-**, **-ki-** can be stressed and can therefore occur as the penultimate syllable.

Its negative form **-sipo-**, however, cannot take stress, so **-ku-** is needed with monosyllabic verbs:

| | |
|---|---|
| Asipokuwa na pesa hatasafiri. | *If he has no money he won't travel.* |
| Wasipokuja hawatamwona mgeni. | *If they don't come they won't see the visitor.* |
| Nazi zake zisipofaa sitazinunua. | *If his coconuts are no good I won't buy them.* |

The first two examples from the dialogue can be translated in a slightly different way:

| ukiwa na nafasi | *you having time* |
| mkiondoka hapa | *you setting off from here* |

**b** These alternative versions of the Swahili examples may help you to link the *if/when* function with another function, which is to refer to ongoing, uncompleted action. This function is performed in English by verbs with the *-ing* ending:

| Nilimwona Regina akinunua matunda. | *I saw Regina buying fruit.* |
| Mama mzee yumo jikoni akipika wali. | *Granny is in the kitchen cooking rice.* |

## 5 Hu- for habitual action

Instead of using **kwa kawaida**, *usually*, with the present tense as in **Kwa kawaida anakaa kwetu siku mbili tu**, *He usually stays just two days with us*, you can use the **hu-** tense. For this you attach **hu-** to the verb-stem; no verb-prefix is needed. There is one occurrence in the dialogue:

Mabasi huondoka kila saa moja.   *Buses usually leave every hour.*

You use the **hu-** tense to refer to habitual or recurrent action not tied to any particular time:

| Ng'ombe hula majani. | *Cows eat grass.* |
| Dada hutafuta panga lake. | *Sister is always/usually/ generally looking for her machete.* |

Notice that **hu-** can be stressed, so monosyllabic verbs do not need their **ku-** prefix.

## 6 'Who', 'which' and 'that': more relative pronouns

**a** In the dialogue Elvan refers to his brother coming and Steve asks **Yule anayekaa Tunduru?** *That one who lives in Tunduru?* The **-ye-** in **anayekaa** means *who*. If Elvan had mentioned more than one brother Steve could have said: **Wale wanaokaa Tunduru?** *Those who live at Tunduru?*

The **-ye-** and **-o-** in these examples are relative pronouns. In these sentences the relative pronoun refers to the subject of the sentence, **yule** and **wale** respectively.

The relative pronouns for all the noun-classes are made from the verb-prefix + o, with the exception of the one for M/WA class singulars. You have already learnt these forms for another function. If you look back to Grammar section 10 of Unit 5 you will find these -o- forms set out (as -o) for all the noun-classes introduced up to that point. You can add to the list the form for U class nouns:

u + o *makes* o

unga uliotoka dukani    *the flour which came from the shop*

The -o- form for plurals of U/N nouns is -zo-, because they are exactly the same as N class plurals:

shanga zilizotoka dukani *the beads that came from the shop*

b The verb-prefixes **ku-**, **pa-** and **mu-** + o:

ku + o *makes* **ko**
pa + o *makes* **po** (also used for time – see Unit 7)
mu + o *makes* **mo**

mahali alipokwenda    *the place where she went*
chumbani alimokaa     *the room in which she stayed*

In these examples the relative pronoun does not refer to the subject. Alternative English versions of these could be *the place she went to* and *the room she stayed in*, leaving out *where* and *which*.

c In spoken English we very often leave out *who*, *which* or *that* when the relative pronoun refers to a word or phrase other than the subject. We usually say *the people I saw* rather than *the people whom I saw* and *the book she bought* rather than *the book which she bought*: in these examples *people* and *book* are objects, not subjects. In Swahili the relative pronoun must always be present.

Watu niliowaona ni          *The people who I saw* (them)
  Wamarekani.               *are Americans.*
Alinipa kitabu alichokinunua. *She gave me the book which*
                            *she bought* (it).

You will notice that the object-prefix is also used, -wa- to refer to **watu**, and -ki- to refer to **kitabu**. In casual speech it is likely to be left out, particularly in sentences like the second one, in which the object refers to a thing, rather than a person.

**d** The relative pronouns can only be used as above, immediately following the tense-marker, with the past, present and future markers **-li-**, **-na-** and **-taka-**. With other tenses, e.g. **-me-**, you have to do something different and this will be explained later.

**e** To make the negative, replace the tense-marker with **-si-**.
This form is timeless, so tends to get used for negatives of a general nature, not tied to a particular time:

Asiyekuwa na tikiti hapandi    *Anyone without a ticket does not*
treni.                         *board the train.* (lit. S/he
                               who does not have a ticket
                               does not board the train.)

Negatives referring to a particular time, like *the driver who didn't come yesterday* are usually made using the relative structure which will be explained later.

## 7 Kusafiri ni kuzuri! – verbs used as nouns

The infinitive form of a verb, e.g. **kusafiri, kuona, kutaka, kupika, kusoma,** can be used as a noun, as in the title of this unit. This **ku-** behaves just like the place-prefix **ku** when it comes before a vowel:

Kupika kwake si kuzuri.    *His cooking is not good.*

Infinitives used in this way form another class of nouns, with **ku-** as the noun-prefix and also the verb-prefix.

# Practice

**1    Somo la jiografia** *A geography lesson*

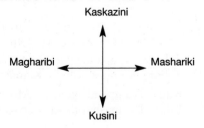

Steve is taken by Elvan to visit the local primary school where he used to be the headteacher. The children try to find out if Steve knows where various towns are. Use the map of Tanzania to check his replies, and write out the correct answers for the ones he gets wrong.

*Example*:

**Mtoto**  Songea iko upande gani wa Njombe?
**Steve**  Songea iko kaskazini ya Njombe.
*Correct reply*: **Songea iko kusini ya Njombe.**

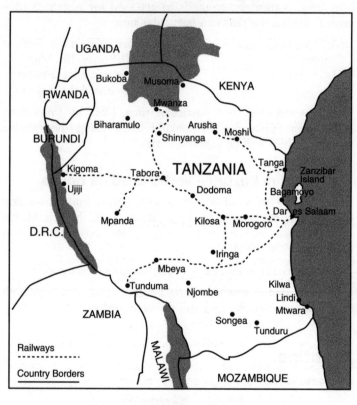

| **Ali** | Iringa iko upande gani wa Dodoma? |
| Steve | Iringa iko kaskazini ya Dodoma. |
| **Apoche** | Tabora iko upande gani wa Kigoma? |
| Steve | Tabora iko mashariki ya Kigoma. |
| **Lajabu** | Kilosa iko upande gani wa Morogoro? |
| Steve | Kilosa iko mashariki ya Morogoro. |

Lunda   Bagamoyo iko upande gani wa Dar es Salaam?
Steve   Bagamoyo iko kusini ya Dar es Salaam.

Grace   Mbeya iko upande gani wa Tabora?
Steve   Mbeya iko kaskazini ya Tabora.

Nanyanja Kilwa iko upande gani wa Mtwara?
Steve   Kilwa iko kaskazini ya Mtwara.

| | |
|---|---|
| somo (MA) | lesson |
| jiografia (N) | geography |
| shule ya msingi (N) | primary school |
| msingi (M/MI) | foundation |

2   Make whole sentences by selecting from the choice on the right to complete the structures listed on the left.

a   Mgeni aliyekuja jana . . .            ni dada zangu.
b   Hatuwezi kula . . .                   tulimpa barua zake.
c   Watoto watakaokwenda mjini . . .     ataondoka kesho.
d   Tulipomwona Mohamed . . .            hawatapata vyumba.
e   Watalii wasiokuja mapema . . .       watanunua nazi sokoni.
f   Wanawake wanaotwanga mahindi . . .   chakula kisichofaa.

3   Complete the following statements about the Dialogue.

a   Si lazima Steve arudi _____ mwisho wa mwezi.
b   Steve atakuwa na _____ huko Dar es Salaam.
c   Anapenda kumtembelea _____ _____.
d   Kaka yake Elvan anakaa _____.
e   Kaka ni mtu wa _____.
f   Steve hapendi kusafiri peke _____.

Note in c and f you will need to change my to his.

4   Using the verb-stems listed on the next page, with hu-prefixed to them, complete the following sentences describing what people always or usually do:

a   Mama mzee _____ chakula cha jioni.
b   Watoto _____ matunda.
c   Wanafunzi _____ vitabu.
d   Mama Fatuma _____ nguo.
e   Watalii _____ vinyago.
f   Wauguzi _____ wagonjwa.

| -shona | -saidia | -nunua | -pika | -soma | -penda |

5 Maswali mengine kuhusu miji ya Tanzania

> **kuhusu** *about, concerning, in connection with*

Steve is back at the school to help with basketball practice. The children have devised a written test for him. Write the word for *north*, *south*, *east* or *west* that he has to fill in to complete these sentences.

a Tanga iko _____ ya Bagamoyo.
b Shinyanga iko _____ ya Arusha.
c Musoma iko _____ ya Mwanza.
d Moshi iko _____ ya Arusha.
e Musoma iko _____ ya Bukoba.
f Ujiji iko _____ ya Kigoma.
g Biharamulo iko _____ ya Bukoba.
h Mbeya iko _____ ya Tunduma.

6 Kwa basi   *By bus*
To refer to methods of travel you use **kwa** followed by the word for the vehicle, or *feet* in the case of going on foot. You already know the words for *bus*, *train*, *aeroplane*, *boat* and *feet*.

KWA NDEGE
BY AIR MAIL
PAR AVION

Complete the following sentences with an appropriate means of travel, using five different ones.

> **baiskeli** (N)   *bicycle*   **mwaka ujao** (M/MI)   *next year*

a   Elvan huenda barabarani _____ _____.
b   Akina mama huenda msituni _____ _____.
c   Steve atakwenda Mtwara _____ _____.
d   Mwaka ujao Steve atarudi Marekani _____ _____.
e   Labda John na Alison watakwenda Zanzibar _____
    _____.

Here are three more words for vehicles which would be useful to learn at this point:

> **gari** (MA)   *vehicle*       **motokaa** (N) or **motakaa**   *car*
> **lori** (MA)   *lorry, truck*

---

### As the saying goes...

Here is another riddle. Even if you don't foresee riddling as a major leisure activity you should learn it as it will help you to remember **-po-**, *when*, and **hu-** for habitual action. You should by now know all the words in the riddle except one.

> **-cheza**   *dance*

Ninapompiga mwanangu watu hucheza.
(The answer is **ngoma**.)

# 09

## safari ya basi
a bus journey

**In this unit you will learn**
- how to tell someone not to worry
- how to talk about where your luggage is stowed on a road journey
- how to ask for a particular cassette or video tape
- how to wish someone a safe arrival

# ▶ Dialogue

**Saa tatu asubuhi.** Steve is talking to Bw. Twaibu, the manager of the small hotel where he has spent the night.

| | |
|---|---|
| **Twaibu** | Usiwe na wasiwasi, bwana. Mabasi ya kwenda pwani huondoka kila saa moja. Tiketi zinauzwa kuanzia asubuhi. Utakwenda Lindi au Mtwara? |
| **Steve** | Nitakwenda Mtwara. |
| **Twaibu** | Vizuri. Mimi nina shughuli kwenye benki. Twende pamoja. Nitakupelekea kituo cha basi. Una mizigo mingine? Au ni huu tu, basi? |
| **Steve** | Ni mfuko huu tu. |
| **Twaibu** | Haya, twende! |

Ten minutes later they are standing in the doorway of the ticket office at the bus station.

| | |
|---|---|
| **Twaibu** | Bila shaka utapanda basi iondokayo saa nne. (*Indicating the young man behind the ticket-office table*:) Huyu ni ndugu yangu na dereva ni ndugu yangu. Utapata nafasi nzuri. Usipopata tiketi hapa ofisini kondakta atakukatia tiketi kwenye basi. Haya bwana, nakwenda sasa. (*He shakes Steve's hand.*) Kwa heri, bwana. Fika salama! |
| **Steve** | Kwa heri bwana. Asante sana! |

**Saa tisa mchana.** Steve is standing outside the bus chatting to a fellow-passenger during a refreshment stop. The driver and a few passengers are having a snack inside a small **hoteli** nearby. Some people are buying fruit, and others are inside the bus ready to continue the journey.

| | |
|---|---|
| **Mama** | Unasafiri mpaka Mtwara, bwana? |
| **Steve** | Ndiyo. Nitakaa Mtwara siku mbili tu. Kesho kutwa nitakwenda Dar es Salaam kwa ndege. |
| **Mama** | Pole kwa kusafiri peke yako! |
| **Steve** | Asante. Nasafiri peke yangu, ila babake rafiki yangu alinisindikiza mpaka barabarani jana. |
| **Mama** | (*Looking up at the bus roof-rack, piled high with boxes, bulging sacks and a bicycle*:) Mizigo yako ipo juu? |
| **Steve** | Hapana. Nina mfuko mmoja tu. Upo chini, ndani ya basi. Naona abiria wengine wana mizigo mingi. |
| **Mama** | Mingi sana. Sisi ambao tumetembelea ndugu shamba, tuna mizigo mingi. |
| **Steve** | (*Seeing the bundles of sugar-cane that she has bought*:) Utaiweka wapi? |

| | |
|---|---|
| **Mama** | Inabidi kumpa mume wangu, aitunze. |
| **Steve** | Ndiye yule bwana ambaye amekaa mbele, karibu na dereva? |
| **Mama** | Ndiye. |
| **Steve** | (*Looking through the window of the driver's cab*:) Mna mizigo mingi sana! |
| **Mama** | Ah, si yote. Vipo vitu ambavyo si mali yetu. Abiria huwapa vitu wale waliopo mbele, wavitunze. Si uliona mzee akimpa mume wangu kikapu, na bwana mmoja akiweka kitu fulani, sijui ...? |
| **Steve** | Kile kilicho chini ni spea ya baiskeli.<br>(*The driver returns to the bus. Steve notices him preparing to change the video.*) |
| **Steve** | Una ukanda wa Lubumbashi Stars? |
| **Dereva** | Ah, hamna, bwana. Vijana Jazz ninao. Unaupenda? Niweke? |
| **Steve** | Weka tu. Utatuchangamsha! |

| | |
|---|---|
| **usiwe na wasiwasi** | *don't worry* (lit. don't have worries) |
| **wasiwasi** (N) | *worry, doubt, disquiet* |
| **tiketi zinauzwa** | *tickets are sold* |
| **kuanzia** | *starting from* |
| **kwenye** | *at* |
| **-pelekea** | *take* (in this context) |
| **mzigo** (M/MI) | *piece of luggage* |
| **iondokayo** | *which sets off* |
| **ndugu** (N) | *close friend* (also relative) |
| **nafasi** (N) | *space, place* (in this context) |
| **kondakta** (MA) | *conductor* |
| **atakukatia tiketi** | *(he) will sell you a ticket* |
| **-kata** | lit. cut (here = *sell*) |
| **kwenye** | *in, at* |
| **Fika salama!** | *Arrive safely!* |
| **kesho kutwa** | *the day after tomorrow* |
| **kesho** | *tomorrow* |
| **peke yako** | *on your own* |
| **babake rafiki yangu** | *my friend's father* |
| **babake (baba yake)** (N) | *his / her father* |
| **-sindikiza** | *accompany part of the way* |
| **juu** | *on the top* |
| **chini** | *on the floor, ground* |
| **ndani ya basi** | *inside the bus* |
| **ndani** | *inside* |

| | |
|---|---|
| **abiria** (N) | *passengers* |
| **sisi ambao tumetembelea** | *we who have visited* |
| **shamba** (no **-ni**) | *(in the) countryside* |
| **inabidi** (**i** = *it*) | *it's best, it's necessary* |
| **mume** (M/WA) | *husband* |
| **-tunza** | *look after, guard* |
| **ndiye yule bwana ...?** | *is he indeed the man ...?* |
| **ambaye amekaa mbele** | *who is sitting at the front* |
| **mbele** | *front* |
| **vitu ambavyo si mali yetu** | *things which are not our property* |
| **mali** (N) | *property* |
| **wale waliopo mbele** | *those who are at the front* |
| **kile kilicho chini** | *that thing which is on the floor* |
| **spea ya baiskeli** | *bicycle spare-part* |
| **spea** (N) | *spare-part* |
| **ukanda** (U/N) | *video or cassette tape* |
| **Lubumbashi Stars** | name of a D.R.C. band |
| **hamna** | *no* (see p.109 **c**) |
| **Vijana Jazz** | name of a Tanzanian band |
| **-changamsha** | *cheer up, make happy* |

# ℹ️ Changes of plan

After reading about Steve's travel plans in the dialogue in Unit 8, you may wonder why he is travelling on his own instead of with Elvan's brother. The following train of events could explain this.

On the day the brother was due to leave home, a distant relative, who lived locally, died. As a senior member of the deceased's clan, Elvan's brother was obliged to stay and help organize the funeral and give support to the man's widow and children. He sent a message to Elvan via a neighbour and a truck driver, which Elvan received two days after his brother had been due to arrive. Elvan decided to accompany Steve at least as far as the nearest town where he would be staying the night. But, before they were able to set off, mama mzee became ill with fever and Elvan could not leave his family.

After waiting a few more days, Steve decided to travel on his own as he had a dated Mtwara–Dar es Salaam plane ticket, bought several weeks earlier in Dar es Salaam, and time was running out. He would not now have time to visit the medieval ruins at Kilwa Kisiwani as he had hoped. As he explains to one of his fellow-passengers in this unit's dialogue, Elvan had accompanied him as far as the main road. From there it would have been relatively easy to hitch a lift to the town with a driver known to Elvan.

Family illness and the death of a relative or friend are among the most common reasons for people having to change their plans. In places where fever can worsen rapidly, where illness ends in death more frequently than it does in more temperate climates, and where medical services are under-resourced, the future seems less sure than it does in more affluent societies. The relationships which link people within their extended family and their clan provide support in time of trouble – support which is dependent upon obligations being regarded as paramount and to be fulfilled without fail.

A second scenario concerns the time of departure. The ten o'clock bus turned out to be already full. Steve missed the eleven o'clock one owing to a misunderstanding about time and finally got a seat on the bus due to leave at midday.

## 🛈 Bus travel

'Luxury' buses on major routes, such as Dar es Salaam to Moshi and Arusha, would not normally carry passengers next to the driver. But elsewhere, if you are lucky enough to be given a seat at the front next to the driver (there is usually enough room for two other people), be prepared for other passengers picked up along the way to ask you to look after one or two things for them.

As on Steve's bus, most of the long-distance ones provide video or music cassette entertainment. Music from D.R.C. is very popular throughout eastern Africa and the lyrics are an interesting mixture of Swahili and French or Lingala and French.

The sort of rural **hoteli** where Steve's bus stopped for half an hour or more would provide food and drink but not accommodation. It is almost always possible to get bottled or canned drinks in a **hoteli** (look for the advert outside) and it is a good idea to take advantage of this in order to conserve the bottled water or fruit you are carrying with you.

| | | | |
|---|---|---|---|
| **ukanda** (U/N) | *tape* (any sort) | **kaseti** (N) | *cassette* |
| **ukanda wa kaseti** | *cassette tape* | **muziki** (N) | *modern music* |
| **ukanda wa video** | *video tape* | **video** (N) | *video* |

(A joking use of **video** is to make it the plural form, with **kideo** as the singular, thus putting it in the KI/VI class. But this is not normal usage.)

# Grammar

## 1 Kwenye, and other -enye words: -enye + noun

**-enye** is one of the qualifier-stems that takes the verb-prefix. It means *having* or *becoming*.

**a** When used with one of the place-prefixes attached to it, and a following noun, it describes a place or condition:

kwenye basi (ku-enye)          *where the bus is* (lit. the place having the bus), *at / in the bus*

As always, **ku-** has a wide range of meanings for place and circumstance. The prefix **pa-** is obligatory after **mahali**.

Mtoto amekaa kwenye majani. *The child is sitting on the grass / among the grass* (in a grassy area).

Mahali penye maji ni pazuri. *A place with water* (a well-watered place) *is good.*

Kwenye miti mtu amejenga nyumba. *Where the trees are* (at the place having trees) *someone has built a house.*

Alifika kwenye kituo cha basi. *He arrived at the bus stop.*

You cannot use **kwenye**, etc. in front of nouns with the **-ni** ending meaning *at*, *on*, *in*. So you can either say **kwenye shamba** or **shambani**. These **-enye** forms with the place-prefixes often get used with nouns that do not take the **-ni** ending; there is one example in the dialogue:

Mimi nina shughuli kwenye benki.          *I have business at the bank.*

**b** The adjective-forming function of **-enye** together with a following noun is clearer when it has prefixes other than those of place.

It is the verb-prefix of the first noun, the noun that is being described, that is placed on the front of **-enye**. As always, the singular of the M/WA class is odd.

(mtu) mwenye mali          *a well-off person, a person with property*

nyumba yenye paa la bati          *a house with an iron roof, an iron-roofed house*

kitabu chenye picha          *a book with pictures in it*
gauni lenye mikono           *a dress with sleeves*

| Noun-class | Sing. | Pl. |
|---|---|---|
| M/WA | **mwenye** (mw + enye) | **wenye** (wa + enye) |
| N | **yenye** (i + enye) | **zenye** (zi + enye) |
| KI/VI | **chenye** (ki + enye) | **vyenye** (vi + enye) |
| (JI)/MA | **lenye** (li + enye) | **yenye** (ya + enye) |
| M/MI | **wenye** (u + enye) | **yenye** (i + enye) |
| U/(N) | **wenye** (u + enye) | (as for N) |
| KU (Infinitive) | as for **ku-** (place) | |

Note that M/WA class **mwenye** and **wenye**, *person/people having*, are used to mean *owner(s)*:

mwenye nyumba          *house owner*
mwenye duka            *shopkeeper*
mwenye gari            *vehicle owner*

## 2 The verb -kata and its various meanings

In the dialogue Bw. Twaibu tells Steve that if he does not get a ticket from the ticket-office, the conductor on the bus **atakukatia tiketi**, *he will sell you a ticket*. Here **-kata**, which usually means *cut*, is in its prepositional form because the ticket will be sold *to someone*. The various meanings of **-kata** are dependent upon the noun that follows. Here are a few of the most common meanings:

-kata hukumu                *pronounce judgement*
-kata kiu                   *quench thirst*
-kata njia                  *take a short cut*
-kata shauri                *make a decision*
-kata tamaa                 *despair*
-kata (kitambaa cha gauni)  *buy (dress material)*

---

**hukumu** (N) *judgement*        **tamaa** (N) *ambition, longing*
**shauri** (MA) *advice, affair*

# 3 More on word order

## a hapa ofisini

When words for *here* and *there* such as **hapa, pale, huku**, etc.,
are used with adverbial nouns, nouns made into adverbs by the
addition of **-ni**, the *here* or *there* word often comes first:

| | |
|---|---|
| hapa ofisini | *here in the office* |
| pale pembeni | *there in the corner* |
| kule mjini | *there in the town* |
| humu mfukoni | *here in the bag* |

## b yule bwana

The words for *this*, *that*, *these*, *those* (see Units 5 and 6) are
sometimes used in front of nouns instead of following them. An
example in the dialogue is **yule bwana**. When this happens, **yule**
(etc.) no longer has a 'pointing' function; all it does is to make
the noun definite, which is what *the* does in English. You can
only use **yule, huyu**, etc., in front of a noun if you and your
listener(s) know which person, or thing, is being talked about.

The **-le**, *over there*, forms are more commonly used to mean *the*
than the **h-** forms are. But the **h-** forms, **huyu, hawa, hii, hizi,
hiki, hivi**, etc, can be used with a *the* purpose if:

* the person or thing has only just been mentioned, perhaps
  in the preceding sentence, and you need to mention the
  word again, or
* the person or thing is extremely important to you at this
  point in the conversation.

It is as if the person or thing denoted by the noun is close to you,
even though not physically near you.

| | | | |
|---|---|---|---|
| yule bibi | *the lady* | bibi yule | *that lady (there)* |
| wale wauguzi | *the nurses* | wauguzi wale | *those nurses (there)* |
| ile nyumba | *the house* | nyumba ile | *that house (there)* |
| vile viti | *the chairs* | viti vile | *those chairs (there)* |

| | |
|---|---|
| huyu mwalimu | *the teacher* (the one you've just mentioned or the one I'm particularly interested in at the moment) NB: The teacher is not present. |
| mwalimu huyu | *this teacher* (for example standing next to the speaker) NB: The teacher is present. |

## c the order of recipients / beneficiaries and objects

In section 6 of the Grammar in Unit 4 you were given the rule
that the word for the person benefiting from the action comes

before the object, in sentences like:

> Nitampa Francis mananasi.     *I will give Francis some pineapples.*

Both -**m**-, in front of the verb-stem, and Francis, refer to the recipient / beneficiary of the action, so they must be as close together as possible.

But you can only do this when, as in this example, the recipient / beneficiary is denoted by a single word. When several words are used they have to go after, rather than before, the object. In the dialogue we have:

> Abiria huwapa vitu wale waliopo mbele.     *The passengers give things to those at the front.*

Here the recipient/beneficiary is **wale waliopo mbele**, *those who are at the front.*

Here is another example with an even longer recipient / beneficiary:

> Nilimpa chakula mgeni aliyetoka Afrika ya Kusini.     *I gave food to the visitor who had come from South Africa.*

## 4 Babake and other contracted forms

**Babake**, *his father*, occurs in the dialogue in the phrase **babake rafiki yangu**, *my friend's father*. It is the contracted form of **baba yake**. In the second dialogue of Unit 1, Mama Fatuma addresses her adult son as **mwanangu**, *my child*; this is the contracted form of **mwana wangu**. Not all words for relatives and friends have these contracted forms using the possessives; among the most common are:

|         | *my*      | *your*    | *his/her* |
|---------|-----------|-----------|-----------|
| mama    | mamangu   | mamako    | mamake    |
| baba    | babangu   | babako    | babake    |
| dada    | dadangu   | dadako    | dadake    |
| mwana   | mwanangu  | mwanako   | mwanake   |
| mwenzi  | mwenzangu | mwenzako  | mwenzake  |
| ndugu   |           | nduguyo   | nduguye   |
| rafiki  |           | rafikiyo  | rafikiye  |
| mke     |           | mkeo      | mkewe     |
| mume    |           | mumeo     | mumewe    |

---

**mke (M/WA)**    *wife*        **mwenzi (M/WA)**    *companion*

## 5 Two meanings of shamba

In this unit's dialogue, **shamba** means *country*, as opposed to *town*. When it has this meaning it does not take the -ni ending.

| Walikwenda shamba. | *They went to the country.* |
| Walikwenda shambani. | *They went to the field/ smallholding/plantation.* |

**Shamba** with the meaning of *country/rural area* is not used everywhere, least of all by people who actually live in a rural area – which is most people in East Africa. It is mainly used by people living in towns to refer to going out of town to the country. You are most likely to hear it used in the Swahili spoken by people in the coastal and island towns where, for centuries, there has been a tradition of urban living supported by the cultivation of crops in the rural hinterland.

## 6 'Who', 'which', 'that' – more about relatives

In section 6 of the Grammar in Unit 8 you had the verb-prefix + **o** forms which have the function of *who*, *which* and *that* in English structures like *The woman who bought the coat* and *The things that I appreciate.* In Unit 8 you had examples in which the relative pronoun followed the tense-marker:

shanga zilizotoka dukani       *the beads that came from the shop*

The relative pronouns (the verb-prefix + **o** forms) can only be used in this position with the three tense-markers **-li-**, **-na-** and **-ta-**.

**a  Sisi ambao tumetembelea ndugu** – the **amba-** relative

In this structure the relative pronoun is attached to the end of a separate stem, **amba-**, and the verb follows.

You can use the **amba-** relative with all tenses, and with **ni** and **si**.

| vitu ambavyo ni mali yetu | *the things which are our property* |
| mtoto ambaye amekwenda sokoni | *the child who has gone to the market* |
| watalii ambao wataondoka kesho | *the tourists who will set off tomorrow* |

Notice that the future-tense marker **-ta-** does not change to **-taka-**.

To make the negative, change the verb into its negative form; the **amba-** form does not change.

| | |
|---|---|
| watoto ambao hawapendi wali | *the children who do not like rice* |
| vitabu ambavyo havikufaa | *the books which were not suitable* |

**b  basi iondokayo saa nne** – the general relative
In this structure there is no tense-marker, and the relative pronoun goes at the end of the verb-stem:

i-ondoka-yo

This is used for general statements. In the dialogue Bw. Twaibu says:

| | |
|---|---|
| Bila shaka utapanda basi iondokayo saa nne. | *Probably you'll get on the bus that leaves at ten.* |

This tells us that a bus leaves at ten every morning. If he had said **itakayoondoka saa nne**, *which will be leaving at ten*, there would be no implication that this happens every day.

| | |
|---|---|
| watu wakaao mjini | *people who live in the town* |
| watu wakaao shamba | *people who live in the country* |
| wiki ijayo (i-ja-yo) | *next week* (the week which will come) |
| mwezi ujao (u-ja-o) | *next month* (the month which will come) |

The negative form using **-si-**, which was introduced in Unit 8, is used as the negative of this general relative, as well as of relatives with **-li-**, **-na-** and **-taka-**.

| | |
|---|---|
| Wagonjwa ni wale wasiokula chakula kizuri. | *The sick people are those who do not eat good food.* |

**c  The general relative with the verb *be***
There is one example in the dialogue of a general relative with a verb meaning *be*:

| | |
|---|---|
| Kile kilicho chini ni spea ya baiskeli. | *That (thing) which is on the floor is a spare-part of a bicycle.* |

When you make a general relative with *be* you have to use **-li-** instead of **kuwa**. This **-li-** is the remnant of an old verb meaning *be* which has almost disappeared from Swahili; do not confuse it with the past-tense marker. The structure is: verb-prefix + **li** + relative pronoun.

| niliye | *I who am* | tulio | *we who are* |
| uliye | *you* (sing.) *who are* | mlio | *you* (pl.) *who are* |
| aliye | *s/he who is* | walio | *they who are* |

Mpe mtu aliye fundi.          *Give (it) to someone who is a craftsman.*

Tunza masanduku yaliyo          *Look after the boxes which are his property.*
mali yake.

For the negative, use **-si-** instead of **-li-**:

tusio wauguzi          *we who are not nurses*
asiye mgonjwa          *the one who is not ill*
wasio watalii          *they who are not tourists*

In the example **kile kilicho chini** from the dialogue it is the identity of the thing that is important. If Steve had been more concerned with its position on the floor, he would have attached a place-marker to **kilicho**: **kile kilichopo chini**. There is one example of this sort in the dialogue:

watu waliopo mbele          *the people who are at the front*

If you are referring to something which is in a place (e.g. **nyumbani, kwenye benki, juu, chini**, etc.) and you want to focus on the thing's position, add a place-marker to the end, as in the case of **kuwa** in Unit 8:

watu waliopo sokoni          *people who are at the market*
mayai yaliyomo kikapuni          *eggs which are in the basket*
miti iliyoko shambani          *trees which are in the field*

## 7 ndi *it is indeed*

If you want to say that something is *indeed, definitely, certainly so*, you use **ndi-**. It is like using **ni** with added emphasis.

When referring to a person you add part of the personal pronoun (**mimi, wewe**, etc.) to it:

| ndimi | *it is I* | ndisi | *it is we* |
| ndiwe | *it is you* (sing.) | ndinyi | *it is you* (pl.) |
| ndiye | *it is s/he* | ndio | *it is they* |

In the dialogue mama says she will have to give her husband the bundles of sugar-cane to look after, and Steve asks:

| Ndiye yule bwana ambaye amekaa mbele, karibu na dereva? | *Is he the gentleman who is seated at the front, near the driver?* |
|---|---|

Mama replies: **Ndiye.** *It is he.*

For inanimates you use the form made with the appropriate verb-prefix + **o**.

This is the same form as in **ninazo, tunacho, analo,** etc. (see Unit 5), and is also the form used for relative pronouns.

| Ndivyo vitabu vyangu. | *They are indeed my books.* |
|---|---|
| Ndizo nguo zake. | *They are definitely her clothes.* |

In the Unit 7 dialogue we had this structure used with **-po-** *when*:

| ndipo utakoroga | *then* (that is when) *you will stir* |
|---|---|

The **ndi-** structure is often used with a relative, which is also a way of emphasizing something:

| Yule ndiye mgeni aliyetoka Mombasa. | *That person is indeed the visitor who came from Mombasa.* |
|---|---|
| Hiki ndicho kitambaa ambacho nilikinunua Nairobi. | *This is indeed the fabric which I bought in Nairobi.* |

## 8 The verb -kaa and its meanings

**Kaa** is used in the dialogue with two different meanings:

**a** *be sitting, in a seated position,* as in **amekaa,** *(he) is sitting.* If you are referring to present time you must use the **-me-** tense because **-kaa**, with this meaning, is one of the verbs of state explained in Unit 5. **Nimekaa** (*I am sitting*) is sometimes used as a polite reply to **Karibu!**, and you need not be sitting, when you say it. Later on there will be a section on how to refer to states such as sitting, standing, feeling tired, etc., in the past.

You could use **-na-** if you were describing someone in the act of sitting down, although it is hard to imagine a context in which you would want to do that, apart perhaps from a commentary on a piece of slow-motion film footage!

**b** *stay* or *live* (somewhere) as in **Nitakaa Mtwara**. (*I will stay at Mtwara*)

In the present tense you would use **-na-**:

> Wanakaa Mombasa.  *They are living in Mombasa.*

**c** Another meaning of **-kaa**, not used in the dialogues, is *last*, *endure*, as in:

> Kitambaa hiki kimekaa sana. *This fabric has lasted a long time/worn well.*

# Practice

**1**  Write about the picture by answering the questions. For **a** to **d** you will need one of the words **ndani**, **mbele**, or **juu**.

*Example*: Masanduku yako wapi? **Masanduku yapo juu.**

    **a**  Baiskeli iko wapi?
    **b**  Magunia yako wapi?
    **c**  Dereva yuko wapi?
    **d**  Wanawake wako wapi (ila mama mwenye kikapu)?
    **e**  Mama mwenye kikapu anaongea na nani?
    **f**  Vijana wanauza nini?

| | | |
|---|---|---|
| **gunia** (MA)  *sack* | **-ongea** (na)  *chat (to)* | |

▶ 2 Steve had never heard the expression **usiwe na wasiwasi** before his conversation with Bw. Twaibu. He decided to make a note of each occurrence of *don't worry, don't let them worry*, etc., that he heard. He did not always have time to make very full notes and also the sentences from different contexts got mixed up. Help Steve sort out his notes by:

* writing **Usiwe/Msiwe/Wasiwe na wasiwasi!**, as appropriate, in response to each of the exclamations **a** to **e**.
* adding an appropriate sentence from the list at the end.

*Example*:
A: Mama huyu hajapata tiketi!
B: **Asiwe na wasiwasi! Kondakta atamkatia tiketi kwenye basi.**

| | | |
|---|---|---|
| | **-kosa** | *miss* (a bus, train, event, etc.) (also *make a mistake*) |
| **msafiri** (M/WA) | | *traveller* |
| | **-umwa** | *be ill* |

a **Wasafiri** Tumekosa basi lile!
  **Mtu** ......
b **Kondakta** Mabibi hawa, pesa zao hazitoshi!
  **Rafiki** ......
c **Msafiri** Nimechelewa sana!
  **Dereva** ......
d **Msafiri 1** Mfuko wangu siuoni!
  **Msafiri 2** ......
e **Mama** Mtoto wangu anaumwa!
  **Bibi** ......

> Mimi ni mwuguzi – nitamsaidia.
> Panda tu.
> Mabasi huondoka kila saa moja.
> Nitawapa shilingi mia.
> Upo hapa chini.

3   Write an English version of the example and your mini-dialogues in question **2**.

4   Find out how well you have understood the dialogue by answering these questions in Swahili:

   **a**   Ni nani aliyekwenda na Steve mpaka kituo cha basi?

   **b**   Steve ana mizigo mingapi?

   **c**   Nani amekaa mbele, karibu na dereva?

   **d**   Kikapu kilicho mbele ni mali ya nani?

   **e**   Dereva ana ukanda gani?

   **f**   Steve atakaa Mtwara siku ngapi?

5   **a**   You are seeing a friend off on a long bus or train journey. What do you say just before she leaves, to wish her a safe arrival?

   **b**   You are seeing a group of friends off at the airport. What do you say to wish them a safe arrival? (If necessary, look back at Unit 4, in section 3 of the Grammar, for plural imperatives.)

6   Now you have a chance to see how well you remember some of the characters and events in previous units. Complete the sentences by filling in the missing words.

   UNIT 1 Mtu aliyewatembelea John na Alison hotelini ni _____.

   UNIT 2 Ambaye alikwenda posta kununua stampu ni _____.

   UNIT 3 Aliyesema anapenda wali kwa _____ ni Alison.

   UNIT 4 Watu ambao wana kiu ni _____ na _____.

   UNIT 5 Ambaye alinunua _____ ndiye John.

   UNIT 6 Ambao walitembea karibu na _____ ndio Bw. Mohamed, Alison na John.

   UNIT 7 Mama mzee ndiye _____ kisamvu. (What is missing means *she who cooked*.)

   UNIT 8 Steve ndiye _____ hapendi kusafiri peke yake. (What is missing means *he who said*.)

# 10

## chumba kizuri!

a good room!

**In this unit you will learn**
- words for furniture and other domestic items
- how to say where things are in a room
- how to say whether you are feeling hot or cold

# ▶ Dialogue

Steve has just booked into a small beach hotel recommended by someone on the bus. He was taken there by a taxi-owning friend of the bus driver, whom they met at the bus station. Makasi, the receptionist-cum-barman, is about to open the bar. A young man, Juma, is taking Steve to his room.

**Juma**    Makasi atafungua baa sasa hivi.

**Steve**    Vizuri. Naona kiu sana.

**Juma**    (*unlocking a door*) Namba sita! Karibu bwana. Swichi hii yawasha taa ya chumba cha kulalia. Swichi hii yawasha taa ya maliwato na hii yawasha feni.

**Steve**    Maliwato iko wapi?

**Juma**    (*opening a door on the far side of the bedroom*) Ipo bafu na choo. Kila kitu safi.

**Steve**    Safi kabisa!

**Juma**    Mimi mwenyewe nilisafisha humu asubuhi.
          (*They return to the bedroom.*)

**Juma**    Beseni ya kunawia ipo pale. Ipo almari hapa, na pembeni pana kabati la nguo.

**Steve**    Vizuri sana, ila sina nguo nyingi!

**Juma**    Kitanda hiki chembamba, lakini godoro ni jipya. Nikunjue chandalua sasa ... Bila shaka matandiko yatatosha. Hutasikia baridi, siyo? Tuna mablanketi ndani ya stoo.

**Steve**    Sitahitaji matandiko mengine. Shuka itatosha. Sioni baridi. Siku zote nasikia joto tu! Haya, Juma. Sasa nitaoga.

**Juma**    Vizuri, bwana. Angalia – nimeweka ufunguo wako juu ya rafu. Je bwana, chakula? Tuna wali kwa samaki na wali kwa kuku. Afadhali uagize sasa. Baada ya nusu saa kitakuwa tayari.

**Steve**    Nipo pwani sasa. Lazima nile samaki!

Soon Steve is sitting with a cold beer at one of the small tables outside, near the bar. He is chatting to Makasi.

**Steve**    Wageni ni wengi siku hizi?

**Makasi**    Si wengi sana.

**Steve**    Wapo wangapi hotelini leo?

**Makasi**    Mmoja tu.

**Steve**    Nani huyo?

**Makasi**    Ndiye wewe.

**Steve**    Mimi tu?

**Makasi**    Ndiyo. Hakuna wageni wengi siku hizi. Ni wakati wa mavuno ya korosho ambapo wengi watakuja hapa. Wanunuzi korosho huja kwa wingi. Meneja amesema kwamba bwana mmoja atakuja kesho. Huja mara kwa mara.

**Steve** Yuko likizoni?

**Makasi** Yuko kazini. Afanya kazi katika kampuni ambayo yauza zana za kilimo. Yeye anajua Kiingereza vizuri sana. Atafurahi kukutana nawe.

(*Juma comes outside to the bar area.*)

**Juma** Chakula tayari, bwana. Utakula ndani ama nikuletee hapa nje?

| | |
|---|---|
| **-fungua** | *unfasten, unlock* |
| **-ona kiu** | *feel thirsty* |
| **namba** (N) | *a written or printed number* |
| **swichi** (N) | *switch* |
| **-washa** | *turn on light, light lamp, light fire* |
| **taa** (N) | *light, lamp* |
| **chumba cha kulalia** (KI/VI) | *bedroom* |
| **-lala** | *lie down, rest, sleep* |
| **maliwato** (N) | *bathroom* |
| **feni** (N) | *(ceiling) fan* |
| **mwenyewe** | *myself* |
| **-safisha** | *clean* |
| **beseni ya kunawia** (N) | *wash basin* |
| **beseni** (N) | *basin* |
| **-nawa** | *wash the hands* |
| **almari** (N) | *chest of drawers* |
| **kabati la nguo** (MA) | *wardrobe, closet* |
| **kabati** (MA) | *cupboard* |
| **godoro** (MA) | *mattress* |
| **-kunjua** | *unfold* |
| **matandiko** (MA) (usually used in the plural form) | *bedding* |
| **-sikia baridi** | *feel cold* |
| **-sikia** | *feel (also hear, understand, and smell)* |
| **baridi** (N) | *cold, cool(ness)* |
| **blanketi** (MA) | *blanket* |
| **ndani ya stoo** | *in the store* |
| **stoo** (N) | *store* |
| **shuka** (N) | *sheet* |

| | |
|---|---|
| **sioni baridi** | *I don't feel cold* |
| **-ona** | *feel (also see, understand, smell and taste)* |
| **siku zote** | *always, all the time* |
| **joto** (JI, no plural) | *heat* |
| **-oga** | *have a bath, shower* |
| **ufunguo** (U/N) | *key* |
| **rafu** (N) | *shelf* |
| **-agiza** | *order* |
| **nani huyo?** | *who's that (the person mentioned)?* |
| **wakati wa** | *during, at the time of* |
| **wakati** (U/N) | *period of time, season* |
| **mavuno** (MA) (usually used in the plural form) | *harvest time* |
| **ambapo** | *when (time at which)* |
| **wanunuzi korosho** | *cashew-nut buyers* |
| **mnunuzi** (M/WA) | *buyer* |
| **kwa wingi** (u-ingi) | *in large numbers, in abundance* |
| **meneja amesema kwamba ...** | *the manager has said that ...* |
| **Yuko likizoni?** | *Is he on holiday?* |
| **likizo** (N) | *holiday, vacation* |
| **kampuni** (N) | *company, firm* |
| **zana** (N) | *tools, implements* |
| **kilimo** (KI) | *agriculture* |
| **tayari** | *ready* |
| **ama** (=au) | *or* |
| **nje** | *outside* |

Note: **huyo** and similar structures will be explained in Unit 11.

**i** By taking advice about hotels from someone on the bus and by mentioning to the driver that he would need transport, Steve arrived safely at the congenial and inexpensive small hotel. It is clean and well equipped and the staff are friendly. Because Mtwara is not a major tourist centre any other guests will mostly be locals, like the sales representative for a firm which imports agricultural machinery, who is due to arrive the following day.

The dialogue contains several words for furniture and other domestic items; you will already know **kitanda** and **chandalua**. Here are some more:

| | |
|---|---|
| **fanicha** (or **samani**) (N) | *furniture* |
| **makuti** (MA) | *coconut-leaf thatch* |
| **mkeka** (M/MI) | *locally-made plaited mat* |
| **mto** (M/MI) | *pillow* |
| **pazia** (MA) | *curtain* |
| **sabuni** (N) | *soap* |
| **taulo** (N) | *towel* |
| **zulia** (MA) | *carpet* (woven) |

**i** **Makuti** is the traditional thatching material for coastal houses. The plural form is always used when referring to what a roof is made of: **paa la makuti**, *a makuti-thatched roof*. You would only use **kuti** to refer to a single leaf of the coconut palm. Large hotels at the coast tend to make use of **makuti** on at least some of their buildings such as the cottage-type accommodation and also for shaded areas near the swimming pool and bar. In Steve's much more modestly priced hotel we may imagine, outside the main building, the small bar at the side of a paved area with seven or eight tables for customers, the whole area shaded by a **makuti** roof. Just below the far edge of the paved area is a small garden, **bustani** (N), and then the beach.

Coastal road

# Grammar

## 1 Doing and undoing

There are two examples in the dialogue of a special form of the verb which involves adding a vowel to the root, or in a few cases, replacing a vowel. This vowel is usually **-u-**. Doing this has the effect of reversing the meaning of the verb. You should be able to recognize the two verbs from the dialogue, as well as a few from the earlier units.

| | | | |
|---|---|---|---|
| -fum- | *weave* | -fumua | *unpick* |
| -fung- | *fasten, lock, tie* | -fungua | *unfasten, unlock, untie* |
| -funik- | *cover* | -funua | *uncover* |
| -kunj- | *fold* | -kunjua | *unfold* |
| -tat- | *tangle* | -tatua | *untangle* |
| -va- | *put on clothes* | -vua | *take clothes off* |
| -zib- | *stop up* | -zibua | *unstop, unblock* |

If the vowel in the verb-root is **-o-** the extra vowel for reversing the meaning is also **-o-**:

| | | | |
|---|---|---|---|
| -chom- | *pierce, prick* | -chomoa | *extract* |

Grammar books call this form of the verb the 'conversive' form. A good way to remember the conversive form is to learn this meaning of -**kunja** and -**kunjua**:

-kunja uso, *frown* (fold up the face)  kunjua uso, *smile* (unfold the face)

---

**uso** (U/N)   *face*

---

## 2 Swichi hii yawasha taa – the -a- indefinite tense

This example from the dialogue means *This switch turns on the light*. The -a- tense-marker is used for general statements which are not tied to a particular time. The structure of **yawasha** is:

i- a-washa (i + a makes ya)

The verb prefix is **i-** because **swichi** is a singular noun in the N class.

*I, you, we,* etc., *turn on (the light)* would be:

| **na**washa | *I turn on* | (ni-a-washa) | (ni + a → na) |
| **wa**washa | *you* (sing.) *turn on* | (u-a-washa) | (u + a → wa) |
| **a**washa | *s/he turns on* | (a-a-washa) | (a + a → a) |
| **twa**washa | *we turn on* | (tu-a-washa) | (tu + a → twa) |
| **mwa**washa | *you* (pl.) *turn on* | (m [w]-a-washa) | (mw + a → mwa) |
| **wa**washa | *they turn on* | (wa-a-washa) | (wa + a → wa) |

Notice that when the verb-prefix is **ni-** you cannot hear any difference, in rapid conversational Swahili, between the **-na-** and **-a-** tenses; for example **ni-na-pika** and **ni-a-pika** both sound like **napika**.

With the other noun-classes the slight changes to the verb-prefix when the **-a-** tense is used are the same as the changes that occur when they are attached to **-a,** *of*:

| kitabu chafaa (ki-a-faa) | *the book is suitable* |
| ngoma yafaa (i-a-faa) | *the drum is suitable* |
| jembe lafaa (li-a-faa) | *the hoe will do* |

The function of this tense is being taken over by the **-na-** tense; fewer and fewer people are using **-a-**. Their negative forms are the same. One thing you need to note, if you are going to be on the Kenya coast, is that some mother-tongue speakers of Swahili use **yu-**, instead of **a-** as the s/he verb-prefix with this tense – as in:

yuaja — *s/he comes*

This tense-marker is one of those that can carry stress, so the **ku-** of the verb is not needed when the verb has just a single syllable:

waja (wa-a-ja) — *they come*

Although you can manage without using this tense, you need to be able to recognize it. One place where you can easily identify it is in newspaper headlines. Reading these is a good way of improving your Swahili, particularly when they are accompanied by pictures which give you a clue to the meaning. Here are some examples:

Sri Lanka yapata serikali mpya. (i-a-pata) — *Sri Lanka gets a new government.*

Tetemeko laua 150. (li-a-ua) *Earthquake kills 150.*
Mechi na Sigara yaahirishwa. *Match against Sigara*
  (i-a-ahirishwa)       *postponed.*

---

| | | | |
|---|---|---|---|
| **tetemeko** (MA) | *earthquake* | **mechi** (N) | *(football) match* |
| **-ua** | *kill* | **-ahirishwa** | *be postponed* |
| **serikali** (N) | *government* | | |

---

This is a typically journalistic use of the **-a-** indefinite tense. The message in headlines is usually about something that has just happened and if someone gave you the same message in a conversation they would use **-me-**.

## 3 Mimi mwenyewe *I myself*

**-enyewe** expresses *myself, yourself, itself,* etc., for emphasis. With the personal pronouns you use **-enyewe** like this:

---

| | | | |
|---|---|---|---|
| mimi mwenyewe | *I myself* | sisi wenyewe | *we ourselves* |
| wewe mwenyewe | *you yourself* | ninyi wenyewe | *you yourselves* |
| yeye mwenyewe | *he himself/ she herself* | wao wenyewe | *they themselves* |

---

Like **-enye** (Unit 9), **-enyewe** takes the verb-prefix and the same slight adjustments are made to it.

| kitanda chenyewe | *the bed itself* |
|---|---|
| taa yenyewe | *the lamp itself* |
| mkeka wenyewe | *the mat itself* |

## 4 In the store and on the shelf

In the dialogue we have **Tuna mablanketi ndani ya stoo,** *We have blankets in the store* and **Angalia – nimeweka ufunguo wako juu ya rafu,** *Look – I've put your key on the shelf.*

In Unit 9 **juu** (*on the top*), as well as **mbele** (*at the front*) and **chini** (*on the floor*), were used as place-adverbs, with no word or phrase following them. In this unit's dialogue we have items being placed in a particular room (store) or on something (shelf). So to describe where they are we need a phrase that includes a word for what the item is in or on. Phrases of this kind are called prepositional phrases, like *in the store, on the* *shelf, under the chair, outside the house*, etc., in English. They are made with a place-adverb, followed by **ya** and then the word for the location.

| | |
|---|---|
| ndani ya kabati | *in the cupboard* |
| juu ya meza | *on the table* |
| chini ya kiti | *under the chair* |
| nje ya nyumba | *outside the house* |
| mbele ya (*or* za) mlango | *in front of the door* |
| nyuma ya shule | *behind the school* |
| katikati ya mji | *in the centre of the town* |
| kati ya hoteli na posta | *between the hotel and the post office* |
| karibu ya (*or* na) basi | *near the bus* |
| mbali ya (*or* na) stesheni | *far from the station* |

Note the three that have an alternative to **ya**.

Miongoni, *among*, is followed by **mwa**:

| | |
|---|---|
| miongoni mwa watoto | *among the children* |

**Katika**, often translated as *in*, does not need **ya** following it. This word can refer to *coming from/out of* or *going in/on to* as well as simply *being in* a place. The precise meaning is largely dependent on the type of location referred to, or the activity:

| | |
|---|---|
| Ziweke katika meza. | *Put them on the table.* |
| Ziweke katika kabati. | *Put them in the cupboard.* |
| Watoto walitoka katika chumba. | *The children came from (inside) the room.* |
| Juma alipanda katika mnazi. | *Juma climbed up (into) the coconut palm.* |
| Akina mama wamo katika kupika. | *The womenfolk are in the middle of cooking.* |

**Katika**, like **kwenye** (Unit 9), cannot be used with an adverbial noun, such as **nyumbani, jikoni, sokoni**, etc. **Katika** and **kwenye** have to be used with a 'plain' noun, without the **-ni** ending. You can either say **kabatini** or **katika kabati** for *in the cupboard*.

Both **katika** and **kwenye** are useful if you are talking about something being in a *small, large, good, blue* (etc.) *place* because you can only use adjectives with 'plain' nouns. You cannot use adjectives with adverbial nouns.

| | |
|---|---|
| Mtoto yumo katika chumba kidogo. | *The child is in the small room.* |

Watakaa katika mji mkubwa. *They will live in a large town.*
Nimetia sukari katika *I have put sugar in the blue cup.*
  kikombe cha buluu.

## 5 Feeling hot and cold

| | |
|---|---|
| **-ona** | *see; understand, smell, taste, feel* |
| **-sikia** | *hear; understand, smell, feel* |

In the box above, the main meaning of each verb is shown first.

Niliona shamba lake. *I saw his field.*
Nilisikia habari zake. *I heard his news.*

Both verbs can be used to refer to *feeling* (e.g hungry or thirsty,
hot or cold). In the dialogue we have:

Hutasikia baridi, siyo? *You won't feel cold, will you?*
Sioni baridi. *I don't feel cold.*
Siku zote nasikia joto tu! *I always just feel hot!*

## 6 -ote *all*

**Siku zote**, in the dialogue, literally means *all days*. The qualifier
of **siku** is **-ote**, with the appropriate prefix on it. The form **-ote**
means *all* and takes the verb-prefix.

watu wote *all the people*
ndizi zote *all the bananas*
chakula chote *all the food*
miti yote *all the trees*

The usual slight adjustments have to be made to the prefix. If
you want to check on what happens when the verb-prefix is
followed by **-o**, turn back to Unit 5, section 10 and Unit 8,
section 6.

The form **-o-ote**, meaning *any at all*, works in the same way (but
note what happens in the case of M/WA singulars):

Mpe mtoto yeyote. *Give (it) to any child at all.*
Hana pesa zozote. *She has no money whatever.*
Sina vitabu vyovyote. *I have no books at all.*

## 7 Meneja amesema kwamba . . .
*The manager has said that . . .*

**Kwamba**, as well as **kuwa** and **kama**, are used to introduce what someone *said, thought, believed, warned, agreed*, etc.

| | |
|---|---|
| Meneja amesema kwamba bwana mmoja atakuja kesho. | *The manager has said that a certain man will come tomorrow.* |
| Walikubali kuwa matandiko yatatosha. | *They agreed that the bedding would be sufficient.* |
| Wanasema kuwa wamechoka. | *They say that they are tired.* |

Notice how they can be used in sentences with **ni** and **si**:

| | |
|---|---|
| Ukweli ni kwamba pesa zimepotea. | *The truth is that the money is lost.* |
| Ni kweli kuwa pesa zimepotea. | *It's true that the money is lost.* |

In Swahili, unlike English, you do not put reported speech referring to the future into the past tense. You use the tense that the speaker originally used. In the example above, beginning **Walikubali . . .**, the people who came to an agreement about the bedding would have used the future tense, **matandiko yatatosha**, *the bedding will be sufficient, there will be enough bedding.*

**Kama** is probably less common than **kwamba** and **kuwa** in sentences like those above. It has a special function of its own, of which there is an example in the Unit 8 dialogue. This is the *if/whether* meaning, as in Steve's first sentence:

| | |
|---|---|
| Sijui kama nitapata nafasi . . . | *I don't know whether I'll have time . . .* |
| Hakusema kama wanafunzi watakuja kesho. | *She didn't say whether the students would be coming tomorrow.* |

As well as following a negative verb, it also has the *if/whether* meaning in questions:

| | |
|---|---|
| Anajua kama wanafunzi watakuja kesho? | *Does she know if the students are coming tomorrow?* |

**Kwamba** and **kuwa** can be used interchangeably. In some areas **kwamba** is more common, and in others **kuwa** is more often used.

## 8 Atafurahi kukutana nawe – na-

Earlier units have already given examples of **na-** with shortened forms of the personal pronouns attached. They are set out here for reference:

| | | | |
|---|---|---|---|
| nami | *with me* | nasi | *with us* |
| nawe | *with you* (sing.) | nanyi | *with you* (pl.) |
| naye | *with him/her* | nao | *with them* |

    pamoja nami        *together with me*
    karibu naye        *near him/her*

With other noun classes it is the verb-prefix + **o** form that gets attached to **na-**.

    Mwalimu alikwenda nacho.   *The teacher took it with him.*
                             (lit. went with it)

You learned these **-o** forms attached to **na-** in Unit 5:

    ninacho   *I have it*        tunazo   *we have them*

# Practice

1    Just as Steve was going to bed, after a good supper and rather a lot of beer, a failure of the local electricity supply put all the hotel lights out. The next morning he found that he had scattered his belongings around and put some of them in very odd places. Write a sentence for each picture.

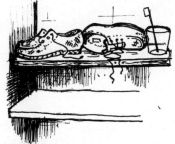

*Example*:
**Viatu vipo juu ya rafu.**             **a**

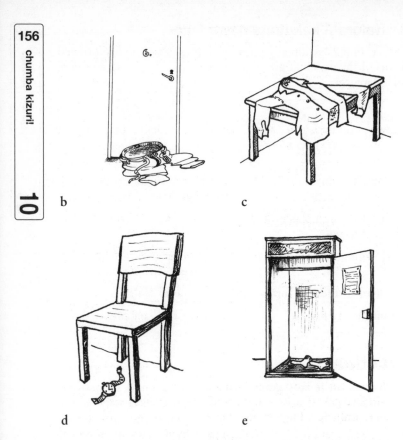

b

c

d

e

*Note:* The word for *trousers* is used in the singular.

2   In a letter to a Swahili-speaking friend you include a description of the house you are living in. Describe what is in the sitting room, **ukumbi** (U/N):
    *... two doors, one window, a large table, a small table, four chairs, a large cupboard, two shelves with (having) French books, and a mat on the floor.*

    **Ukumbi wetu una...**

3   It is the cool season, and two of you are staying in a hotel in the Usambara mountains, inland from Tanga. Fill in your part of the conversation with Aranya, who helps run the hotel.

| Aranya | Matandiko yatatosha? |
|--------|---------------------|
| You | *It* (use the plural) *won't be enough. I shall feel cold at night. I would like another blanket.* (I want/ask for) |
| Aranya | Afadhali niwaletee mawili. |
| You | *OK.* |
| Aranya | Mnahitaji vitu vingine? |
| You | *Please bring us two more pillows. Also* (**tena**) *please show me how to* (**namna ya ku-**) *open this window.* |
| Aranya | (*opening the window*) Unafanya namna hii. Basi, chakula tayari sasa. Nitaleta mablanketi baadaye. |
| You | *Good. We're coming right now.* (*Right now* is in the Unit 7 dialogue.) |

4   Make whole sentences by choosing suitable endings from the list on the right.

a   Masanja ni dereva...                ambalo ni jipya.
b   Tusubilege ni mtoto...              ambao wanatoka Ulaya.
c   Hivi ni vitabu...                       ambaye gari lake ni jeupe.
d   John na Alison ni wageni...     ni Masanja.
e   Godoro lile ndilo...                  ambavyo nilivinunua jana.
f   Ambaye hatakuja nasi...          ambaye yupo shuleni.

*Notes:* Tusubilege is a girl's name.
**ambaye gari lake** = *whose vehicle* (who his vehicle)
In **f**, **ambaye** = the person who

5   Answer these questions about the dialogue:

a   Nani anamwonyesha Steve chumba chake?
b   Ni nani aliyesafisha asubuhi?
c   Kabati la nguo liko wapi?
d   Kitanda ni kipana au chembamba?
e   Kwa nini Steve hatahitaji matandiko mengine?
f   Juma ameweka ufunguo wapi?

6   Find the Swahili equivalents for each of the following in the dialogue:

a   I'm feeling very thirsty.
b   This switch turns on the bedroom light.
c   There's a chest of drawers here.
d   Let me unfold the mosquito net.
e   The sheet will be enough.
f   I really must eat fish!

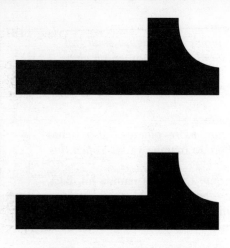

**mialiko**
invitations

**In this unit you will learn**
- how to talk about being invited to take part in or watch an event
- how to talk about actions being done by people
- how to refer to people's dates of birth

# ▶ Dialogue

John and Alison are in Zanzibar, staying at a hotel where Mohamed's brother Faiz is the manager. Much of their time is spent in the company of Faiz's family and friends. Alison is chatting to Faiz's wife, Zubeda, at home.

**Zubeda** Umealikwa ngoma kesho kutwa.

**Alison** Aa, vizuri sana! John pia amealikwa?

**Zubeda** John hakualikwa. Maana ni ngoma ya wanawake tu.

**Alison** Nimealikwa na nani?

**Zubeda** Umekaribishwa na Bi. Salma na dadake, Pili, ambaye ataolewa wiki ijayo. Ni ngoma ya arusi. Chama chetu kinatayarisha mambo yote. Tutacheza ngoma kama chakacha. Kutakuwapo taarabu pia.

**Alison** Pili ataolewa na nani?

**Zubeda** Bwana arusi ni Daudi, ndugu yake Mohamed. Babake ni yule mwenye duka karibu na hoteli. Ni mzee ambaye tuliongea naye jana.

*(Faiz and John come in and greetings are exchanged.)*

**John** *(to Alison)* Tumealikwa mashindano!

**Alison** Mashindano gani?

**Faiz** Mashindano ya ngalawa. Sisi sote tutakwenda forodhani wiki ijayo, tuangalie mashindano. Unajua ngalawa ni kitu gani?

**Alison** Ni aina ya boti? Ni kama jahazi?

**Faiz** Hata kidogo! Si kama jahazi. Majahazi makubwa zaidi. Tena, huundwa kwa mbao.

**Alison** Ngalawa hutengenezwa namna gani?

**Faiz** Huundwa kwa kuchonga gogo, hasa gogo la mwembe. Tena, huwa na ndubi. Katikati pana mlingoti ambao tanga hufungwa. Hutumiwa na wavuvi.

**John** Majahazi yana milingoti miwili?

**Faiz** Si lazima. Mengi yanao mlingoti mmoja tu. Kuna aina nyingi za majahazi. Kila aina huitwa kwa jina lake.

**Alison** Haya, basi. Mashindano hayo yatakuwa siku gani?

**Faiz** Jumamosi ya wiki ijayo.

**Alison** Ala! Tunakusudia kuondoka siku ya Alhamisi!

**Zubeda** Msiondoke kabla ya mashindano! Lazima mwongeze likizo. Kama sisi Waswahili tunavyosema, 'Mwenda bure si mkaa bure, huenda akaokota.'

| umealikwa | *you have been invited* |
| ngoma (N) | *dance* (with drums) |
| pia | *also, too* |
| maana | *because, meaning, reason* |
| umekaribishwa | *you have been invited* |
| ataolewa | *she will be married* |
| arusi or harusi (N) | *wedding* |
| chama (KI/VI) | *association, club* |
| -cheza ngoma | *dance to drumming* |
| chakacha (N) | *women's dance* |
| taarabu (N) | *music played on traditional (coastal) instruments accompanied by singers* |
| bwana arusi (MA) | *bridegroom* |
| mashindano (MA) (usually used in plural form) | *race, competition* |
| ngalawa (N) | *dug-out canoe with outriggers* |
| sisi sote | *all of us* |
| forodhani (forodha-ni) | *(at the) customs jetty* |
| kama | *like* |
| jahazi (MA) | *dhow* |
| hata kidogo | *not a bit, not in the least, not at all* |
| -undwa | *be constructed* |
| mbao (U/N) | *planks* |
| -chonga | *hew, cut to shape* |
| gogo (MA) | *log* |
| hasa | *especially* |
| ndubi (N) (or mrengu) | *outrigger* |
| mlingoti (M/MI) | *mast* |
| tanga (MA) | *sail* |
| mvuvi (M/WA) | *fisherman* |
| aina (N) | *kind, type, sort* |
| -itwa | *be called, referred to* |
| Kama sisi Waswahili tunavyosema | *As we Swahili people say* |

**Mwenda bure si mkaa bure, huenda akaokota.**
*An aimless traveller is not like someone sitting down aimlessly, a traveller may pick up something.*

In a courtyard, Zanzibar

## ℹ️ Tucheze ngoma *Let's dance to the drum!*

The dancing to which Alison is invited, in the dialogue, is one of the celebratory events during the days leading up to a wedding in Muslim communities in East Africa. Much of women's socializing takes place in each other's homes and some of it comes about through helping to organize events such as the one referred to in the first half of the dialogue.

The dance called **chakacha** is for women only, but women of any age – married or unmarried, and including invited guests such as Alison – can take part. It would take place in an open courtyard outside the house. A different kind of women's dance would be restricted to close married friends of the bride and would take place inside. The word **ngoma** is used for the dancing accompanied by drumming as well as for the drum itself. Note that -**cheza** can mean play as well as dance.

The **taarabu** to which Zubeda refers is music for listening. This would be performed on a stage, erected for the purpose in someone's courtyard if it is an entertainment for a family celebration such as a wedding.

The preparations being made by members of the **chama** of which Zubeda is a member might include the purchase of fabric for special costumes or **kanga**, so that all the dancers will be dressed in identical colours or patterns. Some of the functions performed by such women's organizations vary from one area to another and according to the level of prosperity of the members, but what they have in common is the maintenance of the traditional ways of marking the important events in women's lives.

### Ngalawa and majahazi

The world of boats and seafaring is very much a men's world. The making and mending of small boats is something you can observe on the edges of towns and villages along the coasts of the mainland and islands.

The **ngalawa**, described by Faiz in the dialogue, is a more stable craft than the ordinary canoe which is also a dug-out, sometimes used with a small mast and sail but without outriggers. The mango is the favoured tree for providing the huge logs from which these dug-out boats are carved.

**mtumbwi** (M/MI)    *canoe*

The **jahazi** as Faiz points out, is quite different. This has a keel, and the shell of the dhow is made of planks. The large dhows have one or two decks, and nowadays accommodate a diesel engine. Dhows and their forerunners have enabled the east coast of Africa to take part in Indian Ocean trade for more than two thousand years.

One way in which visitors can sample dhow travel is to make the crossing from Dar es Salaam to Zanzibar in one; this is not, however, recommended for anyone prone to seasickness.

## Grammar

### 1 Being invited, being built – the -w- form of verbs

**a** Several verbs in the dialogue have had a **-w-** inserted before the final **-a**. One of these is a verb meaning *invite*:

-alika    *invite*              -alikwa    *be invited*

Bi. Salma alimwalika Alison.   *Bi. Salma invited Alison.*
Alison alialikwa na Bi. Salma.  *Alison was invited by Bi. Salma.*
Faiz atawaalika wageni.         *Faiz will invite the visitors.*
Wageni wataalikwa na Faiz.      *The visitors will be invited*
                                *by Faiz.*

This form of the verb is called the *passive*. As in English, you do not have to say who did the inviting:

Wageni watakaribishwa.     *The visitors will be invited.*

In the dialogue four of the other verbs used with -w- are:

| -funga | *tie, fasten* | -fungwa | *be tied, fastened* |
| -karibisha | *welcome, invite* | -karibishwa | *be welcomed, invited* |
| -tumia | *use* | -tumiwa | *be used* |
| -unda | *construct* | -undwa | *be constructed* |

Towards the end of section 2 of the Unit 10 Grammar section you had the verb meaning *postpone* used with -w-:

| -ahirisha | *postpone* | -ahirishwa | *be postponed* |

And in the Unit 9 dialogue the verb meaning *sell* was used in this way:

| -uza | *sell* | -uzwa | *be sold* |

Another verb used with -w- in this unit's dialogue is one of those that needs something extra attached to the -w-:

| -oa | *marry* | -olewa | *be married* |

When a verb ends in -aa, -oa or -ua, insert -le- or -li- before the -w-:

| -zaa | *give birth, bear fruit* | -zaliwa | *be born* |
| -fua | *wash clothes* | -fuliwa | *be washed* (of clothes) |
| -nunua | *buy* | -nunuliwa | *be bought* |

*Note*: These are verbs whose roots have lost their final -l-.

Whether you insert -le- or -li- depends on what the preceding vowel is. If it is -o- or -e-, insert -le-, otherwise -li-. This is part of the same rule you had for the prepositional form of the verb in Unit 4, and it will turn up again later.

Verbs of Arabic origin ending in -e, -i or -u make their passive form with -iw- or -ew-:

| -samehe | *forgive* | -samehewa | *be forgiven* |
| -hitaji | *need* | -hitajiwa | *be needed* |
| -jibu | *answer* | -jibiwa | *be answered* |
| -ruhusu | *allow, permit* | -ruhusiwa | *be allowed, permitted* |

Those ending in -au add -liw-:

| -sahau | *forget* | -sahauliwa | *be forgotten* |

A final -a always goes at the end, as if they are verbs of Bantu origin.

**b** Using the passive with verbs in the prepositional form.
You have already learnt the prepositional form of these verbs:

| -andika | → | -andikia | *write to* (someone) |
|---|---|---|---|
| -leta | → | -letea | *bring to* or *for* (someone) |
| -nunua | → | -nunulia | *buy for* (someone) |
| -pika | → | -pikia | *cook for* (someone) |

If you want to focus on the person or people being written to, having things bought for them, being cooked for, etc., you can add the passive **-w-**, and the word for the recipient/beneficiary of the action comes at the front:

| Koku aliandikiwa barua. | *Koku had a letter written to her.* |
|---|---|
| Sisi wageni tutaletewa chakula. | *We visitors will have food brought to us.* |
| Ruta amenunuliwa viatu vipya. | *Ruta has had new shoes bought for him.* |

The passive **-w-** always follows any other 'special purpose' forms that are attached to the verb-root, i.e. it always immediately precedes final **-a** (which marks the end of the verb-stem).

## 2 Marrying and being married – -oa and -olewa

In the dialogue Alison asks whom Pili is going to marry. The verb used is **-olewa**, not **-oa**. You can only use **-oa** if you are referring to a man getting married. If you are referring to the bride you have to use **-olewa**.

| **bibi arusi** (MA) | *bride* |
|---|---|

| Bw. Daudi atamwoa Bi. Pili. | *Mr David is going to marry Miss Pili.* |
|---|---|
| Bi. Pili ataolewa na Bw. Daudi. | *Miss Pili is going to be married to* (or *by*) *Mr David.* |

## 3 Sisi sote *All of us*

| sisi sote | *all of us* |
|---|---|
| ninyi nyote | *all of you* (pl.) |
| wao wote | *all of them* |

The qualifier -ote, introduced in Unit 10, can be used with the plural personal pronouns:

**Wote** is the usual word for *all (people)* but **sote** and **nyote** are the ones to use when *us* and *you* (pl.) are referred to. **Sisi** and **ninyi** need not always be used; just saying **sote, nyote** implies *all of us, all of you.*

| | |
|---|---|
| sote wawili | *both of us* |
| nyote watatu | *all three of you* |
| wote wawili | *both of them* |
| wote wamekuja | *all of them have come* |

## 4 Mlingoti ambao tanga hufungwa – more about amba-

The sentence in the dialogue which contains the above words means *In the middle is a mast to which the sail is fixed.* This sort of structure, using **amba-**, is needed if you want to convey the meaning of *to which, in which, on which, for whom, to whom, whose,* etc.:

| | |
|---|---|
| Nimemwona bibi ambaye mwanawe yupo Tanga. | *I have seen the lady whose son is at Tanga.* (the lady who her son...) |
| Tunatafuta lile duka ambalo ndani yake mna mshonaji. | *We are looking for the shop in which there is a tailor.* (the shop which inside it...) |
| Walinipa kitanda ambacho godoro lake ni jipya. | *They gave me a bed the mattress of which was new.* (a bed which its mattress...) |

In very casual conversation you could give the two chunks of information contained in sentences like this in two separate statements:

| | |
|---|---|
| Walinipa kitanda – godoro lake ni jipya. | *They gave me a bed – its mattress was new.* |

But if you want to give a careful account of an event or explain something to people you will find yourself needing **amba-**. It helps to make you sound more organized!

## 5 Mashindano hayo
*Those* (already mentioned) *races*

You have already learnt the words for *that/those over there* (Unit 6) and *this/these here* (Unit 5). There is another set of 'pointing words', or *demonstratives* which, instead of 'pointing' to something as being distant from you or near to you, 'points' to something previously mentioned in the conversation. This set of words is like **hayo**, in that they begin with **h-**, include the verb-prefix and have **-o** at the end.

In the dialogue **hayo** helps us to know that the **mashindano** Alison refers to are the **ngalawa** races and not some other races or competitions which are taking place. In English we do not have a separate demonstrative for this referring-back function; we would use *that/those* or *this/these*.

The structure of the **hayo**-type words is like the *this/these* words introduced in Unit 5: **huyu, hawa; hii, hizi; hiki, hivi,** etc., except that **-o** replaces the final vowel. There are the usual slight changes when a verb-prefix is followed by **-o**.

| Noun-class | *'already mentioned'* | |
|---|---|---|
| | sing. | pl. |
| M/WA | huyo | hao |
| N | hiyo | hizo |
| KI/VI | hicho | hivyo |
| (JI)/MA | hilo | hayo |
| M/MI | huo | hiyo |
| U(N) | huo | (as N class) |
| KU (infinitives) | huko | |
| KU (place) | huko | |
| PA (place) | hapo | |
| MU (place) | humo | |

Like most qualifiers, these follow their noun – but remember that **huko** can also be used to mean *over there* and is often used in front of a place name. This was pointed out in Unit 8. In some areas you may hear **hapo** used in a similar way.

**Hayo** need not refer just to a previously-mentioned word or phrase. It can be used to refer to a whole episode that has been described or several pieces of information that have been reported, and then it can be used on its own:

Ni nani aliyesema hayo?    *Who said that/those thing(s)?*
                           (Who is it who said that /
                           those thing(s)?)

Hayo refers to **mambo,** *matters* or *affairs*, which is a (JI)/MA plural noun. You could say **mambo hayo** in the sentence above but people usually just say **hayo.**

| | |
|---|---|
| Hao hawajafika. | *Those* (already mentioned people) *have not yet arrived.* |
| Hizo, sikuziona. | *Those* (already mentioned bananas or computers, etc.) *I didn't see.* |

## 6 Vizuri – vi – for manner

The word **vizuri** meaning *good* when used on its own and *well* after a verb, has already been introduced, but not explained. The **vi-** prefix, as well as being the noun- and verb-prefix for KI/VI class plurals, is also used to express the manner in which something is done. Prefixing **vi-** to -**zuri,** *good*, makes it into an adverb:

| | |
|---|---|
| Mtoto huyu anasoma vizuri. | *This child reads well.* |
| Wamefanya kazi vizuri sana. | *They have done the work very well.* |

**Vi-** can be used with some other adjective-stems to make adverbs:

| | |
|---|---|
| Aliwatunza watoto vyema. | *She looked after the children well.* |

Note also:

| | |
|---|---|
| Alisema hivi: 'Msiende pale'. | *He said: 'You should not go there'.* |
| Kuona vile, waliondoka mara moja. | *Seeing how things were, they left immediately.* |
| Nifungue vipi, dirisha hili? | *How should I open (it), this window?* |

The **ki-** prefix has a much more restricted function, referring to the manner in which something is done, but it is typically used with -**dogo** to mean *a little* or *slightly*:

| | |
|---|---|
| Wageni walicheza kidogo. | *The visitors danced a little.* |

## 7 Kama sisi Waswahili tunavyosema – -vyo-

In this part-sentence the -**vyo-** is a relative pronoun made from the **vi-** prefix of manner + **o.** The other relative pronouns you have already learnt mean *who, which* or *that.* The relative pronoun **-vyo-** means *the manner* or *way in which*. There are several words which have to be followed by **-vyo-** in the verb.

| | | | |
|---|---|---|---|
| **jinsi** (N) | *manner, way, type* | **kama** | *as, like* |
| **kadiri** (N) | *extent, amount* | **namna** (N) | *method, type* |

**Jinsi, kadiri** and **namna** are all nouns in the N class. The idea of '*the manner in which*' for **-vyo-** needs to be interpreted rather loosely, because following **kadiri** it means *extent to which*.

| | |
|---|---|
| Sijui jinsi walivyounda jahazi lile. | *I do not know how they built that dhow.* |
| Soma kadiri uwezavyo. | *Study as hard as you can.* |
| Ni kama alivyosema. | *It is as she said.* |
| Sipendi namna alivyoshona shati hili. | *I don't like the way she sewed this shirt.* |
| Fanya kama upendavyo. | *Do (it) as you like.* |

Note: Two of these examples use the *general relative* structure (see p. 138).

## 8 Mwenda bure si mkaa bure – nouns from verbs (1)

The proverb quoted by Zubeda at the end of the dialogue contains two nouns which have been made by putting a noun-class-prefix on the front of the verb-stem.

| | | | | |
|---|---|---|---|---|
| -enda | *go* | → | mwenda | *one who goes* |
| -kaa | *sit* | → | mkaa | *one who sits* |

This is the simplest way of making a noun from a verb; there are other ways which will be dealt with later.

| | | | | |
|---|---|---|---|---|
| -ganga | *heal, cure* | → | mganga | *traditional healer* |
| -piga ngoma | *beat a drum* | → | mpiga ngoma | *drummer* |
| -piga picha | *take a photograph* | → | mpiga picha | *photographer* |
| -faa | *be of use, be suitable* | → | kifaa | *useful thing, tool* |
| -nywa | *drink* | → | kinywa | *mouth* |
| -tata | *tangle* | → | matata | *complications, trouble* |

# Practice

1

msikiti          ngalawa          paa

ngoma          shati          jahazi

John's diary entries have become very scrappy. He sometimes just jots down bits of sentences in the hope of filling in the rest later. Help him complete these sentences about things that were made, by putting one of the picture words at the beginning and one of the boxed words or phrases at the end.

Remember that **na** precedes the doer(s) of the action and **kwa** precedes the means by which the action is carried out.

a    _____ lilishonwa na _____.
b    _____ iliezekwa kwa _____.
c    _____ ilichongwa na _____.
d    _____ liliundwa kwa _____.
e    _____ ulijengwa kwa _____.
f    _____ ilipigwa na _____.

> mbao  Alison  Juma na Ali  mawe  mabati  Mohamed

> **mawe** (JI/MA)    *stones*

**2** Faiz gets involved in hosting a party for some locals and a group of visitors from Britain. Here are some of the things he overheard. Fill in the gaps with a phrase, meaning *all of us*, *all of you* or *all of them*.

a _____ mmekaribishwa na Mwalimu Musa?
b _____ waliletewa matunda.
c _____ tuliandikiwa barua.
d _____ mlinunuliwa vinyago?
e _____ walipikiwa chakula cha jioni.
f _____ tumealikwa ngoma.

Now write an English version of each sentence.

▶ **3** Pili, the bride-to-be, is showing Alison some of her new clothes. Fill in Alison's part of the conversation.

**Alison** (*Ask who these dresses were sewn by.*)
**Pili** Mawili haya yalishonwa na fundi. Hili hapa lilishonwa na mama.
**Alison** (*Ask if she has a sewing-machine.*)
**Pili** Tumenunuliwa cherehani kama zawadi ya arusi, lakini bado kutumiwa!
**Alison** (*Ask when she will use it.*)
**Pili** Nitaitumia baada ya arusi!

---

**zawadi** (N)   *gift, present*

---

**4** **Walizaliwa lini?**   *When were they born?*
Under the heading **Siku za kuzaliwa**, *Birthdays*, write a sentence about each of these people to say which date and month they were born.

*Example*: Mwalimu Musa 16/7
**Mwalimu Musa alizaliwa tarehe kumi na sita, mwezi wa saba (or mwezi wa Julai.)**

a Pili 28/6                    d John 29/11
b Mohamed 10/4                 e Faiz 3/12
c Alison 1/2                   f Zubeda 10/10

**5** See how well you understand the dialogue by answering these questions:

a Kwa nini John hakualikwa ngoma? (Use **kwa sababu** or **maana** in your answer.)

**b** Alison alialikwa na nani?
**c** Bwana arusi ni nani?
**d** Watakwenda wapi waangalie mashindano ya ngalawa?
**e** Watakwenda hapo siku gani?

**6** Alison is chatting to Zubeda again. See if you can follow their conversation, and answer the questions at the end.

| | |
|---|---|
| **Zubeda** | Kesho tutamkaribisha mgeni mmoja. |
| **Alison** | Ni nani ambaye utamkaribisha? |
| **Zubeda** | Ni Bw. Athumani, ndugu yangu. |
| **Alison** | Anaishi wapi? |
| **Zubeda** | Anaishi Dar es Salaam. Ni mtu wa biashara. |
| **Alison** | Atakaa kwenu wiki ngapi? |
| **Zubeda** | Atakaa wiki mbili tatu. Anajenga nyumba huko Jambiani. Atakwenda huko aangalie mafundi, jinsi wanavyofanya kazi. |
| **Alison** | Nyumba inajengwa kwa mawe au matofali? |
| **Zubeda** | Inajengwa kwa matofali. |

---

**-ishi**   *live (in a place)*        **matofali** (MA)   *bricks*

---

**a** Bw. Athumani atakaribishwa na nani?
**b** Bw. Athumani anaishi wapi?
**c** Nyumba mpya ya Bw. Athumani inajengwa mahali gani?
**d** Nyumba hiyo inajengwa kwa matofali?

# 12

## hairuhusiwi kuegesha!
### no parking!

**In this unit you will learn**
- how to say you are in difficulty
- how to talk about starting and stopping a vehicle
- how to say a vehicle has broken down
- how to express what would happen if you took a certain course of action

# ▶ Dialogue

Alison is in Dodoma, and about to park a borrowed motorcycle against a wall. She has not seen this notice.

---

### HAIRUHUSIWI KUEGESHA HAPA

---

**Asha**     Bi. Alison! Ni wewe? Hujambo dada?

**Alison**   Aa! Sijambo sana. Za siku nyingi?

**Asha**     Safi kabisa. Sijui wewe?

**Alison**   Njema tu. Mbona upo hapa?

**Asha**     Ninahudhuria mkutano ili nifanye kazi ya uhazili. Na wewe?

**Alison**   Mimi na John tunamtembelea mwenzetu anayefanya kazi hospitalini.

**Asha**     Ni daktari?

**Alison**   Ni daktari, ndiyo. Ni mtaalamu wa magonjwa ya watoto wachanga. Pikipiki hii ni yake.

**Asha**     Unakwenda wapi sasa?

**Alison**   Kwa kweli, siwezi kwenda popote! Nimo katika shida kidogo. Pikipiki imeharibika.

**Asha**     Kuna pancha?

**Alison**   Siyo pancha. Nina hakika ni shauri ya mota. Kwa sababu ya kwenda pale dukani ilinibidi kuizima. Baada ya kutoka katika duka nilijaribu kuwasha, lakini wapi?

**Asha**     Haifanyi kazi?

**Alison**   Haifanyi kazi. Haiendi hata kidogo. Kitu fulani kimevunjika ndani ya mota.

**Asha**     (*looking around in all directions*) Sioni gereji yoyote. Tungejua mahali penye mafundi tungekwenda huko pamoja. Ningekusaidia kusukuma pikipiki.

**Alison**   Afadhali niegeshe hapa. Niende upesi kwa miguu nikamwulize mwenye duka. Labda atajua gereji iko wapi. Hata wajenzi wale waliopo karibu na kituo cha basi, labda watanisaidia.

**Asha**     Usiegeshe hapa. Angalia tangazo ukutani! Kama ungeegesha pikipiki hapa labda ingeondolewa na polisi. Ungerudishiwa pikipiki baada ya kutozwa faini. Basi, tukatafute fundi. (*They go off, with the motorcycle, in search of a mechanic.*)

| | |
|---|---|
| **hairuhusiwi** | *it is forbidden* |
| **-ruhusu** | *permit, allow* |
| **-egesha** | *park a vehicle* |
| **sijui wewe?** | *how about you?* (lit. *I don't know about you*) |
| **-hudhuria** | *attend* (meeting, conference, class) |
| **mkutano** (M/MI) | *meeting, conference* |
| **ili** | *in order (that)* |
| **kazi ya uhazili** | *secretarial work* |
| **daktari** (MA) | *doctor* |
| **mtaalamu** (M/WA) | *expert, specialist* |
| **magonjwa** (MA) | *illnesses, diseases* |
| **watoto wachanga** (M/WA) | *infants* |
| **pikipiki** (N) | *motorcycle* |
| **popote** (pa-o + pa-ote) | *anywhere at all* |
| **nimo katika shida kidogo** | *I'm in rather a difficulty* |
| **-haribika** | *be broken down, spoilt* |
| **pancha** (N) | *puncture* |
| **nina hakika** | *I'm sure* |
| **hakika** (N) | *certainty* |
| **ni shauri ya mota** | *It's something to do with the motor, engine* |
| **mota** (N) | *motor, engine* |
| **kwa sababu ya** | *because of* |
| **ilinibidi** | *I had (to)* (lit. it forced me) |
| **-zima** | *switch off* |
| **-jaribu** | *try* |
| **-washa** | *switch on* (engine, in this context) |
| **wapi?** | *what's the use?* (idiomatic use of *where?*) |
| **kitu fulani** | *something or other* |
| **fulani** | *such and such, so and so* |
| **-vunjika** | *be broken (in pieces)* |
| **gereji** (N) | *garage* |
| **mafundi** (MA) | *mechanics* (in this context) |
| **tungejua** | *if we knew* |
| **tungekwenda** | *we would go* |
| **ningekusaidia** | *I would help you* |
| **-sukuma** | *push* |
| **upesi** | *quickly* |
| **nikamwulize** | *that I may go and ask (him)* |
| **wajenzi** (M/WA) | *builders* |
| **tangazo** (MA) | *notice* |

| kama ungeegesha | *if you parked, were to park* |
| ingeondolewa | *it would be taken away* |
| -ondoa | *take away* |
| ungerudishiwa pikipiki | *you would have the motorcycle returned* |
| -rudisha | *return* (something) *to someone or to place* |
| kutozwa faini | *be fined* |
| -toza | *impose, extract* (fine, penalty, etc.) |
| faini (N) | *fine* |
| tukatafute | *let's go and look for* |

*Note:* **popote** is in agreement with **mahali**, which can be omitted, as in the dialogue.

---

**i** You are likely to encounter 'No Parking' notices only in cities and towns. Brief illegal parking might possibly go unnoticed by the police nine times out of ten but the tenth time could involve you in lengthy negotiations at the police station and the payment of a fine, if your vehicle is impounded. So it is worth checking for written signs, as well as road-markings.

Because Dodoma is the official capital of Tanzania all parliamentary sittings take place there. The meeting for which Asha is doing secretarial work may be a meeting of politicians or perhaps a meeting of a non-governmental organization with a nationwide delegacy. The organizers might have chosen Dodoma as the venue, rather than Dar es Salaam or Arusha (where there is a large international conference centre), because of its relatively central position. It is not a tourist town.

Although Alison was too distracted by the motorcycle problem to explain why she had come into town from her host's house, the main reason was to go to the bus station. She had intended to enquire about the departure time of the daily bus to Arusha and to buy tickets for herself and John. The journey takes a whole day – and usually rather more than twelve hours. They are planning to join an organized group in Arusha, for a trip to a game park.

# Grammar

## 1 Pikipiki imeharibika – the stative form of verbs

Verbs such as -**haribika** and -**vunjika** in the dialogue describe a state and therefore when you are talking about a present state of affairs you need to use the -**me**- tense. You have already learnt one group of verbs expressing a state when used with -**me**- (see Unit 5, Grammar section 8 for verbs denoting being seated, feeling tired or happy, being lost or full, etc.)

This new group of verbs is recognizable by their -**ik**- or -**ek**- ending. You use a stative verb to refer to something being in a particular state – being broken, shut, forgotten about, satisfied, etc. when the agent or instigator of this state of affairs is unknown or irrelevant.

It is useful to compare the stative with the passive, which you already know.

| | |
|---|---|
| -vunj- | *break* |
| -vunjw- | *be broken* (passive) |
| -vunjik- | *be in a broken state* (stative) |

Asha alivunja gilasi.      *Asha broke the glass.*
Gilasi ilivunjwa (na Asha).      *The glass was broken (by Asha).*
Gilasi imevunjika.      *The glass is broken.* (I'm not interested in who did it, I'm more concerned with the fact of the breakage.)

The choice of -**ik**- or -**ek**- is dependent on what the preceding vowel (the last or only vowel in the root) is; this is the same rule as for the choice of vowel in the prepositional verb-form (see Unit 4). The full stem is shown in brackets after each of the following examples so that you can see the difference between the verbs of Bantu and Arabic origin.

Nimetosheka. (-tosha)      *I have had enough to eat.*
Makosa yamesameheka.      *The errors are forgiven.*
  (-samehe)
Kazi hii imefanyika. (-fanya)      *The work is done, has been done.*
Lori limeharibika. (-haribu)      *The truck has broken down.*
Mlango umefungika. (-funga)      *The door is locked.*

In the above examples you can easily identify the two verbs of Arabic origin – the ones that do not have a final -a. The rules for these are:

- If the ending is -i or -u the stative is -ik-, as in -haribika.
- If the ending is -e the stative is -ek-, as in -sameheka.
- If the ending is -au the stative is -lik-:

-sahau          *forget*              -sahaulika          *be forgotten*

When verbs denoting a state are used with a tense other than -me- they express 'potentiality.' Verbs of the kind introduced in Unit 5 – expressing a state but without the special ending – need the -ik-/-ek- inserted for this purpose. Some of the examples are given in the negative because the 'potentiality' function often occurs in negative statements in conversation.

| | |
|---|---|
| Vikombe hivi vinavunjika | *These cups are breakable, liable to break.* |
| Mlango huu haufungiki. | *This door can't be locked.* |
| Nyumba hii inakalika. (-kaa) | *This house is habitable.* |
| Ndizi hizi haziliki. (-la) | *These bananas are inedible.* |

*Note*: A small number of verbs make this potentiality function in the following way. You already know these three in their stem form:

-onekana (-ona)    -patikana (-pata)    -wezekana (-weza)

| | |
|---|---|
| Nyumba yao haionekani. | *Their house can't be seen, is invisible.* |
| Mayai yanapatikana leo? | *Are eggs available today?* |
| Haiwezekani. | *It's not possible.* |

Note that -wezekana was used in the Unit 8 dialogue.

## 2  Magonjwa – more about MA plurals

In the dialogue Alison's host is referred to as being a specialist in infant diseases. You have already been introduced to the stem -gonjwa in mgonjwa (M/WA), *a sick person*. Illness in general is ugonjwa (U); when this is used to refer to a particular illness it has to be qualified with the name of the illness.

| | | |
|---|---|---|
| ugonjwa wa | { kipindupindu (KI) | *cholera* |
| | malaria (N) | *malaria* |
| | ukimwi (U) | *AIDS* |

In conversation people usually use the name of the disease on its own, but in a formal news report or an address to a meeting of health-workers, for example, a speaker might say, **ugonjwa wa ukimwi**.

If you want to refer to a number of diseases, without specifying what they are, use **magonjwa**:

| | |
|---|---|
| magonjwa ya wazee | *old people's diseases* |
| magonjwa ya nchi za kaskazini | *diseases prevalent in the northern countries* |

There are other MA class plurals with a corresponding abstract form in the U class:

| | | | |
|---|---|---|---|
| ugomvi | *quarrelling* | magomvi | *quarrels* |
| uhitaji | *need* | mahitaji | *needs* |

The **ma-** prefix can also be used to refer to a collection of people or things, even if the word is normally used in another class:

rafiki (N)  *friend*

| | |
|---|---|
| Marafiki zetu wametusaidia sana. | *Our network of friends have been very supportive.* |

(Notice the prefix on **-etu**.)

hospitali (N)  *hospital*

| | |
|---|---|
| Mahospitali ya nchi hiyo yana mahitaji mengi. | *The hospitals of that country have many requirements.* |

## 3  A note about -weza

In the dialogue Alison says **siwezi kwenda popote**, *I can't go anywhere at all*. **-weza** followed by a verb in its infinitive form, **ku-** or **kw-**, is an extremely useful structure and you should by now be able to express ability or inability to carry out a variety of actions.

*Note*: There are two important points, though, to note about this verb:

**a** Do not use **-weza** to mean *can* in English polite requests like *Can you open this window?* when you are really asking the person to open the window for you. **Unaweza kufungua dirisha hili?** means *Do you have the ability to open this window?* Instead use the **-e** form of the verb (see Unit 6, Grammar section 4); this is called the subjunctive: **Ufungue dirisha hili.**

**b** The negative form of -weza used on its own, without a following infinitive, means the person or people denoted by the subject is/are not feeling well.

| | |
|---|---|
| Siwezi. | *I'm not feeling too good.* |
| Juma hawezi. | *Juma's not feeling at all well.* |
| Wazee hawawezi. | *The old folks aren't very well.* |

## 4 Tungejua ... tungekwenda – *If we knew...*

**a** In the dialogue Asha looks around, says she can't see a garage, and follows that with the sentence beginning **Tungejua mahali penye mafundi. . .** *If we knew where there were some mechanics. . .*

The *if* part of the sentence expresses a condition and the second part expresses a consequence provided the condition is fulfilled: **. . . tungekwenda huko pamoja, . . .** *we would go together.* Both halves of the sentence need **-nge-** in the tense 'slot'. The use of **kama** in front of the first (expressing the condition) **-nge-** is optional.

| | |
|---|---|
| Tungekuwa na pesa nyingi tungenunua nyumba ile. | *If we had a lot of money we would buy that house.* |
| Ungealikwa kwao ningekushonea gauni. | *If you were invited to their place I would make you a dress.* |
| Wangepata gogo wangechonga ngalawa. | *If they got a log they would carve a canoe.* |

Asha's sentence with one **-nge-**, **Ningekusaidia kusukuma pikipiki** *I would help you to push the motorcycle* also expresses a possible consequence of the condition that they know where to find mechanics.

**b** To make the negative insert **-si-** in front of **-nge-**:

| | |
|---|---|
| Asingesoma magazeti asingejua mambo hayo. | *If he didn't read newspapers he wouldn't know these things.* |
| Nisingekuwa na pesa nyingi ningekaa shamba. | *If I did not have much money I would live in the country.* |
| Nisingekuwa na pesa nyingi nisingekaa mjini. | *If I did not have much money I would not live in town.* |

*Note*: Monosyllabic verbs, like **-wa** (*be*), have to be used with their **ku-** (infinitive) prefix; **-nge-** cannot take stress.

## 5 Niende... nikamwulize – -ka-

In the dialogue Alison says, *Let me go quickly on foot and ask the shopkeeper.* You do not need a separate word for *and*; -ka- joins the meaning of the two verbs and makes it clear that the second action relies on the first action being carried out.

Even when the -ka- verb is on its own it still carries the meaning of being subsequent to and dependent on the subject going somewhere, as in the last sentence of the dialogue, when Asha says, **Basi, tukatafute fundi,** *Right, let's (go and) find a mechanic.*

You can also use -ka- like this, with a verb in the subjunctive, following an imperative:

| Nenda sokoni ukanunue matunda. | *Go to the market and buy some fruit.* |

and following the future tense:

| Tutakwenda mjini tukamnunulie suruali. | *We'll be going to town to buy him some trousers.* |

Another major use of -ka- is in narrative; this will be dealt with later.

## 6 Wajenzi – nouns from verbs (2)

**Wajenzi,** *builders,* is a noun made from the verb-root -**jeng**-, *build.* You should recognize at least one other noun-and-verb pair in the examples below. Prefixing **m-/wa-** to a verb-root and putting -**i** on the end makes a noun denoting a person/people closely associated with the action, usually the doer of the action. Some nouns are made from verb-roots that have already been added to, for example: -**tumik**- in the box below is from -**tum**, *send* or *employ,* with the addition of the stative ending (see section 1 of this Grammar section).

| M/WA nouns made from verbs | | | |
|---|---|---|---|
| **mpishi** | *cook* | -pik- | *cook* |
| **mtumishi** | *servant* | -tumik- | *be employed* |
| **mlevi** | *drunkard* | -lew- | *be drunk* |
| **mwivi** or **mwizi** | *thief* | -ib- | *steal* |
| **mlinzi** | *security guard* | -lind- | *guard* |
| **mzazi** | *parent* | -za- | *give birth* |

| mwuguzi | nurse | -ugu- | become ill |
|---------|-------|-------|------------|
| mshoni | tailor | -shon- | sew |
| mfanyikazi | worker | -fany- kazi | work |
| mjenzi | builder | -jeng- | build |

Notice the changes caused by the attachment of -i. Although -n-, as in -shon-, and -ny-, as in -fany-, do not change, other consonants at the end of the verb-root do:

k *becomes* sh
d *becomes* z
g *becomes* z
w *and* b *become* v *or* z

Three changes not illustrated in the examples but which you may occasionally notice are:

p *becomes* f
t *becomes* s
l *becomes* z

Because -l- changes to -z-, mzazi and mwuguzi have -z-, despite the -l- having disappeared from the end of the verb-root, leaving their roots now as -za- and -ugu-.

Although almost all words for doers of actions made with the -i ending are in the M/WA class there are a few exceptions:

| kinyozi (KI/VI) | barber | -nyoa | shave |
|-----------------|--------|-------|-------|
| kiongozi (KI/VI) | leader | -ongoza | lead |

Be careful with kinyozi, because it has an idiomatic use meaning *a tradesman who cheats* (fleeces) *his customers*.

Another way of making words for actors is to use the ending -aji with M/WA prefixes. Some of these words, but by no means all, denote habitual performers of the action. Some have counterparts in the first group, with the -i ending; mshonaji is one of these.

| **More M/WA nouns made from verbs** | | | |
|-----------------|--------------------|----------|----------------|
| mchungaji | herder, shepherd | -chunga | herd, guard |
| mshonaji | tailor | -shona | sew |
| mwimbaji | singer | -imba | sing |
| mwombaji | beggar, supplicant | -omba | ask for, beg |

# Practice

1 **Kitu gani kimevunjika?** *What's broken?*
Write a sentence for each of the following pictures to say what is broken or what has broken down. Use **-vunjika** for *being broken into pieces*, and **-haribika** for *being broken down or damaged*.

*Example*:
**Pikipiki imeharibika**        a                                b

c                d                e                f

2 Complete the sentences **a** to **f** by adding suitable second parts from the choice listed on the right.

| | | |
|---|---|---|
| a | Tungekuwa na nafasi... | mngekwenda Marekani? |
| b | Baba angekwenda Zanzibar... | nisingekaa hotelini. |
| c | Juma asingekuwa mgonjwa... | ungetozwa faini. |
| d | Kama mngekuwa na pesa za kutosha... | angekaa kwa Faiz. |
| e | Ningehudhuria mkutano huko Nairobi... | tungekwenda Arusha. |
| f | Kama ungeegesha pale... | angefanya kazi hiyo. |

3   Don't do it!

a   Give an English version of the notice shown at the beginning of the dialogue.

Here are some more public notices. Work out what they are prohibiting, with the aid of the vocabulary box, and devise English equivalents for them.

b

**HAIRUHUSIWI KUSIMAMA HAPA**

c

**HAIRUHUSIWI KUKAA HAPA**

d

**HAIRUHUSIWI KUUZA VITU VYA AINA YOYOTE ENEO HILI**

> **-simama**   *stop* (also *stand* but not in this context)
> **eneo** (MA)   *area*

4   See how well you have understood the dialogue by answering these questions:

a   Asha anafanya nini Dodoma?
b   Pikipiki ni mali ya nani?
c   Asha anaweza kuona gereji?
d   Ni watu gani wanaofanya kazi karibu na kituo cha basi?

▶ 5   Fill in your part of the following conversation with a passer-by in a town centre.

> **mpita njia** (M/WA)   *passer-by*

| | |
|---|---|
| **You** | (*Say you're in rather a difficulty.*) |
| **Mpita njia** | Shida gani bibi? |
| **You** | (*Say your car has broken down.*) |
| **Mpita njia** | Pole sana. Kuna pancha? |
| **You** | (*Say it's not a puncture. It's to do with the engine.*) |
| **Mpita njia** | Gari liko wapi sasa? |
| **You** | (*Say it's in Makongoro Road, near the church.*) |

**Mpita njia**  Lipo karibu na gereji ya kaka yangu. Twende huko, basi.

6    You are at the airport, and see this notice for departing passengers. The friend travelling with you knows no Swahili and asks you what it means. Give her an English equivalent. Do not attempt a word-by-word translation – this won't work!

TAFADHALI KWA USALAMA NA RAHA YA KUKAA KWENYE NDEGE ABIRIA ANATAKIWA AWE NA MZIGO MMOJA TU MKONONI. HAIRUHUSIWI ZAIDI YA MMOJA.

NAWATAKIENI SAFARI NJEMA.

| | |
|---|---|
| **tafadhali** | *please* |
| **usalama** (U) | *safety* |
| **raha** (N) | *comfort* |
| **zaidi ya** | *more than* |
| **-takia** | *wish* (someone) lit. want for (someone) |

Notice that the **abiria** are referred to in the singular, whereas we would use the plural in English.

# 13

## kujifunza lugha

learning a language

**In this unit you will learn**
- how to talk about learning a language
- how to ask people to speak more slowly or repeat
- how to say what would have happened if you had taken a certain course of action

# ▶ Dialogue

Steve is back in Nairobi after his vacation in Tanzania. It is Saturday lunchtime, and he is at a crowded open-air café looking for a table. A friend, already seated at a table, sees him.

**Adam** Ebu! Steve! Je, hujambo, bwana?

**Steve** Alaa! Sijambo sana, bwana. Habari yako?

**Adam** Safi kabisa. Habari za safari? (*pulling out a chair for Steve*) Karibu keti.

**Steve** Salama tu. Akina Francis walinikaribisha vizuri.

**Adam** Wazee wake hukaa wapi? Karibu na Dar es Salaam?

**Steve** La! Mbali kabisa, sehemu za kusini. Si mbali na mpaka kati ya Tanzania na Msumbiji.

**Adam** Aa, wewe ni msafiri hodari sasa!

**Steve** (*noticing a French book on the table in front of Adam*) Na wewe, unafanyaje?

**Adam** Najifunza Kifaransa. Nimealikwa kuhudhuria mkutano huko Ufaransa,* mwezi wa tisa. Bora nijaribu kusema kidogo Kifaransa. Ingawa nilifundishwa Kifaransa shuleni nimesahau maneno yote.

**Steve** Mtu akisema Kifaransa utaweza kuelewa?

**Adam** Akisema polepole huenda nitaelewa. Ni kama wewe, jinsi ulivyojifunza Kiswahili. Tulipokutana wakati ule ulijua maneno machache tu. Siku zile ulikuwa ukisema 'Sema polepole! Sema polepole!' au 'Sema tena! Sema tena!'

**Steve** Nakumbuka sana. Lakini siku hizi sisemi hivyo. Ningalikuwa na mwalimu kama wewe mwanzoni ningaliendelea vizuri zaidi.

**Adam** Sasa unaendelea kwa haraka, maana huogopi kusema. Kutosema hakufai mwanafunzi wa lugha. Ukija nami Mombasa mwezi ujao wazee watafurahi kuzungumza nawe. Wameniambia kwamba wana hamu ya kukutana nawe.

**Steve** Nitaelewa, jinsi wasemavyo?

**Adam** Bila shaka utaelewa, ingawa Kimvita na Kiswahili sanifu vinatofautiana kidogo.

**Steve** Matamshi ni tofauti?

**Adam** Tofauti, lakini kidogo tu.
(*A waiter appears.*)

**Steve** Je, ndugu! Saladi za namna gani zinapatikana leo?

*In the recorded material Adam says 'Zaire' instead of 'Ufaransa'.

Lunch time in Nairobi

| | |
|---|---|
| **la** | *absolutely not, not so* |
| **lugha** (N) | *language* |
| **-keti** (= **kaa**) | *sit* |
| **sehemu** (N) | *part, area* (and in this sense used in the plural) |
| **mpaka** (M/MI) | *border, boundary* |
| **unafanyaje?** | *what are you doing?* |
| **bora** | *better, excellent* (used here like **afadhali**) |
| **-jaribu** | *try* |
| **ingawa** | *although* |
| **-fundisha** | *teach* |
| **-sahau** | *forget* |
| **maneno** (MA) | *words* |
| **-elewa** | *understand* |
| **polepole** | *slowly* |
| **huenda** | *perhaps* |
| **wakati ule** | *(at) that time* |
| **siku zile** | *(in) those days* |
| **ulikuwa ukisema** | *you used to say, you were saying* |
| **-kumbuka** | *remember* |
| **hivyo** | *that, thus* (lit. *in the manner referred to*) |
| **mwanzoni** | *at the beginning* |
| **-endelea** | *progress, continue* |
| **vizuri zaidi** | *better* |
| **zaidi** | *more* |

| kwa haraka | *quickly* |
|---|---|
| haraka (N) | *haste, hurry* |
| -ogopa | *fear, be afraid* |
| kutosema | *not speaking, not to speak* |
| -zungumza (= -ongea) | *chat, converse* |
| -ambia | *tell* |
| wana hamu ya | *they very much want* |
| hamu (N) | *desire, need* |
| Kimvita | *Mombasa dialect of Swahili* |
| sanifu | *standard* |
| -tofautiana | *differ* |
| matamshi (MA) | *pronunciation* |
| saladi (N) | *salads* |

**i** In the dialogue Adam makes several important points about learning a foreign language. His experience of forgetting the French he had learnt at school is a common one, largely due to lack of incentive and opportunity to maintain competence in the language. Adam's reply to Steve's question about whether he will understand if someone speaks French to him reflects a common feeling among beginners in a foreign language. 'If s/he speaks slowly perhaps I will understand.'

Steve obviously gets a lot of help from Adam, who is aware of the importance, for successful language-learning, of not being afraid to use the language. Lack of confidence in speaking to people in the early stages of learning a language is really a fear of making mistakes. But making mistakes, whether by using the wrong words or the wrong sentence structure, is a way of constantly increasing your competence in the language. If a mistake is corrected at the time by a sympathetic friend you are likely to remember the correct form next time you need it. You need to ask people to correct any mistakes they notice otherwise they will ignore them out of politeness.

**sahihisha makosa yangu**   *correct my mistakes*

Notice Steve's use of **saladi** in his question to the waiter at the end of the dialogue. The **kachumbari** mentioned in Unit 3 after the second dialogue, although containing a few of the ingredients one might expect in a salad, is not a main course dish. **Saladi** is an established loan-word in the Swahili spoken in cosmopolitan places such as Nairobi and the other capital cities and large towns. The waiter is likely to have a knowledge of English as well as Swahili and several other languages, and will be skilled at recognizing the words for dishes on his menu in whatever language the customer uses.

Adam's invitation to meet his parents, the **wazee** referred to in the dialogue, will give Steve's Swahili another boost. He will probably find that Adam's family and friends will modify their Swahili a little until they find out how much he understands. The Kimvita dialect of Swahili is their mother-tongue, but people like them are a small proportion of the population of Mombasa.

Because standard Swahili is taught in schools and used in the media in Kenya, most people know it to some extent; and Kimvita and the other coastal and island dialects are subject to varying degrees of influence from it. Dialect speakers who are in constant contact, perhaps through their work, with people using standard Swahili – or something approaching it – are a major conduit of this influence.

Steve should have few problems in communicating with people in Mombasa, whether they are members of Adam's family using the local dialect or some of the many people who have come from elsewhere within or outside Kenya to work in that busy commercial and tourist centre.

# Grammar

## 1 Unafanyaje? The function of -je?

Although we would say, *What are you doing?* as the English equivalent of **Unafanyaje?**, **-je** on the end of a verb that asks a question really means something more like *how?*

| | |
|---|---|
| Mnajuaje? | *How do you know?* |
| Tutapataje? | *How will we get (it)?* |
| Mambo yanaendeleaje? | *How are things progressing?* |
| Tufanyeje? | *What should we do?* |
| Amesemaje? | *What did he say?* |

## 2 Ningalikuwa na mwalimu . . .
*If I'd had a teacher . . .*

**-ngali-** is the past-tense equivalent of **-nge-**, introduced in Unit 12. As in the case of **-nge-**, **-ngali-** is used with the verb of both parts of the sentence, the part that states the condition and the part that states the consequence (if the condition is fulfilled).

Both -nge- and -ngali- sentences deal with suppositions.

| | |
|---|---|
| Ningemwona ... | *If I saw him .../Suppose I saw him ...* |
| Ningalimwona ... | *If I had seen him .../Suppose I had seen him ...* |

In the case of -ngali- it is no longer possible for the supposed condition to be realized; it is now too late.

| | |
|---|---|
| Ningalimwona ningalipata habari hizo. | *If I had seen him I would have got that information.* |
| Tungalizungumza naye ungalikasirika. | *If we had chatted to her you would have been angry.* |
| Kama ungalikuwapo ungalimsaidia. | *If you had been there you would have helped him.* |

As with -nge-, the negative is made with -si-:

| | |
|---|---|
| Tusingalikwenda huko tusingalimwona Rais. | *If we had not gone there we would not have seen the President.* |

---

| | |
|---|---|
| **-kasirika** *be angry* | **rais** (MA) *president* |

---

*Note*: An easy way to remember the difference between -nge- and -ngali- is to note that the one which refers to the past contains the past-tense-marker, -li-. In practice usage can vary; do not be surprised to find that people sometimes use -nge- for past reference. But the converse does not usually occur.

## 3 Kutosema – not to speak, not speaking

In the dialogue Adam says, using **kutosema**: *Not speaking is no use to a language-learner*. **Kutosema** is the negative form of the infinitive **kusema**, *to speak*. The negative -to- goes between **ku-** and the verb-stem.

| | |
|---|---|
| Kutomwandikia kutaleta matata. | *Not writing to him will cause* (lit. bring) *trouble.* |
| Kutowasaidia wagonjwa si kuzuri. | *Not helping the sick is bad* (lit. not good). |

## 4 Tulipokutana, vinatofautiana – the reciprocal form of verbs

The ending -an-, attached to the verb-root, changes the meaning of the verb slightly to express that the action is carried out mutually, in interaction, in association with or even (depending on the meaning of the verb) dissociation from.

| -ambi- | tell | -ambiana | tell one another |
| -ju- | know | -juana | know one another |
| -kut- | see, come upon | -kutana | meet (together) |
| -pat- | get | -patana | agree |
| -pend- | love | -pendana | love one another |
| -pig- | hit | -pigana | fight |

Sometimes you will need to use the -an- ending on a verb that has already been extended from its root with one special ending, such as the prepositional:

| -andik- | write |
| andiki- | write to (someone) |
| andikian- | write to each other |
| Waliandikiana kila juma. | They wrote to each other every week. |

Verbs (usually of Arabic origin) ending in -i or -e simply add -an- (and then the final -a that all Bantu stems have):

| -rudi | return | -rudiana | return to each other |
| -samehe | forgive | -sameheana | forgive each other |

Verbs of Arabic origin ending in -u replace it with -i and then add -an-:

| -jibu | answer | -jibiana | answer each other |

Verbs of Arabic origin ending in -a treat the -a as part of -an-:

| -saidia | help | saidiana | help each other |

The reciprocal verb-form -tofautiana, differ, which occurs in the dialogue, is made from a word of Arabic origin, tofauti, which can be used both as a noun to mean difference and as an adjective to mean different.

| Watoto hawa wawili wanatofautiana sana. | These two children are very different (from each other). |

You can use a singular, rather than a plural, subject and put the word for the other person/people involved in the action after the verb, but that word must be preceded by na. For example:

instead of saying:

| Francis na Regina wanapendana. | Francis and Regina love one another. |

you can say:

> Francis anapendana          *Francis and Regina love*
> na Regina.                  *one another.*

Using the reciprocal form in either of these two ways conveys that the loving is mutual, whereas **Francis anampenda Regina** implies only that *Francis loves Regina*; Regina might, for all we know, be quite indifferent.

You will also need to use **na** followed by a noun if the associated action is between two or more people (plural subject) and one or more other people (**na** + a noun):

> Tulikutana na Pendo maktaba.    *We met Pendo in the library.*
> Walipigana na wevi.             *They fought with the thieves.*

## 5 Msafiri, safari, -safiri – word-families

You have probably already made the link between this group of words with the related meanings *traveller*, *journey* and *travel* respectively; the root of all three is of Arabic origin and has the characteristic pattern of three consonants, s-f-r in this case.

Two other words which you have already learnt are related in the same way:

kitabu          *book*          maktaba          *library*

You can add to these:

| **k-t-b** | |
|---|---|
| **katiba** (N) | *constitution* |
| **katibu** (MA) | *secretary of a company, union, association, etc.* |

The verb **-hudhuria**, *attend* (in the Unit 12 dialogue) is related to the two words in the next box:

| **h-dh-r** | | | |
|---|---|---|---|
| **mhadhara** (M/MI) | *lecture* | **mhadhiri** (M/WA) | *lecturer* |

Unlike the relationship between verbs and nouns of Bantu origin, it is not possible to set out rules for deriving one form from another in the case of words of Arabic origin in Swahili. But it may be useful to note that the nouns of Arabic origin tend to have more a's in them than the verbs do.

## 6 Kwa haraka – adverbial phrases made with kwa + noun

You are already familiar with a few such phrases, for example in Unit 8 you had **kwa basi**, *by bus*, **kwa miguu**, *on foot*, etc., and you also know **kwa kweli**, *truly*, *really*, *actually* and **kwa kawaida**, *usually*.

In the dialogue in this unit, Adam says:

Sasa unaendelea kwa haraka ... *Now you are getting on*
*quickly* (lit. with haste)

Here are some more useful adverbials made from **kwa** + a noun; they should help to make your conversations more interesting.

| | | | |
|---|---|---|---|
| **kwa bahati** | fortunately, luckily | **kwa ufupi** | briefly |
| **kwa bahati mbaya** | unfortunately, unluckily | **kwa sauti** | loudly, aloud |
| | | **kwa shida** | with difficulty |

Kwa bahati tulimkuta njiani. *Fortunately we came upon him*
*along the road.*
Sema tena kwa sauti! *Say (it) again loudly!*

# Practice

1   **Unafanyaje? Mnafanyaje?**
    For each of the pictures, make up a mini-dialogue in which you ask the person/people in the pictures what they are doing, and they give you an appropriate reply.

*Example*:

A na B

**You**    Mnafanyaje?
**A na B** Tunajifunza Kifaransa

a Edda          b Steve          c Musa na Saidi

d Rehema        e Kip na Ben        f Agnes

2   How well did you understand the dialogue? Answer these questions about it: **Jibu maswali:**

   a   Ni watu gani waliomkaribisha Steve vizuri?
   b   Watu hao hukaa wapi?
   c   Adam anafanyaje?
   d   Ni nani ambaye haogopi sasa kusema Kiswahili?
   e   Steve anaalikwa kwenda wapi?
   f   Steve anapenda kula nini leo?

3   You are chatting to a local teacher. After an exchange of greetings, the following conversation takes place. Fill in your part of the conversation. You will need these words:

| | |
|---|---|
| **darasa** (MA) | *classroom* |
| **lugha ya kigeni** | *foreign language* |
| **lugha** (N) | *language* |
| **somo** (MA) | *subject, lesson* |
| **wala** | *or* (after a negative, *nor*) |

**You**      (*Ask her what subject she teaches.*)
**Mwalimu**  Nafundisha Kifaransa, pamoja na jiografia kidogo.
**You**      (*Ask her if the students like learning [to learn] French.*)

| Mwalimu | Wanapenda kujifunza Kifaransa, ila wanajifunza kwa shida. |
|---|---|
| You | (Ask why they have difficulty in learning French: model your question on the last part of the teacher's reply.) |
| Mwalimu | Wanajifunza kwa shida, kwa sababu Kifaransa ni lugha ya kigeni. Hawasikii Kifaransa nyumbani wala mjini. |
| You | (Say you do not understand very well – use the present negative of -elewa – and ask her to repeat [it].) |
| Mwalimu | Haya, niseme tena polepole. Nasema hivi: Watoto wanajifunza Kifaransa kwa shida, kwa sababu ni lugha ya kigeni. Watoto hawasikii neno lolote la Kifaransa, ila darasani tu. Na wewe, unafanya kazi gani? |
| You | (Say you are a doctor.) |
| Mwalimu | Aa, karibu kwetu. Kaka yangu ni daktari. Atapenda sana kuzungumza nawe. |

If you are working with someone else, do this as a role-play. Notice the slight difference between the teacher's first mention of the difficulty of learning French and her second reference to it, after you ask her to repeat what she said.

4 Fill in the missing verbs in their reciprocal form. The stems of the verbs to choose from are given in the box. One of them will need the prepositional extra vowel attached to the root and then the reciprocal form.

a Mwaka ujao Alison na Zubeda _____ barua kila mwezi.

b Siku hizi Adam na Steve _____ lugha za kigeni.

c John na Ruth _____ kwenye duka la sanaa jana.

d Daudi na Pili _____ sana; wamekata shauri ku _____.

e Mimi na ndugu zangu hu _____ shambani wakati wa mavuno.

f Watoto wale si wema; _____ sana kila wakati.

---

-kuta  -saidia  -oa  -fundisha  -andika  -penda  -piga

---

5 Find the second half of each sentence from the list on the right.

a Angalimwona...

b Tungalikuwa na pesa za kutosha...

c Nisingalikwenda dukani...

d Asingaliegesha pale...

e Wangalikwenda Nairobi...

f Steve angalikuwa na nafasi...

1 wangalimtembelea Adam.

2 angalikwenda Kilwa.

3 nisingalikosa basi.

4 motakaa yake isingaliondolewa na polisi.

5 angalimpa vile vitabu.

6 tungalisafiri kwa gari moshi.

6 This cutting is from the letters page of a newspaper; it invites readers to send letters for publication. You should be able to work out the meaning of **msomaji** and **wasomaji**. The other new words are in the box below.

Mhariri anakaribisha barua kuhusu jambo lolote linalompendeza au kumkera msomaji. Barua ziandikwe kwa kiswahili sanifu kwa lugha fasaha na zipigwe chapa. Ziwe fupi na za kuchangamsha. Kila barua lazima iwe na sahihi, jina au majina kamili ya msomaji au wasomaji.
Mhariri

Barua za Wasomaji,
Majira
S.L.P.71439 DSM

*Note*: Notice the infinitive **kumkera** in the second line. When you refer to two actions that are closely associated, but the second one is not the result of the first, or subsequent to it, you use the infinitive for the second verb: **linalompendeza au kumkera**.

| | |
|---|---|
| **mhariri** (M/WA) | editor |
| **-pendeza** | attract, have an interest for |
| **-kera** | annoy, irritate |
| **fasaha** (N) | of good style (used of language only) |
| **-piga chapa** | type, print |
| **sahihi** (N) | signature |

If you decide to write a letter to this paper, what criteria must your letter fulfil? You should be able to find five.

*Note:* You will get help with letter-writing later, in Unit 18.

# 14

# siku ya taabu

a day of trouble

**In this unit you will learn**
- how to talk about injuring, or feeling pain in, different parts of the body
- how to give an account of a sequence of related events
- how to say something had already occurred, was happening or used to happen

# ▶ Dialogue

It is Friday evening and Steve has arrived in Mombasa for the weekend with Adam and his brother Yusuf, in whose car they have driven from Nairobi. They arrived in time for Yusuf and Adam to go to the mosque with their father for **magharibi** prayers. Their mother Lela has made Steve a cup of spiced tea and is now chatting to him before joining her daughter in the kitchen where the evening meal is being prepared.

**Steve**    Kwa kweli, tulifikiri tutachelewa sana kwa sababu ya ajali hiyo ya matatu.

**Lela**    Gari lake Yusuf halikugongwa kwa matatu? Naona li zima.

**Steve**    Matatu na motakaa hazikugongana. Tulipoona matatu ilikuwa imeshapinduka. Ilionekana kwamba mahali hapo ni pa hatari kwa sababu lami imeharibika pande zote mbili za barabara. Huenda ikawa dereva alikuwa akiendesha mbio karibu sana na upande wa kushoto. Tena abiria ni wengi mno.

**Lela**    Kwa kuwa Yusuf ni tabibu alisimamisha gari aangalie watu?

**Steve**    Ndiyo. Tulipokaribia matatu Yusuf aliegesha gari, tukashuka upesi tukaenda tukaangalia abiria. Walikuwa wamekaa kando ya barabara. Walituambia matatu ilipinduka polepole hata kila mmoja aliwahi kushika kiti kilichopo mbele yake.

**Lela**    Na dereva, je?

**Steve**    Dereva naye alikuwa amekwenda kituo cha mafuta ampigie simu mwenye matatu. Kondakta alibaki hapo aangalie abiria.

**Lela**    Wengi waliumia?

**Steve**    Si wengi. Wachache walikuwa wamechubuka. Wengine walisema wanaumwa kichwa au shingo, wengine mgongo. Msichana mmoja alikatwa usoni. Yusuf alisafisha jeraha akatia dawa, kisha akalifunika kwa plasta.

**Lela**    Ehe. Hakuna mtu aliyeumia sana?

**Steve**    Hata mmoja, namshukuru Mungu.

**Lela**    Alhamdulillahi. Ajali ilitokea wapi?

**Steve**    Sijui hasa, ila nina hakika ilitokea mashariki ya Makindu. Basi, tuliendelea na safari, tukafika Mtito Andei tukanunua petroli tukaenda mkahawani tupumzike kidogo.
       (*A woman neighbour calls in on the way home from visiting her son in hospital*.)

**Jirani**    Hodi hodi!

**Nuru**    (*from the kitchen nearby*) Karibu!

**Lela**    Karibu!

*(The neighbour hears the women's voices, comes in – not expecting to see any men – and does not immediately notice Steve, who is sitting behind the door.)*

**Jirani** Msalkherini kina mama!

**Lela** Akheri bibi. Waonaje?

**Jirani** Salama tu, mama. Ala! Hujambo, bwana?

**Steve** Sijambo, bibi. Habari za jioni?

**Jirani** Salama bwana.

**Lela** Bwana huyu ni rafikiye Adam. Wanasoma pamoja chuo kikuu.

**Jirani** Ee. Vizuri sana. Karibu Mombasa!

**Lela** Je, habari yake Musa? Yupo hospitalini bado?

**Jirani** Bado yupo. Jana walikata shauri kufanya operesheni. Leo asubuhi na mapema alipasuliwa. Sasa yu macho, lakini hawezi kunena, ila maneno machache tu.

**Lela** Yu dhaifu?

**Jirani** Yu dhaifu. Lakini atapongea, Mungu akimjalia.

**Lela** Inshallah! Leo siku ya taabu, kwelikweli.

| | |
|---|---|
| **-fikiri** | *think* |
| **ajali** (N) | *accident* |
| **matatu** (N) | *privately-owned bus* (Kenya) |
| **-gonga** | *knock, hit* |
| **naona li zima** | *I see it's in one piece* |
| **-zima** | *whole* |
| **ilikuwa imeshapinduka** | *it had already overturned* |
| **-pinduka** | *overturn* |
| **hatari** (N) | *danger* |
| **lami** (N) | *tarmac* |
| **huenda ikawa** | *perhaps* |
| **alikuwa akiendesha** | *(he) was driving* |
| **-endesha** | *drive* |
| **mbio** (= **upesiupesi**) | *very fast* |
| **upande** (U/N) | *side* |
| **kwa kuwa** | *because* |
| **tabibu** (MA) (= **daktari**) | *doctor* |
| **-simamisha** | *stop* (car, bus, etc.) |
| **-karibia** | *come near (to)* |
| **tukashuka** | *and we got out* |
| **-shuka** | *get out of a vehicle* |
| **-ka-** | *and then* |
| **walikuwa wamekaa** | *they were sitting* |
| **kando ya** | *near, not far away from* |
| **hata** | *so that* |
| **-wahi** | *manage* (to do something) |

| | |
|---|---|
| **-shika** | *grasp, hold on to* |
| **dereva naye** | *the driver himself* |
| **alikuwa amekwenda** | *he had gone* |
| **kituo cha mafuta** (KI/VI) | *filling-station* |
| (= **gereji**) **-baki** | *remain* |
| **-umia** | *be injured* |
| **walikuwa wamechubuka** | *were bruised* |
| **-chubuka** | *be bruised, have abrasions* |
| **-umwa** | *feel pain (in)* |
| **shingo** (N) | *neck* |
| **mgongo** (M/MI) | *back (of the body)* |
| **msichana** (M/WA) | *girl, young unmarried woman* |
| **uso** (U/N) | *face* |
| **jeraha** (MA) | *wound* |
| **dawa** (N) | *ointment, medicine* |
| **kisha** | *then* |
| **plasta** (N) | *plaster, adhesive dressing* |
| **ehe** | *'I'm following what you're telling me'* |
| **hakuna mtu ...?** | *there wasn't anyone ...?* |
| **hata mmoja** | *not even one* |
| **namshukuru Mungu** | *I thank God* |
| **Mungu** (M/MI) | *God* |
| **Alhamdulillahi** | *Praise be to God* |
| **-tokea** | *happen, occur* |
| **Makindu** *and* **Mtito Andei** | *(see map on p.210)* |
| **petroli** (N) (also **mafuta**) | *petrol* |
| **jirani** (MA) | *neighbour* |
| **-pumzika** | *rest, have a break* |
| **Msalkherini** | *an afternoon or evening greeting* |
| | *(sing. is **Msalkheri**)* |
| **Akheri** (sing.) | *reply to **Msalkheri(ni)*** |
| **Waonaje? (U-a-ona-je?)** | *How are you feeling? (greeting)* |
| **-soma** | *study (also means read)* |
| **chuo kikuu** (KI/VI) | *university (of Nairobi in this context)* |
| **-kuu** | *great, of high rank* |
| **-operesheni** (N) | *operation* |
| **asubuhi na mapema** | *early in the morning* |
| **-pasua** | *operate on (also tear and split)* |
| **yu macho** | *he is awake (lit. he is eyes)* |
| **-nena** | *speak, utter* |
| **yu dhaifu** | *he is weak* |
| **-pongea** | *recover (from a serious illness)* |
| **Mungu akimjalia** | *God willing, if God enables him* |
| | *(to get better)* |
| **Inshallah** | *If it pleases God* |

# ℹ️ The road to Mombasa

The **matatu** is the Kenyan equivalent of the Tanzanian **daladala**, and is usually – but not invariably – a minibus. They tend to be overloaded, and therefore unstable, and are often driven faster than the large company buses. The **matatu** in the dialogue could have been on a short route between towns or on the Nairobi–Mombasa run which, in normal circumstances, would take not more than a full day, with stops at each town and turn-off. The same journey in an average car might take six hours including a stop. The road is generally good but does have occasional patches where the edges have been undermined by heavy rain and erosion and have crumbled. The **matatu** driver was unlucky in going too near one of these; a more stable vehicle might well not have overturned.

From Mtito Andei the road runs through the Tsavo National Park, an arid area of thorn scrub and occasional baobab trees. There is ample provision for game-watching in this huge area. You are unlikely to see elephants or lions while driving along the main road, but you might glimpse a few passing zebras.

For most of the year it is hot, dry and dusty but the onset of rain suddenly brings it to new life. Most of the time it is not until you reach the beginning of the coastal 'strip' that lush vegetation is to be seen.

**pori** (MA)  *scrub, bush area*  **mbuyu** (M/MI)  *baobab tree*

## Kwa Adam, at Adam's home

Adam and Yusuf's father would have been pleased that they had arrived in time to join him for the special Friday prayers in the mosque. They would have put on **kanzu** and **kofia** and Steve would have been surprised at the sudden transformation in their appearance. Steve, like other foreign visitors, would be impressed at the way in which capital city dwellers slip easily from one lifestyle to another when they visit relatives in other parts of the country.

Adam's family live in a late nineteenth-century house in the densely populated area of narrow streets to the north of Fort Jesus on Mombasa island. This is the old part of the town, and has a predominantly Muslim population. The older women in this cluster of neighbourhoods tend to do their frequent visiting of friends in the afternoon. The neighbour in the dialogue is calling on Lela rather later than she normally would (there is the preparation of the evening meal to be supervised at home) but she knows that Lela would like to know about the boy's operation and will help to pass this important piece of information around the neighbourhood.

The men and women of the family eat their evening meal together unless there are guests who are not close relatives. So Steve will be eating with the menfolk; this will include an elderly man – the friend of a friend of Adam's father – who is passing through Mombasa on his way to Nairobi, and a young man on his way to Tanga in Tanzania, who has been studying at the mosque college on Lamu island. A great deal of visiting takes place between Muslim people living on the islands and along the coastal strip, where cultural and family ties predate the establishment of the political border between Kenya and Tanzania.

# Grammar

## 1 Tulifikiri tutachelewa sana – tenses in reported speech

Although the use of the tenses in reported speech was mentioned in Unit 10, Grammar section 7, it is noted again here, as a reminder.

In English we would have to translate Steve's words **tulifikiri tutachelewa sana** as *we thought we would be very late*. In English it is only when we are quoting a person's actual words (*'direct speech'*) that we use the same tense that they used at the time of speaking – or thinking – as in *We thought 'We will be late'*.

In Swahili the same tense is used for reported speech as would be used for direct speech; in fact there is less distinction between the two than in English. The second of these two examples shows what you would have to do if you needed to make it clear that you are quoting a person's actual words.

Alisema watachelewa.          *He said they would be late.*
                                              (reported)
Alisema hivi: 'Watachelewa'.  *He said, 'They will be late'.*
                                              (direct)

Notice that in casual conversation the words for *that* – **kwamba** and **kuwa** – are very often omitted in reported speech, just as you often omit *that* in English.

## 2 Yu dhaifu – using the verb prefix for 'is'

There are three examples in the dialogue of the verb-prefix, rather than **ni**, being used for *is*. You have already learnt a few structures in which **yu-** occurs instead of the expected **a-**.

| naona li zima | *I see it is in one piece* (lit. whole) |
| yu macho | *he is awake* (lit. he is eyes) |
| yu dhaifu | *he is weak* |

These are typical of the way the verb-prefix can be used for *is*; they all refer to the state of someone or something and the subject is not named. The verb-prefix is not usually used if the subject is present; you would use **ni** instead:

| gari ni zima | *the car is in one piece* |
| lile ni zima | *that's in one piece* |

Using the verb-prefix for *is* is much more common when the (unnamed) subject is a person.

Here are some common uses of the verb-prefix:

| **Yu** (or **yuko**) **tayari?** | *Is s/he ready?* |
| **U** (or **uko**) **tayari?** | *Are you ready?* |
| **Yu mgonjwa?** | *Is s/he ill?* |
| **Yu hai?** | *Is s/he alive?* |

A few structures, like **yu macho** in the dialogue, are idioms.

| Yu maji. | *He is in trouble* (lit. in water) |

The negative, as for **ni**, is **si**. But note that a negative reply to **U(ko) tayari?** *Are you ready?*, is **Bado,** *Not yet.*

## 3 Ilikuwa imepinduka – two-verb tenses

There are several examples in the dialogue of tenses which use two verbs, the first of which is **kuwa**, *be*:

| ilikuwa imepinduka | *it had turned over* |
| alikuwa akiendesha | *he was driving* |
| walikuwa wamekaa | *they were seated* |
| alikuwa amekwenda | *he had gone* |
| walikuwa wamechubuka | *they were bruised* |

The verb **kuwa**, marked with **-li-** for past tense, places the event in the past. The second verb describes the action or state as you would have referred to it at that time, with **-me-** used for the completion of an action (with an action verb) or being in a particular state (with a state verb) and -ki- denoting ongoing action (with an action verb):

| imepinduka | *it has overturned* | (verb expresses state) |
| akiendesha | *(he) driving* | (verb expresses action) |
| wamekaa | *they are seated* | (verb expresses state) |
| amekwenda | *he has gone* | (verb expresses action) |
| wamechubuka | *they are bruised* | (verb expresses state) |

You can use **kuwa** to express past, present or future time, but note that **-nakuwa** means *becoming*.

| Mwaka ujao nitakuwa nikisoma Nairobi. | *Next year I will be studying in Nairobi.* |
| Ukija saa tano usiku tutakuwa tumelala. | *If you come at 11 o'clock at night we will be asleep.* |
| Anapokuwa akisoma watoto hawasemi kwa sauti. | *While he is studying the children do not speak loudly.* |

Sometimes **-na-** is used instead of **-ki-** in the second (or 'main') verb, to indicate ongoing activity, but it is not nearly as common as **-ki-**.

| Zamani alikuwa anasoma gazeti kila siku. | *Ages ago he used to read the newspaper every day.* |

Make **kuwa** negative in the usual way:

| haikuwa imepinduka | *it had not overturned* |
| hakuwa akiendesha | *he was not driving* |
| sitakuwa nikisoma | *I will not be studying* |
| hatutakuwa tumelala | *we will not be asleep* |

## 4 Tukanunua petroli – more about -ka-

You have already met **-ka-** in Unit 12, Grammar section 5. Here is another function of it. The **-ka-** tense is not like the other tenses in that it has no time reference of its own. In narrative sequences it is used to show that its verb denotes an action subsequent in time to, and dependent on, the preceding one.

The first of a sequence of events which happened in the past is usually marked by **-li-** and the subsequent string of verbs by **-ka-**. These are the ones in the dialogue:

| | |
|---|---|
| Yusuf aliegesha gari tukashuka upesi tukaenda tukaangalia abiria. | *Yusuf stopped the car and we got out and went quickly and had a careful look at the passengers.* |
| Basi, tuliendelea na safari tukafika Mtito Andei tukanunua petroli tukaenda mkahawani tupumzike kidogo. | *Well, we continued the journey and arrived at Mtito Andei and bought petrol and went to the café to rest for a bit.* |

You do not need **na** between verbs if you use -ka-; -ka- itself means *and (then)*. Occasionally, for emphasis, you can put in an adverb meaning *finally*, *eventually*, or *then* as in the sequence about Yusuf treating the girl's cut face:

| | |
|---|---|
| Yusuf alisafisha jeraha akatia dawa kisha akalifunika kwa plasta. | *Yusuf cleaned the wound and put on some ointment and then (finally) covered it with a plaster.* |

Including **kisha** here emphasizes the putting on of the adhesive dressing as the culmination of several procedures.

The first tense-marker in a sentence need not necessarily be -li-. It can be -ka- if the verb it is attached to is in sequence with the last verb of the preceding sentence.

The negative counterpart of -ka- is the same as the negative of the -e form of verbs, the so-called subjunctive (see Unit 6 Grammar section 4):

| | |
|---|---|
| Nilikwenda kwa Mama Lela nikapiga hodi nikasubiri kidogo nisimwone. | *I went to Mama Lela's place and called hodi and waited a while and didn't see her.* |

This use of -ka- is typical of informal spoken narrative, in which people tend to recount a sequence of events in the order in which they actually occurred.

The use of -ka- is not restricted to past sequences of events:

| | |
|---|---|
| Mkimpa pesa akazipoteza, mtafanya nini basi? | *If you (all) give him money and he wastes it, what will you do then?* |
| Mzee hufika kwetu kila siku akala nasi. | *The old man comes to our place each day and eats with us.* |

Note that -ka- is one of the tense-markers that can take stress so one-syllable verb-stems, such as -la in the example above, do not need their infinitive ku-.

-ka- can also follow an infinitive. In this case as well as expressing subsequent action -ka- also has a *so that* meaning:

Tutawezaje kumsaidia msichana akaendelea na masomo chuo kikuu?

*How will we be able to help the young lady so that she continues her studies at the university? (... and have her continue her studies...)*

## 5 -nena and maneno – nouns from verbs (3)

There are quite a few nouns made from the verb-root (or an extended root) with the addition of -o, as in -nen-, *speak*, and the noun neno (MA), *word* or *utterance*, both used in the dialogue: ... hawezi kunena, ila maneno machache tu. ... *he can't speak, except for a few words.*

Nouns with the -o ending occur in various classes and usually mean either the result of the action expressed by the verb or, in the case of concrete objects, the means by which the action is carried out. Among the most commonly-used are those in the (JI)/MA class; notice that some -o nouns in this class are typically used in the plural:

| (JI)/MA nouns ending in -o | | | |
|---|---|---|---|
| -elez- | *explain* | **maelezo** | *explanation* |
| -endele- | *continue* | **maendeleo** | *progress* |
| -fundish- | *teach* | **mafundisho** | *teaching* |
| -pigan- | *fight* | **mapigano** | *fighting* |
| -shindan- | *compete* | **mashindano** | *competiton, race* |
| -siki- | *hear* | **sikio** | *ear* |
| -waz- | *think, ponder* | **wazo** | *thought, idea* |
| -za- | *produce* | **zao** | *crop* |
| | | **mazao** | *production* |

| KI/V nouns ending in -o | | | |
|---|---|---|---|
| -funik- | *cover* | **kifuniko** | *lid* |
| -fung- | *fasten* | **kifungo** | *button* |
| -tu- | *alight* | **kituo** | *stopping-place* |
| -zib- | *stop up* | **kizibo** | *plug, stopper* |

| | M/MI nouns ending in -o | | |
|---|---|---|---|
| -chez- | *play, dance* | **mchezo** | *game* |
| -end- | *go* | **mwendo** | *speed, manner of going, behaviour* |
| -ish- | *finish* | **mwisho** | *end* |
| -kutan- | *meet* | **mkutano** | *meeting* |

| | N nouns ending in -o | | |
|---|---|---|---|
| -ot- | *dream* | **ndoto** | *dream* |
| -und- | *construct* | **nyundo** | *hammer* |

| | U/N nouns ending in -o | | |
|---|---|---|---|
| -fagi- | *sweep* | **ufagio** | *broom, brush* |
| -fungu- | *open* | **ufunguo** | *key* |
| -imb- | *sing* | **wimbo (u-imbo)** | *song* |

Understanding how verb–noun pairs are related will help you to work out the meaning of new nouns that you hear. Do not attempt to try to learn all these now; they are given to help you to understand the system. You should be able to recognize quite a few of the verbs.

Other noun-endings to watch out for are **-u**:

| | Nouns ending in -u | | | |
|---|---|---|---|---|
| | Class M/WA | | Class U | |
| -kunjuk-<br>*be unfolded* | **mkunjufu** | *cheerful person* | **ukunjufu** | *amiability* |
| -pote-<br>*be lost* | **mpotevu** | *wasteful person* | **upotevu** | *waste, vandalism* |
| -sahau<br>*forget* | **msahaulifu** | *forgetful person* | **usahaulifu** | *forgetfulness* |
| (-sahau is of Arabic origin) | | | | |

and **-e** which, whatever class the noun is in, helps to make nouns that usually denote the thing or person acted upon:

| | | Nouns ending in -e | |
|---|---|---|---|
| -kat- | *cut* | **mkate** (M/MI) | *loaf of bread* |
| -pet- | *bend* | **pete** (N) | *ring* |
| -shind- | *win, beat* | **mshinde** (M/WA) | *loser* |
| -tum- | *send* | **mtume** (M/MI) | *apostle, prophet* |
| -umb- | *create* | **kiumbe** (KI/VI) | *living creature* (including human) |

## 6 Msalkherini – more greetings

Lela's neighbour uses the plural form of an afternoon-and-evening greeting; the standard reply to one person is **Akheri**. The equivalent morning greeting is **Subalkheri** (sing.) and either the same word or **Akheri** is used to reply it.

A greeting which is used at any time of the day is **Salaam aleik** (to one person) or **Salaam aleikum** (to more than one). The standard reply is **Wa aleik salaam** (to one) or **Wa aleikum salaam** (to more than one).

These greetings tend to be used mainly in Muslim communities. Greeting customs can be quite localized, and differences between men's and women's usage and between the usage of older and younger people can vary from one district or town to another.

## Practice

1 Soon after Steve first arrived in Nairobi he happened to meet a group of young athletes who had come from all over Kenya. He asked them where they came from and then had to find out where some of the places are, in relation to Nairobi. Using the map on page 210, fill in the replies to Steve's questions using **kusini ya** (etc.) **Nairobi** (if necessary, look back to page 123).

    a  **Steve**  Nyeri iko wapi?
         **Jibu**   _____.
    b  **Steve**  Magadi iko wapi?
         **Jibu**   _____.
    c  **Steve**  Isiolo iko wapi?
         **Jibu**   _____.

**d Steve** Kitui iko wapi?
  **Jibu** _____.
**e Steve** Narok iko wapi?
  **Jibu** _____.
**f Steve** Eldoret iko wapi?
  **Jibu** _____.

2 During the Mombasa weekend Yusuf drove Steve one hundred or so kilometres along the Mombasa–Malindi road to see the ruins of a fifteenth-century town at Gedi. They also hoped to go swimming at nearby Watamu but unfortunately did not have time, as they were late setting out from Mombasa.

Fill in the gaps in Steve's diary entry for that day; the verb-stems are provided. Note that he refers to *we* all the time and that there are a few places where **-ka-** is appropriate.

> *Jumamosi (-kata) shauri (-enda) Gedi. (-chelewa) kuondoka,*
> *kwa sababu ya wageni wengi waliopo nyumbani. (-ondoka) saa*
> *saba (-enda) Kilifi (-nunua) petroli. Basi, (-endelea) na safari*
> *(-fika) Gedi. Huko Gedi (-angalia) magofu ya msikiti mkubwa,*
> *msikiti mdogo, nyumba mbalimbali na visima. Kwa bahati mbaya*
> *(-pata) nafasi kuogelea Watamu.*

| | |
|---|---|
| **mbalimbali** *various* | **-ogelea** *swim* |
| **visima** (KI/VI) *wells* | |

3 Fill in the Nairobi–Mombasa and Mombasa–Malindi roads on the map on the next page.

4 How well did you understand the dialogue? Fill in the missing words in **a–c**, and give complete answers for **d–f**.

a Ajali ya matatu ilitokea kati ya _____ na
  _____. (*place names*)
b Dereva wa matatu alikuwa amekwenda _____
  _____ ampigie simu mwenye matatu.
c _____ mmoja alikatwa usoni.

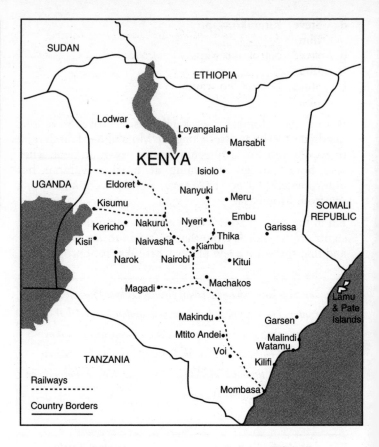

**d** Baada ya kusafisha jeraha na kutia dawa Yusuf alifanya nini?

**e** Wasafiri hao watatu walifanya nini huko Mtito Andei?

**f** Nani yupo hospitalini? (*Begin your answer with* Yupo... .)

5 This is an extract from a folktale about a rich trader – **tajiri** (MA) – who had recently married a second wife. Before going on a journey to buy trade-goods he asked each wife what she would like him to bring back for her. The junior wife asked for a long list of things; the senior wife said he should not go to a lot of trouble but she would like a ring and a *portion of wisdom*, **kipande cha akili** (KI/VI).

> *Basi, tajiri akafunga safari akafika huko alikokuwa akienda.*
> *Kufika huko akanunua vifaa vyake vyote alivyovihitaji kwa duka*
> *lake. Vile vile akanunua vitu vyote kama vile nguo ambavyo bibi*
> *mdogo alimtuma pamoja na pete ya bibi mkubwa. Sasa*
> *akakwama wapi apate kipande cha akili. Akazunguka maduka*
> *yote asipate. Mwishowe hata yeye akaona ni upuuzi kutafuta*
> *kipande hicho.*

| | |
|---|---|
| **-funga safari** | *set off on a journey* |
| **vile vile** | *also* |
| **kama vile** | *such as* |
| **-tuma** | *send (someone) for* |
| **-kwama** | *be stuck, in a fix* |
| **-zunguka** | *go around* |
| **mwishowe** | *finally* |
| **upuuzi** (U) | *nonsense, foolishness* |

Write out the parts of the passage which mean:

a  On arriving there he bought all the utensils he needed for his shop.

b  Now he was in a fix as to where he should get the portion of wisdom.

c  He went round all the shops and did not get it.

6  **Walikuwa wakifanya nini mwaka jana?**  *What were they doing last year?*

Fill in the gaps in these sentences which describe what someone was doing during last year. You will need two verbs for each; the second verb is shown.

a  Mwaka jana Adam (**-soma**) Marekani.

b  Mwaka jana Bw. Yahya (**-fanya**) biashara Malindi.

c  Mwaka uliopita Yusuf (**-kaa**) huko Edinburgh.

d  Mwaka jana Bi. Nuru (**-andika**) kitabu.

e  Mwaka uliopita dada yangu (**-fundisha**) huko Machakos.

7 **Anaumwa shingo! Amekatwa usoni!**

You have just been involved in a road accident. A driver in a passing lorry stops to see if you need help. Write out what you tell him, using the following information. Use -**katwa** and body-part + **ni** for having a cut and -**umwa** and body-part for feeling pain.

*This man's head hurts and the woman has a pain in her neck and shoulders. This child has a cut arm and the one who is sitting over there has a cut on his leg. The driver has a painful chest. Fortunately I'm OK (-**zima**).*

---

**bega** (MA)  *shoulder*          **kifua** (KI/VI)  *chest*

# 15

## katika mbuga ya wanyama
in the game park

**In this unit you will learn**
- how to refer to game animals
- how to use some more colour words
- how to make comparisons
- how to ask for someone's name and address and supply this information about yourself
- how to talk about small and large sizes of things

# ▶ Dialogue

John and Alison are in the Serengeti national park in a four-wheel-drive vehicle with a driver, Robert, and four other visitors, one of whom is Joshua, a Tanzanian journalist. It is the last full day of a five-day safari and, after spending the night in a safari lodge, they will be returning to Arusha. It is late afternoon and Robert has just pulled up not far from a cluster of trees. He notices Alison looking in the notebook where she has been keeping a daily record of the animals she has seen. Robert has a keen sense of humour.

| | |
|---|---|
| **Robert** | Umeona nyumbu wangapi, dada? *(Everyone laughs.)* |
| **Alison** | *(keeping a straight face)* Elfu saba, mia nne, thelathini na mmoja! |
| **Robert** | Ulihesabu kila mmoja? |
| **Alison** | *(laughing)* Kila mmoja. |
| **Joshua** | Kwa kweli sikuona jambo kama tulivyoona asubuhi. Kila tulikokwenda pana nyumbu. Ghafula walikuja – |
| **Robert** | *(whispering)* Tazama pale! |
| **John** | Wapi? |
| **Robert** | Palepale, chini ya mti. |
| **Alison** | Mti upi? |
| **Robert** | Mti ulio mrefu sana. Kuna simba. Wamelala upande wa kulia. |
| **Alison** | Siwaoni. |
| **Robert** | Wamelala kwenye kivuli. Mmoja ni mkubwa kuliko wengine. Ni jike pamoja na watoto wawili. Tazama katikati ya kivuli. Mtaona sehemu yenye rangi ya kahawia-njano; ndiye simba. |
| **Alison** | Ninachokiona ni weusi tu. Sioni simba. Twende karibu kidogo, tupate kuwaona vizuri. |
| **Robert** | Sipendi kuwakurupua. Tusubiri kidogo. Ni desturi yao kuamka wakati huu. Labda wataamka baadaye kidogo. Tukae kimya… |

Two hours later, in the lodge, people are chatting over pre-supper drinks. John seems to have disappeared.

| | |
|---|---|
| **Alison** | Makala ambayo unaiandika inahusu mbuga za wanyama? |
| **Joshua** | Haihusu mbuga tu. Mada nayo ni utalii. Hii ndiyo sababu nitakaa hapa hotelini siku moja zaidi. Hatutaonana kesho asubuhi, maana mtaondoka mapema sana, siyo? |

**Alison**  Sawa. Niambie jina lako kamili, pamoja na anwani yako, nikupelekee picha ambazo nimezipiga leo. (*She gets out her notebook:*) Jina lako nani?

**Joshua**  Jina langu kamili ni Joshua Kisinda; ki-si-nda. Anwani ni hii: Sanduku la Posta, mbili, sita, saba, tisa, sifuri, Dar es Salaam. Utakapopeleka picha lazima uandike anwani yenu.

**Alison**  Kwa nini kamera yako haifanyi kazi leo?

**Joshua**  Bila shaka betri zimekwisha. Kwa bahati ninazo betri spea chumbani mwangu. Nitafurahi sana kupata picha za simba, hasa picha ya yule dume alipowaletea wengine mzoga.

**Alison**  Vilevile nitakupelekea picha zilizopigwa asubuhi, yaani za tembo, nyumbu, punda milia na twiga, pamoja na ile ya joka ambaye tulimwona karibu na jabali kubwa.

**Joshua**  Nitafurahi sana.
(*John comes into the bar.*)

**Alison**  Mbona umechelewa hivi?

**John**  Nilikuwa nikizungumza na Robert. Yuko nje anasafisha gari. Nilimrudishia kijitabu chake cha mbuga za wanyama.

**Joshua**  Mlisoma zile kurasa kuhusu mbuga ya Selous?

**Alison**  Tulisoma, ndiyo. Laiti tungekuwa na nafasi zaidi…

**John**  Na pesa zaidi…

**Alison**  Basi. Mimi nasikia njaa. Twende mezani! Ninyi mnakusudia kukaa hapa baa mpaka saa ya kifunguakinywa?

| | |
|---|---|
| **nyumbu** (N) | *wildebeest (gnu)* |
| **-hesabu** | *count* |
| **kila tulikokwenda** | *everywhere we went* |
| **ghafula** | *suddenly* |
| **mti ulio mrefu sana** | *the tallest tree, the tree which is the tallest* |
| **simba** (N) | *lion* |
| **mmoja ni mkubwa kuliko wengine** | *one is larger than the others* |
| **jike** (JI/MA) (pl. **majike**) | *female* (animal) |
| **kivuli** (KI/VI) | *shadow, shade* |
| **sehemu** (N) | *part, area* |
| **rangi ya kahawia-njano** | *brownish-yellow colour* |
| **ninachokiona ni weusi tu** | *what I see is just blackness (the thing that I see)* **weusi** = **ueusi** |
| **-eusi** | *black* |
| **twende karibu kidogo** | *let's go a bit nearer* |

| | |
|---|---|
| **-karibia** | *go/come near* |
| **tupate kuwaona vizuri** | *so that we manage to see them clearly* |
| **-pata** (= **-wahi**) | *manage, get (to do something)* |
| **-kurupua** | *startle (person, animal) into running away* |
| **desturi** (N) | *custom, habit* |
| **-amka** | *wake up* |
| **kimya** | *quietly (also silence, quiet)* |
| **makala** (N) | *article (journalistic, academic)* |
| **-husu** | *concern* |
| **mbuga ya wanyama** (N) | *game park/reserve* |
| **mada nayo ni utalii** | *the actual topic is tourism* |
| **mada** (N) | *topic* |
| **jina lako kamili** | *your full name* |
| **anwani** (N) | *address* |
| **-piga picha** | *take photograph(s)* |
| **picha** | *picture, photograph* |
| **jina lako nani?** | *what is your name?* |
| **sifuri** (N) | *nought, zero* |
| **kamera** (N) | *camera* |
| **betri** | *battery* |
| **dume** (MA) | *male (animal)* |
| **mzoga** (M/MI) | *carcass* |
| **vilevile** | *also* |
| **yaani** | *that is (to say), i.e.* |
| **tembo** (N), also **ndovu** (N) | *elephant* |
| **punda milia** (N) | *zebra* |
| **twiga** (N) | *giraffe* |
| **joka** (JI/MA) | *large snake* |
| **jabali** (MA) | *rock, rocky outcrop* |
| **-rudishia** | *return (something to someone)* |
| **kijitabu** (KI/VI) | *pamphlet, booklet* |
| **ukurasa** (U/N) | *page* |
| **laiti** | *if only* |
| **mezani** | *to the dining room* |
| **meza** (N) | *table* |
| **kifunguakinywa** (KI/VI), | *breakfast* |
| | *also* **chamshakinywa** (KI/VI) |

A plausible scenario to account for how John and Alison got to the game park with a group is that they encountered the other four travellers in the office of one of the tour companies in Arusha; the six of them decided to team up in order to keep the cost down.

The five-day safari included the Lake Manyara national park and the Ngorongoro crater, which is in a conservation area bordering the Serengeti. The party decided to book rooms in safari lodges in preference to the (cheaper) alternative of making overnight stops at designated self-catering campsites.

Of all the Tanzanian national parks and game reserves the Selous, mentioned by Joshua, the journalist in the dialogue, is the largest. It lies south-west of Dar es Salaam, which is where the relevant tour companies are located.

| | |
|---|---|
| **kampuni ya safari** (N) | *tour company* |
| **mwandishi habari** (M/WA) | *journalist* |
| These might also be useful: | |
| **hema** (N) | *tent* |
| **-piga hema** | *pitch a tent* |
| **msimamizi wa safari** (M/WA) | *tour organizer* |

# Grammar

## 1 Kila tulikokwenda – kila used without a noun

**a** Of the three relative pronouns of place, **-ko-**, **-po-** and **-mo**, **-ko-** is the least definite, and so is the most suitable one to use for a *wherever* function. Joshua had no particular place in mind when he said this so there is no noun denoting place following **kila**. As the noun **mahali**, *place*, need not mean one particular place, he could also have said:

Kila mahali tulipokwenda . . .    *Every place (where) we went. . .*

or

Kila tulipokwenda. . .    *Everywhere we went. . .*

If you want to make a general statement, not tied to a particular time, you should use the 'general' or 'tenseless' relative structure, in which the relative pronoun goes on the end of the verb-stem:

kila tuendako    *wherever we go*

**b** Remember that **-po-** has another function; it is also a relative pronoun of time, as in:

tulipokwenda                    *when we went*

Using **kila** you can say:

kila aliposema                  *whenever he spoke*
kila watakapo                   *whenever they want/like*

The 'missing' noun would be a time-word, such as **mara**:

kila mara aliposema             *every time he spoke*

**c** It is not only nouns of place and time that can be omitted:

kila asemalo                    *everything he says*

The most likely candidate for the 'missing' noun here, which must be a JI/MA singular because of the relative pronoun being **-lo** (from **li + o**) is **neno** (*word* or *utterance*).

## 2 Bigger and biggest – making comparisons

**a** One way of expressing that one thing is bigger, better, longer, more expensive, etc. than another is to use **kuliko**. The first of the examples is from the dialogue:

Mmoja ni mkubwa kuliko          *One is larger than the others.*
   wengine.
Kikapu chako ni kikubwa         *Your basket is larger than hers.*
   kuliko chake.
Mnazi ni mrefu kuliko           *The coconut palm is taller than*
   mchungwa.                       *the orange tree.*

You can also use **zaidi**, *more*, immediately after the adjective and before **kuliko**:

Mmoja ni mkubwa zaidi kuliko wengine.

If you just want to say *one is bigger* use **zaidi** without **kuliko**:

Mmoja ni mkubwa zaidi.

Other ways of expressing a comparison use verbs:

**-zidi** (related to **zaidi**)   *exceed, increase*
**-shinda**                        *surpass, beat*
**-pita**                          *surpass, outstrip*

| | |
|---|---|
| Kikapu chako ni kikubwa kuzidi chake | *Your basket is larger than hers.* (Your basket is large to exceed hers.) |
| Kikapu chako ni kikubwa kushinda chake | *Your basket is larger than hers.* (Your basket is large to beat hers.) |

**b** To say that something is the biggest, best, longest, most expensive, etc., you can either use **sana** as in the example from the dialogue:

| | |
|---|---|
| Mti ulio mrefu sana. | *The tallest tree.* (The tree which is very tall.) |

or **mno,** as in:

| | |
|---|---|
| Nipe papai lililo kubwa mno. | *Give me the largest pawpaw (papaya).* (Give me the pawpaw that is extremely large.) |

Notice the use of **ulio** and **lililo,** *which is* in the last two examples; these relative structures help to make the thing referred to, the tallest tree and the largest papaya, definite.

A note about **mno:** in other circumstances **mno** can mean *too,* as in:

| | |
|---|---|
| Sipendi papai hili, ni dogo mno. | *I don't want this pawpaw, it's too small.* |

The context will usually tell you whether someone means *extremely* or *too.*

You can also use the verb **-shinda,** together with **-ote,** like this:

| | |
|---|---|
| Kikapu chako ni kikubwa kushinda vikapu vyote. | *Your basket is the largest of all the baskets.* (Your basket is large to surpass all the baskets.) |

It is not necessary to use the plural noun after **kushinda;** **-ote** can stand on its own to represent the noun:

| | |
|---|---|
| Kikapu chako ni kikubwa kushinda vyote. | *Your basket is the largest of all.* |
| Papai lile ni kubwa kushinda yote. | *That pawpaw is the largest of all.* |
| Joseph ni mrefu kushinda wote? | *Is Joseph the tallest of them all?* |

c To express that one thing is the same as another with regard to a particular attribute, use either **sawa na**:

| | |
|---|---|
| Paka huyu ni mkubwa sawa na yule. | *This cat is as large as that one.* |
| Paka huyu ni sawa na yule kwa ukubwa. | *This cat is the same size as that one.* |

or **kama**:

| | |
|---|---|
| Paka huyu ni mkubwa kama yule. | *This cat is as big as that one.* |
| Paka huyu ni kama yule kwa ukubwa. | *This cat is the same size as that one.* |

## 3 Mada nayo ni utalii – using na- for emphasis

Although this structure literally means *The topic and it is tourism*, the function of **nayo** here is rather like that of *actual* in the English sentence *The actual topic is tourism*. **Nayo** emphasizes **mada**. In the same way, **naye** emphasizes **dereva** in the Unit 14 dialogue. These verb-prefix + **o** forms attached to **na-** are already familiar to you, but for other functions.

In connection with their emphatic function, notice that they can also be used to mean *too*, *also*, *as well*:

| | |
|---|---|
| Watalii nao walimpa dereva zawadi. | **a** *The tourists* (+ emphasis) *gave the driver a present.* |
| | **b** *The tourists too gave the driver a present* (in addition to the others who gave him one). |
| Mwalimu naye alikwenda nao. | **a** *The teacher* (+ emphasis) *went with them.* |
| | **b** *The teacher went with them as well* (in addition to the others, e.g. parents, who went with them). |

On its own, **na** can be used to emphasize an action when the verb is in the subjunctive, the **-e**, form; **na** precedes the verb:

| | |
|---|---|
| Basi, bila kupoteza wakati na tuanze. | *Right, without wasting time let's begin.* |

## 4 Jina lako nani? *What's your name?*

As you are an English-speaker, you might have expected *What is your name?* to have **nini?** *what?*, rather than **nani?** *who?* This is a small reminder about keeping an open mind when extending your knowledge of Swahili!

If you are asked your name by someone who is going to write it down, you can avoid confusion over spelling it out by offering to write it yourself.

> **Niandike mwenyewe?** *Shall I write it myself?*

*Note*: When trying to ensure that their names get recorded correctly, Swahili speakers usually 'spell' them out syllable by syllable, as Joshua does in the dialogue.

## 5 JI/MA to denote large size – augmentatives

In order to refer to a large or important version of something the noun-stem is put into the JI/MA class like this:

**a** If the noun-stem begins with a vowel, or is a single syllable, **ji-** is prefixed to it, for both singulars and plurals: the **ma-** plural prefix goes in front of **ji-**. The first example is from the dialogue. You may remember **jumba** from the second dialogue in Unit 6.

| | | | | | |
|---|---|---|---|---|---|
| nyoka | snake | joka | large snake | majoka | large snakes |
| nyumba | house | jumba | large building | majumba | large buildings |
| kisu | knife | jisu | large knife | majisu | large knives |
| mtu | person | jitu | giant | majitu | giants |
| mji | town | jiji | city | majiji | cities |

**b** Other types of noun-stem are used in the JI/MA class by losing their singular prefix (if they have one) and having **ma-** as their plural prefix.

| | | | | | |
|---|---|---|---|---|---|
| mdudu | insect | dudu | large insect, pest | madudu | large insects, pests |
| mbuzi | goat | buzi | large goat | mabuzi | large goats |
| kikapu | basket | kapu | large basket | makapu | large baskets |
| paka | cat | paka | large cat | mapaka | large cats |

The augmentative forms denoting people usually take the M/WA class agreement-prefixes on qualifiers and the verb, unless the speaker is making a derogatory statement.

## 6 KI/VI to denote small size: diminutives

To refer to a small or insignificant version of something a noun-stem is put into the KI/VI class like this:

**a** If the noun-stem begins with a vowel or is just one syllable or the noun is already in the KI/VI class the prefixes have to be **kiji-** and **viji-**. The first example is from the dialogue:

| kitabu | book | kijitabu | booklet | vijitabu | booklets |
|--------|------|----------|---------|----------|----------|
| nyoka | snake | kijoka | small snake | vijoka | small snakes |
| mji | town | kijiji | village | vijiji | village |
| mti | tree | kijiti | small stick | vijiti | small sticks |
| mwana | child (of) | kijana | youth | vijana | youths |
| mwiko | wooden cooking spoon | kijiko | spoon | vijiko | spoons |

**b** Other stems take the **ki-** (singular) and **vi-** (plural) prefixes. The first example comes from the dialogue:

| uvuli | shade (in general) | kivuli | shadow, shade | vivuli | shadows |
|-------|--------------------|--------|---------------|--------|---------|
| kombe | serving dish challenge cup | kikombe | cup | vikombe | cups |
| mlima | mountain | kilima | hill | vilima | hills |
| mtoto | child | kitoto | small baby | vitoto | small babies |
| ngoma | drum | kigoma | small drum | vigoma | small drums |

Note: KI/VI nouns denoting people should usually be used with M/WA class agreement-prefixes on qualifiers and the verb unless some special emphasis, such as endearment, is intended. Note that **kitoto** is used only of an unusually small baby, e.g. a premature one, in which case the KI/VI prefixes would be used throughout the sentence. A baby of normal size is **mtoto mchanga**.

# 7  -piga picha, -piga hema – verbs made with -piga + noun

The verb -**piga**, meaning *hit* or *beat* on its own, can be used with a variety of following nouns to form many verb-meanings. As well as the two verbs given above, used in this unit, you should also know -**piga simu** *make a telephone call*, introduced in Unit 3. Here are a few more:

| | |
|---|---|
| -**piga hodi** | *call hodi outside someone's door* |
| -**piga deki** | *wash the floor* |
| -**piga pasi** | *iron (e.g. clothes)* |
| -**piga mstari** | *draw a line* |
| -**piga makofi** | *clap* |
| -**piga magoti** | *kneel* |
| -**piga chafya** | *sneeze* |
| -**piga miayo** | *yawn* |
| -**piga kelele** | *make a noise* |
| -**piga mbio** | *run* |
| -**piga maji** | *be roaring drunk* |
| -**piga bao** | *consult omens, with a divining board* |
| -**piga kura** | *vote* |
| -**piga chapa** | *print* |
| -**piga soga** | *chat, gossip* |

# 8  More colour adjectives

The two colours mentioned in the dialogue are:

| | |
|---|---|
| kahawia-njano | *brownish-yellow* |
| weusi (u-eusi) | *blackness* |

**Kahawia** is a word for *brown*; there is another word with the same meaning – **hudhurungi**. The other half of the compound **kahawia-njano** is part of the word for *yellow*, **manjano**, which also means *turmeric*. The only one of these colour adjectives that takes an agreement-prefix to match its noun is -**eusi**. Another colour adjective that does not need an agreement-prefix is **zambarau**, *purple*.

# Practice

1 This is part of a letter Joshua wrote to a friend referring to one morning's activities in the national park. Write a similar account of your own experience, using the information below, including the types and numbers of animals seen.

> *Tuliondoka saa mbili tukaenda mpaka mtoni. Kati ya saa tatu na saa nne u nusu tuliona tembo watatu, twiga wawili na punda milia sita. Kwa bahati mbaya hatukuona simba yeyote. Tulirudi hotelini saa tano na nusu tukanywa soda.*

*You set off at 7.30 a.m., returned to the hotel (safari lodge) at midday and had a beer.*

2

7

5

wengi

2 How well have you understood the dialogue? Answer the first question in English. Notice that the questions all refer to the past.

a How many wildebeest did Alison tell Robert she had seen?
b Simba walikuwapo wapi?
c Alison alipenda kufanya nini?
d Robert hakupenda kufanya nini?
e Kwa nini kamera ya Joshua haikufanya kazi?
f Alison alisema atampelekea Joshua vitu gani?

3 After he returned to Dar es Salaam, Joshua had his camera stolen and went to the local police station to report the theft. Fill in Joshua's part of the conversation from the information in the dialogue and the clues given here.

| Askari-polisi | Jina lako nani? |
|---|---|
| Joshua | _____. |
| Askari-polisi | Anwani yako? |
| Joshua | (*Write the P.O. Box no. in figures.*) |
| Askari-polisi | Namba ya simu? |
| Joshua | (*Say your phone number is 35602: write it in words.*) |
| Askari-polisi | Unafanya kazi gani? |
| Joshua | (*Say you are a journalist.*) |
| Askari-polisi | Uliibiwa lini? |
| Joshua | (*Say you were robbed that morning.*) |
| Askari-polisi | Saa ngapi? |
| Joshua | (*Say 11.20.*) |
| Askari-polisi | Ulikuwa wapi? |
| Joshua | (*Say you were at Kariakoo.*) |
| Askari-polisi | Uliibiwa kitu gani? |
| Joshua | (*Say you were robbed of a camera.*) |

4

Koku     Bhoke     Aranya

The three women above are often seen together at Joshua's local market in Dar es Salaam. His wife has sometimes mentioned their names but he cannot yet identify them correctly. She makes another attempt to help him match names and people. This is what she says. You fill in the names.

| **-nene** | *fat* |
|---|---|

_____ ni mrefu sana; kwa kweli ni mrefu kushinda wote. _____ ni mfupi kuliko _____, lakini mwanamke ambaye ni mfupi mno ni _____. Kusema kweli, _____ ni mwembamba mno, na_____ ni mnene kushinda wote. Kikapu chake _____ ni sawa na kikapu cha Aranya. Kilicho kikubwa sana ni kikapu chake _____.

5   Fill in the gaps. The missing words in **a–d** are augmentatives and in **e–h** diminutives. Re-read Grammar sections 5 and 6 first; they contain all the words you will need.

   a   Rais hukaa kwenye _____ kubwa.
   b   Joshua anakaa katika _____ la Dar es Salaam.
   c   Bwana yule ni mkubwa mno, tena mrefu sana, hata watoto wanafikiri ni _____.
   d   Wakati wa safari Alison pamoja na wenziwe waliona _____ karibu na jabali.
   e   Koroga chai kwa _____ hiki!
   f   _____ chao kilizaliwa mwezi uliopita. (*She was born prematurely.*)
   g   Mwalimu huwafundisha watoto namna ya kuhesabu anatumia _____ hivi vya rangi.
   h   John amesoma _____ chake Robert.

6   Some of the words in John's hastily pencilled note about the leopard have become obliterated. Help him to reconstruct his notes by filling in the missing words from the list at the end.

| **chui** (N) *leopard* | **-erevu** *cunning* |
|---|---|
| **doa** (MA) *spot, mark* | **-winda** *hunt* |

*Kwa rangi chui ni manjano, mwenye madoa _____.*
*Wakati wa mchana hulala katika _____. Mnyama*
*huyu ni mwerevu sana katika kuwinda wanyama _____*
*Huwinda wakati wa _____.*

| wadogo | meusi | miti | usiku |
|---|---|---|---|

## Utakwenda mbuga ya wanyama?

If so, you might like to learn a few more words for animals you are likely to see.

| | |
|---|---|
| **duma** (N) | *cheetah* |
| **fisi** (N) | *hyena* |
| **kiboko** (KI/VI) | *hippo* |
| **kifaru** (KI/VI) | *rhino* |
| **kima** (N) | various kinds of small monkey |
| **kuru** (N) | *waterbuck* |
| **ngiri** (N) | *warthog* |
| **nyani** (N) | *baboon* |
| **swala** (N) | *gazelle* |
| **swalatomi** (N) | *Thomson's gazelle* |
| **tumbili** (or **tumbiri**) (N) | *vervet monkey* |

# 16

## mlimani:
## kuna nini?

on the mountain: what's the matter?

**In this unit you will learn**
- how to ask what is the matter, what's wrong
- some more expressions describing symptoms and pain
- how to refer to people's ages.
- how to refer to causing something to happen
- how to warn people/someone against doing domething

# ▶ Dialogue

Steve is visiting Tanzania again and is about 4,000 metres up Mt Kilimanjaro with a group of friends, a mountain guide and two porters. They are walking across a fairly flat area on their way to the top hut. Steve and Dominic, the guide, are slightly ahead of the others.

**Dominic**    Natumaini karibu tutawaona kundi la watu wanaoshuka. Kiongozi wao ni ndugu yangu. Ndipo tutapata habari ya hali ya hewa huko juu, hasa hali ya theluji.

**Steve**    Tutafika Kibanda cha Kibo saa ngapi?

**Dominic**    Labda tutafika kunako saa kumi. Inategemea mwendo wetu. Tusiende haraka. Kwa bahati mmeanza kwenda polepole sasa!

**Steve**    Si kama siku ya kwanza. Siku ile tulipokuwa tukipita mwituni tulisahau kabisa ushauri wako. Ingawa ulituonya tusiende kwa haraka, kwa kuwa sisi sote ni wazima hatuna neno, tulianza kwenda mbio.

    (*Dominic turns round to check that the others are following.*)

**Dominic**    Kumbe wamesimama! Paul amekaa chini. Basi, tukamwangalie.

    (*They walk back to the others.*)

**Dominic**    Kuna nini?

**Jane**    Paul hawezi! Kichwa kinamwuma, tena amepatwa na kichefuchefu.

    (*Paul shows them his hands.*)

**Steve**    Mikono imefura.

**Paul**    (*trying to joke*) Shauri ya uzee...

**Jane**    Si shauri ya uzee. Una miaka arobaini tu.

**Dominic**    Ugonjwa huu hauhusu umri hata kidogo. Umetapika?

**Paul**    Ndiyo. Nimetapika.

**Steve**    Tumsaidie vipi?

**Dominic**    Tumpe maji. Anywe maji kidogo.

**Paul**    Sipendi maji zaidi. Nimekunywa mengi. Lazima niendelee. Sitaki kuwachelewesha.

**Dominic**    Tumpe tunda. Mna matunda? Wapagazi wanabeba matunda katika mizigo, lakini sipendi kufungua mizigo sasa.

**Steve**    Mimi nina tofaa. Tukate vipandevipande. Kisu changu kimeingia kutu. Nani ana kisu safi?

**Dominic**    (*offering his penknife*) Kata kwa kisu hiki. Angalia! Ni kikali sana. Usijikate mkono.

(*Paul tries to eat a piece of apple, but feels sick again*.)

**Dominic** Lazima ashuke mpaka Horombo. Hawezi kupona hapa. Avute pumzi mahali panapo oksijeni zaidi.

**Jane** Basi, niende naye. Tushuke pamoja.

**Paul** La! La! Uendelee kupanda juu na wenzako...

(*Dominic looks ahead and sees a group of climbers in the far distance coming towards them on their way down the mountain*.)

**Dominic** Tazama kulee! Ni wale wanaorudi Horombo. Paul, afadhali uende nao. Kiongozi ni ndugu yangu, atakusaidia. Ukae Horombo siku mbili. Sisi tutarudi huko kesho jioni. Kesho kutwa sisi sote tutashuka chini pamoja. Unakubali? Utafikiri marafiki zako wamekutupa?

**Paul** Sitafikiri hivyo. Nitafurahi kushuka kidogo. Mahali hapa ni kama jangwa, lakini baridi.

(*They sit and wait for the other party to reach them*.)

| | |
|---|---|
| **-tumaini** | *hope, expect* |
| **karibu** | *soon* |
| **kundi** (MA) | *group* |
| **-shuka** | *descend* |
| **kiongozi** (KI/VI) | *guide, leader* |
| **hali ya hewa** (N) | *weather (lit. state of the air)* |
| **hewa** (N) | *air* |
| **theluji** (N) | *snow* |
| **Kibanda cha Kibo** | *Kibo Hut (the top hut)* |
| **kunako** | *at about* |
| **Inategemea mwendo wetu** | *It depends on our speed* |
| **bahati (kwa** is sometimes omitted) | *fortunately* |
| **tulipokuwa tukipita mwituni** | *when we were going through the forest* |
| **-pita** | *go along, through, by* |
| **mwitu** (M/MI) | *forest* |
| **ushauri** (U) | *advice* |
| **ingawa** | *although* |
| **ulituonya tusiende kwa haraka** | *you warned us not to go quickly* |
| **-onya** | *warn* |
| **kwa kuwa** | *because* |
| **sisi sote ni wazima** | *we were all fine (with)* |
| **hatuna neno** | *no problem* |
| **Kumbe ...!** | *an expression of surprise* |

| | |
|---|---|
| **Kuna nini?** | *What's the matter?* |
| **Kichwa kinamwuma** | *his head is hurting* (lit. head is hurting him) |
| **amepatwa na kichefuchefu** | *he feels nauseous* (lit. he has been overcome by nausea) |
| **-fura** | *swell up* |
| **Shauri ya uzee\*** | *It's to do with old age* |
| **Una miaka arobaini tu** | *You're only forty* |
| **umri** (U) | *age* |
| **hata kidogo** | *(not) at all* (only used after negatives) |
| **-tapika** | *vomit* |
| **vipi?** | *how?* |
| **-chelewesha** | *make* (people) *late* |
| **wapagazi** (M/WA) | *porters* |
| **-beba** | *carry* |
| **tofaa** (MA) | *apple* |
| **Kisu changu kimeingia kutu** | *My knife is rusty* |
| **Ni kikali sana** | *It's very sharp* |
| **Usijikate mkono** | *Don't cut your hand* |
| **Horombo** | *Horombo Hut* |
| **-pona** | *get better* |
| **-vuta pumzi** | *breathe in* |
| **mahali panapo oksijeni zaidi** | *a place that has more oxygen* |
| **oksijeni** (N) | *oxygen* |
| **-panda** | *climb up* |
| **kulee** (**kule** with a lengthened **e**; the longer the **e** the greater the distance referred to) | *right over there, in the distance* |
| **-tupa** | *abandon* (lit. throw) |
| **jangwa** (JI/MA) | *desert* |

\*For this function **shauri** is used in the N class.

# ℹ️ Mlimani

The location of the dialogue is the barren expanse of land between Kibo and Mawenzi peaks known as the Saddle, which has to be crossed by climbers using the Marangu route up Kilimanjaro. It seems interminable and Paul is not far wrong in comparing it to a desert.

Paul's symptoms are among the classic ones of mountain sickness, caused by shortage of oxygen. Dominic, as an experienced guide, can see that Paul is suffering from a particularly acute attack and will only recover by descending to a lower altitude. This sickness can be experienced by anyone, regardless of age or climbing experience. You can reduce the likelihood of getting it by walking slowly and first spending a few days acclimatizing on the lower slopes, in one of the hotels, guest houses or camp sites outside the national park area.

Maasai men a few miles from the foot of Mt. Kilimanjaro

# Grammar

## 1 Kunako, panapo, mnamo – Time and place

In the dialogue **kunako** refers to time and **panapo** refers to place. All three forms are general or 'tenseless' relatives, with the place prefix attached to -**na**- and the relative pronoun -**ko** (from **ku + o**), -**po** (from **pa + o**) or -**mo** (from **mu + o**) coming at the end. They can all be used to refer to time as well as place. There is generally less distinction between their meanings when used with time expressions than with expressions referring to a place; for some speakers they are more or less interchangeable, for others **mnamo** implies more precision in the time reference than the other two.

**Time:**

| | |
|---|---|
| kunako jioni | *some time during the evening* |
| panapo saa sita | *at about 12 o'clock* |
| mnamo saa tisa | *at about 3 o'clock* |

**Place:**

| | |
|---|---|
| Atatafuta kazi huko kunako mahoteli mengi. | *He will look for work there where there are a lot of hotels.* (at some place which has...) |
| Tukae pale panapo kivuli. | *Let's sit over there where there is some shade.* (in the place which has...) |
| Tia mnamo maji. | *Put (it) where there is some water.* (inside which has...) |

# 2 Ulituonya tusiende – warning against, forbidding and preventing actions

Verbs meaning *warn against*, *forbid* or *prevent* an action require the following verb, the verb denoting the unwise or forbidden action, to be in its negative subjunctive form. Two verbs of this kind are:

| | |
|---|---|
| **-kataza**  *forbid* | **-zuia**  *prevent* |

| | |
|---|---|
| Ametukataza tusiende haraka. | *He has forbidden us to go quickly.* |

(Notice that **haraka** is sometimes used without **kwa** in front of it, when it means *quickly*).

| | |
|---|---|
| Walimzuia asianguke. | *They prevented her from falling.* |

# 3 Kichwa kinamwuma
## *His head hurts* – and other pains

**a** This is another way of expressing the same general meaning as **anaumwa kichwa** (see Unit 14), but putting **kichwa** first, as the subject of the verb, focuses attention on the person's head. Notice that you do not need words for his/her, my, your, etc. Instead, you use the object-marker referring to the person who is feeling pain:

| | |
|---|---|
| Mkono unaniuma. | *My hand hurts.* |
| Miguu inakuuma? | *Do your feet/legs hurt?* |
| Mgongo unamwuma. | *His back hurts.* |
| Bega linaniuma. | *My shoulder hurts.* |

Here are a few more words for parts of the body:

| | | | | |
|---|---|---|---|---|
| **kidole** (KI/VI) | *finger* | | **mdomo** (M/MI) | *lip* |
| **kinywa** (KI/VI) | *mouth* | | **pua** (N) | *nose* |
| **koo** (MA) | *throat* | | **tumbo** (MA) | *stomach* |

**b** A similar structure, using the object-marker for the person, with no possessive for the body-part, is:

| | |
|---|---|
| Damu inamtoka kichwani. | *He is bleeding from the head.* |
| Damu inamtoka. | *He is bleeding.* |

With rather less emphasis on the extent of the bleeding you can also say:

| | |
|---|---|
| Anatoka damu puani. | *His nose is bleeding.* |
| Anatoka damu. | *He is bleeding.* |

| | | | |
|---|---|---|---|
| **-toka damu** | *bleed* | **damu** (N) | *blood* |

**c Usijikate mkono**   *don't cut your hand*

This example from the dialogue also uses the object-marker for the person; the word for the body-part is just tacked on at the end. The object-marker here is **-ji-** because the subject and the object refer to the same person. Interpreted literally, the sentence means: *Do not cut yourself (-ji) as far as your hand is concerned.*

Here are a few examples in which subject and object are not the same.

| | |
|---|---|
| Usimkate mkono. | *Don't cut his hand.* |
| Asimkate kichwa. | *Don't let her cut his head.* |
| Nisimkate kidole. | *Don't let me cut his finger.* |

## 4 Amepatwa na kichefuchefu – and other attacks

**a** The passive form of **-pata**, *get*, is a very common way of referring to someone having been *seized/assailed/overcome* by an illness. Another verb which is used for the same purpose is:

| | |
|---|---|
| **-shika** | *grasp, hold, seize* |

| | |
|---|---|
| Mtoto wake Juma amepatwa na homa. | *Juma's child has got a fever/ high temperature.* |
| Bahati mbaya wachezaji wawili wameshikwa na malaria. | *Unfortunately two players have gone down with malaria.* |
| Siku zile wengi walipatwa na kipindupindu. | *In those days many contracted cholera.* |

The use of this structure implies a rather more serious view of the illness, or the sudden nature of the attack, than is implied by the use of **ana homa**, etc.

**b** Some illnesses are described by means of a verb, or a verb-phrase (verb + noun).

| | |
|---|---|
| **-hara** *have diarrhoea* | **-hara damu** *have dysentery* |

| | |
|---|---|
| Kwa kuwa mtoto anahara wamempelekea zahanati. | *Because the child has diarrhoea they have taken him to the clinic.* |

**zahanati** (N) *dispensary, clinic*   **kliniki** (N) is also sometimes used

## 5 Una miaka arobaini tu *You're only forty*

In Swahili you talk about someone having a certain age, and there are two ways of asking how old someone is.

| | |
|---|---|
| Ana umri gani? | *What age is he?* |
| Ana umri wa miaka ishirini. | *He is twenty.* |
| Ana miaka mingapi? | *How old is she?* |
| Ana miaka hamsini na mitano. | *She is fifty-five.* |
| Mzee aliyefariki Jumatano, alikuwa na umri gani? | *The old man who passed away on Wednesday, how old was he?* |

| | |
|---|---|
| **-fariki** | *die* (used only of humans, like 'pass away', 'pass on') |
| **-fa** | *die* (can be used for humans and animals) |

## 6 Vipi? *How?*

There is another example of **vipi** in Grammar section 6 of Unit 11. It is made up of the **vi-** prefix of manner attached to **-pi**. When prefixed by a verb-prefix, **-pi** means *which... ?* as in **baa**

**ipi?** (see Unit 2 Practice question 5), **mtoto yupi?** *which child?* **tofaa lipi?** *which apple?* etc.

So **vipi?** literally means *in which manner?*

| | |
|---|---|
| Nitapika vipi bila ya maji? | *How shall I cook without water?* |
| Tuanze vipi kazi hii? | *How should we start this work?* |

## 7 Sitaki kuwachelewesha – the causative form of verbs

You have already had some forms of the verb in which the meaning is given an extra function when you add a particular vowel or consonant, or both, to the root or to a 'special function' form that has already been added to the root.

The causative form works in this way, and is used to express a range of meanings, not just the meaning of causing something to happen, but also of making/helping/encouraging/letting someone do something.

The extra sound which makes a verb causative is either -**sh**- or -**z**- or, in a few cases, -**y**-. You should be able to recognize quite a few verbs among the examples below, including some causatives which have occurred in earlier units. When an extra vowel is needed it is either -**i**- or -**e**-, according to the rule given in Unit 4 for the prepositional form of the verbs, and referred to again for statives in Unit 12.

**a** In most verbs where the final consonant is -**k**- it changes into -**sh**- to make the causative form. The -**k**- might be the final consonant of the root, or it might be the stative ending as in the case of -**waka** which is the stative form of -**waa**, a verb hardly used any more. Not all -**k**- verbs behave like this, though, for example the roots of -**andika** and -**cheka** in the list below.

| | | **-sh-** | |
|---|---|---|---|
| -amk- | *wake up* | -amsha | *wake (someone) up* |
| -andik- | *write* | -andikisha | *register* |
| -chek- | *laugh* | -chekesha | *amuse* |
| -chelew- | *be late* | -chelewesha | *delay (someone)* |
| -chemk- | *be boiling* | -chemsha | *boil (something)* |
| -kop- | *borrow* | -kopesha | *lend* |
| -kumbuk- | *remember* | -kumbusha | *remind* |
| -wak- | *be lit, burning* | -washa | *light (lamp), switch on, kindle a fire* |
| -wez- | *be able* | -wezesha | *enable, empower* |

One reason why the -sh- form is the one you are likely to use most frequently is that it is used for making nouns, adjectives and adverbs into causative verbs:

| bahati | *luck* | -bahatisha | *try one's luck, guess* |
| fupi | *short* | -fupisha | *shorten* |
| hakika | *certainty* | -hakikisha | *make sure* |
| safi | *clean* | -safisha | *clean* (something) |
| sahihi | *correct, correctly* | -sahihisha | *correct errors* |
| sawa | *equal* | -sawazisha | *equalize* |
| tayari | *ready* | -tayarisha | *get ready* |

Just as -k- turns into -sh- to make the causative form of some of the verbs in the first group above, so -l- turns into -z- in many of the verbs in the next group. It so happens that the -l- has long since disappeared from the end of many verb-roots; the exception here is -lal-, which still has its final -l-.

|  |  | -z- |  |
| --- | --- | --- | --- |
| -ele- | *be clear, understood* | -eleza | *explain to* |
| -ja- | *be full* | -jaza | *fill* (something) *up* |
| -kata- | *refuse, decline* | -kataza | *forbid, prohibit* |
| -kimbi- | *run away* | -kimbiza | *chase* |
| -lal- | *lie down* | -laza | *lay down, put to bed* |
| -pungu- | *get less* | -punguza | *make less, reduce* |
| -ugu- | *be ill* | -uguza | *nurse* (a sick person) |
| -um- | *hurt* | -umiza | *cause pain to* |

Not quite all verbs that have lost their root-final -l- put -z- where the -l- used to be. In a few verbs the -l- is 'put back' and either -sh- or -z- is used for the causative, preceded by the appropriate vowel:

| -ju- | *know* | -julisha | *inform* |
| -ka- | *sit* | -kalisha | *get* (s.one) *to sit down* |
| -za- | *give birth* | -zalisha | *assist at a birth* |

Only verb-roots with -n- as the final consonant take the -y- form of the causative:

| | | -y- | |
|-------|----------|-----------|--------------------------|
| -gawan- | *share* | -gawanya | *divide up, share out* |
| -kan- | *deny* | -kanya | *reprimand* |
| -on- | *see* | -onya | *warn* |
| -pon- | *get well* | -ponya | *cure* |

Notice that **-ona** has two causative forms, the one given here and **-onyesha**, *show*. The reciprocal verb **-gawana** is one of the few exceptions to the rule given in section **b** below.

**b** The causative form of reciprocal verbs.
Verbs in their reciprocal form (see Unit 13) have **-n-** as their final consonant, but nearly always make their causative form with **-sh-**:

| -patan- | *be in agreement* | -patanisha | *reconcile people* |
|----------|----------------------------|-------------|-----------------------------------------------|
| -pendan- | *love, like each other* | -pendanisha | *reconcile, promote harmony between people* |
| -pigan- | *fight* | -piganisha | *cause a fight* |

**c** The causative form of monosyllabic verbs.
Only about half of the monosyllabic verbs have causative forms and not all of those are in common use. The most useful ones are:

| -l- | *eat* | -lisha | *feed* (someone) |
|-------|---------|-----------|-------------------------------------------|
| -nyw- | *drink* | -nywesha | *give a drink to, supply with liquid* |

Utawalisha watoto hapa?     *Will you feed the children here?*
Tuliwanywesha wagonjwa maji. *We got the sick people to drink some water.*

## 8 Kisu changu kimeingia kutu – colloquial usage

If you think of **-ingia** as including among its meanings *enter into a state*, it is easier to understand the above example from the dialogue, as well as similar examples in which the subject and object of **-ingia** seem, to English-speakers, to be the wrong way round. Note that **kutu** is an N class noun, meaning *rust*.

| Miguu imeingia baridi. | *(My) feet have become cold.* |
| Nchi ile imeingia homa ya kuhara. | *That country (or area) has an outbreak of typhoid.* |
| Mji umeingia watalii. | *The town is overrun with tourists.* |

Another verb that describes a state is **-jaa**. It makes no difference to the basic meaning which noun is at the front, as the subject:

| Kisima kimejaa maji. Maji yamejaa kisima. } | *The well is full of water.* |

Here are a few more examples of colloquial usage:

| Wamekwenda kuitwa. | *Someone has gone to call them./ They are being called now.* |
| Kuni zimekwenda kukatwa. | *Someone has gone to cut firewood./ Firewood is being cut now.* |
| Basi moja inapanda watu mia na hamsini! | *A hundred and fifty people climb on to one bus!* |

Sentences like the last example are likely to occur in only the most casual sort of conversation, when the speaker is talking in an entertaining way and even, as here, exaggerating. The speaker is focusing attention on the state of the buses in a place he has visited. It is not advisable for beginners to attempt sentences like the last one; just note that they occasionally occur.

If these structures seem a little strange to you, remember that in English we can say: *This tent sleeps four, Your essay reads well, Flight 194 is boarding now*, etc.

# Practice

1   When Steve returned to Nairobi after climbing Kilimanjaro, Adam plied him with questions. Fill in the gaps in the conversation, writing any figures in words.

---

**kilele** (KI/VI) *summit, peak*   **mwinuko** (M/MI) *rise, elevation*
**mita** (N) *metre*   **urefu** (U) *height*
**mpanda-mlima (M/WA)** *climber*

---

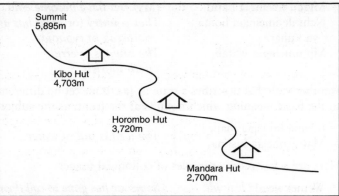

**Adam** Mlima una urefu gani?
**Steve** Una urefu wa mita _____
**Adam** Wapanda-mlima hukaa wapi wakati wa safari?
**Steve** Hukaa katika _____ (*One word.*)
**Adam** Kuna vibanda vingapi?
**Steve** _____
**Adam** Kibanda cha mwanzo kipo urefu wa mita ngapi?
**Steve** Kipo urefu _____
**Adam** Nimesikia kila kibanda kina jina lake; vinaitwaje?
**Steve** Kibanda cha mwanzo kinaitwa _____, cha pili
_____, _____
**Adam** Kibanda cha mwisho kipo urefu wa mita ngapi?
**Steve** _____
**Adam** Ni mwinuko wa mita ngapi kutoka kibanda cha
mwisho mpaka kilele?
**Steve** _____

2   It is 2003. Answer the questions about these people's ages.

a   Mama Fatuma alizaliwa mwaka 1956. Ana umri gani?
b   Mzee Yohanna alizaliwa mwaka 1949. Ana miaka mingapi?
c   Pendo alizaliwa mwaka 1982. Ana miaka mingapi?
d   Yahya na Nuru ni pacha. Walizaliwa mwaka 1992.
    Wana umri gani?
e   Francis alizaliwa mwaka 1971. Ana umri gani?
f   Mohamed alizaliwa mwaka 1980. Ana miaka mingapi?
g   Tusubilege alizaliwa mwaka uliopita. Ana umri gani?
h   Bibi alizaliwa mwaka 1941. Ana miaka mingapi?

---

**pacha** (N)      *twins* (also **ma-**)

---

3    Match the questions on the left, about the dialogue, with the
     answers on the right.

     a  Nani ni kiongozi?              1 Aliyekuwa amekaa chini
                                         ni Paul.
     b  Walikuwa wakipita wapi,        2 Alikuwa na umri wa miaka
        siku ya kwanza?                  arobaini.
     c  Nani alikuwa amekaa chini?    3 Alisema ni kama jangwa.
     d  Paul alikuwa na umri gani?    4 Dominic ndiye kiongozi.
     e  Steve alikuwa na tunda gani?  5 Alikuwa na tofaa.
     f  Paul alisema walipokuwa        6 Walikuwa wakipita
        ni kama mahali gani?             mwituni.

4    **Kuna nini?** You are one of a group of climbers, some of
     whom have fallen ill or injured themselves. You meet
     another group and in reply to their **Kuna nini?** tell them that
     Robert is not well, his back is hurting. Also tell them that
     Dunstan has been overcome by nausea and his face is
     swollen, Anna's finger is broken, Ruth's nose is bleeding and
     Simon's foot is bleeding. (Note that this is *not* a typical
     Kilimanjaro scenario!)

     | | |
     |---|---|
     | **-vunjika** | *be broken* |
     | **amevunjika mkono** | *his/her arm is broken* |

5    **Matayarisho**  *Preparations*
     Fill in the gaps with causative verbs; the meanings you will
     need are given at the end in the correct order.

     Asubuhi na mapema Regina aliwa_____ watoto. Anastasia
     alimsaidia mamake ku_____ moto, a_____e maji. Ruth
     ali_____ chakula cha safari. Mtoto ambaye ni mdogo sana
     alitaka kuwa_____ kuku. Regina alimw_____ kwamba
     watu wote wataondoka saa moja akawa_____ watoto
     wote wasiende nje tena. Francis ali_____ gari akakata
     shauri ku_____ petroli baadaye, barabarani. Hatimaye
     waliwa_____ watoto ndani ya gari na kutia mizigo. Kabla
     hawajaondoka Regina alimw_____ Francis asi_____ mbio
     safari hii.

     | | |
     |---|---|
     | **hatimaye** | *eventually* |

     *wake, light, boil, prepare, chase, explain, forbid, clean, fill
     up (with), get seated, warn, drive*

**6   Una nini?**   *What's the matter with you?*

You have a nightmare in which you suffer from various ailments and injuries. The final episode involves the sudden appearance of a nurse, who asks you '**Una nini?**' You tell her you have a painful stomach and head (use **vi-** as the verb-prefix if you decide to make the body-parts the subject), your feet are bleeding, you have an attack of fever, you have diarrhoea and, moreover, you have a cut hand.

Mercifully, at this point you wake up – and start writing down what you said to the nurse.

**7**   This is an extract from a textbook on the geography of Tanzania.

Sura ya nchi ya Tanzania inatofautiana sana kutoka mahali hata mahali. Karibu na mji wa Moshi, mlima Kilimanjaro, wenye urefu wa mita 5,950, unajitokeza juu mawinguni kwa utukufu mkubwa. Mlima huo, ambao ni wa asili ya volkeno, ni mrefu kuliko yote katika Afrika. Kibo, ambacho ni kimoja kati ya vilele vyake vitatu, Kibo, Mawenzi na Shira, kimefunikwa na barafu na theluji.

| | | | |
|---|---|---|---|
| **sura** (N) | *appearance* | **utukufu** (U) | *majesty, glory* |
| **-tofautiana** | *differ* | **asili** (N) | *origin, source* |
| **-tokeza** | *project* | **volkeno** (N) | *volcano* |
| **wingu** (MA) | *cloud* | (also **volkano**) | |

(Some sources give the height of Kilimanjaro as 5,895m.)

**a**   Write down the part-sentence that means: *(it) rises majestically up into the clouds.*

**b**   Write out the sentence which contains the information that (1) Kilimanjaro has a volcanic origin and (2) it is the highest mountain in Africa.

**c**   Mlima Kilimanjaro una vilele vingapi? Vinaitwaje? (*Answer in Swahili.*)

**d**   What is Kibo peak covered with? (*Answer in English.*)

## As the saying goes ...

Here is one last proverb for you to learn. If you are living in a Swahili-speaking area you may have heard it already. It would be highly suitable for Dominic to quote to his climbers.

> Haraka haraka haina baraka.
> *Hurry, hurry has no blessing.*
> (Rather like 'More haste less speed'.)

**baraka** (N)     *blessing*

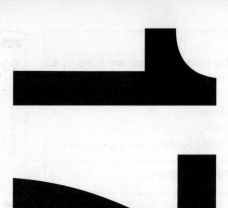

# 7

## mchezaji soka
## na wachezaji
## ngoma

a soccer player and some dancers

**In this unit you will learn**
- some kinship terms
- how to refer to natural events
- how to talk about types of things and actions

# ▶ Dialogue

It is Saturday afternoon. John and Alison have come with Francis to an open-air performance of dances from different areas, to be followed by a play. They are waiting for Joseph, who has stopped to greet a friend.

**Alison**   Joseph ni mpwa wako?

**Francis**  Ndiyo, ni mwana wa dadangu. Kwa kawaida anacheza mpira Jumamosi.

**John**     Ni mchezaji soka katika timu ya ligi?

**Francis**  Ndiyo, na mimi ni mwanachama wa klabu yake! Alitarajia kucheza mechi ya kirafiki leo, siyo ya ligi. Imeahirishwa kwa sababu ya mvua nyingi usiku. Ameambiwa kwamba uwanja umejaa maji. Ni kama mafuriko huko. Hata hapa pana tope. Tusimame pale kando tujikinge tope.

**Alison**   Kumeanuka sasa.

**Francis**  Ndiyo. Mawingu hayaonekani. Kama mvua itanyesha tena tutatumia mwavuli wangu. Tazama, ni mkubwa kabisa!

**Alison**   Joseph yuko wapi? Simwoni sasa.

**Francis**  Yupo pale mlangoni. Anapiga soga tu. (*He walks towards Joseph:*) Harakisha bwana! Kiwanjani panajaa watazamaji. Tutafute viti karibu na jukwaa!
(*Joseph says goodbye to his friend, joins the others and they make their way to seats near the stage.*)

**Joseph**   Watacheza ile ngoma ya Kisukuma ya kutumia nyoka? Ni ngoma ya kupendeza sana.

**Francis**  Bila shaka wataicheza. (*Explaining to John and Alison:*) Huweka kikapu jukwaani. Wakati wanapocheza, nyoka anaonekana kujitokeza.

**Alison**   Tutaona ngoma nyinginezo?

**Francis**  Hatutaona nyingine za kutumia nyoka. Nyingine zitakuwa za aina mbalimbali za kikabila. Moja ni ya Kinyakyusa, nyingine ni za Kibena, Kimeru, Kihaya na kadhalika. Katika ngoma wanazozicheza Wahaya, wachezaji huruka juu sana, kana kwamba ni ndege. Mtaona ngoma nyingi leo.

**Alison**   Inawezekana kutakuwa kumekuchwa kabla tamthilia haijaanza!

**Francis**  Inawezekana, lakini pana taa kubwa za umeme kwenye jukwaa, pale . . . na pale . . . mnaona? Aa! Rafiki yangu Augustine yupo palepale pembeni. Mnamwona mrefu yule? Ni meneja wa kikundi cha wachezaji. Tulisoma pamoja shuleni. Baadaye mtakutana naye. Michezo inaanza sasa hivi.

| | |
|---|---|
| **mpwa** (M/WA) | *a man's sister's child* |
| **-cheza mpira** | *play football* |
| **mpira** (M/MI) | *ball, rubber, ball-game* |
| **mchezaji soka** (M/WA) | *soccer player* |
| **soka** (N) | *soccer (association football)* |
| **timu** (N) | *team* |
| **ligi** (N) | *association football league* |
| **mwanachama** (M/WA) | *club member* |
| **klabu** (N *or* KI/VI) | *club (mainly used for sports clubs and drinking clubs)* |
| **-tarajia** (also **-taraji**) | *expect* |
| **mechi ya kirafiki** (N) | *friendly match* |
| **uwanja** (U/N) | *pitch, stadium* |
| **mafuriko** (MA) | *flood* |
| **tope** (MA) | *mud (sometimes used in the plural)* |
| **kando** | *aside, at the side, to one side* |
| **-kinga** | *protect (from)* |
| **kumeanuka** | *the weather has cleared up* |
| **mwavuli** (M/MI) | *umbrella* |
| **mlango** (M/MI) | *gate, door, entrance* |
| **Harakisha!** | *Hurry up!* |
| **Kiwanjani panajaa watazamaji** | *The ground is getting filled up with spectators* |
| **kiwanja** (KI/VI) | *open area, plot of ground* |
| **watazamaji** (M/WA) | *audience, spectators, onlookers* |
| **jukwaa** (MA) | *stage, platform* |
| **Kisukuma** | *Sukuma-type* |
| **ngoma nyinginezo** | *other dances of the same kind* |
| **kikabila** | *ethnolinguistic type, tribal* |
| **kabila** (MA) | *ethnolinguistic group, tribe* |
| **Kinyakyusa** | *Nyakyusa-type* |
| **Kibena** | *Bena-type* |
| **Kimeru** | *Meru-type* |
| **Kihaya** | *Haya-type* |
| **na kadhalika** | *and so on, etc.* |
| **-ruka** | *jump, leap* |
| **kana kwamba** (also **kama kwamba**) | *as if* |
| **kutakuwa kumekuchwa** | *the sun will have set* |
| **-chwa** | *set (of the sun)* |
| **tamthilia** (N) | *play, drama* |
| **umeme** (U) | *electricity* |
| **palepale** | *right there (repetition of **pale** for emphasis)* |
| **kikundi** | *group, troupe* |
| **Tulisoma pamoja shuleni** | *We were at school together* |

# **i** Maonyesho *Performances*

Professional performances involving dancing to the drum and singing are popular among town-dwellers and tourists. But the situations of these performances, whether on stage or in an arena, are very different from the family and community contexts of which they have traditionally been, and still are, an important part. At weddings, celebrations of births, funerals, initiations and healings, for example, there is much less distinction between the roles of performer and onlooker. Weddings in particular give people an opportunity to improvise songs which incorporate topical social and political comment.

The singing which accompanies routine work done rhythmically also provides an opportunity for improvisation. Work of this sort includes hoeing, threshing, hauling in nets and pounding grain.

Singing is also sometimes a component of story-telling, the songs being 'performed' by characters in the story. Even when there is no singing in a folktale there is always a large amount of dialogue, and a good narrator will modify the pitch and tempo of her voice as she switches from one character to another. And strong characterization is one of the features of a dramatic performance, **tamthilia**, which audiences enjoy.

# Grammar

## 1 Mpwa and other kinship terms

Note that **mpwa** is used only by men, to refer to a sister's child. You already know some kinship terms. Here are a few more, including two which involve words you already know:

| | | |
|---|---|---|
| **babu** (N) | *grandfather,* also used for *ancestor* with **ma-** for plural | |
| **mjukuu** (M/WA) | *grandchild* (male and female) | |
| **mke** (M/WA) | *wife* | |
| **mume** (M/WA) | *husband* | |
| **binti** (N) | *daughter* | |

| **Parents' generation** | |
|---|---|
| **baba mdogo** (N) also **ami** (N) | *paternal uncle* |
| **mjomba** (M/WA) | *maternal uncle* |
| **mama mdogo** (N) | *maternal aunt* |
| **shangazi** (N) | *paternal aunt* |

NB Some people only use **baba mdogo** if the paternal uncle is younger than their father, referring to an older uncle as **baba mkubwa**.

| **In-laws** | |
|---|---|
| **mkwe** (M/WA) | a close in-law; used for *parent-in-law* as well as *son-* or *daughter-in-law* |
| **shemeji** (N) also **shemegi** | *spouse's brother or sister* |
| **wifi** (N) | *sister-in-law*; used by a woman to refer to her husband's sister or her brother's wife |

Although it is not a kinship term, note the following word:

| **bikizee** (N) | *very old woman* |
|---|---|

Although in theory **mzee** can refer to an old man or an old woman, in practice it is more often used for men. An elderly woman, not quite old enough to be a **bikizee** might be referred to and addressed as **mama mzee**, like Francis' grandmother (his **bibi** or **nyanya**) in the Unit 7 dialogue.

Two words are in use for *family*:

| **familia** (N) *nuclear family* | **jamaa** (N) *extended family* |
|---|---|

## 2 Mwanachama – compound words using mwana (son/daughter)

You already know a few compounds made from **mwana** with another word attached to it; **mwana** always comes first. Here are a few more common ones, all in the M/WA class.

| **mwanamaji** | *sailor* | **mwanasheria** | *lawyer* |
|---|---|---|---|
| **mwananchi** | *citizen* | **mwanasoka** | *soccer-player* |

## 3 Ki- for manner and type – more on adverbs and adjectives

**a** Manner (adverb)

The **ki-** prefix was noted at the end of grammar section 6, Unit 11, as a means of making the adjective **-dogo** into an adverb. It is also commonly used for making nouns into adverbs. If the noun has a prefix, **ki-** replaces it.

| | |
|---|---|
| Alisema **ki**toto. | *She spoke in a childish way.* |
| Waliimba **Ki**zungu. | *They sang in a European way.* |
| Amevaa **Ki**hindi. | *She is dressed in Indian style.* |

Notice that this function of **ki-** includes its use for ways of speaking – names of languages: **Kiswahili, Kiingereza, Kichina, Kinyamwezi**, etc. (see Unit 3 Grammar section 10, and Unit 5 Grammar section 9).

**b** Type (adjective)

There are five examples in the dialogue of adjectival phrases made from **-a**, *of*, followed by an adjective made from **ki-** + noun:

| | |
|---|---|
| ya **ki**rafiki | *friendly* |
| ya **Ki**sukuma | *Sukuma-type* |

Similarly:

| | |
|---|---|
| desturi za **Ki**bantu | *Bantu customs* |
| michezo ya **ki**toto | *childish games* |
| nguo za **ki**taifa | *national costume* |

| | | |
|---|---|---|
| **taifa** (MA) | | *nation* |

## 4 Ku- and the natural world

In the dialogue there are two references to natural events in which the verb-prefix is **ku-**: with **-anuka**, *clear up, stop raining* and **-chwa**, *set* (of the sun). Note that **-chwa** is a monosyllabic verb and requires the infinitive **ku-** in front of it with certain tenses (see the Appendix). Two more 'natural event' verbs, similar in meaning, are:

| | |
|---|---|
| **-cha** | *rise (of the sun)* |
| **-pambazuka** | *get light, dawn, be daytime* |

| Kumekucha. | *The sun has risen.* |
| Hakujakucha. | *The sun's not up yet.* |
| Kunapambazuka. | *It's getting light.* |
| Kumepambazuka; twende pwani. | *It's daylight; let's go to the beach.* |

With -cha and -chwa you can use jua (*sun*) as the subject; if you do this the verb prefix is li-:

| Jua limekuchwa. | *The sun has set.* |

## 5 Kiwanjani panajaa watazamaji – -na- for process

Up to now -jaa, *be full up*, and other verbs denoting state have mostly been used with the -me- tense, to denote that the process of getting into that state is completed:

| Debe limejaa maji. | *The container is full of water.* |

But these verbs can also be used with the -na- tense to indicate that the process is happening at the moment:

| Debe linajaa maji. | *The container is filling up with water.* |
| Mwanafunzi analewa. | *The student is getting drunk.* |
| Tunapotea. | *We are getting lost.* |

This difference, between using -me- when referring to a state and -na- when referring to the process of getting into that state, was pointed out for -vaa in Unit 5. The same distinction applies to -kaa, *sit*, -simama, *stand*, and other verbs describing posture.

## 6 Ngoma nyinginezo – other dances of the same kind

The basic structure of nyinginezo is: -ingine + -o

| -ingine | (takes the noun-prefix) | '*other*' |
| -o | (takes the verb-prefix) | refers back |

| michezo mingineyo (i + o → yo) | *other games of this sort* |
| watu wengineo (wa + o → o) | *other people like these* |
| matunda mengineyo (ya + o → yo) | *other fruit of that type* |

## 7 Ngoma wanazozicheza Wahaya – putting the subject after the verb

In this structure, and the following examples, the relative pronoun refers to the object:

| | |
|---|---|
| vitabu ali**vyo**vileta Juma | *the book which Juma brought* |
| miti wali**yo**iona watoto | *the trees which the children saw* |
| wali ali**o**upika Rehema | *the rice that Rehema cooked* |

There is also a subject-noun: **Juma, watoto** and **Rehema**. Instead of being in its usual place, before the verb, the subject-noun is put after the verb. This means that the relative pronoun, -**vyo**-, -**yo**- and -**o**- in the three examples, is as close as possible to the word it refers back to.

If everyone in the conversation knows who you are talking about you will not be using the subject-noun anyway:

| | |
|---|---|
| vitabu alivyovileta | *the books he brought* |
| miti waliyoiona | *the trees which they saw* |
| wali alioupika | *the rice that she cooked* |

The object-marker is usually included because the object is definite and is the focus of the speaker's attention.

*Notes:*

1 If you use the **amba**-relative the subject-word does not need to be shifted (see Unit 9, Grammar section 6):

    vitabu ambavyo Juma alivileta
    miti ambayo watoto waliiona
    wali ambao Rehema aliupika

2 Another way of focusing on the subject is to use the passive (see Unit 11, Grammar section 1):

    vitabu vilivyoletwa na Juma
    miti iliyoonwa na watoto
    wali uliopikwa na Rehema

# Practice

1

    **a**   Katika picha hii wachezaji wako wapi?

    **b**   Wachezaji wangapi wanaonekana wamevaa nguo nyeupe na kofia?

    **c**   Wale wachezaji wawili wanaocheza upande wa kulia, wanashika kitu gani?

    **d**   Watazamaji wangapi wanaonekana hapa mbele?

2   See how well you have understood the dialogue.

    **a**   Ni nani ambaye huchezaji soka Jumamosi?

    **b**   Kwa nini hachezi leo?

    **c**   Nani amekuja na mwavuli?

    **d**   Mawingu yanaonekana sasa?

    **e**   Francis amemwambia nani aharakishe?

    **f**   Francis amemwona nani pembeni?

3   Make up a leave-taking dialogue in which Joseph tells his friend that he (Joseph) must go now. The friend says they will be seeing each other at Peter's place on Tuesday evening. Joseph points out that if it rains a lot he might be late. They exchange goodbyes.

4 This is the heading of a newspaper advert:

# TANGAZO TANGAZO

**Tangazo** (MA) means *advertisement* or *announcement*.

a Suggest the verb that **tangazo** has been made from.
b Use this verb in writing the Swahili equivalent of:
  1 Dancing is advertised in the newspaper. (Assume this means traditional dancing, with a drum.)
  2 They haven't yet announced the date of the final.

> **fainali** (N)   *final* (final match in a league competition)

5 Find the second half of each sentence, then write out the completed sentences.

| | | |
|---|---|---|
| a Kumekuchwa; | 1 | tuwashe taa. |
| b Hakujakucha; | 2 | karibu tutaauona mlima. |
| c Kunapambazuka; | 3 | sioni kitu, hata kidogo. |
| d Kunakuchwa; | 4 | tusiondoke bado. |

6 From the sports page of a newspaper:

> Timu ya soka ya Asante Kotoko kutoka Ghana iliwasili juzi jijini Dar es Salaam kwa ziara ya mechi nne nchini ambapo itapambana na Simba na Yanga mwishoni mwa wiki.
>
> Kikosi cha Kotoko kilichowasili juzi kina wachezaji 18, kati yao saba ni wachezaji wa timu ya taifa ya Ghana 'Black Stars'.

> | | | | |
> |---|---|---|---|
> | **timu** (N) | *team* | **ziara** (N) | *visit* |
> | **-wasili** | *arrive* | **-pambana na** | *confront* |
> | **juzi** (MA) | *day before yesterday* | **kikosi** (KI/VI) | *squad* |

a Wachezaji wageni wanatoka nchi gani?
b Wachezaji wangapi wamekuja, kwa jumla?
c Timu ambayo iliwasili juzi inaitwaje?
d Andika majina ya timu mbili za Tanzania.

On page 254 is a poem for you to read and enjoy, and perhaps come back to later. Poetry – **ushairi** (U) – is the oldest literary form in Swahili, and is very popular today. This poem is a modern one that does not conform to the complex conventions that make traditional verse-forms so challenging for poetry-writers and sometimes difficult for Swahili-learners to understand.

The poem has an air of mystery about it, until the last line. The poet contemplates a deserted dancing-place, in which only remnants of the trimmings from the dancers' costumes are to be seen, scattered on the ground.

### Ngoma ya Kimya

Wacheza ngoma wamekwishaondoka
Kilichobaki ni uwanja uliokauka majani,
Njuga, manyoya na kindu zilizodondoka
Toka kwa wachezaji waliozidisha mbwembwe
Nao watazamaji wakipiga kelele na vigelegele.
Ni jana tu walikuwa hapa.
Wachezaji sasa wafikiria ngoma ijayo.
Watazamaji hawayakumbuki maneno
Ya nyimbo zote zilizoimbwa.
Zilizobaki ni taswira hai na vivuli.

Lakini labda miti hii michache yakumbuka.
Nitaviokota nitengeneze vazi langu
Kisha nitacheza ngoma yangu kimyakimya
Katika uwanja huu mpana ulioachwa wazi
Bila watazamaji
Nao upepo ukinifundisha lugha ya kimya
Maana yule mwanamke amekwishajifungua.

| | |
|---|---|
| **-kauka** | *dry up, become dry* |
| **njuga** (N) | *small bells* |
| **manyoya** (MA) | *feathers* |
| **kindu** (U/N) | *leaves of wild date palm* |
| | (used for plaiting, e.g. mats) |
| **-dondoka** | *drop off, bit by bit* |
| **mbwembwe** (N) | *display, spectacle* |
| **vigelegele** (KI/VI) also | *ululation* (done by women at times |
| **ugelegele** | of celebration) |
| **-fikiria** | *think about* |
| **taswira** (N) | *image, picture* |
| **hai** | *living, alive* |
| **-okota** | *pick up* |
| **wazi** | *empty, open, clear* |
| **upepo** (U/N) | *wind, breeze* |
| **-jifungua** | *give birth* |

# 8

## barua zimewasili!

**In this unit you will learn**
- how to congratulate someone
- how to wish someone a Happy Christmas, New Year, Idi
- how to write letters

# ▶ Dialogue

Alison and John have been home from Africa for several months. Thekla, a niece of Francis, is staying with them. They speak Swahili on alternate days during her visit, and today is a Swahili day. Some letters have just been delivered.

**Thekla**  Barua zimewasili!

**John**  (*from the kitchen*) Vizuri! Zilete hapa, tupo hapa jikoni!

**Alison**  Ni barua zetu au zako?

**Thekla**  Mbili ni eafomu. Nimeandikiwa moja tu. Eafomu nyingine ni yenu, pamoja na bahasha hizi tatu za kawaida.

**Alison**  Imetoka kwa Mohamed! Kumbe, alibandika stempu nyingi mno!

(*She opens the letter and starts reading it.*)

**John**  Soma kwa sauti.

**Alison**  Haya, sikiliza. (*Reading aloud:*)

Wapendwa ndugu,

Salaam nyingi zitokazo kwetu, na baada ya wingi wa salamu natumaini nyote hamjambo hapo nyumbani? Mama hajambo sana. Bado anashona nguo! Ijapokuwa mzee lakini ana nguvu. Anawasalimu.

Habari zetu ni hivi. Nimeachilia mbali kazi ya benki. Siku hizi ninashughulikia kazi ya duka la baba. Naye baba amestaafu kwa ajili ya udhaifu wake baada ya ugonjwa. Alishikika vibaya hata hakuweza kufunga. Tena amezeeka. Ana wasaidizi wema dukani lakini hawaelewi kinaganaga mambo ya bidhaa ziingizao toka nje, yaani uingizaji. Baba aliona bora nichukue madaraka. Siku hizi nipo dukani siku nenda siku rudi. Wateja sasa wameongezeka. Kwa ufupi, mimi ni mfanyibiashara halisi!

Juzijuzi nilikutana na kijana mmoja, Mmarekani. Anafahamiana na Francis, rafiki yenu. Anasema Kiswahili vizuri sana, kana kwamba ni mwenyeji. Huyu kijana amesoma Chuo Kikuu cha Nairobi, tena amekizuru Chuo Kikuu hapa, kwa ajili ya utafiti wake. Ataondoka wiki ijayo. Kabla hajarudi Marekani atakizuru Chuo Kikuu cha Cardiff. Nimempa anwani yenu na namba ya simu. Kwa hisani yenu msaidieni kadiri mwezavyo. Sina zaidi. Mimi na familia yangu twawatakia salamu za kheri kwa Krismasi na baraka ya mwaka mpya.

Wasalaam,
Ndimi rafiki yenu,
Mohamed

**John** Inaonekana hatimaye Mohamed atakuwa milionea!

**Alison** (to Thekla) Na wewe, umepokea barua ya kupendeza?

**Thekla** Ndiyo, imetoka kwa mjomba.

**John** Francis?

**Thekla** Ndiyo. Amenipongeza kwa kufaulu mtihani, tena ametoa habari za nyumbani. Aidha amewaandikia ujumbe mfupi: (Reading aloud the message for Alison and John:)

Wapendwa marafiki,
Salamu za heri na fanaka ziwafikie hapo mlipo. Sisi huku kuna joto jingi sana. Mmarekani mmoja atawasili Heathrow tarehe 16. Ni yule ambaye alinizuru zamani chuoni nikampeleka kuwatembelea wazee sehemu za kusini. Ni kijana mwema. Nimempa namba ya simu yenu. Iwapo atawapigia simu msaidieni kadiri mwezavyo. Hajui mtu yeyote Uingereza. Jina lake Steve Robinson.

Kesho nitakwenda kwa wazee niangalie marekebisho. Wakati wa masika shamba, ghala na nyumba ya nyanya vilikuwa vimeharibika. Sina zaidi, nisije nikachelewa kwenda posta.
Wasalaam,
Francis

**Alison** Ni tarehe gani leo?

**John** Tarehe kumi na sita.
(The telephone rings.)

Shopping

| | |
|---|---|
| -wasili | *arrive* |
| eafomu (N) | *air letter form, aerogramme* |
| bahasha (N) | *envelope* |
| -bandika | *stick on* |
| -sikiliza | *listen* |
| salamu (N) | *greetings* |
| Bado anashona nguo! | *She's still sewing clothes!* |
| Ijapokuwa, also ijapo | *Even though, although* |
| Anawasalimu | *She greets you* |
| -achilia mbali | *leave, give up altogether* |
| -shughulikia | *be concerned with* |
| -staafu | *retire (from work)* |
| udhaifu (U) | *frailty* |
| Alishikika vibaya | *He was taken very ill* |
| -funga | *fast* (during Ramadhan, in this context) |
| -zeeka | *become old* |
| kinaganaga | *in detail, thoroughly* |
| bidhaa ziingiazo toka nje | *imported goods* |
| bidhaa (N) | *trade commodities* |
| uingizaji | *importation* |
| bora (= afadhali) | *better* |
| madaraka (MA) | usually used in plural form *responsibility* |
| siku nenda siku rudi | *all the time, day in day out* |
| wateja (M/WA) | *customers* |
| mfanyibiashara (M/WA) | *businessman* |
| halisi | *complete* |
| juzijuzi | *recently* |
| mwenyeji (M/WA) | *local person* |
| -zuru | *visit* |
| utafiti (U) | *research* |
| kwa hisani yenu | *by your kindness* |
| kadiri mwezavyo | *as much as you can* |
| salamu (N) | *greetings* |
| Wasalaam also Wasalamu | formulaic letter-ending, meaning *with greetings* |
| milionea (MA) | *millionaire* |
| -pongeza | *congratulate* |
| -faulu | *pass* (an examination), *succeed* |
| mtihani (M/MI) | *examination* |
| aidha | *moreover* |
| ujumbe (U/N) | *message* |
| fanaka (N) | *prosperity, success* |
| iwapo | *if* |
| marekebisho (MA) | *repairs* |
| ghala (N) | *store* (e.g. grain-store) |
| nisije | *lest* |

# Grammar

## Kuandika barua

**a** Addressing your correspondent
**Mpendwa,** as used in the dialogue, is a typical way of starting an informal letter to a friend or acquaintance:

| | |
|---|---|
| Mpendwa Ruth, | *Dear Ruth,* |
| Mpendwa dada/kaka, | (to a friend of the same generation) |
| Mpendwa Bi. Thekla, | |
| Mpendwa Mwalimu, | |

Note that **Mwalimu** is a term of respect and you can use it as a form of address even if you are not writing to him or her in their capacity as a teacher. The abbreviation of **Mwalimu** is **Mwl.** when writing a teacher's name and address on an envelope, for example. For an addressee who is a close family member or an intimate friend:

| | |
|---|---|
| Mpenzi wangu, | *My dearest,* |
| Mpenzi Zena, | *Dearest Zena,* |
| Mpenzi Baba/Mama, | *Dearest Father/Mother,* |
| | (also for older friend) |

For a formal letter or a brief note to a colleague, you either use the addressee's title and name alone:

Bwana A. Omari,
Bi. Amina,
Profesa Khamisi,
Mwalimu N. Ali,

or:

Kwa Bwana A. Omari,
Kwako Bibi Amina,

**b** Greetings
The first paragraph of an informal letter must contain greetings, as in the first two letters in the dialogue. The greetings in Francis' brief note are minimal. Overleaf is another example:

*Salamu nyingi sana.
Natumaini wewe na
wanafunzi wako ni wazima.
Wote hawajambo
nyumbani? Sisi hapa
hatujambo sana. Nilirejea
salama salimini nyumbani
kwetu, ila tulichelewa
Nairobi kwa sababu ya
kifundi. Hatujaanza kulima
bado.*

*Warm greetings. I hope you
and your students are well.
Is everyone fine at home?
We're all fine here. I
returned home safely, apart
from being held up at
Nairobi because of technical
problems. We have not yet
started ploughing.*

In a letter to a person much older than yourself, you could start the greetings with **Shikamoo** (introduced in Unit 1).

These greetings are very important and must not be skipped in an informal letter. Formal letters do not need them.

**c Closing the letter**
**Wasalaam**, followed by the signature on the line below, is a good standby for any sort of letter including formal ones.

Only in letters to friends or family would you substitute for it, or add to it (on the line below) any of the following:

> Ni mimi,
> Ndimi,
> Mimi rafiki / ndugu yako,

In a letter to a family member or intimate friend you can use:

> Mimi nikupendaye,
> Wako akupendaye,
> Akupendaye,
> Mpenzi wako.

Formal letters end with either **Wasalaam** or **Wako,** above the signature.

**d Kadi za kusalimu** – greetings cards

The last sentence of Mohamed's letter contains a standard greeting for Christmas and New Year. A variation on this for a single recipient, including the substitution of *send* for *wish*, is:

Nakuletea salamu za heri kwa Krismasi na baraka na fanaka ya mwaka mpya.

*I send you happy greetings for Christmas and blessings and prosperity in the new year.*

A greeting for Idi, the Muslim festival at the end of the fasting month of Ramadhan, is:

Idi Mubarak.

A general greeting is:

Nakutakia kila la kheri (*or* heri).

*I wish you all the best.*

# Grammar

## 1 Bado anashona nguo!
*She is still sewing clothes!*

**Bado** is used with a verb, or with a word substituting for a verb, to mean that the action or state is still continuing. The position of **bado** is very flexible.

Watoto wamelala bado.
Walikuwa bado kusoma zile barua.
Mukami yumo jikoni bado.
Bado yu mtoto.

*The children are still asleep.*
*They were still reading the letters.*
*Mukami is still in the kitchen.*
*He is still a child.*

The *not yet* meaning of **bado**, with the **-ja-** tense, was introduced in Unit 6.

## 2 Ijapokuwa and other ways of saying 'although'

**Ijapokuwa**, the related word **ijapo**, and **ingawa**, which was used in Unit 16, all mean *although*, *even though* or *even if*. They look like verbal structures with **i-** as the verb-prefix; this is what they were but they have 'fossilized' into words which do not vary in their prefix.

Ijapokuwa hana pesa nyingi
amevaa nguo maridadi.

*Even though she hasn't
much money she is
wearing elegant clothes.*

---

**maridadi**   *elegant, attractive* (does not take a prefix)

---

Ijapo atashindwa mtihani
atapewa kazi dukani.

Ingawa meneja yupo ofisini
mwake, lakini hawezi kuongea
nawe sasa.

*Even if he fails the exam he will
be given work in the shop.*

*Although the manager is in
his office he cannot talk to
you now.*

**Ingawaje** is an alternative to **ingawa**.

Notice that in Swahili **lakini** can be used with any of the
*although* words, whereas in English there is a tendency not to
use *but* after *although*.

## 3 Sikiliza – another function for the causative verb-form

The causative ending which can be attached to verb-roots (see
Unit 16) has another, non-causative, function. It is used to show
an intensifying of the meaning of the verb. Do not attempt to
make up causatives for this purpose; just note the following
common verbs:

| | | | |
|---|---|---|---|
| -l- | *eat* | -lisha | *graze* |
| -ny- | *emit, let fall* | -nyesha | *rain* |
| -nyama- | *be quiet* | -nyamaza | *be very quiet* |
| -siki- | *hear* | -sikiliza | *listen* |
| | | (or, occasionally, -sikiza) | |

Nyamazeni, watoto!
Mbuzi wanalisha pale.

*Be very quiet, children!*
*The goats are grazing over there.*

## 4 Nimeachilia mbali – another function for the prepositional verb-form

The prepositional ending, introduced in Unit 4, can also be used
for the intensifying function noted above for the causative. In
some cases the **i / e** ending is doubled, **ili/ele**:

| | | | |
|---|---|---|---|
| -ach- | *leave, stop* | -achilia | *leave, stop completely* (also *forgive*) |
| -og- | *bathe* | -ogelea | *swim* |
| -shik- | *hold, grasp* | -shikilia | *hold on to* |
| -tup- | *throw* | -tupilia | *throw right away* |
| -va- | *wear, dress* | -valia | *dress up* |

**-tupilia** is often followed by **mbali**, *far*, to mean *throw away completely* and the addition of **mbali** to **-achilia**, as in Mohamed's letter in the dialogue, also adds to the finality of the action.

Hakuiacha kazi yake, bali aliishikilia kwa nguvu.

*He did not leave his job, on the contrary he held on to it firmly.*

| | | | |
|---|---|---|---|
| **bali** | *on the contrary* | **nguvu** (N) | *strength, firmness* |
| **kwa nguvu** | *firmly, strongly* | | |

Watacheza dansi, ndiyo sababu Kitwana amevalia.

*They're going to have a dance, that's why Kitwana is all dressed up.*

| | |
|---|---|
| **-cheza dansi** | *dance to a live band, taped disco music, etc.* |

## 5 Bidhaa ziingiazo *Incoming goods*

This is a reminder of just how important relative structures are in Swahili. You will often need a relative, either the general relative as in the above example, or a past-tense relative, to express a meaning for which you would use an adjective in English.

| | |
|---|---|
| bidhaa zitokazo | *outgoing goods* |
| shanga zilizopotea | *lost beads* |
| ndoo iliyojaa maji | *a full bucket of water* |
| mwezi ujao | *next month* |
| nyumba isiyokalika (-kaa) | *an uninhabitable house* |
| nyumbu wasiohesabika (-hesabu) | *innumerable wildebeest* |

| | |
|---|---|
| **ndoo** (N) | *bucket* |

## 6 Multiple subjects – which verb-prefix?

When you use more than one subject-noun and the two, or three, nouns are in different classes the choice of verb-prefix should be as follows:

- If the nouns denote concrete things, as in the dialogue example; use **vi-**:

  **shamba** (MA), **ghala** (N) **na nyumba ya nyanya** (N) **vilikuwa vimeharibika.**
  In this case you treat the items as being **vitu**. An alternative is to use the prefix matching the last-mentioned subject-noun.

- If your subject-nouns are abstract and not all in the U class you can use: **zi-**, **u-** or the prefix matching the last subject-noun.

Try to avoid mixing human and non-human nouns:

| | |
|---|---|
| Watoto hawatasahauliwa wala nyimbo zao. | *The children will not be forgotten nor will their songs.* |

## 7 Ways of saying: 'If...'

You have now seen several ways of making 'If . . .' sentences. Two of them are 'fossilized' verbal structures with the **i-**, *it*, prefix.

| | |
|---|---|
| Ikiwa atakuja mpe vitabu hivi. | |
| Iwapo atakuja mpe vitabu hivi. | *If she comes give her* |
| Kama atakuja mpe vitabu hivi. | *these books.* |
| Akija mpe vitabu hivi. | |

# Practice

1

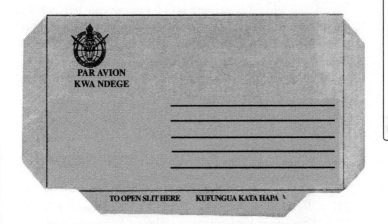

Andika kwenye eafomu jina na anwani ya Daudi Mhina, ambaye ni mwalimu. Anakaa Mpwapwa, Mkoa wa Dodoma, Tanzania.Wiki iliyopita alipata sanduku la posta; namba yake ni elfu mbili, mia saba, hamsini na tatu.

2

| **-tumbukia** *fall into* |
|---|

This is the back of an aerogramme. You should be able to work out what the warning says (in upper-case letters below the sender's address). Say or write what you think it means in English, but do not attempt a word-by-word translation.

3 Correct and rewrite these false statements about the dialogue.

    a    John na Alison wapo shambani.
    b    Barua sita zimewasili nyumbani.
    c    Katika barua Mohamed anasema kwamba mamake bado anapiga picha.
    d    Babake Mohamed amestaafu kwa ajili ya wajukuu.
    e    Mohamed ameachilia mbali kazi ya kufundisha Kichina.
    f    Wasaidizi kwenye duka la babake Mohamed hawaelewi kinaganaga mambo ya kuhesabu pesa.

4 How well did you understand the rest of the dialogue?

    a    Katika barua Mohamed anasema nini kuhusu wale wateja?
    b    Mohamed alikuwa amekutana na nani juzijuzi?
    c    John anafikiri kwamba hatimaye Mohamed atakuwa mtu wa namna gani?
    d    Thekla ni mtoto wa nani?
    e    Kwa nini Thekla amepongezwa?
    f    Ni nani ambaye atawasili Heathrow tarehe kumi na sita?

5 Congratulations!

To congratulate someone use **pongezi,** a class N noun made from **-pongeza,** a verb used by Thekla in the dialogue.

    Pongezi kwa kufaulu       *Congratulations on passing*
       mtihani!                 *the exam!*

When reporting that someone was congratulated use either **-pongeza,** as Thekla does, or **-pa pongezi:**

Francis alimpa pongezi.       *Francis congratulated her.*

Find the second half of each sentence and write out the completed sentences:

| | | | |
|---|---|---|---|
| a | Tulimpa mzee pongezi | 1 | kwa kupata kazi. |
| b | Mwalimu alimpongeza Thekla | 2 | kwa kurekebisha ghala na nyumba ya nyanya. |
| c | Mama Nuru alipewa pongezi | 3 | kwa kustaafu. |
| d | Nilimpongeza yule kijana | 4 | kwa kufaulu mtihani. |
| e | Elvan alimpongeza Francis | 5 | kwa kujifungua mtoto wa kiume. |

**mtoto wa kiume** (M/WA)  *boy*   **mtoto wa kike** (M/WA)  *girl*

Now write down the actual words that were said to:

- the old man
- the young man

Note: **-hongera** (N), **-pa hongera** are similarly used for giving congratulations.

6   a   Write a message suitable for a Christmas card that you (singular) are sending to a Kenyan family.

b   Write a message for a Christmas card that you (plural) are sending to a student whom you met in Tanzania and who has written to tell you that she passed her examination.

**Hongera!**
You should now have sufficient competence in Swahili to be able to participate in most everyday situations in eastern Africa – and to build on these basic 'nuts and bolts' to extend your knowledge of the language.

**key to the exercises**

## Unit 1

**1 a** Marahaba. **b** Habari za safari? **c** Sijambo. **d** Habari za asubuhi? **e** Hodi! **f** Hatujambo. **g** Salama tu/nzuri/njema/safi. **h** Karibu! **i** Habari za nyumbani? **j** Karibuni! **2 a** Natoka (*or* ninatoka) Marekani. **b** Unatoka wapi? **c** Anatoka Liverpool. **d** Wanatoka Kenya? **e** Wanatoka Nairobi. **f** Mnatoka wapi? **g** Anatoka Ujerumani? **h** Mnatoka Uganda? **3** Kenya – Mkenya. Uchina – Mchina. Uingereza – Mwingereza. Uganda – Mganda. Ufaransa – Mfaransa. Tanzania – Mtanzania. Urusi – Mrusi. Ujerumani – Mjerumani. **4 a** Hodi! **b** Hamjambo? **c** Habari za – ? **d** Habari za safari? **e** Mnatoka wapi? **f** Hujambo? **g** Shikamoo. **h** Wewe ni Mwingereza? **i** Wewe si Mmarekani? **6 A** Jeanne na Pierre ni watalii. **B** Bw. Musa ni mpokeaji. **C** Mama Amina ni mfinyanzi. **D** Bw. Ramadhani ni mwalimu. **E** Bi. Bertha ni mwuguzi. **F** Lulu na Abdu ni wanafunzi. **a** Siyo, Bi. Bertha si mtalii, ni mwuguzi. **b** Siyo, Pierre si mpokeaji, ni mtalii. **c** Ndiyo, Bw. Ramadhani ni mwalimu. **d** Siyo, Lulu na Abdu si wapokeaji, ni wanafunzi. **e** Ndiyo, Jeanne ni mtalii. **f** Siyo, Mama Amina si mwuguzi, ni mfinyanzi. **g** Ndiyo, Bw. Musa ni mpokeaji. **h** Ndiyo, Abdu ni mwanafunzi.

## Unit 2

**1 a** Nenda moja kwa moja, halafu pinda kushoto. Nenda moja kwa moja halafu utaona benki upande wa kulia. **b** Nenda moja kwa moja, halafu pinda kulia. Nenda moja kwa moja halafu utaona hoteli upande wa kushoto. **c** Nenda moja kwa moja, halafu pinda kushoto. Nenda moja kwa moja halafu utaona hoteli upande wa kushoto.
**d** Nenda moja kwa moja, vuka barabara, halafu utaona posta upande wa kushoto. **e** Nenda moja kwa moja, vuka barabara, halafu utaona benki upande wa kulia.

**2 a** Wageni wako wapi? **b** Chai iko wapi? **c** Mbuzi yuko wapi?
**d** Mtoto yuko wapi? **e** Kahawa iko wapi? **f** Posta iko wapi?
**g** Wajerumani wako wapi? **h** Dada yuko wapi? **3** This exercise gives
you some freedom of choice in the answers, so those below are
sample ones. **a** Baba yuko wapi? Baba yuko Kampala **b** Wanafunzi
wako wapi? Wanafunzi wapo baa. **c** Mzee yuko wapi? Mzee yupo
posta. **d** Bw. Omari yuko wapi? Bw. Omari yuko Mombasa. **e** Ali na
Amina wako wapi? Ali na Amina wapo benki. **f** Mama yuko wapi?
Mama yupo stesheni. **g** Askari yuko wapi? Askari yumo baa.
**h** Wauguzi wako wapi? Wauguzi wako Dar es Salaam. **4 a** Juma
hayupo posta, yupo stesheni. **b** Watalii hawako Dar es Salaam, wapo
Tanga. **c** Bi. Ruth hayuko Nairobi, yupo Mombasa. **d** Wanafunzi
hawapo sinema, wapo baa. **e** Mfaransa hayupo stesheni, yumo baa.
**5** Examples of possible sequences using sentences from Practice 3
questions and their sample answers: Q. Mzee yuko wapi? A. Yupo
posta. Q. Posta ipi? A. Karibu na benki. Q. Ali na Amina wako
wapi? A. Wapo benki. Q. Benki ipi? A. Karibu na sinema. Q. Mama
yuko wapi? A. Yupo benki. Q. Benki ipi? A. Karibu na baa.
**6 a** Shilingi ishirini. **b** Shilingi thelathini. **c** Shilingi mia nane.
**d** Shilingi mia tatu. **e** Shilingi mia nane na hamsini.
**7 a** Shilingi sitini na nne. **b** Shilingi mia moja na tisini.
**c** Shilingi mia saba na sabini.

## Unit 3

**1 a** Shilingi elfu thelathini. **b** (1) cheque, (2) signature. **c** I have
received. **2** a4, b6, c1, d8, e2, f7, g3, h5. **3 a** After *hujambo/sijambo*
and *habari* greetings: *Bw.* C: Naomba chumba cha mtu mmoja. *Mp.*:
Ghorofa ya pili itafaa? *Bw.* C: Ndiyo, itafaa. **b** After greetings: *Bw.* R:
Naomba chumba cha watu watatu; mmoja ni mtoto mdogo. *Mp*:
Tuna chumba kikubwa chenye vitanda viwili; kitafaa? *Bw. R*: Kitafaa.
**4 a** Askari ni hodari sana. **b** Mbuzi wadogo hawa ni wake? **c** Visu
vikubwa ni ghali; vidogo ni rahisi. **d** Njia za Nairobi si nyembamba,
ni pana sana. **e** Kisu hakifai; nitapata kisu kipya. **f** Kila mwalimu ana
nyumba yake. **5** Sipendi nyama lakini napenda samaki. Napenda
wali, lakini sipendi ugali. Sipendi iliki lakini napenda dalasini.
Napenda maandazi lakini sipendi vitumbua. Sipendi vitunguu, lakini
napenda nyanya.

## Unit 4

**1** *You*: Unahitaji mananasi? *Mama F*: Ndiyo, nahitaji mananasi
mawili. *You*: Unahitaji ndizi? *Mama F*: Sihitaji ndizi, kuna migomba
mingi shambani. *You*: Unahitaji malimau? *Mama F*: Ndiyo, nahitaji
malimau matano. *You*: Unahitaji mayai? *Mama F*: Hapana, sihitaji
mayai. Rafiki yangu aliniletea. **2** Regina alimpa mwuzaji Sh. mia sita,

sabini na tano. **3 a** Asha alimpikia chakula (*or* wali, ugali, pilau, biriani, *etc.*) **b** Juma alimfulia nguo. **c** Francis alimpigia simu. **d** Ruth alimletea soda. **e** Khadija alimnunulia nanasi. **f** John alimsomea.
**4** Kaka! Lete chai moja ya rangi, kahawa tatu na soda moja; vitumbua viwili, kibibi kimoja na maandazi mawili. *(If in Kenya substitute* ndugu *for* kaka*).* **5** a6, b3, c7, d5, e1, f2, g8, h4.
**6 a** Mwalimu aliwapa watoto vitabu. **b** Tulimpa mgonjwa matunda. **c** Nilimfulia mama nguo. **d** Baba atanipigia simu kesho. **e** Mgeni wetu alitununulia soda mkahawani. **f** Bi. Khadija alininunulia sukari dukani. **a** The teacher gave the children some books. **b** We gave the sick person some fruit. **c** I washed the clothes for mother. **d** Father will phone me tomorrow. **e** Our visitor bought us 'soda' in the café. (Or fizzy drink/fruit drink instead of 'soda'). **f** Khadija bought some sugar for me in the shop.

## Unit 5

**1** Mzee Khamisi anavaa kofia. Mtalii amevaa kofia. Bi. Pendo anavaa viatu. Mama Lela amevaa kanga. Mama Zubeda amevaa gauni. Bw. Francis anavaa koti. **2 b** Bi. Alison hapendi rangi nyekundu. **c** Bi. Alison hapendi magauni dukani kwa sababu mikono ni myembamba sana, tena ni ghali sana. **d** Msaidizi anamwonyesha Bi. Alison vitambaa. **e** Bw. John ametoka sokoni. **f** Kinyago kikubwa cha Kimakonde kinampendeza. **g** Bw. John hakinunui kinyago kikubwa cha Kimakonde kwa sababu ni kizito. **h** Anapenda kununua mfinyango badala ya kinyago. **3 a** Bi. Asha ameninunulia kitambaa hiki. **b** Utanisaidia kupika maharagwe haya? **c** Msaidizi alituonyesha vitabu hivi. **d** Rafiki yangu ameniandikia barua hii. **e** Akina mama wanamtafuta mtoto huyu. **f** Tutapata machungwa mengi, mwaka huu. **g** Nyumba kubwa hizi zinawapendeza wageni. **h** Jembe hili limenisaidia sana shambani.
**a** Asha has bought me this fabric. **b** Are you going to help me cook these beans? **c** The assistant showed us these books. **d** My friend has written me this letter. **e** The womenfolk are searching for this child. **f** We shall get a lot of oranges, this year. **g** The visitors like these large houses. (These large houses please the visitors.) **h** This hoe has helped me a lot in the plantation. **4** *Ana*: Hatuna./Tunavyo./ Tunazo./ Tunazo./Hatuna. **5** Mto umejaa maji. Hoteli imejaa watalii. Nyumba za walimu zimejaa wazee. Baa imejaa wanafunzi. Sisi na Bw. Juma tumo shuleni. Chakula kimekwisha!

## Unit 6

**1 a** saa moja; **b** saa tano u nusu; **c** saa saba; **d** saa tatu kasa robo; **e** saa kumi na robo; **f** saa kumi na mbili u nusu. **2 a** 4.30 p.m. **b** She has been looking for her white beads. **c** A timetable of boat-sailings to

Zanzibar. **d** Because the flight only takes 20 minutes. **e** Friday.
**f** Wednesday or Thursday. **g** Saa kumi na moja u nusu. **h** He is going to
the mosque to pray. **3 a** Shanga zake Bi. Alison zimepotea. **b** Dada
amewapikia watoto uji huu. **c** Nywele zake ni ndefu.
**d** Mama ana ufagio mzuri. **e** Watoto wanapenda nyimbo za Kifaransa.
**f** Watakarabati ukuta wa kanisa. **4 a** John amekwenda posta kununua
stampu (*or* anunue). **b** Tulimpa Alison pesa alete matunda. **c**
Ninawatafuta wageni niwape barua zao. **d** Regina alinunua mchele
apike pilau. **e** Mwalimu alinipa kitabu cha Kiswahili nisome. **f**
Tulimnunulia Otto gazeti lile asome Kiswahili. **5 a** Friday.
**b** 8.00 p.m. **c** place. **d** Tarehe ishirini na tatu, mwezi wa Agosti, mwaka
wa elfu mbili na mbili. (*You can use* nane *instead of* Agosti). **e** giraffe.

## Part Two

## Unit 7

**1 a** *Mimi*: Unafanya nini? *Thekla*: Ninakoroga kisamvu. **b** *Mimi*:
Unafanya nini? *Kasembe*: Ninashona shati. **c** *Mimi*: Mnafanya nini?
*Francis & Nzunda*: Tunaezeka nyumba. **d** *Mimi*: Unafanya nini?
*Alison*: Ninajifunza Kiswahili. **e** *Mimi*: Unafanya nini? *Maria*:
Ninaandika hadithi. **f** *Mimi*: Mnafanya nini? *Bwenje & Joshua*:
Tunachuma machungwa. Adding to the dialogues: *for a,b,d and e –*
*Mimi*: Nikusaidie? *Reply*: Haya, karibu! *For c and f Mimi*:
Niwasaidie? *Reply*: Haya, karibu! **2 a** Baada ya kutia majani funika
chungu. **b** Alipotuona alitupa korosho. **c** Watakapopata pesa
watanunua mabati. **d** Njooni mchemshe maji! **e** Tutakapofika Nairobi
tutakwenda benki. **f** Watakapopata matofali watakarabati kanisa.
**g** Watalii waliporudi hotelini walikula chakula cha jioni. **h** Mama
alikasirika sana tuliposahau kuosha sufuria. **3 a** Kuchambua majani
ya muhogo ni kazi ya mama mzee. **b** Mama mzee alichuma majani ya
muhogo. **c** Steve anajifunza namna ya kupika kisamvu. **d** Regina
anapika ugali juu ya jiko la makaa. **e** Atakaporudi Nairobi Steve
atajipikia kisamvu. **f** Francis yupo. **4 a** Mjini kuna wageni kutoka
Ujerumani. **b** Kikapuni mna mayai kumi. **c** Kanisani pana watu
wengi. **d** Baharini kuna boti nyingi. **e** Mfukoni mna pesa kidogo.
**f** Jikoni pana kuni za kutosha. **5** Grace, njoo uchemshe maji! Adam,
njoo ukatekate nyanya hizi! Maria, nipe chumvi! Nitatayarisha
samaki hawa, halafu nitatengeneza maji ya machungwa.

## Unit 8

**1** *Reply to Ali*: Iringa iko kusini ya Dodoma. *Reply to Lajabu*: Kilosa
iko magharibi ya Morogoro. *Reply to Lunda*: Bagamoyo iko
kaskazini ya Dar es Salaam. *Reply to Grace*: Mbeya iko kusini ya
Tabora. **2 a** Mgeni aliyekuja jana ataondoka kesho. **b** Hatuwezi kula
chakula kisichofaa. **c** Watoto watakaokwenda mjini watanunua nazi

sokoni. **d** Tulipomwona Mohamed tulimpa barua zake. **e** Watalii wasiokuja mapema hawatapata vyumba. **f** Wanawake wanaotwanga mahindi ni dada zangu. **3 a** Si lazima Steve arudi Nairobi mwisho wa mwezi. **b** Steve atakuwa na shughuli huko Dar es Salaam. **c** Anapenda kumtembelea rafiki yake. **d** Kaka yake Elvan anakaa Tunduru. **e** Kaka ni mtu wa biashara. **f** Steve hapendi kusafiri peke yake. **4 a** Mama mzee hupika chakula cha jioni. **b** Watoto hupenda matunda. **c** Wanafunzi husoma vitabu. **d** Mama Fatuma hushona nguo. **e** Watalii hununua vinyago. **f** Wauguzi huwasaidia wagonjwa (*or* husaidia). **5 a** Kaskazini **b** Magharibi **c** Kaskazini **d** Mashariki **e** Mashariki **f** Kusini **g** Kusini **h** Mashariki **6 a** Elvan huenda barabarani kwa baiskeli. **b** Akina mama huenda msituni kwa miguu. **c** Steve atakwenda Mtwara kwa basi. **d** Mwaka ujao Steve atarudi Marekani kwa ndege (*or* eropleni). **e** Labda Alison na Steve watakwenda Zanzibar kwa boti.

## Unit 9

**1 a** Baiskeli ipo juu. **b** Magunia yapo juu. **c** Dereva yupo mbele. **d** Wanawake wamo ndani. **e** Mama mwenye kikapu anaongea na Steve. **f** Vijana wanauza ndizi. **2 a** *Mtu:* Msiwe na wasiwasi! Mabasi huondoka kila saa moja. **b** *Rafiki:* Wasiwe na wasiwasi! Nitawapa shilingi mia. **c** *Dereva:* Usiwe na wasiwasi! Panda tu. **d** *Msafiri 2:* Usiwe na wasiwasi! Upo hapa chini. **e** *Bibi:* Usiwe na wasiwasi! (*or* asiwe)! Mimi ni mwuguzi – nitamsaidia. **3** Example – This lady hasn't got a ticket yet! – She needn't worry! The conductor will sell her one on the bus. **a** *Traveller:* We've missed that bus! *Someone:* Don't worry! Buses leave every hour. **b** *Conductor:* These ladies, they haven't enough money! *Friend:* They mustn't worry! I'll give them Sh 100. **c** *Traveller:* I'm very late! *Driver:* Don't worry. Hop on. **d** *1st Traveller:* I can't see my bag! (My bag, I can't see it!) *2nd Traveller:* Don't worry! It's here on the floor. **e** *Older woman:* My child's feeling ill! *Younger woman:* Don't worry (*or* don't let him/her worry)! I'm a nurse – I'll help him/her. **4 a** Ni Bw. Twaibu aliyekwenda na Steve mpaka kituo cha basi. **b** Steve ana mzigo mmoja tu. **c** Mumewe mama amekaa mbele, karibu na dereva. **d** Kikapu kilicho mbele ni mali ya mzee. **e** Dereva ana ukanda wa Vijana Jazz. **f** Steve atakaa Mtwara siku mbili. **5 a** Fika salama! **b** Fikeni salama! **6** *Unit 1*: Mtu aliyewatembelea John na Alison hotelini ni Bw. Mohamed. *Unit 2*: Ambaye alikwenda posta kununua stampu ni John. *Unit 3*: Aliyesema anapenda wali kwa samaki ni Alison. *Unit 4*: Watu ambao wana kiu ni Francis na John. *Unit 5*: Ambaye alinunua mfinyango ndiye John. *Unit 6*: Ambao walitembea karibu na bahari ndio Mohamed, John na Alison. *Unit 7*: Mama mzee ndiye aliyepika kisamvu. (*Or:* ambaye alipika) *Unit 8*: Steve ndiye aliyesema hapendi kusafiri peke yake. (*Or:* ambaye alisema)

## Unit 10

**1 a** Mfuko upo ndani ya beseni ya kunawia. **b** Suruali ipo nje ya mlango (*or* ipo chini). **c** Shati lipo juu ya meza (*or* mezani). **d** Saa ipo chini ya kiti. **e** Soksi zimo katika kabati (*or* ndani ya kabati *or* kabatini). **2** Ukumbi wetu una milango miwili, dirisha moja, meza kubwa, meza ndogo, viti vinne, kabati kubwa, rafu mbili zenye vitabu vya Kifaransa, na mkeka chini. **3** *You*: Hayatatosha. Nitasikia (*or* nitaona) baridi usiku. Naomba blanketi jingine./ Haya./Tuletee mito miwili mingine. Tena, nionyeshe namna ya kufungua dirisha hili./ Vizuri. Tutakuja sasa hivi! **4 a** Masanja ni dereva ambaye gari lake ni jeupe. **b** Tusubilege ni mtoto ambaye yupo shuleni. **c** Hivi ni vitabu ambavyo nilivinunua jana. **d** John na Alison ni wageni ambao wanatoka Ulaya. **e** Godoro lile ndilo ambalo ni jipya. **f** Ambaye hatakuja nasi ni Masanja. **5 a** Juma anamwonyesha Steve chumba chake. **b** Ni Juma aliyesafisha asubuhi. **c** Kabati la nguo lipo pembeni. **d** Kitanda ni chembamba. **e** Steve hatahitaji matandiko mengine kwa sababu anaona (*or* anasikia) joto. **f** Juma ameweka ufunguo juu ya rafu. **6 a** Naona kiu sana. **b** Swichi hii yawasha taa ya chumba cha kulalia. **c** Ipo almari hapa. **d** Nikunjue chandalua. **e** Shuka itatosha. **f** Lazima nile samaki!

## Unit 11

**1 a** Shati lilishonwa na Alison. **b** Paa iliezekwa kwa mabati. **c** Ngalawa ilichongwa na Juma na Ali. **d** Jahazi liliundwa kwa mbao. **e** Msikiti ulijengwa kwa mawe. **f** Ngoma ilipigwa na Mohamed. **2 a** Ninyi nyote mmekaribishwa na Mwalimu Musa? **b** Wao wote walieletwa matunda. **c** Sisi sote tuliandikiwa barua. **d** Ninyi nyote mlinunuliwa vinyago? **e** Wao wote walipikiwa chakula cha jioni. **f** Sisi sote tumealikwa ngoma. **a** Have all of you been invited by Teacher Musa (Moses)? **b** They all had fruit brought for them. **c** We all had letters written to us. **d** Were carvings bought for you all? **e** They all had an evening meal cooked for them. **f** We have all been invited to the dancing. **3** *Alison*: Magauni haya yalishonwa na nani?/Una cherehani?/ Utaitumia lini? **4 a** Pili alizaliwa tarehe ishirini na nane, mwezi wa sita (*or* mwezi wa Juni) **b** Mohamed alizaliwa tarehe kumi, mwezi wa Aprili (*or* mwezi wa nne). **c** Alison alizaliwa tarehe moja (or mosi), mwezi wa pili (*or* mwezi wa Februari). **d** John alizaliwa tarehe ishirini na tisa, mwezi wa Novemba (*or* mwezi wa kumi na moja). **e** Faiz alizaliwa tarehe tatu, mwezi wa kumi na mbili (*or* mwezi wa Disemba). **f** Zubeda alizaliwa tarehe kumi, mwezi wa Oktoba (*or* mwezi wa kumi). **5 a** John hakualikwa ngoma kwa sababu (*or* maana) ni ngoma ya wanawake tu. **b** Alison alialikwa na Bi. Salma na dadake Pili. **c** Bwana arusi ni Daudi. **d** Watakwenda forodhani. **e** Watakwenda hapo Jumamosi (ya wiki ijayo).

6 a Bw. Athumani atakaribishwa na Zubeda (na Faiz). b Bw. Athumani anaishi Dar es Salaam. c Nyumba mpya ya Bw. Athumani inajengwa Jambiani. d Ndiyo, nyumba hiyo inajengwa kwa matofali.

## Unit 12

1 a Basi limeharibika. b Kikombe kimevunjika. c Lori limeharibika. d Gilasi imevunjika. e Motokaa imeharibika (or motakaa.) f Dirisha limevunjika. 2 a Tungekuwa na nafasi tungekwenda Arusha. b Baba angekwenda Zanzibar angekaa kwa Faiz. c Juma asingekuwa mgonjwa angefanya kazi hiyo. d Kama mngekuwa na pesa za kutosha mngekwenda Marekani? e Ningehudhuria mkutano huko Nairobi nisingekaa hotelini. f Kama ungeegesha pale ungetozwa faini. 3 a No parking here. b It is forbidden to stop here. *Or:* No stopping here. *Or:* Stopping here is prohibited. c It is forbidden to stay here. *Or* (possibly): sit here *Or:* Staying here is prohibited. d The selling of goods of any kind in this area is prohibited. 4 a Asha anahudhuria mkutano ili afanye kazi ya uhazili. b Pikipiki ni mali ya daktari ambaye ni mwenzi wa John na Alison. c Siyo. Asha hawezi kuona gereji yoyote. d Ni wajenzi wanaofanya kazi karibu na kituo cha basi. 5 *You:* Nimo katika shida kidogo./Motokaa imeharibika. (*Or* gari limeharibika.)/Siyo pancha. Ni shauri ya mota./Lipo Makongoro (Road) karibu na kanisa. 6 For your safety and comfort while on board passengers are requested to have only one piece of hand luggage. More than one is not allowed. Have a good journey.

## Unit 13

1 a You: Unafanyaje? Edda: Ninajifunza Kigiriki. b You: Unafanyaje? Steve: Ninakula saladi. c You: Mnafanyaje? Musa na Saidi: Tunachonga ngalawa. d You: Unafanyaje? Rehema: Ninaandika barua. e You: Mnafanyaje? Kip na Ben: Tunajifunza Kirusi. f You: Unafanyaje? Agnes: Ninajifunza Kijerumani. 2 a Ni akina Francis waliomkaribisha Steve vizuri. b Watu hao hukaa sehemu za kusini, karibu na mpaka kati ya Tanzania na Msumbiji. c Adam anajifunza Kifaransa. d Ni Steve ambaye sasa haogopi kusema Kiswahili. e Steve anaalikwa kwenda Mombasa (kwa wazee wake Adam). f Steve anapenda kula saladi. 3 *You:* Unafundisha somo gani?/Wanafunzi wanapenda kujifunza Kifaransa?/Kwa nini wanajifunza Kifaransa kwa shida?/ Sielewi vizuri. Sema tena!/Mimi ni daktari.
4 a wataandikiana b wanafundishana c walikutana d wanapendana, kuoana e husaidiana f wanapigana (*or* hupigana) 5 a5, b6, c3, d4, e1, f2 6 Your letter must be in standard Swahili; have a good style; be typed; be short; be interesting.

## Unit 14

1 a Nyeri iko kaskazini ya Nairobi. b Magadi iko kusini ya Nairobi.
c Isiolo iko kaskazini ya Nairobi. d Kitui iko mashariki ya Nairobi.
e Narok iko magharibi ya Nairobi. f Eldoret iko kaskazini ya Nairobi
(or kaskazini – magharibi.). 2 tulikata; kwenda; Tulichelewa;
Tuliondoka; tukaenda; tukanunua; tuliendelea (or tukaendelea);
tukafika; tuliangalia (or tukaangalia); hatukupata. 4 a Makindu; Mtito
Andei. b kituo cha mafuta (or gereji). c Msichana. d Baada ya
kusafisha jeraha na kutia dawa Yusuf alilifunika kwa plasta.
e Wasafiri hao watatu walinunua petroli wakaenda mkahawani
wapumzike kidogo. f Yupo Musa, mtoto wake jirani. 5 a Kufika huko
akanunua vifaa vyake vyote alivyovihitaji kwa duka lake.
b Sasa akakwama wapi apate kipande cha akili. c Akazunguka maduka
yote asipate. 6 a alikuwa akisoma. b alikuwa akifanya.
c alikuwa akikaa. d alikuwa akiandika. e alikuwa akifundisha. (In any
of these you can use -na- instead of -ki-.) 7 Bwana huyu anaumwa
kichwa na mama anaumwa shingo na mabega. Mtoto huyu amekatwa
mkononi na yule ambaye amekaa pale amekatwa mguuni. Dereva
anaumwa kifua. Kwa bahati mimi mzima.

## Unit 15

1 Tuliondoka saa moja u nusu tukaenda mpaka mtoni. Kati ya saa tatu
na saa nne u nusu tuliona simba wawili, twiga saba, punda milia
watano, na nyumbu wengi. Kwa bahati mbaya hatukuona tembo
yeyote. Tulirudi hotelini saa sita tukanywa bia. 2 a Alison told Robert
she had seen 7,431 wildebeest. b Simba walikuwapo chini ya mti,
upande wa kulia; wamelala kwenye kivuli. c Alison alipenda kwenda
karibu kidogo. d Robert hakupenda kuwakurupua simba. e Kamera
yake Joshua haikufanya kazi kwa sababu betri zimekwisha.
f Alison alisema atampelekea Joshua picha za wanyama. (Or ... picha
alizozipiga). 3 *Joshua*: Jina langu Joshua Kisinda./ Anwani yangu ni
Sanduku la Posta 26790, Dar es Salaam./ Namba ya simu ni tatu, tano,
sita, sifuri, mbili./ Mimi ni mwandishi-habari./ Niliibiwa asubuhi./Saa
tano na dakika ishirini./Nilikuwepo Kariakoo./ Niliibiwa kamera.
4 Koku; Bhoke; Koku; Aranya; Koku; Bhoke; Koku; Bhoke.
5 a jumba. b jiji. c jitu. d joka. e kijiko. f Kitoto.
g vijiti. h kijitabu. 6 meusi/ miti/ wadogo/ usiku.

## Unit 16

1 *Steve replies*:
Una urefu wa mita elfu tano, mia nane, tisini na tano./Hukaa katika
vibanda./Kuna vibanda vitatu./Kipo urefu wa mita elfu mbili, mia
saba./ Kibanda cha mwanzo kinaitwa Mandara, cha pili kinaitwa
Horombo, cha mwisho kinaitwa Kibo./Kipo urefu wa mita elfu nne

mia saba na tatu./Ni mwinuko wa mita elfu moja, mia moja, tisini na mbili kutoka kibanda cha mwisho mpaka kilele. **2 a** Mama Fatuma ana umri wa miaka arobaini na saba. **b** Mzee Yohanna ana miaka hamsini na minne. **c** Pendo ana miaka ishirini na mmoja. **d** Yahya na Nuru wana umri wa miaka kumi na mmoja. **e** Francis ana umri wa miaka thelathini na miwili. **f** Mohamed ana miaka ishirini na mitatu. **g** Tusubilege ana umri wa mwaka mmoja. **h** Bibi ana miaka sitini na miwili. **3** a4, b6, c1, d2, e5, f3. **4** Robert hawezi, mgongo unamwuma (*or* anaumwa mgongo). Dunstan amepatwa na kichefuchefu, tena uso umefura. Anna amevunjika kidole, Ruth anatoka damu puani na Simon anatoka damu mguuni.

**5** Asubuhi na mapema Regina **aliwaamsha** watoto. Anastasia alimsaidia mamake **kuwasha** moto, **achemshe** maji. Ruth **alitayarisha** chakula cha safari. Mtoto ambaye ni mdogo sana alitaka **kuwakimbiza** kuku. Regina **alimweleza** kwamba watu wote wataondoka saa moja **akawakataza** watoto wote wasiende nje tena. Francis **alisafisha** gari akakata shauri **kujaza** petroli baadaye, barabarani. Hatimaye **waliwakalisha** watoto ndani ya gari na kutia mizigo. Kabla hawajaondoka Regina **alimwonya** Francis **asiendeshe** mbio safari hii. **6** Tumbo na kichwa vinaniuma (*or* ninaumwa tumbo na kichwa). Ninatoka damu miguuni, nimeshikwa (*or* nimepatwa) na homa, ninahara, tena nimekatwa mkononi. **7 a** Unajitokeza juu mawinguni kwa utukufu mkubwa. **b** Mlima huo, ambao ni wa asili ya volkeno, ni mrefu kuliko yote katika Afrika. **c** Mlima Kilimanjaro una vilele vitatu. Vinaitwa Kibo, Mawenzi na Shira. **d** Kibo peak is covered with ice and snow.

## Unit 17

**1 a** Wachezaji wako jukwaani. **b** Wachezaji sita wanaonekana wamevaa nguo nyeupe na kofia. **c** Wale wachezaji wawili wanaocheza upande wa kulia wanashika kanga. **d** Watazamaji wawili wanaonekana hapa mbele. **2 a** Ni Joseph ambaye hucheza soka Jumamosi. **b** Hachezi leo kwa sababu uwanja umejaa maji. (*or* kwa sababu ya mvua nyingi). **c** Francis amekuja na mwavuli. **d** Siyo. Mawingu hayaonekani sasa. **e** Francis amemwambia Joseph aharakishe. **f** Francis amemwona Augustine, ambaye ni rafiki yake. **3** (This is a possible dialogue; yours may be slightly different:) *Joseph*: Haya, lazima niende sasa. *George*: Haya bwana. Tutaonana kwa Peter, Jumanne jioni. *Joseph*: Kama mvua itanyesha kwa wingi labda nitachelewa. (*or* ikinyesha.) *George*: Haya basi. Kwa heri bwana! *Joseph*: Kwa heri! **4 a** -tangaza. **b** (*1*) Kucheza ngoma kunatangazwa gazetini. (*2*) Hawajatangaza tarehe ya fainali. **5** a3, b4, c2, d1. **6 a** Wachezaji wageni wanatoka Ghana. **b** Wachezaji kumi na wanane wamekuja. **c** Timu ambayo iliwasili jana inaitwa Asante Kotoko. **d** Simba na Yanga.

## Unit 18

1 Mwl. Daudi Mhina, S.L.P. 2753, Mpwapwa, Mkoa wa Dodoma, Tanzania. 2 a This aerogramme should have nothing enclosed in it; if it does it will not be sent by air. (*Or*: Nothing should be enclosed in this aerogramme; if it is ... . etc., *or some other version in a formal style giving the two pieces of information*.) 3 a John na Alison wapo jikoni. b Barua tano zimewasili nyumbani. c Katika barua Mohamed anasema kwamba mamake bado anashona nguo. d Babake Mohamed amestaafu kwa ajili ya udhaifu wake baada ya ugonjwa. e Mohamed ameachilia mbali kazi ya benki. f Wasaidizi kwenye duka la babake Mohamed hawaelewi kinaganaga mambo ya bidhaa ziingiazo toka nje, yaani uingizaji. 4 a Katika barua Mohamed anasema wateja wameongezeka. b Mohamed alikuwa amekutana na Steve juzijuzi. c John anafikiri kwamba hatimaye Mohamed atakuwa milionea. d Thekla ni mtoto wa dadake Francis. e Thekla amepongezwa kwa sababu alifaulu mtihani. f Ni Steve ambaye atawasili Heathrow tarehe kumi na sita. 5 a3, b4, c5, d1, e2. *Old man*: Pongezi kwa kustaafu! *Young man*: Pongezi kwa kupata kazi! 6 a Nawatakia salamu za heri kwa Krismasi na baraka ya mwaka mpya. b Twakutakia salamu za heri kwa Krismasi na baraka ya mwaka mpya. Pongezi kwa kufaulu mtihani! (*You could use* -letea *instead of* -takia; *include* fanaka; *spell* heri *as* kheri.)

## Monosyllabic verbs

The verbs with stems of a single syllable are:

| | | | |
|---|---|---|---|
| ku-cha | *to be afraid of* | ku-la | *to eat* |
| ku-cha | *to rise* (sun) | ku-nya | *to excrete, fall* (rain) |
| ku-chwa | *to set* | ku-nywa | *to drink* |
| ku-fa | *to die* | ku-pa | *to give to* |
| ku-ja | *to come* | ku-wa | *to be, become* |

The verbs **-enda** (*go*) and **-isha** (*be finished*) follow the same rules.

**i** Include the infinitive-marker **ku-** when using these verbs with:

| | | |
|---|---|---|
| Past tense | -li- | walikunywa |
| Present | -na- | wanakunywa |
| Perfect | -me- | wamekunywa |
| Future | -ta- | watakunywa |
| Conditionals | -nge- | wangekunywa |
| | -ngali- | wangalikunywa |
| Relative pronouns | | waliokunywa |
| | | aliyekunywa |
| | | watakapokunywa |

except when the relative pronoun is at the end of the stem, i.e. in the 'general' or 'tenseless' relative structure (see below).

**ii** Leave out the infinitive-marker **ku-** when using these verbs with:

| | | |
|---|---|---|
| Past negative | -ku- | hawakunywa |
| If/when | -ki- | wakinywa |

| Narrative | -ka- | wakanywa |
|---|---|---|
| Habitual | hu- | hunywa |
| Subjunctive | | wanywe |
| | | wasinywe |
| Present | -a- | wa(a) nywa |
| Present negative | | hawanywi |
| Object marker | | waliyanywa (-ya- referring to maji or maziwa) |
| The 'general' relative | | wanywao |
| | | anywaye |

iii Either include or omit **ku-** when using these verbs with:

| 'Not yet' | -ja- | hawajakunywa or hawajanywa |
|---|---|---|

## Summary of verb-root suffixes

The suffixes (endings) which can be attached to verb-roots are shown with the verb **kufunga** (*to close, fasten, tie up, lock up,* etc.). The root of the verb is:

**-fung-**

| Niliufunga mlango | *I closed the door.* |
|---|---|
| Walimfunga. | *They locked him up.* |

*Prepositional (or Applicative) -(l)i- or (l)e- (Unit 4)*
| Nilimfungia mlango. | *I closed the door for him.* |
|---|---|

*Conversive -u- or -o- (Unit 10)*
| Alifungua mlango. | *He opened the door.* |
|---|---|

*Passive -(li)w- or -(le)w- (Unit 11)*
| Mlango ulifungwa. | *The door was closed (by somebody).* |
|---|---|

*Stative -ik- or -ek- (Unit 12)*
(Denotes state when used with **-me-**, otherwise denotes potentiality.)

| Mlango umefungika. | *The door is closed (is in a closed state).* |
|---|---|
| Mlango unafungika. | *The door is closable.* |
| Mlango haufungiki. | *The door cannot be closed.* |

*Note:* A few verbs use the Stative with the Reciprocal (see below), -ikan- or -ekan-, to denote potentiality (e.g. **-julikana** (be known/knowable); **-nenekana** (be expressible in words); **-onekana** (be visible); **-patikana** (be obtainable).

*Reciprocal -an- (Unit 13)*

| | |
|---|---|
| Nyuzi zinafungana. | *The threads are tied together.* |

*Causative -(i)sh-, -(e)sh-, -(i)z-, -(e)z- or -y- (Unit 16)*

| | |
|---|---|
| Walimfungisha. | *They had him locked up.* |
| Waliufungisha mlango. | *They had the door closed (had someone close the door).* |

*Reciprocal + Causative -fung-an-y-*

| | |
|---|---|
| Tutafunganya (mizigo) jioni. | *We're going to get the packing done this evening.* |

*Note*: **-funga mizigo** = *tie up loads*, i.e. *get luggage ready*. The extended form **-funganya** can be used on its own, without **mizigo**.

*Conversive + Causative -fung-u-z-*

| | |
|---|---|
| Walitufunguza. | *They set us free (had us set free).* |

*Conversive + Causative + Passive -fung-u-z-w-*

| | |
|---|---|
| Tulifunguzwa. | *We were set free (by someone).* |

*Note:* A few suffixes were not included in the units:

*Static -am- expresses inactivity.*

| | | | |
|---|---|---|---|
| -funga | *tie* | -fungama | *be in a fixed position* |
| -kwaa | *stumble* | -kwama | *be stuck, jammed* |

(Note the example of **-kwama** in Practice 5 of Unit 14.)

*Contactive -at-*

| | | | |
|---|---|---|---|
| -kama | *squeeze* | -kamata | *grab hold of, arrest* |
| -fumba | *close together* | -fumbata | *put arms round,* |
| | (e.g. eyelids, lips) | | *enclose* |

*Inceptive -p- made from adjective stems, denotes entering into a state*

| | | | |
|---|---|---|---|
| -nene | *fat* | -nenepa | *get fat* |
| -oga | *nervous, afraid* | -ogopa | *be frightened* |

*Note:* All verbs (including those of non-Bantu origin) extended by one or more suffixes after the root always have a final **-a**, just as simple stems of Bantu origin, e.g. **-funga**, *do*.

## NOUN CLASS AGREEMENT PREFIXES

| Noun classes → | M/WA (Unit 1) | | N (Unit 2) | | KI/VI (Unit 3) | | (JI)/MA (Unit 4) | |
|---|---|---|---|---|---|---|---|---|
| | mtu | watu | nyumba | nyumba | kiti | viti | chungwa | machungwa |
| **The noun-prefix is used with** | m | wa- | nasal prefix | | ki | vi | ji or no pfx | ma |
| qual. adjectives → | mwema | wema | njema | njema | chema | vyema | jema | mema |
| numbers 1–5 & 8 → | mmoja | wawili | moja | mbili | kimoja | viwili | moja | mawili |
| -ingi & -ingine → | mwingine | wengine | nyingine | nyingine | kingine | vingine | jingine | mengine |
| -ngapi? → | | wangapi? | | ngapi? | | vingapi? | | mangapi? |
| **The verb-prefix is used with** | ni-<br>ku-<br>a-/yu- | wa- | i | zi | ki | vi | li | ya |
| -a (of), etc. → | wa* | wa | ya | za | cha | vya | la | ya |
| place markers → | yuko* | wako | iko | ziko | kiko | viko | liko | yako |
| possessives e.g. -ake- → | wake* | wake | yake | zake | chake | vyake | lake | yake |
| this, these → | huyu | hawa | hii | hizi | hiki | hivi | hili | haya |
| that, those → | yule | wale | ile | zile | kile | vile | lile | yale |
| -enye & -enyewe → | mwenye* | wenye | yenye | zenye | chenye | vyenye | lenye | yenye |
| -ote → | | wote | | zote | | vyote | | yote |
| pronoun forms with -o as in: | | | | | | | | |
| -o -ote → | ye yote | wo wote | yo yote | zo zote | cho chote | vyo vyote | lo lote | yo yote |
| h-o → | huyo | hao | hiyo | hizo | hicho | hivyo | hilo | hayo |
| ndi- → | ndiye | ndio | ndiyo | ndizo | ndicho | ndivyo | ndilo | ndiyo |
| rel. pronouns → | -ye- | -o- | -yo- | -zo- | -cho- | -vyo- | -lo- | -yo- |
| na-o (also nina-, una-, etc.) → | naye | nao | nayo | nazo | nacho | navyo | nalo | nayo |
| | nami | | | | | | | |
| | nasi | | | | | | | |
| | nawe | | | | | | | |
| | nanyi | | | | | | | |

*Note special cases

# NOUN CLASS AGREEMENT PREFIXES (CONTINUED)

| Noun classes → | M/MI (Unit 5) mti / miti | | U/(N) (Unit 6) wimbo / nyimbo | | Place classes (Unit 7) mahali | | | KU Inf. (Unit 8) kusafiri |
|---|---|---|---|---|---|---|---|---|
| **The noun-prefix is used with** | m | mi | u | nasal | ku | pa | mu | ku |
| qual. adjectives ↑ | mwema | myema | mwema* | njema | kwema | pema | | kwema |
| numbers 1–5 & 8 ↑ | mmoja | miwili | mmoja* | mbili | | pamoja | | |
| -ingi & -ingine ↑ | mwingine | mingine | mwingine* | nyingine | kwingine | pengine | | kwingine |
| -ngapi? ↑ | | mingapi? | | ngapi? | | pangapi? | | |
| **The verb-prefix is used with** | u | i | u | zi | ku | pa | mu | ku |
| -a, (of) etc. ↑ | wa | ya | wa | za | kwa | pa | mwa | kwa |
| place-markers ↑ | uko | iko | uko | ziko | | | | |
| possessives e.g. -ake ↑ | wake | yake | wake | zake | kwake | pake | mwake | kwake |
| this, these, ↑ | huu | hii | huu | hizi | huku | hapa | humu | huku |
| that, those ↑ | ule | ile | ule | zile | kule | pale | m(u)le | kule |
| -enye & -enyewe ↑ | wenye | yenye | wenye | zenye | kwenye | penye | mwenye | kwenye |
| -ote ↑ | | yote | | zote | kote | pote | mwote | kote |
| pronoun forms with -o, as in: | | | | | | | | |
| -o -ote ↑ | wo wote | yo yote | wo wote | zo zote | ko kote | po pote | | ko-kote |
| h-o ↑ | huo | hiyo | huo | hizo | huko | hapo | humo | huko |
| ndi- ↑ | ndio | ndiyo | ndio | ndizo | ndiko | ndipo | ndimo | ndiko |
| rel. pronouns ↑ | -o- | -yo- | -o- | -zo- | -ko- | -po- | -mo- | -ko- |
| na-o (also mina-, una- etc.) ↑ | nao | nayo | nao | nazo | nako | napo | namo | nako |

*Note special cases

Verbs are shown in their stem form, without the infinitive **ku**.
Hyphens are used only in front of qualifiers that take a prefix.
Except for the N class of nouns, plural prefixes are generally
shown in brackets, although in a few cases the full form of a
plural noun is given.

-a *of*
-a kwanza *first*
-a mwisho *last*
-a pili *second*
abiria *passenger*
adhuhuri *midday*
afadhali *better, preferable*
Afrika *Africa*
agiza *(to) order*
Agosti *August*
ahadi *promise*
ahirisha *(to) postpone*
aidha *moreover*
aina *kind, type*
ajali *accident*
ajili *reason, sake*
-ake *his, her, its*
akina *see **kina***
-ako *your*
ala  expression of suprise
alasiri *afternoon*
alfajiri *dawn*
Alhamisi *Thursday*
alika *(to) invite*
almari *chest of drawers*
ama *or*
ama ... ama *either ... or*
amba- *who, which*
ambia *(to) tell*
amka *(to) wake*

andazi (ma) *doughnut*
andika *(to) write*
angalia *(to) take care, observe*
-angu *my*
anwani *address*
anza *(to) begin*
anzia *(to) start from*
-ao *their*
Aprili *April*
arobaini *forty*
arusi *wedding*
asante *thank you*
asili *origin, source*
askari *soldier, policeman*
asubuhi *morning*
au *or*
au ... au *either ... or*

baa *bar*
baada ya *after*
baadaye *afterwards*
baba *father*
baba mdogo *uncle* (paternal)
babu (ma) *ancestor*
badala ya *instead of*
bado *still, (not) yet*
bafu *bath, shower*
bahari *sea, ocean*
bahasha *envelope*
bahati *luck, fortune*

baiskeli *bicycle*
baki *(to) remain*
bandari *port*
bandika *(to) stick on*
Bara Hindi *India*
barabara *major road*
baraka *blessing*
baridi *cold, coolness*
barua *letter*
basi *so, now, well*
basi (ma) *bus*
bati (ma) *corrugated iron*
batiki *batik*
-baya *bad*
beba *(to) carry*
bega (ma) *shoulder*
bei *price*
beseni *basin*
betri *battery*
bia *beer*
biashara *trade*
bibi (ma) *lady, grandmother*
bibi arusi *bride*
bidi *(to) be compelled*
bila *without*
binadamu *human being*
biriani *rice dish*
bizari *curry powder*
  (& ingredients of)
blanketi (ma) *blanket*
bora *good, better*
boti *boat*
buibui *outer garment*
  (Muslim women)
buluu *blue*
bure *useless, uselessly*
bwana (ma) *gentleman, Mr, sir*
bwana arusi *bridegroom*

-chache *few*
chai *tea*
chakacha *women's dance*
chakula (vy) *food*
chama (vy) *association,*
  *political party*
chambua *(to) sort out*
chamshakinywa (vy) *breakfast*
chandalua (vy) *mosquito net*
-changa *young*
changamka *(to) feel more cheerful*
changamsha *(to) cheer sy. up*

changu *kind of sea fish*
chelewa *(to) be late*
chemka *(to) be boiling*
chemsha *(to) boil* (something)
chenji *change* (coins)
cherehani *sewing machine*
cheti (vy) *note, certificate*
cheza *(to) dance, play*
chini *down, on the floor*
chini ya *under*
chinja *(to) slaughter*
choka *(to) get tired*
chonga *(to) carve* (wood)
choo (vy) *lavatory, excrement*
chubuka *(to) be bruised*
chui *leopard*
chukua *(to) take, carry*
chuma *(to) gather, pluck*
chumba (vy) *room*
chumvi *salt*
chungu (vy) *cooking-pot*
chungwa (ma) *orange*
chuo kikuu (vy) *university*
chupa *bottle*
chwa *(to) set* (sun)

dada *sister*
dafu *young coconut*
dakika *minute*
daktari (ma) *doctor*
daladala *private bus* (Tanz.)
dalasini *cinnamon*
damu *blood*
darasa (ma) *class, classroom*
dawa *medicine, treatment*
debe (ma) *large oil-tin*
deni (ma) *debt*
dereva (ma) *driver*
Desemba *December*
desturi *custom, habit*
dhaifu *frail, weak*
dhuru *(to) harm*
dirisha (ma) *window*
Disemba see **Desemba**
divai *wine*
doa (ma) *spot, mark*
-dogo *small*
dudu (ma) *large insect, pest*
duka (ma) *shop*
duma *cheetah*
dume *male animal*

ebu! *hi there!*

egesha *(to) park*

-ekundu *red*

elewa *(to) understand*

eleza *(to) explain*

elfu *thousand*

-ema *good*

-embamba *narrow*

embe (ma) *mango*

enda *(to) go*

endelea *(to) continue, progress*

endesha *(to) drive*

eneo (ma) *area*

-enye *having*

-enyewe *self*

-enu *your* (pl.)

-erevu *cunning*

-etu *our*

-eupe *white*

-eusi *black*

ezeka *(to) roof a building*

fa *(to) die*

faa *(to) be suitable, useful*

fagia *(to) sweep*

fanaka *success*

fanya *(to) do, make*

fanya kazi *(to) work*

fariki *(to) die* (humans)

faulu *(to) succeed, pass an exam*

Februari *February*

fedha *money, silver*

feni *fan*

fika *(to) arrive*

fikiri *(to) consider, think*

fisi *hyena*

forodha *customs office*

fua *(to) wash clothes*

fuata *(to) follow*

fuatana *(to) accompany*

fulani *someone/thing*

fuma *(to) weave*

fumua *(to) unpick*

fundi (ma) *skilled worker*

fundisha *(to) teach*

funga *(to) close, tie, fasten*

fungua *(to) open, untie*

funika *(to) cover*

funua *(to) uncover*

-fupi *short*

fura *(to) swell*

ganga *(to) heal, cure*

gani? *what* (kind)?

gari (ma) *vehicle*

gari moshi (ma) *train*

gauni (ma) *dress, frock*

gawanya *(to) give up*

gazeti (ma) *newspaper*

gereji (ma) *garage*

ghafula *suddenly*

ghala *store, warehouse*

ghali *expensive*

ghorofa *floor, storey*

gilasi *glass*

godoro (ma) *mattress*

gofu (ma) *ruin* (building)

gogo (ma) *log*

gonga *(to) knock*

goti (ma) *knee*

-gumu *hard*

gunia (ma) *sack*

habari *news*

hadithi *story*

hakika *certainty*

halafu *then, afterwards*

hali *state, condition*

halisi *genuine, true*

hamsini *fifty*

hamu *need, desire*

hapa, hapo *here*

hapana *no*

hapo *then, there*

hara *(to) have diarrhoea*

   hara damu *(to) have dysentery*

haribika *(to) be broken*

haribu *(to) destroy, spoil*

harusi see **arusi**

hasa *particularly, exactly*

hata *until, so, (not) even*

hatari *danger*

hatimaye *eventually*

hawa/hao *these* (people, animals)

Haya! *Okay! Right! Fine!*

haya, hayo *these*

hebu! see **ebu!**

hela *money* (not much used)

hema *tent*

heri *happiness, good luck*

   Kwa heri! *Goodbye!*

hesabu *(to) count*

hewa *air, atmosphere*

hii, hiyo *this*
hiki, hicho *this*
hili, hilo *this*
hisani *kindness*
Hispania *Spain*
hitaji *(to) need*
hivi, hivyo *these, thus*
hizi, hizo *these*
hodari *able, brave, efficient*
Hodi! *May I/we come in?*
hoteli *hotel*
hudhuria *(to) attend*
huenda *perhaps*
huko *over there (at)*
huku *around here*
hukumu *judgement, sentence*
humu, humo *in here*
hundi *cheque*
hundi ya posta *postal order*
husu *(to) concern*
huu, huo *this*
huyu, huyo *this* (person, animal)

iba *(to) steal*
Ijumaa *Friday*
ijapo *although, even though*
ijapokuwa *although, even though*
ikiwa *if*
ila *but, except*
ile *that*
ili *in order that*
iliki *cardamom*
imba *(to) sing*
ingawa *although*
-ingi *many*
ingia *(to) enter*
-ingine *some, other*
isha, kwisha *(to) be finished*
ishirini *twenty*
ita *(to) call, name*
iwapo *if, supposing*

ja *(to) come*
jaa *(to) be full*
jahazi (ma) *dhow*
jambo (mambo) *matter, thing*
jana *yesterday*
jangwa (ma) *desert*
jani (ma) *leaf*
Januari *January*
Je! *Well! Now then!*

-je? *how?*
jembe (ma) *hoe*
jenga *(to) build*
jeraha (ma) *wound, sore*
jibu (ma) *answer*
jibu *(to) reply*
jicho (macho) *eye*
jifungua *(to) give birth*
jifunza *(to) learn*
jiji (ma) *city*
jike (ma) *female animal*
jiko (meko) *kitchen, cooker, stove*
jina (ma) *name*
jino (meno) *tooth*
jinsi *manner, type*
jiografia *geography*
jioni *evening*
jirani (ma) *neighbour*
jiwe (mawe) *stone*
joto *heat*
jua (ma) *sun*
jukwaa (ma) *stage*
Julai *July*
Jumamosi *Saturday*
Jumanne *Tuesday*
jumba (ma) *large building*
jumba la makumbusho(ma) *museum*
jumla *total*
Juni *June*
juu *above, up*
juu ya *on*
-a juu *top*
juzi *day before yesterday*
juzijuzi *recently*

kaa (ma) *lump of charcoal*
kaa *(to) sit, stay, live*
kabati (ma) *cupboard*
kabila (ma) *tribe*
kabisa *completely, entirely*
kabla *before*
kabla ya *before*
kadiri *extent, amount*
kahawa *coffee* (drink)
kahawia *brown*
kaka *brother*
kama *like, such as, if*
kamba *rope*
kamera *camera*
kamili *complete, exact, exactly*
kampuni (ma) *company, firm*

kana *(to) deny*
kando *aside, away from*
kando ya *near, next to*
kanga *patterned cloth* (women)
kanisa (ma) *church*
kanzu *long garment* (Muslim men)
kaptura *shorts*
karabati *(to) renovate*
karani (ma) *clerk*
karibia *(to) move near to*
karibisha *(to) welcome sy.*
Karibu! *Welcome!*
karibu *near, soon*
kaseti *cassette*
kasha (ma) *chest (storage)*
kasirika *(to) be angry*
kaskazi *N.E. monsoon*
kaskazini *north*
kata *(to) cut, buy, sell*
  kata hukumu *(to) pronounce
    judgement*
  kata kiu *(to) quench thirst*
  kata njia *(to) take a short cut*
  kata shauri *(to) make a decision*
  kata tamaa *(to) despair*
kataa *(to) refuse, decline*
kataza *(to) forbid*
katiba *constitution*
katibu *secretary* (company,
  committee, etc.)
katikati *in the middle*
kati ya *between*
kawaida *custom*
kazi *work*
kera *(to) annoy*
kesho *tomorrow*
kesho kutwa *day after tomorrow*
keti *(to) sit*
kiangazi *hot season*
kiasi *amount*
kiatu (vi) *shoe*
kiazi (vi) *sweet potato*
kibanda (vi) *hut*
kibibi (vi) *small pancake*
kiboko (vi) *hippopotamus*
kichefuchefu *nausea*
kichwa (vi) *head*
kidato (vi) *form* (sec. school)
kidogo *a little, slightly*
kidole (vi) *finger, toe*
kifaa (vi) *tool*

kifaru (vi) *rhinoceros*
kifua (vi) *chest, chest ailment*
kifungo (vi) *button*
kifunguakinywa (vi) *breakfast*
kifuniko (vi) *lid*
kijana (vi) *young person*
kijani *green*
kijiji (vi) *village*
kijiko (vi) *spoon*
kijitabu (vi) *booklet, pamphlet*
kikapu (vi) *basket*
kikoi (vi) *men's sarong*
kikombe (vi) *cup*
kila *every, each*
kile *that*
kilele (vi) *peak, summit*
kilima (vi) *hill*
kilimo *agriculture*
kilo *kilo*
kima *small monkey*
kimbia *(to) run away from*
kimbilia *(to) run to*
Kimvita *Mombasa dialect of Swahili*
kimya *quiet, quietly*
kina *associates of sy.*
  kina baba *menfolk*
kinaganaga *explicitly, in detail*
kinu (vi) *mortar, mill*
kinyago (vi) *carving*
kinyozi (vi) *barber*
kinywa (vi) *mouth*
kinywaji (vi) *drink*
kiongozi (vi) *leader, guide*
kipande (vi) *piece*
kipindupindu *cholera*
kipofu (vi) *blind person*
kipupwe *cool season*
kisamvu *cooked cassava leaves*
kisha *then*
kisima (vi) *well, bore-hole*
kisu (vi) *knife*
Kiswahili *the Swahili language*
kitabu (vi) *book*
kitambaa (vi) *cloth, fabric*
kitanda (vi) *bed*
kitendawili (vi) *riddle*
kiti (vi) *chair*
kitumbua (vi) *rice bun*
kitunguu (vi) *onion*
kitoto (vi) *very small baby*
kitu (vi) *thing*

kituo (vi) *stopping-place*
  kituo cha ndege  *airport*
  kituo cha polisi  *police-station*
kiu *thirst*
kiungo (vi) *seasoning, spice*
kivuli (vi) *shadow, shade*
kiwete (vi) *lame person*
kizibo (vi) *plug, stopper*
kiziwi (vi) *deaf person*
kofia *hat*
kombe (ma) *serving dish,*
  *challenge cup*
kompyuta *computer*
kondakta (ma) *conductor* (train/bus)
koo (ma) *throat*
kopa *(to) borrow*
kopesha *(to) lend*
koroga *(to) stir*
korosho *cashew nut*
kosa (ma) *error, fault*
kosa *(to) miss, make an error*
koti (ma) *jacket, coat*
kubali *(to) agree, accept*
-kubwa *large*
kucha *whole night*
kuhusu *concerning, about*
kuku *chicken, hen*
kulia *right (side)*
kuliko *than*
kumbuka *(to) remember*
Kumbe! *expression of surprise*
kumi *ten*
kundi (ma) *group*
kuni *firewood* (pl.)
kunja *(to) fold*
kunjua *(to) unfold*
kuro *water buck*
kurupua *(to) startle*
kushoto *left (side)*
kusini *south*
kusudia *(to) intend*
kutana *(to) meet*
kutu *rust*
kutwa *whole day*
-kuu *great*
kwa *with, to, from, at*
  kwa ajili ya  *because of*
  kwa heri  *goodbye*
  kwa kuwa  *because*
  kwa nini?  *why?*
  kwa sababu  *because*

kwama *(to) become stuck*
kwanza *first*
kweli *truth, true, truly*
kwenu *your (pl.) home*
kwetu *our home*

la *(to) eat*
La! *Certainly not!*
labda *perhaps*
laini *smooth, soft*
laiti *if only*
lakini *but*
lala *(to) lie down, sleep*
lami *tar, tarmac*
lazima *necessary, necessity*
leo *today*
leta *(to) bring*
lewa *(to) be drunk*
likizo *holiday, vacation*
lile *that*
limau (ma) *lemon*
linda *(to) guard*
lipa *(to) pay*
lisha *(to) graze, feed*
lori (ma) *lorry, truck*
lugha *language*

maana *meaning, cause*
maarifa *knowledge*
Machi *March*
mada *topic*
madaraka *responsibility*
maelezo *explanation*
maendeleo *development, progress*
mafundisho *teaching*
mafuta *oil*
mafuta ya taa *kerosene, paraffin*
magharibi *west*
magomvi *quarrelling*
maharagwe *kidney beans*
mahali *place*
mahindi *maize* (sweetcorn)
mahitaji *needs, requirements*
majani *grass, leaves*
maji *water*
majivu *ash*
makaa *charcoal*
makala *written article*
maktaba *library*
malaria *malaria*
mali *wealth, property*

maliwato *bathroom*
maliza *(to) finish*
mama *mother*
mama mdogo *aunt (maternal)*
manjano *yellow, turmeric*
manufaa *usefulness, advantage*
mapema *early*
mapigano *fighting*
mapokezi *reception desk/counter*
mara *time, occasion*
mara *suddenly*
marahaba! *reply to* shikamoo!
Marekani *USA*
marekebisho *repair*
maridadi *elegant, smart*
mashariki *east*
mashindano *competition, race*
masika *season of heavy rain*
maskini *poor*
maskini! *expression of sympathy*
matamshi *pronunciation*
matandiko *bedding*
matata *trouble, complications*
matatizo *problems*
matatu *private bus* (Kenya)
matembezi *walk, stroll*
mavuno *harvest-time*
mazao *production*
mbali *far*
mbalimbali *various*
mbele *in front, ahead*
mbele ya *in front of*
mbili *two*
mbio *fast, speedily*
mboga *vegetable*
mbona? *why ...?*
 (surprise or displeasure)
mbu *mosquito*
mbuga ya wanyama *game-park/
 reserve*
mbuyu (mi) *baobab tree*
mbuzi *goat*
bmwa *dog*
mchana *daytime*
mchele *husked uncooked rice*
mchezo (mi) *game*
mchi (mi) *pestle*
mchicha *spinach-like vegetable*
Mchina (Wa) *Chinese (person)*
mchungaji (wa) *shepherd, herder*
mchungwa (mi) *orange tree*

mdomo (mi) *lip*
mdudu (wa) *insect*
mechi *match* (sport)
Mei *May*
meneja (ma) *manager*
mfano (mi) *example*
mfanyabiashara see **mfanyibiashara**
mfanyakazi (wa) see **mfanyikazi**
mfanyibiashara (wa) *trader*
mfanyikazi (wa) *worker*
Mfaransa (Wa) *French person*
mfinyango (mi) *pottery figure*
mfinyanzi (wa) *potter*
mfuko (mi) *bag, pocket*
Mganda (Wa) *Ugandan (person)*
mgeni (wa) *guest, stranger*
mgomba (mi) *banana plant*
mgongo (mi) *back, backbone*
mgonjwa (wa) *ill person*
mguu (mi) *foot and leg*
mhadhara (mi) *lecture*
mhadhiri (wa) *lecturer*
Mhindi (Wa) *Indian (person)*
mhindi (mi) *maize plant*
mia *hundred*
milionea *millionaire*
mimi *I, me*
miongoni mwa *among*
Misri *Egypt*
mita *metre*
mjenzi (wa) *builder*
Mjerumani (Wa) *German (person)*
mji (mi) *town, settlement*
mjomba (wa) *uncle (maternal)*
mjukuu (wa) *grandchild*
mkahawa (mi) *café*
mkate (mi) *loaf, bread*
mke (wa) *wife*
Mkenya (Wa) *Kenyan (person)*
mkono (mi) *hand and arm, sleeve*
mkoa (mi) *region*
mkorosho (mi) *cashew-nut tree*
Mkristo (Wa) *Christian (person)*
mkungu (mi) *hand (stem)
 of bananas*
mkunjufu (wa) *cheerful person*
mkutano (mi) *meeting, conference*
mlango (mi) *door*
mlevi (wa) *drunkard*
mlima (mi) *mountain*
mlimau (mi) *lemon tree*

mlingoti (mi) *mast*
mlinzi (wa) *guard, watchman*
Mmarekani (Wa) *American* (person)
mnamo *at, in, about*
mnanasi (mi) *pineapple plant*
mnazi (mi) *coconut palm*
mno *extremely, too*
mnunuzi (wa) *buyer*
mnyama (wa) *animal*
-moja *one*
   moja kwa moja *straight ahead*
   -mojawapo *any one* (of)
   -moja -moja *singly*
moshi (mi) *smoke*
mota *motor, engine*
moto (mi) *fire*
moyo (mi) *heart*
mpagazi (wa) *porter*
mpaka (mi) *border, boundary*
mpaka *up to, until*
mpanda (wa) *climber*
mpigaji ngoma (wa) *drummer*
mpigaji picha (wa) *photographer*
mpishi (wa) *cook*
mpita njia (wa) *passer-by*
mpokeaji (wa) *receptionist*
mpotevu (wa) *wasteful person*
mpwa *nephew*
mrengu (mi) *outrigger*
Mrusi (Wa) *Russian* (person)
msafiri (wa) *traveller*
msahaulifu (wa) *forgetful person*
msaidizi (wa) *assistant, helper*
msalkheri! *evening greeting*
mshikaki (mi) *kebab*
mshinde (wa) *loser*
mshonaji (wa) *tailor*
mshoni (wa) see **mshonaji**
msichana (wa) *young unmarried woman*
msimamizi (wa) *organizer, foreman*
msingi (mi) *foundation*
msitu (mi) *woodland*
mstari (mi) *line*
Msumbiji *Mozambique*
mtaalamu (wa) *expert, specialist*
mtalii (wa) *tourist*
mtama (mi) *millet*
Mtanzania (Wa) *Tanzanian* (person)
mteja (wa) *customer*
mti (mi) *tree*

mtihani (mi) *examination*
mtindo (mi) *style*
mto (mi) *river, pillow*
mtoto (wa) *child*
   mtoto wa kike *boy*
   mtoto wa kiume *girl*
mtumbwi (mi) *dug-out canoe* (no outriggers)
mtume (mi) *apostle, prophet*
mtumishi (wa) *employee, servant*
muda (mi) *period of time*
   muda wa *during*
muhogo (mi) *cassava*
mume (wa) *husband*
Mungu (mi) *God*
muwa (mi) *sugar-cane*
muziki *modern music*
mvi *grey hair*
mvua *rain*
mvulana (wa) *young man*
mvuvi (wa) *fisherman*
mwaka (mi) *year*
mwalimu (wa) *teacher*
mwana (wa) *son or daughter*
mwanafunzi (wa) *student, pupil*
mwanamke (wanawake) *woman*
mwanamume (wanaume) *man*
mwandishi (wa) *writer*
   mwandishi habari (wa) *journalist*
mwanzo (mi) *beginning, onset*
mwembe (mi) *mango tree*
mwendo (mi) *movement, speed*
mwenye (wa) *owner*
mwenyeji (wa) *native, local resident*
mwenyewe (wa) *him/herself*
mwenzi (wa) *companion*
mwezi (mi) *month*
mwili (mi) *body*
mwimbaji (wa) *singer*
Mwingereza (Wa) *Briton*
mwinuko (mi) *rise, elevation*
mwisho (mi) *end*
   mwishowe *finally*
Mwislamu (Wa) *Muslim* (person)
mwitu (mi) *forest*
mwivi (wevi) see **mwizi**
mwizi (wezi) *thief*
mwombaji (wa) *beggar, supplicant*
mwuzaji (wa) *seller, stall-holder*
mwuguzi (wa) *nurse*
mzazi (wa) *parent*

mzee (wa) *old person*
mzigo (mi) *piece of luggage, load*
mzoga (mi) *carcass*
Mzungu (Wa) *European* (person)

na *and, with, by*
nafasi *opportunity, space*
nakshi *decoration, pattern*
namba *number* (written)
namna *type*
nanasi (ma) *pineapple*
-nane *eight*
nani? *who?*
nawa *(to) wash the hands*
nazi *coconut*
nchi *country*
ndani *inside*
ndi- *am/is/are* (emph.)
ndipo *then, there*
ndiyo *yes, it is so*
ndizi *banana*
ndoo *bucket*
ndoto *dream*
ndovu *elephant*
ndubi *outrigger*
ndugu *relative, close friend*
nena *(to) speak*
nenda! *go!*
-nene *fat*
neno (ma) *word, utterance*
ngalawa *dug-out canoe with
    outriggers*
ngano *wheat*
-ngapi? *how many?*
ngiri *warthog*
ngoja *(to) wait*
ngoma *drum, dance*
ng'ombe *cow*
nguo *garment, cloth*
nguru *kingfish*
nguvu *strength*
ni *am/are/is*
nini? *what?*
ninyi *you* (pl.)
njaa *hunger*
nje *outside*
njia *road, path*
njoo! *come!*
-nne *four*
Novemba *November*
nunua *(to) buy*

nusu *half*
nyama *meat*
nyamaa *(to) be quiet*
nyani *baboon*
nyanya *grandmother, tomato*
nyesha *(to) rain*
nyoa *(to) shave*
nyoka *snake*
nyuma *behind, at the back*
nyuma ya *behind, at the back
    of sthg.*
nyumba *house*
nyumbu *wildebeest*
nyundo *hammer*
nywa *(to) drink*

oa *(to) marry* (man)
ofisi *office*
oga *take a bath, shower*
ogelea *(to) swim*
ogopa *(to) be afraid* (of)
okota *(to) pick up, find*
oksijeni *oxygen*
Oktoba *October*
olewa *(to) be married* (woman)
omba *(to) ask for, beg, pray*
ona *(to) see, feel*
ondoa *(to) remove*
ondoka *(to) set off, leave*
onekana *(to) be visible, be evident*
ongea *(to) chat, talk*
ongeza *(to) increase, add to*
ongoza *(to) lead*
onya *(to) warn*
onyesha *(to) show*
operesheni *operation*
osha *(to) clean*
ota *(to) dream, grow*
-ote *all*
-o-ote *any*

pa *(to) give*
paa *roof*
paka *cat*
palilia *(to) weed, hoe*
pamoja *together*
pana *there is/are*
-pana *wide*
pancha *puncture*
panda *(to) board, climb*
panga (ma) *machete*

papai (ma) *pawpaw, papaya*
pasua *(to) split, tear, operate on*
pata *(to) get*
patana *(to) be in agreement*
patikana *(to) be obtainable*
peke *alone*
peleka *(to) send, take*
pembe *corner*
penda *(to) like, love*
pendeza *(to) please*
pesa *money*
peta *(to) bend*
pete *ring*
petroli *petrol* (USA *gas*)
-pi? *which?*
picha *picture, photograph*
piga *(to) hit, beat*
  piga bao *(to) consult omens*
  piga chafya *(to) sneeze*
  piga chapa *(to) print*
  piga deki *(to) wash floor*
  piga hema *(to) pitch a tent*
  piga hodi *(to) ask to come in*
  piga kelele *(to) make a noise*
  piga kura *(to) vote*
  piga magoti *(to) kneel*
  piga maji *(to) get very drunk*
  piga makofi *(to) clap*
  piga mbio *(to) run*
  piga miayo *(to) yawn*
  piga mstari *(to) draw a line*
  piga ngoma *(to) beat a drum*
  piga pasi *(to) iron* (clothes, etc.)
  piga simu *(to) telephone*
  piga soga *(to) chat, gossip*
pigana *(to) fight*
pika *(to) cook*
pikipiki *motorcycle*
pilipili *pepper*
pinda *(to) turn, bend*
pinduka *(to) be overturned*
pita *(to) go along, through, by*
plasta *plaster, adhesive dressing*
poa *(to) get cool, recover*
pokea *(to) receive*
pole! *sorry!*
polepole *slowly*
pombe *local beer*
pona *(to) recover*
ponda *(to) pound*
pongea *(to) recover*

pongeza *(to) congratulate*
ponya *(to) cure*
pori (ma) *bush, scrub area*
posta *post office*
potea *(to) be lost*
poteza *(to) waste, spoil*
pua *nose*
pumzika *(to) rest*
punda milia *zebra*
pungua *(to) decrease*
punguza *(to) reduce sg.*
pwani *beach, coast*
-pya *new*

rafiki *friend*
rafu *shelf*
raha *comfort*
rahisi *easy, cheap*
rais (ma) *president*
ramani *map*
rambirambi expr. of condolence
rangi *colour*
ratiba *timetable*
-refu *long, tall, high, deep*
rekebisha *(to) repair*
robo *quarter*
rudi *(to) return*
rudisha *(to) return sth.*
ruhusa *permission*
ruhusu *(to) allow, permit*
ruka *(to) jump*

saa *hour, clock, watch*
saba *seven*
sababu *reason*
sabini *seventy*
safari *journey*
safi *clean*
safiri *(to) travel*
safisha *(to) clean*
saga *(to) grind grain*
sahau *(to) forget*
sahihisha *(to) correct*
saidia *(to) help*
saladi *salad*
salama *safely*
salamu *greetings*
salimu *(to) greet*
samahani! *sorry!*
samaki *fish*
sambusa *samosa*

samehe *(to) forgive*
sana *very*
sanaa *art, artistry*
sanduku (ma) *box*
sanifu *standard*
sasa *now*
sauti *sound, voice*
sehemu *part, section*
senti *cent*
Septemba *September*
serikali *government*
shaka (ma) *doubt*
shamba (ma) *farm, plantation*
shangazi *aunt* (paternal)
shati (ma) *shirt*
shauri (ma) *advice, problem
    needing discussion*
shiba *(to) be satisfied*
shida *difficulty, trouble*
shika *(to) hold, grasp*
shikamoo *greeting to an
    older person*
shilingi *shilling*
shinda *(to) win, succeed*
shindana *(to) compete*
shingo *neck*
shiti *sheet*
shona *(to) sew*
shughuli *duties, commitments*
shugulika *(to) be busy*
shuka *sheet*
shuka *(to) descend, leave vehicle*
shukuru *(to) thank*
si *am/are/is not*
sifuri *zero, nought, nil*
sikia *(to) hear*
sikiliza *(to) listen*
sikio (ma) *ear*
siku *day* (24 hours)
simama *(to) stand, stop*
simamisha *(to) stop a vehicle*
simba *lion*
simu *telephone*
sindikiza *(to) accompany part of
    the way, see sbdy. off*
sisi *we, us*
sita *six*
sitini *sixty*
siyo *no*
soda *non-alcoholic drink*
soko (ma) *market*

soksi *sock*
soma *(to) read, study*
somo (ma) *lesson, subject*
spea *spare-part*
staafu *(to) retire from employment*
stampu *postage stamp*
stempu see **stampu**
stesheni *station*
stoo *store*
subiri *(to) wait, be patient*
sufuria *metal cooking-pot*
sukari *sugar*
sukuma *(to) push*
sura *face, appearance*
suruali *trousers*
swala *gazelle*
swali (ma) *question*
swara see **swala**
swichi *switch*

taa *light* (electric, oil)
tabibu (ma) *doctor*
tafadhali *please*
tafuta *(to) look for*
taka *(to) want*
tamaa *desire*
tamthilia *play* (drama)
tanga (ma) *sail*
tangazo (ma) *notice, advertisement*
tango (ma) *cucumber*
tangu *since*
-tano *five*
tapika *(to) vomit*
tarabu *music* (coastal) *for listening*
tarehe *date* (of month)
taslim *cash payment*
tata *(to) tangle*
tatua *(to) untangle*
-tatu *three*
tayari *ready*
tayarisha *(to) get sg. ready*
tazama *(to) look at*
tegemea *(to) depend on*
teksi *taxi*
tembea *(to) walk*
tembelea *(to) visit*
tembo *elephant*
tena *again, also*
tengeneza *(to) prepare, repair*
tetemeko (ma) *earthquake*
thelathini *thirty*

theluji *snow*
themanini *eighty*
tia *(to) put*
tiketi *ticket*
tisa *nine*
tisini *ninety*
tofaa (ma) *apple*
tofali (ma) *brick*
tofauti *difference*
tofautiana *(to) differ*
toka *from, since*
toka *(to) leave* (a place)
  toka damu *(to) bleed*
tokea *(to) happen*
tokeza *(to) protrude*
tosha *(to) be enough, suffice*
toza *(to) fine, tax*
treni *train*
tu *just, only*
tua *(to) alight, land*
tui *coconut juice*
tuma *(to) send*
tumaini *(to) hope, expect*
tumbili *vervet monkey*
tumbo (ma) *stomach*
tumbukia *(to) tumble into*
tumika *(to) be of service, employed*
tunda (ma) *single fruit*
tunza *(to) take care of*
tupa *(to) throw*
twanga *(to) pound grain*
twiga *giraffe*

ua *(to) kill*
ubao (mbao) *plank, blackboard*
ubaya *badness, evil*
Ubelgiji *Belgium*
Uchina *China*
udhaifu *frailty, weakness*
udogo *smallness*
udongo *soil, clay*
ufagio (fagio) *broom, brush*
Ufaransa *France*
ufunguo (funguo) *key*
ugali *polenta*
Uganda *Uganda*
Ugiriki *Greece*
ugomvi *quarrelling*
ugonjwa *illness*
ugua *(to) become ill*
uhazili *secretarial work*

uhitaji *need, requirement*
Uingereza *U.K., Britain*
Ujerumani *Germany*
uji *liquid porridge, gruel*
ujinga *stupidity*
ujumbe (jumbe) *message*
ukanda (kanda) *tape* (video etc.)
ukimwi *AIDS*
ukubwa *size*
ukumbi (kumbi) *sitting-room*
ukunjufu *amiability, cheerfulness*
ukuni (kuni) *stick of firewood*
ukurasa (kurasa) *page*
ukuta (kuta) *wall*
Ulaya *Europe*
ule *that*
ulimi (ndimi) *tongue*
uliza *(to) ask*
uma *(to) hurt*
umba *(to) create*
umeme *electricity*
umia *(to) be injured*
umiza *(to) cause pain to somebody*
umri *age*
umwa *(to) be ill, feel pain*
unda *(to) construct*
unga *flour*
unywele (nywele) *single hair*
upande (pande) *side, direction*
upesi *quickly*
upotevu *waste, vandalism*
upuuzi *foolishness, nonsense*
urefu *height, length*
Urusi *Russia*
usahaulifu *forgetfulness*
usalama *safety*
ushanga (shanga) *bead*
usiku (siku) *night*
uso (nyuso) *face*
utafiti *research*
utoto *childhood*
utukufu *glory*
uwanja (wanja) *pitch* (games)
uza *(to) sell*
uzee *old age*

vaa *(to) dress, be wearing*
vazi (ma) *garment*
vibaya *badly*
video *video*
vile *those, thus*

vilevile *also*
vipi? *how?*
vizuri *well*
volkeno *volcano*
vua *(to) undress*
vuka *(to) cross*
vuli *season of light rain*
vunja *(to) break*
vunjika *(to) be broken*
vuta *pull*
   vuta pumzi *(to) breathe in*

wa *(to) be*
wa na *(to) have*
wahi *(to) do sthg. in time*
waka *(to) burn, blaze*
wakati (nyakati) *time, period*
wala *nor* (with negative tense)
wale *those* (people, animals)
wali *cooked rice*
wao *they*
wapi? *where?*
washa *(to) light fire, lamp*
wasili *(to) arrive*
wasiwasi *worry*
wavu (nyavu) *net*
waza *(to) think, ponder*
wazi *open*
wazo (ma) *thought, idea*
weka *(to) put* (aside)
wekesha *(to) reserve, book*
wewe *you* (sing.)
weza *(to) be able to do sthg.*
wezekana *(to) be possible*

wiki *week*
-wili *two*
wimbo (nyimbo) *song*
winda *(to) hunt*
wingi *abundance*
wingu (ma) *cloud*

ya *of*
yaani *that is to say, i.e.*
yai (ma) *egg*
yale *those*
yeye *s/he*
yu *s/he is*
yule *that* (person, animal)

za *of*
zaa *(to) give birth, produce*
zahanati *clinic, dispensary*
zaidi *more*
zamani *long ago*
zambarau *purple*
zana *tools, appliances*
zao (ma) *crop*
zawadi *gift, present*
zeeka *(to) become old*
ziba *(to) stop up, plug*
-zima *whole, well*
-zito *heavy*
zoea *(to) be familiar with*
zuia *(to) prevent*
zunguka *(to) go round*
zungumza *(to) converse*
-zuri *good*
zuru *(to) visit*

*able* (*be*) ku-weza
*above* juu
*accident* ajali
*accompany* ku-fuatana
*accompany part way* ku-sindikiza
*address* anwani
*advantage* manufaa
*advertise* ku-tangaza
*advertisement* tangazo (ma)
*advice* shauri (ma)
*advise* ku-shauri
*afraid* (*be*) ku-ogopa
*Africa* Afrika
*after* baada ya
*afternoon* alasiri
*afterwards* baadaye
*again* tena, halafu
*age* umri
*agree* (*to*) ku-kubali
*agreement* (*be in*) ku-patana
*agriculture* kilimo
*AIDS* ukimwi
*air* hewa
*all* -ote
*allow* ku-ruhusu
*alone* peke -angu, -ake, etc.
*aloud* kwa sauti
*also* tena, vilevile
*although* ingawa, ijapo, ijapokuwa
*am* ni
*American* (*person*) Mmarekani
*among* miongoni mwa
*amount* kiasi
*ancestor* babu (ma)
*and* na, tena, -ka-
*angry* (*be*) ku-kasirika

*animal* mnyama (wa)
*announce* ku-tangaza
*announcement* tangazo (ma)
*annoy* ku-kera
*another* -ingine
*answer* jibu (ma)
*any* -o -ote
*appearance* sura
*apple* tofaa (ma)
*April* Aprili
*are* ni
*area* eneo (ma)
*arm* mkono (mi)
*arrive* ku-fika, ku-wasili
*art* sanaa
*article* (*written*) makala
*ash* majivu
*aside* (*to one side*) kando
*ask* ku-uliza
*assistant* msaidizi (wa)
*association* chama (vy)
*at* kwa, kwenye
*attend* ku-hudhuria
*August* Agosti
*aunt* (*maternal*) mama mdogo
*aunt* (*paternal*) shangazi

*baobab tree* mbuyu (mi)
*baboon* nyani
*baby* mtoto mchanga (wa)
*back* (*phys.*) mgongo (mi)
*back* (*at the*) nyuma
*bad* -baya
*badly* vibaya
*badness* ubaya
*bag* mfuko (mi)

*banana*  ndizi
*banana plant*  mgomba (mi)
*bar (for alcohol)*  klabu, baa
*barber*  kinyozi (vi)
*basin*  beseni
*basket*  kikapu (vi)
*bath (have a)*  ku-oga
*bath*  bafu
*bathroom*  maliwato
*battery*  betri
*be*  ku-wa
*beach*  pwani
*beads*  shanga
*bean*  haragwe (ma)
*beat*  ku-piga
*because*  kwa sababu, kwa kuwa
*bed*  kitanda (vi)
*bedding*  matandiko
*beer*  bia, pombe
*before*  kabla
*beg*  ku-omba
*beggar*  mwombaji (wa)
*begin*  ku-anza
*beginning*  mwanzo (mi)
*behind*  nyuma
*bend*  ku-pinda
*best*  bora
*between*  kati ya
*bicycle*  baiskeli
*birth (give)*  ku-zaa
*black*  -eusi
*blackboard*  ubao (mbao)
*blanket*  blanketi (ma)
*bleed*  ku-toka damu
*blessing*  baraka
*blind*  -pofu
*blood*  damu
*blue*  buluu
*boat*  boti
*body*  mwili (mi)
*boil*  ku-chemka
*boil sthg.*  ku-chemsha
*book*  kitabu (vi)
*booklet*  kijitabu (vi)
*border*  mpaka (mi)
*borrow*  ku-kopa
*boundary*  mpaka (mi)
*box*  sanduku (ma)
*boy*  mtoto wa kiume (wa)
*brave*  hodari
*bread*  mkate (mi)

*break*  ku-vunja
*breakfast*  chamshakinywa
*breathe*  ku-vuta pumzi
*brick*  tofali (ma)
*bride*  bibi arusi (ma)
*bridegroom*  bwana arusi (ma)
*bring*  ku-leta
*Britain*  Uingereza
*British (person)*  Mwingereza
*broken (be)*  ku-vunjika
*broken down (be)*  ku-haribika
*broom*  ufagio (fagio)
*brother*  kaka
*brown*  kahawia, hudhurungi
*bruised (be)*  ku-chubuka
*bucket*  ndoo
*build*  ku-jenga
*builder*  mjenzi (wa),
  mwashi (wa)
*building*  jengo (ma)
  *large building*  jumba (ma)
*burn*  ku-waka
*bus*  basi (ma), daladala, matatu
*bush (area)*  pori (ma)
*bus-stop*  kituo cha mabasi
*busy (be)*  ku-shughulika
*but*  lakini, ila
*button*  kifungo (vi)
*buy*  ku-nunua
*buyer*  mnunuzi (wa)

*café*  mkahawa (mi)
*call*  ku-ita
*camera*  kamera
*canoe*  mtumbwi (mi)
*canoe with outriggers*  ngalawa
*car*  motokaa, gari (ma)
*carcass*  mzoga (mi)
*cardamom*  iliki
*care for*  ku-tunza
*carry*  ku-beba, ku-chukua
*carve*  ku-chonga
*carving*  kinyago (vi)
*cashew nut*  korosho
*cashew tree*  mkorosho (mi)
*cassava*  muhogo (mi)
*cassette*  kaseti
*cat*  paka
*cause*  maana, sababu
*cent*  senti
*certainty*  hakika

*certificate* cheti (vy)

*chair* kiti (vi)

*change (money)* chenji

*charcoal (lump)* kaa (ma)

*chat* ku-ongea, ku-zungumza

*cheap* rahisi

*cheerful* -kunjufu

*cheerfulness* ukunjufu

*cheer up* ku-changamka

*cheer (sb) up* ku-chamgamsha

*cheetah* duma

*cheque* hundi

*chest (phys.)* kifua (vi)

*chest (storage)* kasha (ma)

*chest of drawers* almari

*chicken* kuku

*child* mtoto (wa)

*childhood* utoto

*China* Uchina

*Chinese (person)* Mchina (Wa)

*cholera* kipindupindu

*Christian (person)* Mkristo (Wa)

*church* kanisa (ma)

*city* jiji (ma)

*clap* ku-piga makofi

*class* darasa (ma)

*classroom* darasa (ma)

*clay* udongo

*clean* ku-safisha

*clean* safi

*clerk* karani (ma)

*climb* ku-panda

*climber* mpanda (wa)

*clinic* zahanati, kliniki

*clock* saa

*close* ku-funga

*cloth* kitambaa (vi), nguo

*cloud* wingu (ma)

*coast* pwani

*coat* koti (ma)

*coconut* nazi, dafu (ma)

*coconut juice* tui

*coconut palm* mnazi (mi)

*coffee (drink)* kahawa

*cold* baridi

*colour* rangi

*come* ku-ja

*come!* njoo!

*comfort* raha

*commitments* shughuli

*companion* mwenzi (wa)

*company* kampuni (ma)

*compete* ku-shindana

*competition* mashindano

*complete* kamili

*completely* kamili

*complications* matata

*computer* kompyuta

*concern (be -ed with)* ku-husu

*concerning* juu ya, kuhusu

*condition* hali

*conductor* kondakta (ma)

*conference* mkutano (mi)

*congratulate* ku-pongeza

*congratulations* hongera, pongezi

*consider* ku-fikiri

*constitution (pol.)* katiba

*construct* ku-unda

*continue* ku-endelea

*cook* ku-pika

*cook* mpishi

*cooking-pot* chungu (vy), sufuria (metal)

*cool* baridi

*cool season* kipupwe

*corner* pembe

*correct sthg.* ku-sahihisha

*correct* sawa

*corrugated iron* bati (ma)

*count* ku-hesabu

*country* nchi, shamba (rural area)

*cover sthg.* ku-funika

*cow* ng'ombe

*create* ku-umba

*crop* zao (ma)

*cross* ku-vuka

*cucumber* tango (ma)

*cultivate* ku-lima

*cunning* -erevu

*cup* kikombe (vi), kombe (ma)

*cupboard* kabati (ma)

*cure* ku-ganga, ku-ponya

*curry powder* bizari

*custom* desturi, kawaida

*customer* mteja (wa)

*customs office* forodha

*cut* ku-kata

*dance* ku-cheza ngoma

*dance* ngoma, dansi

*danger* hatari

*date (calendar)* tarehe

*daughter*  mwana (wa), binti
*dawn*  alfajiri
*day* (24 hrs)  siku
*daytime*  mchana
*deaf*  -ziwi
*debt*  deni (ma)
*December*  Desemba, Disemba
*decline* (e.g. invitation)  -kataa
*decoration*  nakshi
*decrease*  ku-pungua
*decrease sthg.*  ku-punguza
*deny*  ku-kana
*depend on*  ku-tegemea
*descend*  ku-shuka
*desert*  jangwa (ma)
*desire*  tamaa, hamu
*despair*  ku-kata tamaa
*destroy*  ku-haribu
*detail* (*in*)  kinaganaga
*dhow*  jahazi (ma)
*diarrhoea* (*have*)  ku-hara
*die* (*humans*)  ku-fa, ku-fariki
*differ*  ku-tofautiana
*difference*  tofauti
*difficulty*  shida
*dig*  ku-lima
*direction* (*in the – of*)  upande wa
*dish*  kombe (ma)
*dispensary*  zahanati
*distress*  taabu
*divide*  ku-gawa, ku-gawanya
*doctor*  mganga (wa), daktari, tabibu
 (ma)
*dog*  mbwa
*door*  mlango (mi)
*doubt*  shaka (ma)
*doughnut*  andazi (ma)
*down*  chini
*downwards*  chini
*dream*  ku-ota
*dream*  ndoto
*dress*  gauni (ma)
*drink*  ku-nywa
*drink*  kinywaji (vi)
*drive*  ku-endesha
*driver*  dereva (ma)
*drum*  ku-piga ngoma
*drum*  ngoma
*drummer*  mpigaji ngoma (wa)
*drunk* (*be*)  ku-lewa
*drunkard*  mlevi (wa)

*during*  muda wa, wakati wa
*duties* (*work*)  shughuli
*dysentery* (*to have*)  ku-hara damu

*each*  kila
*ear*  sikio (ma)
*early*  mapema
*earthquake*  tetemeko (ma)
*east*  mashariki
*easy*  rahisi
*eat*  ku-la
*editor*  mhariri (wa)
*egg*  yai (ma)
*Egypt*  Misri
*eight*  -nane
*eighty*  themanini
*either*  au, ama
*elder*  mzee (wa)
*electricity*  umeme
*elephant*  ndovu, tembo
*elevation*  mwinuko (mi)
*employed* (*be*)  ku-tumika
*employee*  mtumishi (wa)
*end*  mwisho (mi)
*engine*  injini, mota
*enough* (*be*)  ku-tosha
*enter*  ku-ingia
*entirely*  kabisa
*envelope*  bahasha
*error*  kosa (ma)
*especially*  hasa
*Europe*  Ulaya
*European* (*person*)  Mzungu (Wa)
*evening*  jioni
*eventually*  hatimaye
*every*  kila
*evident* (*be*)  ku-onekana
*exactly*  kamili
*examination* (school, etc.)  mtihani
 (mi)
*example*  mfano (mi)
*except*  ila
*excreta*  choo (vy)
*expect*  ku-tumaini
*expensive*  ghali
*expert*  mtaalamu (wa)
*explain*  ku-eleza
*explanation*  maelezo
*explicitly*  kinaganaga
*extent*  kadiri
*extremely*  mno

*eye* jicho (macho)

*fabric* kitambaa (vi), nguo
*face* uso (nyuso), sura
*familiar* (be – with) ku-zoea
*family* familia, jamaa
*fan* feni
*far* mbali
*farm* shamba (ma)
*fast* ku-funga
*fasten* ku-funga
*fat* -nene (*humans*), -nono (*animals*)
*father* baba
*February* Februari
*feed* ku-lisha
*feel* (e.g. hot) ku-ona, ku-sikia
*female* -ke, -a kike
*female animal* jike
*few* -chache
*fifty* hamsini
*fight* ku-pigana
*fighting* mapigano
*fill sthg. up* ku-jaza
*final* -a mwisho
*finally* mwishoni, mwishowe
*find* ku-ona, ku-pata
*fine* ku-toza
*finger* kidole (vi)
*finish sthg.* ku-maliza
*finished* (be) ku-isha
*fire* moto (mi)
*firewood* kuni
*first* -a kwanza
*firstly* kwanza
*fish* ku-vua
*fish* samaki
*fisherman* mvuvi (wa)
*five* -tano
*flour* unga
*fold* ku-kunja
*follow* ku-fuata
*food* chakula (vy)
*foolishness* upuuzi
*foot* mguu (mi)
*forbid* ku-kataza
*foreign* -geni, -a kigeni
*foreigner* mgeni (wa)
*foreman/woman* msimamizi (wa)
*forest* mwitu (mi)
*forget* ku-sahau
*forgetful* -sahaulifu

*forgive* ku-samehe
*form* (sec. sch.) kidato (vi)
*forty* arobaini
*foundation* msingi (mi)
*four* -nne
*frail* dhaifu
*frailty* udhaifu
*France* Ufaransa
*French* (*person*) Mfaransa
*Friday* Ijumaa
*friend* rafiki, ndugu
*frog* chura (vy)
*from* toka
*front* mbele
   *in front of* mbele ya
*fruit* tunda (ma)
*full* (be) ku-jaa

*game* mchezo (mi)
*game-park/reserve* mbuga ya
   wanyama
*garage* gereji
*garment* nguo, vazi (ma)
*gather* ku-chuma
*gazelle* swala, swara
*gentleman* bwana (ma)
*genuine* halisi
*geography* jiografia
*German* (*person*) Mjerumani,
   Mdachi
*Germany* Ujerumani
*get* ku-pata
*get on* (e.g. bus) ku-panda
*get used to* ku-zoea
*gift* zawadi
*giraffe* twiga
*girl* mtoto wa kike (wa)
*give* ku-pa
*give birth* ku-jifungua
*glass* gilasi
*go* ku-enda
*go!* nenda!
*go around* ku-zunguka
*go near* ku-karibia
*goat* mbuzi
*God* Mungu
*good* -zuri, -ema
*goodbye* kwa heri
*goodness* wema, hisani
*gossip* ku-piga soga
*government* serikali

*grandchild* mjukuu (wa)
*grandfather* babu
*grandmother* bibi (ma), nyanya
*grasp* ku-shika
*grass* majani
*graze* ku-lisha
*great* -kuu
*Greece* Ugiriki
*Greek (person)* Mgiriki
*green* kijani
*greet* ku-salimu
*greetings* salamu
*grind (grain)* ku-saga
*group* kundi (ma), kikundi (vi)
*grow* ku-ota, ku-mea
*gruel* uji
*guard sthg.* ku-linda
*guard* mlinzi (wa)
*guest* mgeni (wa)
*guide* kiongozi (vi)

*hair* nywele
*half* nusu
*hammer* nyundo
*hand* mkono (mi)
*happen* ku-tokea
*happiness* heri
*harbour* bandari
*harm* ku-dhuru
*harvest (crop)* zao (ma)
*harvest time* mavuno
*hat* kofia (ma)
*have* ku-wa na
*having* -enye
*he* yeye, a-
*head* kichwa (vi)
*hear* ku-sikia
*heart* moyo (mi)
*heat* joto
*heavy* -zito
*height* urefu
*help* ku-saidia
*hen* kuku
*her* yeye, -ake, -m-
*herder* mchungaji (wa)
*here* hapa, huku
*herself* mwenyewe
*high* -refu
*hill* kilima (vi)
*him* yeye, -m-
*himself* mwenyewe

*hippopotamus* kiboko (vi)
*his* -ake
*hit* ku-piga
*hoe* ku-palilia
*hold* ku-shika
*holiday* likizo, livu
*hope* ku-tumaini
*hot* moto
*hot season* kiangazi
*hotel* hoteli
*hour* saa
*house* nyumba
*how?* vipi? -je?
*how many?* -ngapi?
*human being* binadamu
*hundred* mia
*hunger* njaa
*hungry (be)* ku-wa na njaa
*hunt* ku-winda
*hurt* ku-uma
*husband* mume (wa)
*hut* kibanda (vi)
*hyena* fisi

*I* mimi, ni-
*idea* wazo (ma)
*if* ikiwa, iwapo, kama
*ill (become)* ku-ugua
*illness* ugonjwa, maradhi
*immediately* mara moja, sasa hivi
*increase* ku-ongeza
*India* Bara Hindi
*Indian (person)* Mhindi (Wa)
*injured (be)* ku-umia
*injury* jeraha (ma)
*insect* mdudu (wa)
*inside* ndani
*instead of* badala ya
*intend* ku-kusudia
*invite* ku-alika, ku-karibisha
*iron sthg.* ku-piga pasi
*iron* pasi
*is* ni
*its (possession)* -ake

*January* Januari
*join* ku-unga
*journalist* mwandishi-habari (wa)
*journey* safari
*judgement* hukumu
*July* Julai

*jump* ku-ruka
*June* Juni

*kebab* mshikaki (mi)
*Kenyan* (*person*) Mkenya (Wa)
*kerosene* mafuta ya taa
*key* ufunguo (funguo)
*kill* ku-ua
*kilo* kilo
*kindness* hisani
*kingfish* nguru
*kitchen* jiko (meko)
*knee* goti (ma)
*kneel* ku-piga magoti
*knife* kisu
*knock* ku-gonga
*know* ku-jua
*knowledge* maarifa, habari

*lady* bibi (ma)
*lamp* taa
*land* ku-tua
*language* lugha
*large* -kubwa
*last* -a mwisho
*late* (*be*) ku-chelewa
*lavatory* choo (vy), msala (mi)
*lead* ku-ongoza
*leader* kiongozi (vi)
*leaf* jani (ma)
*learn* ku-jifunza
*leave* ku-toka, ku-ondoka
*lecture* mhadhara (mi)
*lecturer* mhadhiri (wa)
*left* (*direction*) kushoto
*leg* mguu (mi)
*lemon* limau (ma)
*lemon tree* mlimau (mi)
*lend* ku-kopesha
*length* urefu
*leopard* chui
*lesson* somo (ma)
*letter* barua
*library* maktaba
*lid* kifuniko (vi)
*light* (e.g. fire) ku-washa
*like* ku-penda
*like* kama, namna
*line* mstari (mi)
*lip* mdomo (mi)
*listen* ku-sikiliza

*live* ku-kaa, ku-ishi
*load* mzigo (mi)
*loaf* mkate (mi)
*local* (*person*) mwenyeji (wa)
*log* gogo (ma)
*long* -refu
*long ago* zamani
*look after* ku-angalia, ku-tunza
*look* (*at*) ku-tazama, ku-ona
*look for* ku-tafuta
*lorry* lori (ma), gari (ma)
*loser* mshinde (wa)
*lost* (*be*) ku-potea
*love* ku-penda
*luck* bahati
*luggage* (*piece of*) mzigo (mi)

*machete* panga (ma)
*maize* mahindi
*maize plant* mhindi (mi)
*make* ku-fanya, ku-tengeneza
*malaria* malaria, homa ya malaria
*male* -ume, -a kiume
*male animal* dume
*man* mwanamume (wanaume)
*manager* meneja (ma)
*mango* embe (ma)
*mango tree* mwembe (mi)
*many* -ingi
*map* ramani
*March* Machi
*mark* doa (ma)
*market* soko (ma)
*marry* (*men*) ku-oa
*marry* (*women*) ku-olewa
*mast* mlingoti (mi)
*match* kibiriti (vi)
*match* (*sport*) mechi
*matter* jambo (mambo)
*mattress* godoro (ma)
*May* Mei
*me* mimi, -ni-
*meaning* maana
*meat* nyama
*medicine* dawa
*meet* ku-kutana
*meeting* mkutano (mi)
*message* ujumbe (jumbe)
*metre* mita
*midday* adhuhuri
*middle* (*in the*) katikati

*mill*  kinu (vi)
*millet*  mtama (mi)
*minibus*  daladala, matatu
*minute*  dakika
*miss* (e.g. bus)  ku-kosa
*mistake* (*make a*)  ku-kosa
*mistake*  kosa (ma)
*money*  fedha, pesa
*monkey*  kima, tumbili
*month*  mwezi (mi)
*more*  zaidi
*moreover*  aidha
*morning*  asubuhi
*mortar*  kinu (vi)
*mosquito*  mbu
*mosquito net*  chandalua (vy)
*mother*  mama
*motor*  mota, injini
*motorcycle*  pikipiki
*mountain*  mlima (mi)
*mouth*  kinywa (vi)
*movement*  mwendo (mi)
*Mozambique*  Msumbiji
*museum*  jumba la makumbusho
*music*  muziki, tarabu
*Muslim* (*person*)  Mwislamu (Wa)
*my*  -angu

*name*  jina (ma)
*narrow*  -embamba
*nausea*  kichefuchefu
*near*  karibu
*necessary*  lazima
*necessities*  mahitaji
*need sthg.*  ku-hitaji
*need*  uhitaji
*needlessly*  bure
*neighbour*  jirani (ma)
*neck*  shingo
*nephew*  mpwa
*net*  wavu (ngavu)
*new*  -pya
*news*  habari
*newspaper*  gazeti (ma)
*next to*  kando ya
*night*  usiku (siku)
*nine*  tisa
*no*  siyo, hapana, la
*nonsense*  upuuzi
*north*  kaskazini
*nose*  pua

*note* (*chit*)  cheti (vy)
*notice*  tangazo (ma)
*notify*  ku-tangaza, ku-arifu
*not yet*  bado
*nought*  sifuri
*November*  Novemba
*now*  sasa
*number*  namba, nambari, tarakimu
*nurse*  mwuguzi (wa)

*observe*  ku-angalia
*obtainable* (*be*)  ku-patikana
*occur*  ku-tokea
*ocean*  bahari
*October*  Oktoba
*of*  -a
*office*  ofisi
*oil*  mafuta
*old*  -zee (people)
*old* (*become*)  ku-zeeka
*on*  juu ya
*once*  mara moja
*onion*  kitunguu (vi)
*only*  tu
*open*  ku-fungua
*open*  wazi
*operation*  operesheni
*opportunity*  nafasi
*or*  au, ama
*orange*  chungwa (ma)
*orange tree*  mchungwa (mi)
*order*  ku-agiza
*origin*  asili
*other*  -ingine
*our*  -etu
*outrigger* (*for canoe*)  mrengu (mi), ndubi
*outside*  nje
*overturned* (*be*)  ku-pinduka
*owner*  mwenye (wa), mwenyewe (wa)
*oxygen*  oksijeni

*page*  ukurasa (kurasa)
*pain* (*feel*)  ku-umwa
*pamphlet*  kijitabu (vi)
*paraffin*  mafuta ya taa
*parent*  mzazi (wa), mzee (wa)
*park* (*vehicle*)  ku-egesha
*part*  sehemu, kipande
*particularly*  hasa

*party* (political)  chama (vy)
*pass* (*by, along, through*)  ku-pita
*pass* (*exam*)  -faulu, -shinda
*passenger*  abiria
*passer-by*  mpita njia (wa)
*path*  njia
*patient*  mgonjwa (wa)
*pattern*  nakshi
*pawpaw* (*papaya*)  papai (ma)
*pawpaw tree*  mpapai (mi)
*pay*  ku-lipa
*peak*  kilele (vi)
*pepper*  pilipili
*perhaps*  huenda, labda
*period*  muda (mi), wakati
  (nyakati)
*permission*  ruhusa
*permit*  ku-ruhusu
*pest*  dudu (ma)
*pestle*  mchi (mi)
*petrol*  petroli
*photograph* (*take a*)  ku-piga picha
*photograph*  picha
*pick up*  ku-okota
*piece*  kipande (vi), sehemu
*pillow*  mto (mi)
*pineapple*  nanasi (ma)
*pineapple plant*  mnanasi (mi)
*pitch* (*games*)  uwanja (wanja)
*pitch* (*tent*)  ku-piga hema
*place*  mahali, pahali
*plank*  ubao (mbao)
*plantation*  shamba (ma)
*plaster* (*dressing*)  plasta
*platform*  see *stage*
*play*  ku-cheza
*play* (*drama*)  tamthilia
*please*  ku-pendeza
*please*  tafadhali
*plenty*  wingi
*plough*  ku-lima
*pluck*  ku-chuma
*plug sthg.*  ku-ziba
*plug*  kizibo (vi)
*pocket*  mfuko (mi)
*poetry*  ushairi
*polenta*  ugali
*policeman/woman*  polisi, askari
  polisi
*police-station*  kituo cha polisi (vi)
*poor*  maskini

*port*  bandari
*porter*  mpagazi (wa)
*possible* (*be*)  ku-wezekana
*post office*  posta
*postage stamp*  stampu, stempu
*postal order*  hundi ya posta
*postpone*  ku-ahirisha
*potato*  kiazi (vi)
*potter*  mfinyanzi (wa)
*pottery figure*  mfinyango
*pound*  ku-ponda
*pound grain*  ku-twanga
*pray*  ku-omba, ku-sali
*preferable*  afadhali
*prepare*  ku-tayarisha,
  ku-tengeneza
*president*  rais
*prevent*  ku-zuia
*price*  bei
*print*  ku-piga chapa
*problem*  tatizo (ma), shauri (ma)
*produce*  ku-zaa
*production*  mazao
*progress*  ku-endelea
*progress*  maendeleo
*promise*  ku-ahidi
*promise*  ahadi
*pronunciation*  matamshi
*property*  mali
*protrude*  ku-tokeza
*provisions*  manufaa
*pull*  ku-vuta
*puncture*  pancha
*purple*  zambarau
*push*  ku-sukuma
*put*  ku-tia, ku-weka

*quarrel*  ku-gombana
*quarrelling*  magomvi
*quarter*  robo
*question*  swali (ma)
*quick*  -a upesi
*quickly*  kwa haraka, upesi, mbio
*quiet* (*be*)  ku-nyamaa
*quiet*  kimya, -tulivu
*quietly*  kimya, polepole
*quietness*  kimya, utulivu

*race*  shindano (ma)
*rain*  ku-nyesha
*rain*  mvua

*rainy season (heavy)* masika
*rainy season (light)* vuli
*read* ku-soma
*ready (get)* ku-tayarisha
*ready* tayari
*real* halisi
*reason* sababu, maana
*receive* ku-pokea
*recently* juzijuzi
*reception (hotel)* mapokezi
*recover* ku-pona, ku-poa
*red* -ekundu
*reduce (lessen)* ku-punguza
*refuse* ku-kataa
*region* mkoa (mi)
*relation (relative)* ndugu
*remain* ku-baki
*remember* ku-kumbuka
*remove* ku-ondoa
*renovate* ku-karabati
*repair* ku-rekebisha
*repairs* marekebisho
*reply* ku-jibu
*requirements* mahitaji
*research* utafiti
*reserve (e.g. a room)* ku-wekesha
*responsibility* madaraka
*rest* ku-pumzika
*retire (from work)* ku-staafu
*return* ku-rudi
*return sthg.* ku-rudisha
*rhinoceros* kifaru (vi)
*rice* mpunga (plant), mchele
   (husked), wali (cooked)
*riddle* kitendawili (vi)
*right (direction)* kulia
*ring* pete
*river* mto (mi)
*road* njia, barabara (main)
*roof (put on a)* ku-ezeka
*roof* paa
*room* chumba (vy)
*rope* kamba

*sack* gunia (ma)
*safely* salama
*safety* usalama
*sail* tanga (ma)
*salad* saladi
*salt* chumvi
*samosa* sambusa

*satisfied (be)* ku-shiba
*Saturday* Jumamosi
*saucepan* sufuria
*say* ku-sema
*sea* bahari
*search* ku-tafuta
*season* majira, msimu (mi)
*second* -a pili
*secretary* mhazili (wa) karani (ma)
*section* sehemu
*see* ku-ona
*self* -enyewe
*sell* ku-uza
*send* ku-peleka, ku-tuma
*September* Septemba
*servant* mtumishi (wa)
*set (sun)* ku-chwa
*seven* saba
*seventy* sabini
*sew* ku-shona
*sewing-machine* cherehani
*shade* kivuli (vi)
*shadow* kivuli (vi)
*shave* ku-nyoa
*she* yeye, a-
*sheet* shuka, shiti
*shelf* rafu
*shepherd* mchungaji (wa)
*shilling* shilingi
*shirt* shati
*shoe* kiatu (vi)
*shop* duka (ma)
*short* -fupi
*shorts* kaptura
*shoulder* bega (ma)
*show* ku-onyesha
*shower* bafu
*side* upande (pande), kando
*silence* kimya
*silver* fedha
*since* tangu, toka
*sing* ku-imba
*singer* mwimbaji (wa)
*singly* -moja -moja
*sister* dada
*sit* ku-kaa
*sitting room* ukumbi (kumbi)
*six* sita
*sixty* sitini
*size* ukubwa
*skilled worker* fundi (ma)

*slaughter* ku-chinja
*sleep* ku-lala usingizi
*sleeve* mkono (mi)
*slightly* kidogo
*slowly* polepole
*small* -dogo
*smallholding* shamba (ma)
*smart* maridadi
*smooth* laini
*snack-bar* mkahawa (mi), hoteli
*snake* nyoka
*sneeze* ku-piga chafya
*snow* theluji
*socks* soksi
*soft* laini
*soft drink* soda
*soil* udongo
*soldier* askari jeshi
*some (part of)* -ingine
*son* mwana (wa)
*song* wimbo (nyimbo)
*soon* karibu
*sore* jeraha (ma)
*sorry (be)* ku-sikitika
*sorry!* samahani!
*sort (type)* aina, jinsi, namna
*sort out* ku-chambua
*sound* sauti
*south* kusini
*space* nafasi
*Spain* Hispania
*spare-part* spea, speapati
*speak* ku-sema, ku-nena
*specialist* mtaalamu (wa)
*speed* mwendo (mi)
*spice* kiungo (vi)
*split* ku-pasua
*spoil* ku-haribu
*spoon* kijiko (vi)
*spot* doa (ma)
*stage* jukwaa (ma)
*stall-holder* mwuzaji (wa)
*stand* ku-simama
*standard* sanifu
*start* ku-anza
*startle sy.* ku-kurupua
*state* hali
*station* stesheni
*stay* ku-kaa
*steal* ku-iba
*stick sthg. on* ku-bandika

*still (ongoing)* bado
*stir* ku-koroga
*stomach* tumbo (ma)
*stone* jiwe (mawe)
*stop* ku-simama
*stopper (bottle)* kizibo (vi)
*store* ghala, stoo
*storey* ghorofa
*story* hadithi
*straight (on)* moja kwa moja
*stranger* mgeni (wa)
*strength* nguvu
*student* mwanafunzi (wa)
*study* ku-soma
*stupid* -jinga
*stupidity* ujinga
*style* mtindo (mi)
*succeed* ku-shinda
*success* fanaka
*sudden* -a ghafula
*suddenly* kwa ghafula
*suffice* ku-tosheka
*sugar* sukari
*sugar-cane* muwa (mi)
*suitable (be)* ku-faa
*summit* kilele (vi)
*sun* jua
*sweep* ku-fagia
*swell* ku-fura
*swim* ku-ogelea
*switch* swichi
*sympathy* rambirambi (zako)
  *(expr. of, to a mourner)*

*tailor* mshonaji (wa), mshoni (wa)
*take* ku-chukua
*take away* ku-ondoa
*talk* ku-ongea, ku-zungumza
*tall* -refu
*tangle* ku-tata
*Tanzanian (person)* Mtanzania (Wa)
*tape (video, etc.)* ukanda, tepu
*tarmac* lami
*taxi* teksi
*tea* chai
*teach* ku-fundisha, ku-funza
*teacher* mwalimu (wa)
*teaching* mafundisho
*tear* ku-pasua
*telephone* ku-piga simu
*telephone* simu

*tell*  ku-ambia
*ten*  kumi
*tent*  hema
*terminus*  kituo (vi)
*thank*  ku-shukuru
*thanks*  asante
*that*  yule, ile, kile, etc.
*their (people's)*  -ao
*them (people)*  wao, -wa-
*then*  halafu, kisha, ndipo
*there*  kule, pale, huko
*these*  hawa, hizi, hivi, etc.
*they*  wao, wa-
*thief*  mwizi (wezi), mwivi (wevi)
*thing*  kitu (vi)
*think*  ku-fikiri, ku-waza
*thirst*  kiu
*thirty*  thelathini
*this*  huyu, hii, hiki, etc.
*those*  wale, zile, vile, etc.
*thought*  wazo (ma)
*thousand*  elfu (ma)
*three*  -tatu
*throat*  koo (ma)
*throw*  ku-tupa
*Thursday*  Alhamisi
*ticket*  tiketi
*tie*  ku-funga
*time*  saa, wakati
*timetable*  ratiba
*tired (be)*  ku-choka
*today*  leo
*toe*  kidole (vi)
*together*  pamoja
*tomato*  nyanya
*tomorrow*  kesho
*too (much)*  mno
*tool*  kifaa (vi), zana
*tooth*  jino (meno)
*top*  -a juu
*topic*  mada
*total*  jumla
*tourist*  mtalii (wa)
*town*  mji (mi)
*trade (engage in)*  ku-fanya biashara
*trade*  biashara
*trader*  mfanya/mfanyi
  biashara (wa)
*train*  gari moshi (ma), treni
*travel*  ku-safiri
*traveller*  msafiri (wa)

*treat (illness)*  ku-ganga, ku-tibu
*tree*  mti (mi)
*tribe*  kabila (ma)
*trouble*  taabu, matata, shida
*trousers*  suruali
*truck*  lori (ma), gari (ma)
*true*  kweli
*truly*  kweli, kwa kweli
*Tuesday*  Jumanne
*turmeric*  manjano
*turn*  ku-pinda
*twenty*  ishirini
*twice*  mara mbili
*two*  -wili
*type*  aina, jinsi, namna

*Ugandan (person)*  Mganda (Wa)
*umbrella*  mwavuli (mi)
*uncle (maternal)*  mjomba (wa)
*uncle (paternal)*  baba mdogo
*uncover*  ku-funua
*under*  chini ya
*understand*  ku-elewa
*undress*  ku-vua
*unfold*  ku-kunjua
*university*  chuo kikuu
*unravel*  ku-fumua
*untangle*  ku-tatua
*untie*  ku-fungua
*until*  hata, mpaka
*up*  juu
*up to*  mpaka
*us*  sisi, -tu-
*USA*  Marekani
*useful (be)*  ku-faa
*usefulness*  manufaa
*useless*  bure
*usually*  kwa kawaida, hu-

*vacation*  likizo, livu
*vandalism*  upotevu
*various*  mbalimbali
*vegetables*  mboga
*vehicle*  gari (ma)
*very*  sana
*video*  video
*village*  kijiji (vi)
*visible (be)*  ku-onekana
*visit*  ku-tembelea, ku-zuru
*voice*  sauti
*volcano*  volkeno

*vomit*  ku-tapika
*vote*  kupiga kura

*wait*  ku-ngoja, ku-subiri
*wake up*  ku-amka
*walk*  ku-tembea
*walk (a stroll)*  matembezi
*wall*  ukuta (kuta)
*want*  ku-taka
*warehouse*  ghala, stoo
*warn*  ku-onya
*warthog*  ngiri
*wash (clothes)*  ku-fua
*wash (hands)*  ku-nawa
*waste*  ku-poteza
*wasteful*  -potevu
*water*  maji
*water buck*  kuro
*we*  sisi, tu-
*weak (frail)*  dhaifu
*weakness*  udhaifu
*wear*  ku-vaa
*weave*  ku-fuma
*wedding*  harusi, arusi
*weed*  ku-palilia
*week*  wiki, juma (ma)
*welcome*  ku-karibisha
*welcome!*  karibu!
*well (do sthg. –)*  vizuri
*well (water)*  kisima (vi)
*well (in health)*  -zima
*west*  magharibi
*what kind (of)?*  gani?
*wheat*  ngano
*where?*  wapi?
*which?*  -pi?, gani?
*white*  -eupe
*who?*  nani?

*whole*  -zima
*why?*  kwa nini?
*wide*  -pana
*wife*  mke (wa)
*win*  ku-shinda
*window*  dirisha (ma)
*wine*  divai, mvinyo
*with*  na, kwa, pamoja na
*woman*  mwanamke (wanawake)
*woodland*  msitu (mi)
*word*  neno (ma)
*work*  ku-fanya kazi
*work*  kazi
*worker*  mfanya/mfanyi kazi (wa)
*worry*  wasiwasi
*wound*  jeraha
*write*  ku-andika
*writer*  mwandishi

*yawn*  ku-piga miayo
*year*  mwaka (mi)
*yellow*  manjano
*yes*  ndiyo
*yesterday*  jana
   *day before yesterday*  juzi
*yet*  bado
*you*  wewe, u-, -ku-
*you (pl.)*  ninyi, m-, -wa-
*young*  -changa
*young man*  kijana (vi), mvulana (wa)
*young woman*  msichana (wa)
*your (sing.)*  -ako
*your (pl.)*  -enu

*Zanzibar*  Unguja, Zanzibar
*zebra*  punda milia
*zero*  sifuri

useful phrases for visitors

*Note*: Some Swahili phrases are not direct translations of the English, but are suitable equivalent phrases for the context of use.

## Greetings

An exchange of greetings is an essential preliminary to any conversation. Note that Swahili-speakers tend to use terms of address to the people they are speaking to, so **bwana** *sir*, **bibi** or **mama** *madam* and **mzee** *venerable old man* function rather like *Monsieur* and *Madame* in French; they can follow any of the greetings and responses shown below, e.g. **Hujambo, mama? Sijambo, bwana.**

| | |
|---|---|
| *Hello, how are you?*<br>  *(to one person)* | **Hujambo?** |
| *I'm fine.* | **Sijambo.** |
| *Hello, how are you?*<br>  *(to more than one)* | **Hamjambo?** |
| *We're fine.* | **Hatujambo.** |
| *How's everyone at home?*<br>  *(as a follow-up)* | **Hawajambo nyumbani?** |
| *They're fine.* | **Hawajambo.** |
| Special greeting to a person<br>  much older than yourself | **Shikamoo.** |
| The reply of thanks to<br>  this greeting | **Marahaba.** |

A **jambo**-type greeting is sufficient if you happen to see an acquaintance in a busy town street and neither of you has time to stop for a chat, but in other circumstances you should follow up with one (or more) of the **habari** greetings below.

| | |
|---|---|
| *What's new? / How are things?* | **Habari gani?** |
| *How are things at home?* | **Habari za nyumbani?** |
| *How's everything at work?* | **Habari za kazi?** |
| *How was your trip?* | **Habari za safari?** |
| *How are things this morning?* | **Habari za asubuhi?** |
| *How are things today?* | **Habari za mchana?** |
| *How are things this evening?* | **Habari za jioni?** |

Use any of the following in reply to **habari** greetings: **njema, salama, safi, nzuri.** As a reply to a greeting they all imply *fine.* They can be strengthened, if you wish to indicate that you're on top of the world, by the addition of **sana** or **kabisa** e.g. **safi kabisa.**

There are more greetings than these, but tourists are unlikely to need them, and long-staying visitors will gradually pick up locally-appropriate greetings.

## A few basics

| | |
|---|---|
| *Yes* | **Ndiyo** (it is as you say) |
| *No* | **Hapana** or **La** |
| *Please* | **Tafadhali** |
| *Thank you (very much)* | **Asante (sana)** |

(Be careful with **tafadhali** and **asante**; neither is used as much as *please* and *thank you* are in British English. Polite requests using the -e form of verbs don't also need **tafadhali** unless you want to convey great deference, and thanks for a gift needn't be expressed by **asante** if you receive it politely i.e. with both hands.)

| | |
|---|---|
| *Do you speak _____?* | **Unasema _____?** |
| Swahili | **Kiswahili** |
| English | **Kiingereza** |
| French | **Kifaransa** |
| German | **Kijerumani** |
| Arabic | **Kiarabu** |
| Chinese | **Kichina** |
| Japanese | **Kijapani** |
| *I don't speak _____.* | **Sisemi _____.** |
| *Does anyone here speak ____?* | **Kuna mtu hapa anayesema ____?** |
| *Please help me.* | **Nisaidie.** |
| *Please help us.* | **Tusaidie.** |
| *We're desperate for help.* | **Tunaomba msaada.** |
| *I have lost my _____.* | **Nimepoteza _____.** |
| *We have lost our _____.* | **Tumepoteza _____.** |

|  |  |
|---|---|
| *bag* | **mfuko** |
| *camera* | **kamera** |
| *credit card* | **kadi ya mkopo** |
| *handbag* | **mkoba / begi** |
| *luggage* | **mizigo** |
| *money* | **pesa** |
| *passport* | **pasipoti** |
| *purse, wallet* | **pochi** |

| | |
|---|---|
| *I have had my _____ stolen.* | **Nimeibiwa _____ .** |
| *We have had our _____ stolen.* | **Tumeibiwa _____ .** |
| *Where is the police-station?* | **Kituo cha polisi kiko wapi?** |
| | or **Stesheni ya polisi iko wapi?** |
| *I'm not feeling very well / I'm a bit off-colour.* | **Siwezi.** |

1 **moja**; 2 **mbili**; 3 **tatu**; 4 **nne**; 5 **tano**; 6 **sita**

*Note*: For more on numbers and money see Unit 2; for the time, Unit 6.

## If you're invited into someone's home...

(Remember to use the greetings after you've been welcomed inside.)

| | |
|---|---|
| *May I/we come in?* | **Hodi!** |

(Stand outside the door and call out **hodi** once or twice. If you are in a town, and the door is closed, you will need to knock as well.)

| | |
|---|---|
| *Come in! (to one person)* | **Karibu!** |
| *Come in! (to more than one)* | **Karibuni!** |
| *Have a seat.* | **Karibu keti.** |
| *This is my _____ .* | **Huyu ni _____ .** |

|  |  |
|---|---|
| *brother* | **kaka yangu** |
| *child* | **mwanangu** |
| *colleague* | **mwenzangu** |
| *father* | **babangu** |
| *friend* | **rafiki yangu** |
| *girl/boyfriend* | **mpenzi wangu** |
| *husband* | **mume wangu** |
| *mother* | **mamangu** |
| *relative/close friend* | **ndugu** |
| *sister* | **dadangu** |
| *wife* | **mke wangu** |

| | |
|---|---|
| *Meet _____ .* | **Kutana na _____** (informal). |
| *I'd like to introduce you to ____ .* | **Nikujulishe na ____ .** |
| *I'm very pleased to meet you.* | **Nimefurahi kukutana nawe.** |

| | |
|---|---|
| What is your name? | Jina lako nani? |
| My name is _____ . | Jina langu ni _____ . |
| Would you mind speaking more slowly? | Useme polepole. |
| When did you arrive? | Ulifika lini? |
| I arrived _____ . | Nilifika _____ . |
| yesterday | jana |
| last week | wiki iliyopita |
| last month | mwezi uliopita |

(*Note*: Use English names for months.)

| | |
|---|---|
| When will you leave? | Utaondoka lini? |
| I will leave _____ . | Nitaondoka _____ . |
| We will leave _____ . | Tutaondoka _____ . |
| tomorrow | kesho |
| next week | wiki ijayo |
| next month | mwezi ujao |
| Monday | Jumatatu |
| Tuesday | Jumanne |
| Wednesday | Jumatano |
| Thursday | Alhamisi |
| Friday | Ijumaa |
| Saturday | Jumamosi |
| Sunday | Jumapili |
| That's enough, thanks. | Basi. |
| I'm full up. | Nimeshiba. |
| I don't eat meat. | Sili nyama. |
| I'm sorry (for making a mistake, causing a problem, etc.). | Samahani. |
| Please forgive me. | Nisamehe. |
| Please forgive us. | Tusamehe. |
| I'm sorry for you (to someone who is ill, upset or has experienced some other mishap). | Pole! (one person) Poleni! (more than one) |
| Standard reply to pole | Nimeshapoa. |
| I don't know. | Sijui. |
| It doesn't matter. | Haidhuru or Si kitu. |
| O.K. then. | Haya. |
| Greetings (to you) from Mr A/Ms B. | Salamu zako kutoka kwa Bw A/Bi B. |
| Greetings (to more than one person). | Salamu zenu... |

| | |
|---|---|
| *Give A/B my best wishes* (spoken to one person). | **Unisalimie A/B.** |
| *Give A/B my best wishes* (spoken to more than one). | **Mnisalimie A/B.** |
| *I'm sorry, but I / we really have to go now.* | **Samahani, ni lazima niende/ twende sasa.** |
| *Come again!* | **Karibu / Karibuni tena!** |
| *Goodbye!* (to one person) | **Kwa heri!** |
| *Goodbye!* (to more than one) | **Kwa herini!** |
| *Goodbye until we meet again!* | **Kwa heri ya kuonana!** |
| *Have a good trip!* | **Fika salama!** (Used when seeing people off on a longish journey; its literal meaning is 'Arrive safely'.) |
| *Sleep well!* | **Lala vizuri!** |
| *Come to our place for ____ .* | **Karibu(ni) kwetu kwa ____ .** |
| *lunch* | **chakula cha mchana** |
| *supper* | **chakula cha jioni** |

## Travelling and sightseeing

(Remember to use a preliminary greeting.)

| | | |
|---|---|---|
| *In which direction is the _____?* | | **_____ iko upande gani?** |
| | *coast* | **Pwani** |
| | *game-park* | **Mbuga ya wanyama** |
| | *harbour* | **Bandari** |
| | *ruins* | **Magofu** |
| | *waterfall* | **Maporomoko ya maji** |
| *Where is the _____ ?* | | **_____ iko wapi?** |
| | *bus-stop/stand* | **Kituo cha basi** |
| | *church* | **Kanisa** |
| | *... Embassy* | **Balozi la ...** |
| | *garage* (repairs) | **Gereji** |
| | *garage* (petrol / gas) | **Kituo cha petroli** |
| | *... Guest House* | **Gesti ya ...** |
| | *... High Commission* | **Balozi la ...** |
| | *... Hotel* | **Hoteli ya ...** |
| | *market* | **Soko** |
| | *mosque* | **Msikiti** |
| | *museum* | **Jumba la Makumbusho** |
| | *Parliament Building* | **Bunge** |
| | *railway station* | **Stesheni ya gari moshi** (Tanz.) |
| | | **Stesheni ya treni** (Ken.) |
| | *State House* | **Ikulu** (Tanz.) |
| | *taxi-rank* | **Kituo cha teksi** |

(**iko** in the above questions is not strictly correct with all the places given in the lists, e.g. 'Where is the market?' should really be **Soko liko wapi?** But when you're lost or short of time desperate measures are needed!)

| | |
|---|---|
| *DANGER* | **HATARI** |
| *NO SMOKING* | **USIVUTE SIGARA** |
| *NO PARKING HERE* | **HAIRUHUSIWI KUEGESHA HAPA** |
| *NO STOPPING HERE* | **HAIRUHUSIWI KUSIMAMA HAPA** |
| *ARRIVALS* | **WANAOWASILI** |
| *DEPARTURES* | **WANAOONDOKA** |

| | |
|---|---|
| *Our vehicle has broken down.* | Gari letu limeharibika. |
| *The car is near the _____ .* | Gari liko karibu na _____ . |

| | |
|---|---|
| airport | uwanja wa ndege |
| crossroads | njia panda |
| school | skuli (Ken.) |
| | shule (Tanz.) |

| | |
|---|---|
| *Just a minute./Wait a moment.* | Subiri kidogo. |
| *We need a mechanic.* | Tunataka fundi wa gari. |
| *Can you repair it?* | Unaweza kuitengeneza? |
| *What is the fare to _____ ?* | Nauli ni kiasi gani kwenda _____? |
| *Please stop here (taxi-driver).* | Usimame hapa. |
| *I'm/We're looking for _____ .* | Natafuta/Tunatafuta _____ . |

| | |
|---|---|
| a guest-house | gesti/nyumba ya wageni |
| a hotel | hoteli |
| our friends | marafiki zetu |
| our leader | kiongozi wetu |
| a restaurant | mkahawa |

| | |
|---|---|
| *Do you have any vacancies?* | Kuna nafasi ya chumba? |
| *I/We want a _____ .* | Nataka/Tunataka _____ . |

| | |
|---|---|
| single room | chumba cha mtu mmoja |
| double room | chumba cha watu wawili |
| room with toilet and bath/shower | chumba chenye choo na bafu |
| room for one night | chumba kwa usiku mmoja |

| | |
|---|---|
| *How much per _____?* | Bei gani kwa _____ ? |

| | |
|---|---|
| night | usiku |
| week | wiki |

| | |
|---|---|
| *May I/We see the room?* | Niangalie/Tuangalie chumba? |
| *I'm sorry, it's not suitable.* | Samahani, hakifai. |
| *O.K., that's fine.* | Sawa. |

# Eating and drinking

| | |
|---|---|
| *Are you hungry/thirsty?* (to one p.) | **Una njaa/kiu?** |
| *Are you hungry/thirsty?* (to more than one) | **Mna njaa/kiu?** |
| *Do you like* _____ ? (to one p.) | **Unapenda** _____ ? |
| *Do you like* _____ ? (to more than one) | **Mnapenda** _____ ? |

| | |
|---|---|
| *African food* | chakula cha Kiafrika |
| *beans (kidney)* | maharagwe |
| *beef* | nyama ya ng'ombe |
| *biriani* | biriani |
| *chapati* | chapati |
| *cheese* | jibini/chizi |
| *chicken* | kuku |
| *coastal food* | chakula cha pwani |
| *curry* | mchuzi wa viungo |
| *egg(s)* | yai (ma-) |
| *fish* | samaki |
| *kebab(s)* | mshikaki (mi-) |
| *lamb* | nyama ya kondoo |
| *omelette* | kiwanda (vi-) |
| *pilaff/pilau* | pilau |
| *polenta* | ugali |
| *pork* | nyama ya nguruwe |
| *rice* | wali |
| *samosa(s)* | sambusa |
| *sauce/relish (of chicken, vegetables, etc.)* | kitoweo/mchuzi |

| | |
|---|---|
| *I like* _____ . | **Napenda** _____ . |
| *I don't eat* _____ . | **Sili** _____ . |
| *What do you want?* | **Unataka nini?** |
| *What will you eat?* | **Utakula nini?** |
| *I'd like* _____ . | **Nataka** _____ . |

To call a waiter use **bwana, kaka** or **ndugu** (or **mzee** if he is elderly); if you have a waitress use **bibi** or **mama** if she is an older woman.

| | |
|---|---|
| *Please bring* _____ . | **Lete** _____ . |
| *one cheese omelette* | **kiwanda kimoja cha jibini** |
| *two samosas* | **sambusa mbili** |
| *two samosas each* | **sambusa mbilimbili** |
| *rice with chicken for each of us* | **wali kwa kuku, kwa kila mmoja** |

| | |
|---|---|
| *Please bring us two birianis:* | Tuletee biriani mbili: moja ya |
| *one chicken and one beef.* | kuku, moja ya nyama ya ng'ombe. |
| *Thank you, I've had sufficient.* | Asante, nimetosheka. |
| *Thanks for the food.* | Asante kwa chakula. |
| *drink(s)* | kinywaji (vi-) |
| *beer (bottled)* | bia |
| *beer (locally-brewed)* | pombe |
| *coffee (black)* | kahawa (bila maziwa) |
| *mineral water* | maji safi (ya chupa) |
| *orange/mango juice* | maji ya machungwa/ maembe |
| *soft drink* | soda |
| *tea (without milk)* | chai (ya rangi) |
| *tea (with lemon)* | chai na limau |
| *wine (red / white)* | mvinyo (nyekundu/ nyeupe) |
| *glass* | gilasi |
| *What will you drink?* (to one p.) | Utakunywa nini? |
| *What will you drink?* (to more than one) | Mtakunywa nini? |
| *I'd like an orange juice.* | Nataka maji ya machungwa. |
| *O.K. Please bring us one coffee, one beer and a glass of orange juice.* | Haya. Tuletee kahawa moja, bia moja na maji ya machungwa gilasi moja. |
| *I'd like to pay now.* | Nataka kulipa sasa. |
| *Keep the change.* | Chukua hizi zilizobaki. |
| *Many thanks* (to one p.). | Nakushukuru. |
| *Many thanks* (to more than one). | Nawashukuru. |
| *We've really enjoyed it!* | Tumefurahi kabisa! |

## Getting medical help

Note: Once you get to a doctor, dentist or pharmacist you should be able to use English, but you may need Swahili at a rural clinic/dispensary.

| | |
|---|---|
| *What's the matter?* | Kuna nini? |
| *What's your problem?* | Una tatizo gani? |
| *I/We need a doctor (quickly).* | Ninahitaji/Tunahitaji daktari (kwa haraka). |
| *Where is the hospital?* | Hospitali iko wapi? |
| *Where is the clinic/dispensary?* | Zahanati/kliniki iko wapi? |

| | |
|---|---|
| *S/he has a temperature/fever.* | **Ana homa.** |
| *S/he has diarrhoea.* | **Anahara.** |
| *S/he has dysentery.* | **Anahara damu.** |
| *S/he feels nauseous.* | **Anataka kutapika.** |
| *My _____ hurts.* | **Ninaumwa _____ .** |
|    *arm/hand* | **mkono** |
|    *back* | **mgongo** |
|    *chest* | **kifua** |
|    *head* | **kichwa** |
|    *leg* | **mguu** |
|    *stomach* | **tumbo** |
|    *throat* | **koo** |
| *I have a pain here.* | **Naumwa hapa.** |
| *S/he has been cut on the ___ .* | **Amekatwa ___ ni.** |
|    *hand etc.* | **mkononi etc.** |
| *I'm allergic to _____ .* | **Nina mzio wa _____ .** |
|    *e.g. penicillin* | **e.g. penisilini** |
| *dentist* | **daktari wa meno** |
| *Can you recommend a dentist?* | **Nielekeze daktari wa meno?** |
| *pharmacy* | **duka la dawa** |
| *I'm looking for a pharmacy.* | **Natafuta duka la dawa.** |
| *I have / S/he has _____ .* | **Nina / Ana _____ .** |
|    *a blister* | **lengelenge** |
|    *a headache* | **maumivu ya kichwa** |
|    *a sore throat* | **maumivu ya koo** |

## Shopping

### At the market **Sokoni**

(*Note:* You are expected to bargain for things at the market. Stall-holders will not expect you to accept the first asking-price.)

| | |
|---|---|
| *Where is the market?* | **Soko liko wapi?** |
| *How much?* | **Bei gani?** |
| *That's too expensive!* | **Ghali sana!** |
| *That's much too expensive!* | **Ghali mno!** |
| *Please reduce the price, sir/madam.* | **Upunguze bei, bwana / mama.** |
| *O.K. then, I'll pay _____ .* | **Basi, nitalipa _____ .** |
|    *20 shillings* | **shilingi ishirini** |
|    *10 shillings each* | **shilingi kumi kumi** |
| *Give me _____ .* | **Nipe _____ .** |
|    *6/7/8/9* | **sita/saba/nane/tisa** |
| *fruit* | **matunda** |
| *banana* | **ndizi** |

| | |
|---|---|
| lemon | limau (ma-) |
| lime | ndimu |
| mango | embe (ma-) |
| orange | chungwa (ma-) |
| papaya/pawpaw | papai (ma-) |
| pineapple | nanasi (ma-) |
| sugar-cane | muwa (mi-) |
| vegetables | mboga |
| cabbage | kabichi |
| corn-cob | gunzi la hindi (ma-) |
| onion(s) | kitunguu (vi-) |
| potato(es) | kiazi (vi-) ulaya |
| spinach | mchicha |
| sweet potato | kiazi (vi) |
| tomato | nyanya |

(*Note*: Meat at the market is sold by the kilo.)

*Give me one kilo of* _____ .   **Nipe kilo moja ya _____ .**

## In a shop **Dukani**

*We're looking for a* ____ *shop.* **Tunatafuta duka la ____ .**

| | |
|---|---|
| book | vitabu |
| clothes | nguo |
| craft | sanaa |
| fabric | kitambaa |
| shoe | viatu |

*I'd like to buy* _____ .   **Nataka kununua _____ .**

| | |
|---|---|
| a basket | kikapu (vi-) |
| a bag | mfuko (mi-) |
| batiks | batiki |
| a carving | kinyago (vi-) |
| a dress | gauni (ma-) |
| a drum | ngoma |
| fabric | kitambaa |
| a hat | kofia |
| kangas | kanga |
| a pot | chungu (vy-) |
| a pair of sandals | ndara |
| a shirt | shati (ma-) |
| a pair of trousers | suruali |

| | |
|---|---|
| *How much is this per metre?* | **Mita kiasi gani?** |
| *Can I try this hat on?* | **Niijaribu kofia hii?** |
| *I'd like one like this.* | **Nataka kama hii.** |

**adjective** A term used for words which refer to the attributes (or 'qualities') of the people and objects denoted by nouns, e.g. tall, heavy, good etc. In Swahili an adjective stem has to have the same prefix as the noun it qualifies, e.g. *mtu mrefu, kisu kirefu, miti mirefu, ndizi ndefu* etc. Adjectival phrases such as *ya mboga*, 'of vegetables' in *biriani ya mboga* 'vegetable biriani', *za kutosha* 'of to be enough' in *ndizi za kutosha*, 'enough bananas', do the work of adjectives; the linking item *-a*, which helps to form the adjectival phrase, has to 'agree' with the noun that is being described – *biriani* and *ndizi* in the examples – by using the verb-prefix appropriate to its class rather than the noun-prefix.

**adverb** A term used for words which qualify (or 'modify') verbs i.e. they specify where, when, how or why the action denoted by a verb took place. Swahili adverbial structures include: the *vi-* prefix attached to adjective stems to make single-word adverbs, e.g. *vizuri, vibaya*, 'well' and 'badly' when used following a verb; adverbial phrases made with *kwa* + noun, e.g. *kwa haraka* 'quickly'; structures involving the place-prefixes *pa-, ku-, mu-*, and the suffix *-ni* (for these place structures see the entry **locatives** in this list).

**affix** A word-forming element that has to be attached to a word-root or stem, and cannot function on its own. One type of affix is the **prefix**, and another is the **suffix** (see the entries for these in this list).

**clause** A structural unit which forms part of a sentence but is larger than a word or phrase. Grammarians refer to main clauses and subordinate (or 'dependent') clauses, e.g. in *Tukimwona tutampa kitabu*, 'If we see her we'll give her the book', the main clause is *tutampa kitabu* 'we'll give her the book' and the subordinate clause is *Tukimwona*, 'if we see her'. A main clause can function grammatically on its own as a complete sentence, whereas a subordinate clause cannot. So *Tutampa kitabu* could, in one context, be the main clause in a sentence and, in a different context, it could function as a complete sentence on its own.

**conditional** A term referring to a type of clause which expresses a condition or hypothesis, e.g. clauses beginning with 'if'. One of the functions of Swahili *-ki-* is to express a condition, e.g. *Tukimwona tutampa kitabu.* Clauses with *-nge-* or *-ngali-* express a suppositional condition, e.g. *Tungekuwa na pesa* 'If we had some money'; *Tungalikuwa na pesa* 'If we had had some money'. The *-nge-* and *-ngali-* affixes occur in both clauses of the sentence in these suppositional structures, e.g. *Tungekuwa na pesa tungenunua samaki* 'If we had some money we would buy fish' (the supposition may still be realized); *Tungalikuwa na pesa tungalinunua samaki*, 'If we had had some money we would have bought fish' (the supposition has not been realized).

**conjunction** A joining word for connecting words, phrases and clauses, e.g. 'and' as in 'bread and cheese'; 'or' as in 'the large blue ones or the small green ones'; 'because' as in 'I can't come then because I'll be collecting the children'. Examples of Swahili conjunctions are *na* (expressing association) as in *wanawake na watoto* 'women and children'; *au* as in *kahawa au chai* 'tea or coffee'; *'wala'* as in *Hakuna sukari wala maziwa* 'There is neither sugar nor milk'; *lakini* as in *John amemlipa lakini wewe hujamlipa* 'John has paid him but you haven't yet paid him'. Many joining functions in Swahili are achieved either through phrases, e.g. with *kwa* as in *kwa sababu* 'because', *kwa hiyo* 'therefore', or in the verb, e.g. *Nenda sokoni ukanunue nyama* 'Go to the market and buy some meat'; *Alikwenda sokoni akamwona mgeni wetu* 'She went to the market and saw our visitor'.

**demonstrative** A set of words which can qualify (or 'modify') nouns to indicate whether the person or object denoted by a noun is near to or distant from the speaker. In Swahili, as well as the 'this/these' and 'that/those' demonstratives, e.g. *huyu/hawa* and *yule/wale*, there is a third set, used for referring back to someone or something that has already been mentioned, e.g. *huyo/hao*. Like most other qualifiers (or 'modifiers') of nouns, Swahili demonstratives follow their noun. As well as qualifying a noun a demonstrative can function as a pronoun and be the subject or object of a verb, e.g. *Huyu amekuja sasa hivi* 'This one (i.e. person) has just come'; *Nilimpa yule* 'I gave (it) to that one (i.e. person)'.

**imperative** A type of sentence used to express orders, and the form of the verb used for this purpose. For addressing one person in Swahili the verb is used in the minimal stem form, i.e. verb-root plus final -*a*, e.g. *Simama*! 'Stand!' For addressing more than one person the final -*a* changes to -*eni*, e.g. *Simameni!*

**infinitive** A form of the verb which is not marked for tense or number, i.e. it does not indicate when the action took place or whether the subject of the verb is singular or plural. In English the infinitive is the 'base' form of the verb, e.g. 'go', 'take', 'swim' etc.; it is sometimes used with 'to' as in 'They wanted to swim' and sometimes without 'to' as in 'We watched them swim'. In Swahili the infinitive form of the verb is composed of the minimal stem, i.e. verb-root + *a* (like the imperative form) together with the prefix *ku-*, e.g. *kusoma* 'to read', *kuleta* 'to bring'. The negative form of the imperative ('not to read', 'not to bring') is made by adding -*to*- between *ku*- and the stem: *kutosoma, kutoleta*.

**locative** A term used to refer to a variety of structures in Swahili which function as adverbs or adverbial phrases of place; they express where an action, event or state took place, e.g. the suffix -*ni* as in *nyumbani* 'at the house'; structures involving the locative affixes *ku-*, *pa-* and *mu-* as in *Asha yupo hapa* 'Asha is here'. Swahili sentences can have locative subjects, e.g. *Nyumbani pamejaa watu* 'The house is full of people' (notice that in cases like this the verb must have a locative verb-prefix).

**noun** A word denoting a person, place, thing, idea etc. or the plural of any of these. A noun can occur with a variety of qualifiers, e.g. adjectives and adjectival phrases, demonstratives, relative clauses, etc. A noun with its accompanying qualifiers is often referred to in grammar-books as the 'noun phrase' (and sometimes as the 'nominal group'), e.g. 'that very attractive child'. Nouns and noun phrases can function as subject of the verb as in, e.g. 'That very attractive child has just hit her little brother' or as object of the verb as in 'I'm going to punish that very attractive child'. In Swahili, qualifiers almost always follow their noun, e.g. *watu warefu* 'tall people'; *watu wenye mali* 'prosperous people'; *watu wa kutosha* 'enough people'; *watu waliokuja jana* 'the people who came yesterday'. The last example functions as subject of the verb in *Watu waliokuja jana ni Wajerumani* 'The people who came yesterday are German' and as object of the verb in *Hatujawaona watu waliokuja jana* 'We haven't yet seen the people who came yesterday'.

**object** A term used to refer to the major element of sentence structure which represents the receiver, beneficiary or goal of an action denoted by a verb. In the Swahili sentence *John anasoma kitabu* 'John's reading a book' the object of the verb is *kitabu* 'a book'. In *Mwalimu alimpa John kitabu* 'The teacher gave John a book', in which another person is involved, i.e. the teacher carrying out the action of giving, with John as the beneficiary, traditional grammar-books would call '*kitabu*' the direct object and John the indirect object.

**passive** A term referring to a sentence, clause or verb form in which the grammatical subject is the recipient or goal of the action denoted by the verb (and not the doer of the action), e.g. 'The house was sold by his brother', contrasting with the 'active' sentence 'His brother sold the house'. In English the passive is made with the verb 'be' (am/are/is/was/were etc.), e.g. 'I am haunted by the local cats', 'These machines are sold by trained personnel', 'I was stung by a bee'. In Swahili the passive is indicated by the affixation of *-w-* between the verb root and final *-a*; when the verb root is extended by one or more suffixes *-w-* has to be the last one before *-a*, e.g. *-fung-u-z-w-a*, as in *Tulifunguzwa* 'We were set free'. If the doer ('agent') of the action needs to be mentioned, the noun or noun phrase denoting the doer is preceded by *-na*, functioning like 'by' in English, e.g. *Tulifunguzwa na askari* 'We were released by a soldier'.

**prefix** An affix which is added initially to a root or stem. Examples of Swahili prefixes are: the affixes at the front of nouns which show noun-class membership, e.g. *m-* in *m-toto*, *wa-* in *wa-toto*, *ma-* in *ma-tandiko*, *mi-* in *mitumbwi* etc.; the affixes in front of a verb stem indicating subject of the verb, tense, relative pronoun (if needed) and object pronoun (if needed), e.g. *a-li-ye-zi-pika* 's/he who cooked them'.

**preposition** One of a set of words used in phrases which express a place, time, instrument or cause relation between two entities, one of which is denoted by the noun or noun phrase that is part of the prepositional phrase, e.g. in 'Alan waited at the wrong station', the prepositional phrase is 'at the wrong station', composed of the preposition 'at' followed by the noun phrase 'the wrong station'. The relation here is one of place. Other English prepositions include 'with, in, of, at, from, in spite of, because of' etc. In Swahili *kwa* has a wide range of prepositional functions, e.g. *kwa kisu* 'with a knife', *kwa miguu* 'on foot', *kwa Asif*, 'at Asif's place'. *Na* can also function as a preposition (as well as a conjunction) with the meaning of 'by' or 'with', e.g. *ndoo hizi zililetwa na Asha* 'These buckets were brought by Asha'; *Watakwenda naye* (*na yeye*) 'They will go with him'. Other prepositions include those made from an adverb followed by *ya*, e.g. *mbele ya* 'in front of', *nyuma ya* 'behind' *zaidi ya* 'more than'.

Apart from the single-word and compound prepositions a particular form of the Swahili verb has a preposition-like function, i.e. *-andika* 'write', *-andikia* 'write to'; *-soma* 'read', *-somea* 'read to'; *-pata* 'get', *-patia* 'get for' etc. The prepositional (or 'applied') form of the verb is made by suffixing *i/e* to the verb root, i.e. before final *-a*. Among its many meanings are 'to, for, on behalf of, to the detriment of', and with these meanings an indirect object (the receiver of the action denoted by the prepositional verb) is used in the sentence, e.g. *Nilimwandikia Robert barua ndefu* 'I wrote Robert a long letter'. (Robert is not grammatically essential, because the object-marker *-mw-* is present.)

**pronoun** A term used for a word in one of the sets of words that can substitute for a noun or noun phrase. The personal pronouns form one of these sets: 'I, you, s/he, it, we, you, they'. 'She', for example, could replace either 'Polly', or 'The one with the jade earrings' or 'The woman who arrived on a blue bicycle' as the subject of the sentence '—turned out to be a neurologist'. In Swahili the obligatory verb-prefix, which agrees with the subject noun, acts as a pronoun if the subject is not named, e.g. *Mwuguzi* could be omitted from *Mwuguzi atakupa dawa* 'The nurse will give you medicine'; '*Atakupa dawa*' would be understood as 'She will give you medicine'. This means that the personal pronouns *mimi*, *wewe*, *yeye*, etc. are mostly used for emphasis, e.g. *Mimi nilimwambia* 'I told him' (in which the subject 'I' would be stressed in spoken English). In sentences without a full verb a personal pronoun **would** be needed, e.g. *Yeye ni mwuguzi* 'He is a nurse' or a one-word reply, e.g. '*Mimi!*' in answer to the question *Nani yuko?* 'Who's there?' Object-markers, e.g. *-ni-*, *-ku-*, *-m-* etc. can also function as pronouns, e.g. *Tulimpa John vitabu* 'We gave John the books'; *Tulimpa vitabu* 'We gave him the books'. As in the case of subjects, a self-standing personal pronoun used as object of a full verb will indicate emphasis on the person/people denoted by the pronoun.

For noun-classes other than M/WA (and 'human nouns' in other classes) the subject and object-markers are the same, i.e. the verb-prefix is used to indicate both subject and object, e.g. *i-/zi-*, *ki-/vi-*, *li-/ya-* etc.

Other words with a pronominal function which also contain the verb-prefix in their structure include: demonstratives, e.g. *hiki/hivi* and possessives, e.g. *changu/vyangu*.

Relative pronouns, too, are formed with the verb-prefix but are not separate words as in English; they have a separate entry under 'relative' in this list.

**reflexive** A verb or clause structure in which the subject and object of the verb refer to the same entity, e.g. 'She cut herself'. In Swahili the reflexive prefix *-ji-* occurs in the object-marker position, i.e. immediately before the verb-stem: *Alijikata* 'She cut herself'. The *-enyewe* adjectival stem (prefixed by the verb-prefix except when qualifying M/WA singular nouns in which case it takes *mw-*) is sometimes translated into English as a reflexive pronoun, e.g. 'myself', 'themselves', 'itself' etc. but what it does is emphasize the identity or distinctness of the person or object denoted by the noun it qualifies, e.g. *Mimi mwenyewe nilivileta* 'I myself brought them'; *Sanduku lenyewe lilikuwepo hapa* 'The box itself was here'. *-enyewe* can co-occur with the *-ji-* reflexive prefix: *Alijikata mwenyewe* 'She cut herself'.

**relative** A term referring to a pronoun which introduces (occurs at the beginning of) a qualifying clause within a noun phrase; it is also used to refer to the clause itself. Relative pronouns in English include 'who, which, that, whom, whose' in sentences such as 'The people who helped him took the next train': the relative clause is 'who helped him' and it is part of the noun phrase 'the people who helped him' which is the subject of the verb 'took'. The relative clause functions as a qualifier, and in this example is part of the subject. In Swahili the relative pronouns are prefixes in the verb, immediately after the tense-prefix and, when an object-marker is present, the relative pronoun prefix precedes it, e.g. *wa-li-o-fika* 'they-past-WHO-arrive', i.e. 'they who arrived'. Except for the singular of M/WA nouns (which has a few irregular agreements such as the relative pronoun *-ye-*) the relative pronoun is composed of: verb-prefix + *o*, e.g. *-cho* (*ki* + *o*) in *kiti kilichouzwa* 'the chairs which were sold', *matunda yaliyouzwa* 'the fruit which was sold' (Swahili uses the plural). In *Nilipenda kiti kilichouzwa* the relative clause is part of a noun phrase functioning as the **object** in the sentence, i.e. the object of *-penda* 'like'. The other way of making relative clauses in Swahili is to attach the pronoun to *amba-*; this is obligatory with certain tenses, e.g. *-me-* (Perfect tense). For example: *kiti ambacho kiliuzwa, matunda ambayo yaliuzwa, watu ambao walifika*; these examples show how *amba* + relative pronoun follow the 'head' noun and precede the verb in its usual form – you do not need to affix the relative pronoun to the verb if you use *amba-*.

**root** The base form of a word, with no affixes attached to it – the irreducible minimum. For example, the noun root *-tu*, which can only be used as a word if it has a prefix, e.g. *m-* as in *mtu* 'person', *wa-* as in *watu* 'people', *ki-* as in *kitu* 'thing' or *vi-* as in *vitu* 'things'; the verb-root *-pik-* without any prefixes, e.g. *a-li-ye* or suffixes, e.g. *ish-a*. The root is the part of a word that carries the main component of meaning.

**stem** Part of the structure of a word, to which affixes may be attached. Unlike the root, the stem may be composed of several parts, e.g. *-pikisha* 'get something cooked' which has the causative suffix and the final *-a* following the root. To this stem prefixes may be attached to produce, in the case of the above example, *a-li-ye-pikisha* 's/he who had something cooked'.

**subject** A term for the grammatical function in a sentence of the noun or noun phrase which represents the 'doer' or 'instigator' of the action, or the 'sufferer' or cause of the state, denoted by the verb, e.g. 'The person who baked it' in 'The person who baked it is cutting the cake'; 'Money' in 'Money attracts scroungers'. In Swahili the subject noun or noun phrase is 'copied' onto the front of the verb through the verb-prefix (often referred to in grammatical descriptions of Swahili as the 'subject-prefix'), e.g. in *Vitabu vitatu vya Kifaransa vimepotea* 'Three French books are lost' the verb *-potea*, 'be lost', is made to agree with its subject *Vitabu vitatu vya Kifaransa* by means of the verb-prefix *vi-*. If the subject is not named (because speaker and hearer know its identity) *vi-* assumes its pronominal function, and acts as the subject.

**subjunctive** A term for a verb-form no longer much used in English, which does not have the usual 3rd person singular ending ('-s' in 'lives', 'works', 'comes' etc.) on verbs in the present tense, whether with present or future reference. It occurs in rather formal contexts, e.g. in subordinate clauses such as 'she send in an application form' in the sentence 'We recommended she send in an application form'. These clauses tend to express uncertainty or tentativeness about the outcome of the action denoted by the verb. The subjunctive also occurs in some 'formulaic' expressions in English, e.g. 'So be it', 'Come what may' etc. In Swahili the so-called subjunctive can be used to express purpose, suggestion, obligation or polite request, and its structure is: verb prefix + (obj.) + verb root + *e*. There is no tense prefix, and when there is no need for an object prefix the verb-prefix comes immediately in front of the verb-root, e.g. *Twende!* (*tu-ende*) 'Let's go!' *Azipike* 'Let her cook them / She should cook them'. The structure of the negative form is: verb prefix + *si* + (obj.) + verb root + *e*, e.g. *Asiende* 'She shouldn't go', *Usifungue dirisha* 'Please don't open the window / I'd rather you didn't open the window'.

**suffix** The term referring to an affix which is added to the end of a root or stem, e.g. the locative suffix *-ni* as in *nyumbani* 'In/at the house'; the verb suffixes (sometimes called verb extensions) which can be attached to a verb-root to alter the meaning in some way, and are always followed by the final *-a*, e.g. *-som-* 'read' *-somea* 'read to', *-wez-* 'be able' *-wezesha* 'enable', *-pend-* 'love' *pendana* 'love one another' etc. The suffix *-a* which comes at the end of verbs of Bantu origin is best thought of as a marker of 'verbness'; when verbs that are not of Bantu origin, e.g. *-sahau* 'forget', are extended with one or more of the meaning-shift suffixes the verbness-marker *-a* is added on, e.g. *-sahauliwa* 'be forgotten'.

**tense** A grammatical category referring to the means by which verbs indicate **when** (past, present, future) an action denoted by a verb was carried out, or when an event occurred, or a state of affairs was ongoing. The three most basic tense-markers in Swahili are *-li-* (past), *-na-* (present) and *-ta-* (future) and these prefixes follow immediately after the verb-prefix in the chain of prefixes in front of the verb-root. There is a much closer relationship between tense-marking and real time in Swahili than there is in English; the English present tenses can refer to future action, e.g. 'We fly to Australia next week', 'Next month we are going to Boston' etc. In Swahili *-ta-* (or *-taka-* in relative clauses) **must** be used whenever future actions, events etc. are referred to, e.g. *Mwezi ujao tutakwenda Nairobi* 'Next month we will go to / we go to / we are going to / we will be going to / Nairobi'. Some markers which can be used in the tense-prefix 'slot' have functions other than the indication of time, e.g. one of the functions of *-me-* is to indicate, with verbs denoting an action, the completion of that action.

**verb** A member of the class of words denoting an action, event, state etc. and that can indicate tense, number (singular or plural subject) etc. It usually co-occurs with a noun, pronoun or noun phrase functioning as subject. The basic element of the Swahili verb is the root, e.g. *-som-* 'read' to which the prefixes indicating the subject of the verb, the tense, the object etc. and the meaning-shifting and passive suffixes can be attached.

**taking it further**

## Travel guides

Some guides provide a wealth of useful and well-presented information for the visitor to the countries of East Africa, although details such as prices tend to become out of date fairly quickly. There are rather more guides to Kenya than Tanzania, and Uganda is mostly featured only in guides to the whole region.

Among the most useful are: *Lonely Planet, Rough Guides, Bradt Travel Guides, Insight Guides, Footprint Guides, Globetrotter Travel Guides, Nelles Guides, Berlitz, A.A. Essential Guides*. Useful websites: www.lonelyplanet.com and www.roughguides.com.

## Other books

A small selection of titles for you to sample:

- Chimera, Rocha (1998) *Kiswahili. Past, Present and Future Horizons*, Nairobi University Press, Nairobi.
- Mazrui, A. A. & Mazrui, A. M. (1999) *Political Culture of Language. Swahili, Society and the State*, Institute of Global Cultural Studies, Binghampton Univ., New York.
- Sarakikya, Eva (1996) *Tanzania Cook Book*, Tanzania Publishing House, Dar es Salaam.
- Smyth, A. & Seftel, A. (1999) *Tanzania, The Story of Julius Nyerere*, Fountain Publishers, Kampala.
- Taabu, Alice (2001) *Mke Nyumbani – Alice Taabu's Cookery Book*, East African Educational Publishers, Nairobi.

Books published in Africa can be obtained through either: Africa Book Centre, 38 King Street, Covent Garden, London

WC2E 8JT or African Books Collective, The Jam Factory, 27 Park End Street, Oxford OXD1 1HU (E-mail: abc@africanbookscollective.com). Websites: www.africabookcentre.com    www.africanbookscollective.com.

For second-hand books, by mail order, about East and Central African countries, try Risborough Books; phone 01844 343165.

## More websites

- For information on Swahili programmes in the BBC World Service: www.bbc.co.uk/Swahili
- For current news items on East Africa in English and Swahili: www.ippmedia.com
- Africa Confidential (fortnightly publication) news website: http//www.africa-confidential.com

For information on Swahili courses at the School of Oriental and African Studies, University of London:

- non-degree courses in the Language Centre (evening courses at various levels, short intensive daytime courses, one-to-one tuition etc.): lc@soas.ac.uk
- degree-level courses in the Africa Dept: wm@soas.ac.uk

For information on Swahili courses (including one-to-one tuition) in the Centre for African Language Learning at the Africa Centre, London: www.africacentre.org.uk

I hope you have enjoyed using *Teach Yourself Swahili*, whether you started on it as a complete beginner or needed to revise what you had once learnt.

Inevitably the needs of language-learners vary greatly, depending on their previous experience, their reasons for wanting to learn the language, the amount of time they can devote to it and the extent to which they have contact with native speakers. It is doubtful if any self-teaching book can meet the particular needs of all its individual users, but feedback from readers can go a long way towards identifying aspects of the book which could be improved. For example, if you have found the index reasonably easy to use, it is because a reader working in Tanzania suggested improvements to the one in the earlier edition. I welcome any comments you may have. Please send them to me care of Hodder & Stoughton, 338 Euston Road, London, NW1 3BH, or through the website www.madaboutbooks.com.

Joan Russell

Maswali hapa chini yahusu marafiki zako waliomo kwenye Mazungumzo (yaani *Dialogues*). Jibu maswali yote kwa Kiswahili.

1 Jibu maswali yafuatayo. Yote yahusu mambo ndani ya Mazungumzo 1–6.
  a John hakupenda kununua kinyago kikubwa kwa sababu gani?
  b Alipokuwa akitafuta posta John alimwuliza nani njia?
  c Kwa nini Regina hakununua ndizi sokoni?
  d Mamake Mohamed, jina lake nani?
  e Walipokuwepo njiani wakiangalia kanisa, John alimwambia Bw. Mohamed kwamba Alison amekwenda mahali fulani.
    i Alikuwa amekwenda wapi?
    ii Alikusudia kufanya nini pale?
  f Katika chumba cha kulia hotelini, marafiki zetu watatu walikaa wapi?

2 Jibu maswali yaliyopo hapa chini. Yote yahusu Mazungumzo 7–12.
  a Kwa nini Bw. Elvan alitaka kuangalia ramani?
  b Asha alikuwa akifanya kazi gani huko Dodoma?
  c Akina mama (ila mama mzee) walikwenda mwituni kwa sababu gani?
  d Bw. Twaibu alifikiri kwamba Steve atapanda basi lipi?
  e Ngalawa inatofautiana vipi na jahazi?
  f Juma alipokuwa anamwonyesha Steve kila kitu ndani ya chumba namba 6, alikunjua kitu gani?

3 Jibu maswali yafuatayo. Yote yahusu Mazungumzo 13–18.
  a Steve atakapokwenda Mombasa ni watu gani watakaofurahi kukutana naye?
  b Tafuta sentensi katika mojawapo ya Mazungumzo ambazo maana yake ni hivi:

'An American will be arriving at Heathrow on the 16th. He's the one who visited me some time ago at the college and I took him to visit my parents down south. He's a very nice young man. I've given him your phone number.'

c  Wale wapanda mlima Kilimanjaro walifanya nini siku ya kwanza, ingawaje Dominic aliwaonya wasifanye hivyo?

d  Mahali palipotokea ajali njiani ni mahali pa namna gani?

e  Siku ya kuangalia michezo jukwaani, mpwa wake Bw. Francis alikuwa ametarajia kucheza mpira. Kwa nini hakucheza?

f  Katika mbuga ya wanyama Robert aliwaona simba. Je, simba hao walikuwa wamelala wapi hasa?

# HELP!

If you find that you need remedial help, consult the information given below. Remember to use the vocabulary box which follows each dialogue, and also the word-lists at the end of the book.

The questions in 'Test your Swahili' are about information in the Dialogues, as follows:

1  a Unit 5 Dialogue 2  b Unit 2 dialogue 1  c Unit 4 Dialogue 1
   d Unit 1 Dialogue 2  e Unit 6 Dialogue 1  f Unit 3 Dialogue 2
2  a Unit 8  b Unit 12  c Unit 7  d Unit 9  e Unit 11  f Unit 10
3  a Unit 13  b Unit 18  c Unit 16  d Unit 14  e Unit 17  f Unit 15

If you need to revise any grammatical structures used in the questions – or any that you will need for your answers – you can find them in the Grammar sections (and two in the Practice sections), as follows:

1  a  Unit 3 section 7 for past tense negatives; Unit 5 Practice question 2 for **kwa sababu**.
   b  Unit 14 section 3 for two-verb tenses; Unit 7 section 1 for the relative pronoun -**po**; Unit 9 section 6a and Unit 11 section 4 for the **amba-** relative structure.
   c  Unit 3 section 10 for **kwa nini-?**; Unit 3 section 7 for past tense.
   d  Unit 9 section 4 for contracted forms like **mamake**; Unit 15 section 4 for **Jina lake nani?**.
   e  Unit 14 section 3 for two-verb tenses; Unit 6 section 3 and Unit 7 section 3e for the -**le** demonstrative; Unit 8 section 4b for -**ki**-.

f   Unit 7 section 6 for **chumba cha kulia**; Unit 3 section 3 and Unit 12 section 2 for N class humans with possessives, like **marafiki zetu**.

2  a   Unit 3 section 10 for **kwa nini-?**.
   b   Unit 14 section 3 for two-verb tenses; Unit 8 section 2 for **huko** + place-name.
   c   Unit 3 section 11 for **(a)kina-**; Unit 5 Practice question 2 for **kwa sababu**.
   d   Unit 9 section 6b for the general/'tenseless' relative; Unit 10 section 7 for **kwamba**; Unit 2 Practice question 5 for **-pi?**.
   e   Unit 13 section 4 for reciprocal verb-forms; Unit 16 section 6 for **vipi?**.
   f   Unit 14 section 3 for two-verb tenses; Unit 7 section 1 for the relative pronoun **-po-**.

3  a   Unit 7 section 1 for **-po-** with the future tense.
   b   Unit 9 section 6a and Unit 11 section 4 for the **amba-** relative structure; Unit 11 section 6 for **hivi**.
   c   Unit 8 section 11 for nouns derived from verbs; Unit 16 section 2 for the negative subjunctive.
   d   Unit 7 section 3 and Unit 16 section 1 for **palipotokea**.
   e   Unit 3 section 1 for the locative suffix **-ni**. Unit 17 section 1 for **mpwa**; Unit 14 section 3 for two-verb tenses.
   f   Unit 5 section 11 for demonstratives **hao** etc.; Unit 14 section 3 for two-verb tenses.

# Key to test your Swahili

1  a   *John hakupenda kununua kile kinyago kikubwa kwa sababu ni kizito.*
   b   *Alipokuwa akitafuta posta ni dereva ambaye John alimwuliza njia.*
   c   *Regina hakununua ndizi sokoni kwa sababu ipo migomba shambani mwake.*
   d   *Mamake Mohamed, jina lake Mama Fatuma.*
   e   i   *Alison alikuwa amekwenda maktaba.*
       ii  *Alikusudia kusoma magazeti ya Kiingereza.*
   f   *Marafiki zetu watatu walikaa karibu na dirisha.*

2  a   *Bw. Elvan alitaka kuangalia ramani ili kumwonyesha Steve wako wapi hasa.*
   b   *Asha alikuwa akifanya kazi ya uhazili.* **OR** *Kazi ambayo Asha alikuwa akifanya huko Dodoma ni uhazili.*

c *Akina mama (ila mama mzee) walikwenda mwituni wakate kuni.* **OR** *... ili kukata kuni.*

d *Bw. Twaibu alifikiri kwamba Steve atapanda basi liondokalo saa nne.*

e *Ngalawa ni ndogo zaidi kuliko jahazi. Ndiyo inaundwa kwa kuchonga gogo, lakini jahazi huundwa kwa mbao.*

f *Alipokuwa anamwonyesha Steve kila kitu ndani ya chumba alikunjua chandalua.* **OR** *Kitu ambacho Juma alikikunjua ndani ya chumba hicho ni chandalua.*

3 a *Ni wazazi wa Adam ambao watafurahi kukutana na Steve.*

b *'Mmarekani mmoja atawasili Heathrow tarehe 16. Ni yule ambaye alinizuru zamani chuoni nikampeleka kuwatembelea wazee sehemu za kusini. Ni kijana mwema. Nimempa namba ya simu yenu.'*

c *Walikwenda kwa haraka.* **OR** *Walikwenda mbio.*

d *Mahali palipotokea ajali hiyo njiani ni mahali pa hatari, kwa sababu lami ilikuwa imeharibika pande zote mbili za barabara.*

e *Hakucheza mpira kwa kuwa mechi iliahirishwa sababu ya mvua, yaani uwanja umejaa maji.*

f *Simba hao walikuwa wamelala katika kivuli karibu na mti mrefu sana, upande wa kulia.*